CRITICAL ISSUES
IN
HOMELAND SECURITY

CRITICAL ISSUES IN HOMELAND SECURITY

A Casebook

Edited by

James D. Ramsay

EMBRY-RIDDLE AERONAUTICAL UNIVERSITY

Linda Kiltz

WALDEN UNIVERSITY

WESTVIEW PRESS

A MEMBER OF THE PERSEUS BOOKS GROUP

Westview Press was founded in 1975 in Boulder, Colorado, by notable publisher and intellectual Fred Praeger. Westview Press continues to publish scholarly titles and high-quality undergraduate- and graduate-level textbooks in core social science disciplines. With books developed, written, and edited with the needs of serious nonfiction readers, professors, and students in mind, Westview Press honors its long history of publishing books that matter.

Copyright © 2014 by Westview Press
Published by Westview Press,
A Member of the Perseus Books Group

Find us on the World Wide Web at www.westviewpress.com.
Every effort has been made to secure required permissions for all text, images, maps, and other art reprinted in this volume.

Westview Press books are available at special discounts for bulk purchases in the United States by corporations, institutions, and other organizations. For more information, please contact the Special Markets Department at the Perseus Books Group, 2300 Chestnut Street, Suite 200, Philadelphia, PA 19103, or call (800) 810-4145, ext. 5000, or e-mail special.markets@perseusbooks.com.

Designed by Linda Mark
Library of Congress Cataloging-in-Publication Data

Ramsay, James D.
  Critical issues in homeland security : a casebook / James D. Ramsay, Linda A. Kiltz.
    pages cm.
  Includes bibliographical references and index.
  ISBN 978-0-8133-4827-8 (pbk.) — ISBN 978-0-8133-4828-5 (ebook)
  1. United States. Department of Homeland Security—Case studies. 2. National security—United States—Case studies. 3. United States—Politics and government—Case studies. 4. United States—Foreign relations—Case studies.
I. Kiltz, Linda Ann. II. Title.
  HV6432.4R35 2014
  363.34'560973—dc23
                                                                2013029846

10 9 8 7 6 5 4 3 2 1

*To my eternally patient and understanding wife, Trish,
and my terrific kids, Margo and David, who regularly
remind me of the most important things in life.*
—Jim

*To my wonderful husband, Don,
for his love and support in everything that I do.*
—Linda

Contents

PART II OPERATIONAL CHALLENGES IN HOMELAND SECURITY

Foreword

Thank you for taking a moment to read through the table of contents and to ponder how this text might benefit your program. The purpose of this foreword is to illustrate the logic of this book's organization and to suggest how it might be used by your students across the core curriculum. The homeland security enterprise, as it has come to be known, is a large interconnected network of public and private organizations, academic disciplines, and a wide variety of practitioners. Practical applications and examples of real-life homeland security challenges not only add value to the classroom experience but provide exciting examples of classroom principles in practice and enable students to imagine how they might have thought about or handled a real situation differently had they been involved or in charge.

Our aim in putting this book together was to present case studies that facilitate such enhanced learning and show instructors how to engage their audiences. There were two fundamental approaches to how such a text might be organized. The more traditional style would have been to present case studies completely dedicated to a singular focus or application discipline—all intelligence cases, for example. We chose the second approach instead: the book is organized into seven application or focus areas (i.e., chapters), and the challenges facing each of those areas is highlighted with two robust case studies. This approach yields not only fourteen outstanding case studies representing the challenges that face the homeland security enterprise and its practitioners but also offers to academic programs an efficient and economically viable alternative to the "one book, one topic" structure.

You'll notice that the fourteen case studies are organized into seven chapters and two parts. Our thinking in organizing the text this way is twofold; first, from an economic perspective, this organization allows academic programs to acquire one text that can be used in seven or more classes. With the chapter titles "Law and Policy," "Terrorism," "Environmental Security," "Intelligence," "Critical Infrastructure Protection," "Transportation Security," and "Emergency Management," it is easy to imagine how this book might align itself with several core courses in most homeland security programs. In addition, each case study includes thoughtful and provocative questions that the instructor can use to motivate and structure class discussion. The instructor guide provides not only sketch answers to each of these questions but many helpful tips and resources to help you use the case study approach in your classes.

We hope you find this text to be an innovative, creative, and fun teaching tool that helps your students see the richness and complexity of the many wicked problems they will encounter as homeland security professionals.

Jim Ramsay and Linda Kiltz

Acronyms

APT	advanced persistent threat
AQAP	Al-Qaeda in the Arabian Peninsula
ATF	Bureau of Alcohol, Tobacco, and Firearms
AUMF	Authorization to Use Military Force
CDC	Centers for Disease Control and Prevention
CDEMA	Caribbean Disaster Emergency Management Agency
CIA	Central Intelligence Agency
CIKR	critical infrastructure and key resources
CIP	critical infrastructure protection
DHS	Department of Homeland Security
DoD	Department of Defense
DOT	Department of Transportation
DPC	Directorate for Civil Protection (Haiti)
ELF	Earth Liberation Front
ERD	Emergency Response Division
FBI	Federal Bureau of Investigation
FDNY	Fire Department of New York
FEMA	Federal Emergency Management Agency
FISA	Foreign Intelligence Surveillance Act
GWOT	Global War on Terrorism
HPH	health care and public health
HSPD	Homeland Security Presidential Directive
HTUA	high-threat urban area
IC	incident commander

ICE	Immigration and Customs Enforcement
ICS	incident command system
IE	Internet Explorer
IPCC	Intergovernmental Panel on Climate Change
ISP	Internet service provider
JTTF	Joint Terrorism Task Force
MDE	Maryland Department of the Environment
MTA	Metropolitan Transit Authority
NGO	non-governmental organization
NIPP	National Infrastructure Protection Plan
NIST	National Institute of Standards and Technology
NRC	Nuclear Regulatory Commission
NSA	National Security Agency
NSPD	National Security Presidential Directive
NTSB	National Transportation Safety Board
NYCT	New York City Transit
NYPD	New York Police Department
OEM	Office of Emergency Management
PATH	Port Authority Trans-Hudson
SBIMAP	South Baltimore Industrial Mutual Aid Plan
TCP/IP	Transmission Control Protocol/Internet Protocol
TIH	toxic inhalation hazards
TSA	Transportation Security Administration
TTD	text to donate
UAV	unmanned aerial vehicle
UN	United Nations
UNCLOS	United Nations Convention on the Law of the Sea
WHO	World Health Organization
WTC	World Trade Center

Illustrations

Introduction

JAMES RAMSAY AND LINDA KILTZ

Life is like riding a bicycle.
To keep your balance, you must keep moving.

—Albert Einstein

Threats to security and safety are constant companions in life. They can come from natural events, from technology and man-made systems, or from mindful, premeditated criminal behavior like terrorism or organized crime. History has shown us that how well a society manages the risks posed by such threats is often the main predictor of whether that society thrives or fails. Since the terrorist attacks of September 11, 2001, the United States has spent over $1.4 trillion on the global war on terror,[1] and yet Al-Qaeda still exists, threats from similar organizations abound, many Americans are still concerned about terrorism, and as Hurricane Sandy proved yet again, Americans are still concerned about their ability to survive the aftermath of severe natural disasters. One might surmise that despite record-setting spending and massive popular support for military operations, the collective sense of safety and security within our nation and within our communities has been fundamentally challenged. Indeed, even a casual observation of the rhetoric of the 2012 presidential election campaign demonstrates that the nation

1

is still coming to terms with the uncertainty of how to deal with the specter of transnational terrorism in the United States or the consistently looming threat posed by nature.

In this environment, both students and practitioners of homeland security and emergency management must learn not only how to prepare for an uncertain future but also how to best deal with the systemic stresses that homeland security and natural or technological disasters place on society and the government. In other words, they must use lessons learned from the past to know how best to move forward into the future.

The economic health of the United States greatly influences both the capacity and the efficiency of the homeland security and emergency management communities. Indeed, the fiscal austerity imposed on federal spending in 2013 is certain to challenge practitioners for the next ten years as they strive to do more with less—that is, to cope with smaller budgets and larger obligations. If either homeland security or emergency management professionals are to deal effectively with these types of complex challenges, they must be creative, know how to work across disciplines, and become skilled in higher-level thinking and reasoning. Thus, the use of critical thinking is vital to successfully navigating both the routine and the complex situations encountered in their day-to-day responsibilities. Failure to adapt adequately can lead to mass casualties, widespread destruction of property, and significant loss of public trust, as we witnessed after the 9/11 terrorist attacks in 2001 and again after Hurricane Katrina in August 2005.

Critical Issues in Homeland Security: A Casebook allows students and practitioners to enhance their critical thinking skills through the use of case studies and by providing real-world examples that highlight theories, practices, and principles in the field of homeland security. The homeland security discipline writ large and its body of knowledge seem to be in a nascent stage of development. Such is evident by the lack of both a well-accepted theory of homeland security and a universally accepted definition of it.[2] Part of the debate about what homeland security is, and what it is not, seems to be due to the multidisciplinary nature of the field. For example, as seen in the structure of and interplay between the Department of Homeland Security (DHS), the federal law enforcement community, the intelligence community, the Department of Defense (DoD), the public and environmental health communities, and so on, the field of homeland security clearly comprises a number of academic disciplines—including criminal justice, political science, emergency management, public and environmental health, international relations, risk management, military science, sociology, computer science, and law—each of which contributes to theory, best practices, and policy. The cases in this textbook are written by scholars from a variety of disciplines and thus bring unique perspectives to the problems faced in homeland security.

So as to represent the multidisciplinary nature of homeland security, the text is divided into two parts. Highlighting the legal and policy challenges in homeland security, the chapters in Part I are dedicated to law and policy, terrorism, and environmental security. Part II covers the operational challenges in homeland security, with chapters on intelligence, critical infrastructure protection, transportation security, and emergency management. Each chapter contains two case studies that demonstrate not only the complexity and interconnectedness of the homeland security enterprise but also the challenges of implementing policies, strategies, and programs meant to prevent, deter, respond to, and recover from a vast array of disasters. At the end of each case are discussion questions that provide the reader with an opportunity to review, synthesize, and debate major concepts and issues.

In reading the cases, the reader will find that clear black-and-white answers or solutions to the problems posed by homeland security are rarely, if ever, possible. In fact, there are often multiple solutions and several possibilities, depending on one's perspective. The cases should be seen as problems for students to attempt to solve using the knowledge, concepts, and skills they are learning in their coursework. Each case is designed to engage students through debate, group discussions, and problem-solving. Thus, this case method strategy promotes social change as students reflectively and critically examine their own thoughts in relation to course material and other students' responses. Finally, since many cases focus on real-life problems and dilemmas, students should be able to transfer this information to other settings, such as their work environment. It is our sincere hope that all readers will enjoy and benefit from this text.

NOTES

1. Amy Belasco, "The Cost of Iraq, Afghanistan, and Other Global War on Terror Operations Since 9/11," Congressional Research Service report 7-5700, March 29, 2011, http://www.fas.org/sgp/crs/natsec/RL33110.pdf (accessed November 20, 2012).

2. Linda Kiltz and James Ramsay, "Perceptual Framing of Homeland Security," *Homeland Security Affairs* 8, article 16 (August 2012), http://www.hsaj.org/?article=8.1.16 (accessed November 20, 2012).

PART I

Legal and Policy Challenges in Homeland Security

On September 11, 2001, nineteen men affiliated with Al-Qaeda, an Islamic terrorist organization, hijacked four passenger jets. Two of these planes crashed into the World Trade Center in New York City, causing its collapse; one plane crashed into the Pentagon in Arlington County, Virginia, killing 184 people; and the last aircraft crashed into a field near the town of Shanksville in rural Somerset County, Pennsylvania, as passengers and members of the flight crew attempted to retake control of their plane from the hijackers. Excluding the nineteen hijackers, a confirmed 2,973 people died and thousands were injured as a result of these attacks.[1]

The idea that this event could have been a terrorist attack was not evident in the initial news reports of the first aircraft striking the North Tower of the World Trade Center, even though in 1993 Ramzi Yousef, a nephew of Khalid Sheikh Mohammed (the mastermind behind the 9/11 attacks), and six co-conspirators had detonated a 1,500-pound bomb in the underground parking garage of the World Trade Center that killed six people and injured more than a thousand.[2]

The 1993 World Trade Center bombing was conducted by a small, autonomous cell associated with the Egyptian terrorist organization Islamic Jihad, which was associated with Al-Qaeda. The goal of the 1993 attack was to devastate the foundation of the North Tower in such a way that it would collapse onto its twin, thus causing the collapse of both.[3] As a nation in 2001, we initially did not perceive that we were under attack by Al-Qaeda, although this organization had been responsible for carrying out a number of highly destructive suicide bombing attacks against the United States before 9/11, including the 1993 WTC attack; attacks in 1998 against the American embassies in Nairobi, Kenya, and Dar es Salaam, Tanzania; and the attack on the USS *Cole* off the coast of Yemen on October 12, 2000. Thus, an understanding of homeland security in the United States must include knowledge about the domestic and transnational terrorist threats we have faced in the past and will face in the future. To this end, our chapter on terrorism in Part I presents two cases—one focused on the domestic threat of ecoterrorism and the other on the first WTC attack by transnational terrorists affiliated with Al-Qaeda.

Since the 2001 attacks, homeland security has been a dominant policy issue impacting the lives of people in the United States and abroad. Fear of future terrorist attacks spawned the development and creation of massive government programs, multiple agencies, and policies aimed at protecting the homeland. Among the most significant policies were the declaration on September 20, 2001, of a "Global War on Terrorism" by President George W. Bush, which has led to a military campaign against Al-Qaeda and the Taliban in Afghanistan that has lasted for more than a decade; the passage of the Homeland Security Act of 2002, which created the Department of Homeland Security from the merger and reorganization of twenty-two distinct federal agencies; and the passage in October 2001 of the USA PATRIOT Act, which expanded the meaning of "terrorist organization" under federal law and expanded the surveillance powers of the federal government. These and other policies have fundamentally changed our daily lives. For instance, we now accept long waits in security lines and personal searches at airports, searches through our purses and backpacks at guarded entrances to public facilities and sporting arenas, and constant surveillance by security cameras in public spaces throughout our communities. Americans seem to be willing to accept government imposition into their daily lives even if it extends to personal liberties. Warrantless surveillance, detention without trial, enhanced interrogations, renditions, military commissions, and targeted killings have succeeded in preventing another terrorist attack on the homeland, but these policies have also undermined our legal traditions and rights guaranteed under the US Constitution.[4]

Homeland security provides some of the most complex legal and policy challenges faced by our federal, state, and local government agencies. Our nation's homeland security efforts go to the core of long-standing, intentionally designed tensions within our constitutional system of governance: security versus liberty, federalism in intergovernmental relations and constraining presidential power. In Chapter 1, on law and policy, two cases highlight presidential power and authority in responding to catastrophic incidents, whether natural or man-made, including terrorism. The case featuring the presidential disaster declaration authority compares and contrasts the presidential declarations of major disaster or emergency of President George W. Bush and President Barack Obama. Such presidential declarations have far-reaching consequences because they determine which jurisdictions are eligible to receive federal disaster assistance in the event of a disaster or emergency. The first case in Chapter 1 raises profound questions about the use of remotely piloted aircraft, or drones, for the targeted killing of suspected terrorists, including those who are American citizens. This case looks at the legality of such strikes under both US and international law.

Following 9/11, homeland security policy in the United States focused primarily on responding to the global terrorist threat posed by Al-Qaeda and preventing future terrorist attacks. This is clearly seen in the 2002 *National Strategy for Homeland Security*, which defines homeland security as "a concerted national effort to prevent terrorist attacks within the United States, reduce America's vulnerability to terrorism, and minimize the damage and recover from attacks that do occur."[5] This definition has been expanded under President Obama to include other hazards after the catastrophic events of Hurricane Katrina (highlighted in a case in Chapter 3).

Following Hurricane Katrina, Americans had already begun to realize that even natural disasters can be so traumatic, expensive, and disruptive that they too are potential homeland security concerns—particularly given the need in large disasters for federal assistance through the Federal Emergency Management Agency (FEMA), an integral part of DHS. The Obama administration's current strategy focuses on terrorism as the foremost of many threats, defining homeland security as "a concerted national effort to ensure a homeland that is safe, secure, and resilient against terrorism and other hazards, where

American interests, aspirations, and way of life can thrive."[6] Perhaps one of the new hazards we must consider is that posed by global climate change. Global warming and the resultant, varying climate change around the world will be among the biggest challenges humanity faces. Chapter 3 looks at the links between environmental security and homeland security through two cases—one on Hurricane Katrina and the other on Arctic security.

NOTES

1. National Commission on Terrorist Attacks upon the United States, *The 9/11 Commission Report: Final Report of the National Commission on Terrorist Attacks upon the United States* (New York: W. W. Norton, 2004).

2. Peter Lance, *Triple Cross: How Bin Laden's Master Spy Penetrated the CIA, the Green Berets, and the FBI* (New York: Morrow/Regan, 2006), 243.

3. Simon Reeve, *The New Jackals: Ramzi Yousef, Osama bin Laden, and the Future of Terrorism* (Boston: Northeastern University Press, 2002), 4.

4. Jack Goldsmith, *Power and Constraint: The Accountable Presidency After 9/11* (New York: W. W. Norton, 2012), x.

5. Office of Homeland Security, *National Strategy for Homeland Security* (Washington, DC: The White House, July 2002).

6. US Department of Homeland Security, *Quadrennial Homeland Security Review* (Washington, DC: The White House, 2010), 13.

CHAPTER 1

Law and Policy

The attacks of September 11, 2001, acted as a catalyst for major changes in US security efforts. The attacks altered not only how the nation identified and prepared for threats but also how it worked to prevent them. In the ten years after these devastating attacks, many new laws were passed and policies implemented to enhance homeland security, to protect key assets and critical infrastructure, to secure US borders, and to be better prepared to respond to and recover from a variety of threats and disasters. The primary goal of these new laws and policies was the protection of citizens within the homeland. Indeed, as Bentley suggests, citizens in a free society operate within legal checks and balances on governmental power. She goes on to suggest that those working in homeland security or emergency management need to understand the structure and the limitations of government.[1] The cases in this chapter focus on two very different yet important areas of law and policy, while raising concerns about presidential power and authority, particularly in times of war and disaster.

National emergencies and war invariably shift power to the presidency. President George W. Bush's counterterrorism initiatives, such as warrantless surveillance, detention without trial, enhanced interrogations, renditions, military commissions, and targeted killings, succeeded in preventing another attack on the homeland, but at what cost to our legal traditions and rights guaranteed under the US Constitution? Although Senator Barack Obama

9

campaigned against the Bush approach to counterterrorism, as president he has continued almost all of his predecessor's counterterrorism policies, including the use of drones for targeted killings.[2]

For years the US government has relied on unmanned aerial vehicles (UAVs), or drones, to find, target, and kill high-value terrorists in Afghanistan, Pakistan, Yemen, and other countries. While relentless drone attacks have decimated the top leadership of Al-Qaeda, they have created a great deal of controversy as well, not only because of the amount of collateral damage they have caused (the deaths of innocent civilians), but also because they have been used to kill American citizens. The first case in this chapter, "The Use of Drones in Counterterrorism: The Case of Anwar al-Awlaki," first discusses the benefits and challenges of the use of drones in counterterrorism and then focuses on the legal issues surrounding the killing of Anwar al-Awlaki, a US citizen and Al-Qaeda terrorist. Finally, a future scenario is introduced in which the domestic use of drones has become necessary.

The law and policy of US disaster management accords the president a great deal of flexibility and discretion to decide what does or does not constitute a declarable "major disaster" or "emergency," as highlighted in the second case, "Presidential Declaration of Disaster Decisions: The Case of Turndowns." The first half of the case discusses all aspects of presidential disaster declarations, including the laws and policies involved, the process used by governors to seek a presidential declaration, the criteria used by the Federal Emergency Management Agency (FEMA) to guide presidential decisions, and the justification for turndowns and their impact on governors and states. The second half of the case presents data (from FEMA) collected on turndowns from 1953 to 2011, with specific focus on the turndowns of President George W. Bush and President Barack Obama. The case concludes with observations on the factors and possible motivations involved for both presidents and governors in their disaster declaration decision-making.

NOTES

1. Emily Bentley, "Homeland Security Law and Policy," in *Introduction to Homeland Security*, ed. Keith Logan and James Ramsay (Boulder, CO: Westview Press, 2012), 19.

2. Jack Goldsmith, *Power and Constraint: The Accountable Presidency After 9/11* (New York: W. W. Norton, 2012), x.

The Use of Drones in Counterterrorism

The Case of Anwar al-Awlaki

TOBIAS T. GIBSON

Introduction

On September 11, 2001, the United States was attacked by a group of nineteen terrorists with ties to the Middle East. This group, using only small blades, took over four airplanes and flew those planes into the Twin Towers of the World Trade Center in New York City, the Pentagon in Arlington County, Virginia, and, after a passenger revolt, into a field in Pennsylvania. The crashes killed all on board the four commercial planes; counting the casualties from the Pentagon and the World Trade Center, more than 2,900 lives were lost all told.[1]

The response by the Bush administration was swift: an invasion of Afghanistan in October 2001 and an invasion of Iraq in March 2003 after declaration of the Global War on Terrorism (GWOT).[2] Major portions of the Global War on Terror were fought by special and covert operators, utilizing new tactics and technology on the battlefield against Al-Qaeda and its affiliates.

One of these new technologies is the use of unmanned aerial vehicles (UAVs, or more commonly "drones") to surveil and to kill suspected terrorists. On November 2, 2002, the CIA first used a UAV to kill Qaed Salim Sinan al-Harethi, an Al-Qaeda terrorist leader who was suspected in the bombing of the USS *Cole*, a US Navy destroyer, in 2000.[3] Since then, the program to kill terrorists has expanded as more people have been targeted and as the drone program has been extended to several more countries. It is estimated that the total number of people killed by American drones may be up to 3,247, including several hundred civilians.[4]

While US soldiers have been deployed to Afghanistan and Iraq over the past decade, drones have been used to kill terrorist combatants affiliated with Al-Qaeda in a number of other nation-states. For example, drones were first used to kill terrorist enemies in Yemen. Also, although the United States went to war in Afghanistan and Iraq, many lethal drone attacks have been in Pakistan, with the permission of the Pakistani government.[5] Strikes in Yemen are increasingly common under the Obama administration, and strikes have begun in Somalia as well, with the rise of the Al-Qaeda offshoot Al-Shabaab in that country. According to Daniel Klaidman, "When Obama accepted the Nobel Prize in December 2009, he had authorized more drone strikes than George W. Bush had approved during his entire presidency."[6] Indeed, the use of UAVs seems to be one of President Obama's most common foreign policy tools. In the wake of violent protests in North Africa and the Middle East in September 2012, the United States sent drones to surveil those responsible for the death of US diplomat Christopher Stevens in Benghazi, Libya.[7]

Arguably, the single most important issue with regard to homeland security for the United States in the upcoming decade is the legality of using UAVs to target and kill suspected terrorists who are US citizens.[8] This case study will discuss the benefits and challenges in using drones as a tool of counterterrorism. It will then focus on the legal issues surrounding the killing of Anwar al-Awlaki, a US citizen and Al-Qaeda terrorist. Finally, the case will set out a hypothetical scenario, based on perceived terrorist threats and newsworthy factual stories related to terror and the domestic use of drones, in which the domestic use of drones has become necessary.

The single most important question to ask when reading this case is: what is the appropriate trade-off between liberty and security?[9]

Benefits and Challenges to the Use of Drones

As with any new security technology, there are both benefits and challenges to the use of drones. To be sure, some of the criticism of drone use, with the attendant fears, is scathing. Perhaps the most important criticism is that drone attacks have resulted in the deaths of noncombatants who were not targeted by the US government. For example, award-winning journalist Simon Rogers of *The Guardian* estimates that of the 3,247 dead from drone attacks, perhaps 852 have been civilians.[10] While estimates vary widely, one database tracking civilian deaths caused by drone attacks estimates that as many as nearly half of the people killed by drones in 2008 were civilians.[11] While this estimate is likely to be high, it does give pause when considering the effectiveness of the use of drones by the United States, and particularly when coupling the loss of civilian lives with the realization that such collateral damage may lead to further recruitment by terrorists and strained relationships between the United States and other nation-states, including our allies.[12]

Another negative unintended consequence of the accidental killing of civilians by UAVs may be internal civil unrest due to mass protests and international diplomatic difficulties. For example, although the United States has received permission from the current and former presidents of Pakistan to use UAVs in the elimination of hostiles, their use has strained relationships with the country for a variety of reasons. First, as noted earlier, there is a wide discrepancy between the official US death count of civilians and data from other sources. For example, a May 6, 2011, strike killed only militants, with no civilian causalities, according to the US government. However, both Pakistani and British journalists reported the deaths of six civilians and the destruction of a school, a restaurant, and a house.[13]

As a result of the Pakistani ambivalence—and sometimes outright loathing—toward US drone strikes, it has become evident that securing a strong relationship with Pakistan is essentially out of the question at this juncture. Indeed, Pakistanis regard former president Bush more highly than President Obama . . . and Bush's approval rating in Pakistani polls was only 19 percent.[14] The diplomatic and strategic importance of strong relations between the United States and Pakistan is difficult to overstate. First, Pakistan borders Afghanistan and Iran, two countries with which the United States has either gone to war or has long-standing tensions. This is especially critical as the United States attempts to withdraw its military forces from Afghanistan and Iran continues to seek a nuclear weapons program. Second, Pakistan has long been a refuge for Al-Qaeda and Taliban fighters fleeing the US-led war in Afghanistan. Thus, a continued diplomatic trust between the United States and Pakistan may be important to continue to find and eradicate terrorists in Pakistan, such as Osama bin Laden, who was found and killed in the Pakistani city of Abbottabad. Third, Pakistan is a nuclear power and is in a long-term standoff with fellow nuclear power—and US ally—India over the disputed area of Kashmir. Thus, if the United States is to continue to be trusted by both India and Pakistan and help resolve diplomatic disputes between these two nuclear countries, it must maintain strong ties to Pakistan.

The use of UAVs as a counterterrorism tool and tactic has not only hampered relations with Pakistan and other countries, largely owing to the number of noncombatants killed in these attacks, but also has had a negative impact on the American ground-based pilots operating the drones. Klaidman quotes one drone pilot as saying, "I used to fly my own air missions. . . . I dropped bombs, hit my target, but had no idea who I hit. [With drones], I can look at their faces . . . see these guys playing with their kids and wives. . . . After the strike, I see the bodies being carried out of the house. I see the women weeping and in positions of mourning." Indeed, then, it might be of no surprise that nearly one in three drone pilots suffers from "burnout," and that nearly one in five is "clinically distressed."[15] Given this burnout rate, it may be difficult to recruit and train enough UAV pilots to meet future needs.

Though a number of risks are associated with the use of UAVs, there are a clear number of benefits. Perhaps the most important benefit is that there is no physical risk to the pilot. Indeed, the pilot is often "hundreds even thousands of miles away in perfect safety."[16] And as Rosa Brooks notes, it is "presumably a good thing" to be able to kill a hostile without exposing your own personnel to harm.[17]

Moreover, the cost of drones versus "real" airplanes allows the United States to secure the borders and project force globally at a fraction of the cost of fighters and bombers. This is particularly important during times of national economic hardship. According to the *New York Times,* "the shift [to drones] is also a result of shrinking budgets"; although the drone operation price tag was probably about $10 billion in 2011, "those costs are tiny compared with the price of the big wars."[18]

Finally, an undisputed fact is that drones have been used to kill top terrorist threats to the United States. The best-known example may be Anwar al-Awlaki (or Aulaqi), who was the chief cleric and head of Al-Qaeda in the Arabian Peninsula (AQAP). Additionally, Abu Yahya al-Libi, who was suspected of plotting at least two attacks against New York City, was killed by a drone.[19] Suspected USS *Cole* bomber Fahd al-Quso, a senior Al-Qaeda operative in Yemen, was reportedly killed by a UAV in 2012.[20] In other words, for all the potential downsides, drone attacks have successfully killed all of these terrorists, without exposing US military personnel to physical harm. When coupled with the comparative cost, it is no surprise that the Obama administration has used the UAV as a foreign policy tool in countering the terror threat.

Anwar al-Awlaki:
The Targeted Killing of an American Citizen

Despite the increased use of the drone program overseas since 2002, the most unsettling uses of UAVs will come in the future within our own homeland; indeed, with little media coverage, they may already have begun. The Department of Homeland Security has used surveillance drones over US borders since 2005.[21] Moreover, there are reports of over sixty UAV bases on American soil,[22] and more than three hundred Federal Aviation Administration (FAA) certificates of authorization were reportedly issued for drone flights over US soil in 2012; estimates put that number at thirty thousand by 2020.[23] Of course, some of these FAA certificates of authorization are issued to state and local law enforcement agencies to enhance public safety and to universities for research purposes.[24]

The questions and concerns regarding the domestic use of UAVs is particularly important as the United States increases its use of drones in a variety of ways that may include spying on or killing American citizens. The Obama administration, in a break from prior understandings of citizenship protections, was the first presidential administration to allow the killing of citizens via UAVs. On September 30, 2011, a US drone killed an American citizen, Muslim cleric Anwar al-Awlaki. The strike, which also killed Samir Khan, another US citizen and editor of AQAP's online magazine *Inspire,* was hailed by President Obama as "a major blow to Al Qaeda's most active operational affiliate."[25] While drones were used in these cases to kill known terrorists, they have also been used to kill children who are not suspected terrorists.

On October 14, 2011, another drone strike killed al-Awlaki's sixteen-year-old son.[26] His son had no history of terrorism and was not suspected of terrorist activities. Very little is known about the reasons behind this attack. In contrast to the death of his father, which was "trumpeted" by the Obama administration and other government officials, no official reason has been given for the attack on this young American citizen.[27] There was also backlash from some official quarters. For example, Senator Ron Wyden (D-OR) of the

Senate Intelligence Committee sent a letter to Attorney General Eric Holder expressing his frustration that the administration refused to inform Congress of its legal justification for killing al-Awlaki and targeting other American citizens.[28] While the drone attack on al-Awlaki's son should be considered both unethical and illegal, many justify the targeted killing of a known terrorist such as al-Awlaki as necessary for national security.[29]

Anwar al-Awlaki was born in Las Cruces, New Mexico, and lived there until he was seven, when his family moved to Yemen. He returned to the United States to attend Colorado State University; though he dropped out, he did return to earn a degree after becoming a full-time cleric. The *9/11 Commission Report* noted that two of the 9/11 hijackers attended al-Awlaki's mosque in San Diego and that all three of the men moved to Virginia at about the same time. The two future hijackers again prayed at al-Awlaki's mosque, this time in Falls Church, Virginia. The commission's final report concluded that this contact was coincidental. There was some dispute, however, about this claim. According to one FBI agent, the American-born cleric was linked directly to the hijackers' plans, may have had knowledge of the 9/11 plot, and kept "the hijackers spiritually focused."[30]

Al-Awlaki was deemed a high-value target because he was directly involved in supporting terror plots against the United States: he had ties to Umar Farouk Abdulmutallab, the so-called Underwear Bomber who attempted to blow up an airplane in flight to Detroit, and to Major Nidal Hasan, the Army officer who killed thirteen military personnel at Fort Hood.[31] Farouk was one of al-Awlaki's students, and Hasan and al-Awlaki had email exchanges prior to the shooting spree at Fort Hood in November 2009. In fact, there were several distressing signs pointing to Hasan's plans, all of which stemmed from electronic surveillance of al-Awlaki.[32] Additionally, Zachary A. Chesser, an American citizen accused of trying to join jihadi efforts in Somalia, said that he too had had email correspondence with al-Awlaki prior to his arrest.[33]

Al-Awlaki had long been targeted by the Obama administration, having been placed on a "kill list" by the president no later than June 2010 and perhaps as early as January of that year.[34] According to Stuart Levy, the US Department of Treasury's undersecretary for terrorism and financial intelligence, al-Awlaki had "involved himself in every aspect of the supply chain of terrorism" and was "extraordinarily dangerous."[35] Going so far as to say that al-Awlaki was the number-one threat to the homeland, according to President Obama, Daniel Klaidman quotes the president as telling advisers at a terrorism briefing, "I want Awlaki. Don't let up on him." Importantly, according to government attorneys in the US Department of Justice's Office of Legal Counsel, al-Awlaki was to be killed "only if it were not feasible to take him alive."[36]

The Legal Explanation and Debate Around the Death of al-Awlaki

Al-Awlaki's record of terrorism, combined with his calls for more attacks, presented President Obama with an urgent question: could he order the targeted killing of an American citizen, in a country with which the United States was not at war, in secret, and without the benefit of a trial? Al-Awlaki's death by a US drone strike differs from the elimination of other Al-Qaeda operatives in Afghanistan and Pakistan in two critical ways: (1) al-Awlaki was not technically in a battleground or "hot zone," and (2) he was an American citizen. In fact, al-Awlaki was the first American targeted under the Obama administration's campaign against Al-Qaeda and its affiliates. This case is compelling because as Americans we must ask ourselves: were the president's actions legal under domestic and international law and were his actions constitutional?

Most Americans believe that as US citizens we have a fundamental constitutional right not to be killed by the state without the exercise of due process. This is clearly stated in the Fifth Amendment of the US Constitution: "No American shall be . . . deprived of life, liberty or property without due process of law." According to *Black's Law Dictionary*, due process of law is "law in its regular course of administration through courts of justice" and includes "a course of legal proceedings according to . . . rules and principles which have been established . . . for the enforcement and protection of private rights." And furthermore, for those proceedings to have "any validity, there *must be a tribunal competent by its constitution*" (emphasis mine).[37] As a US citizen, al-Awlaki should have been guaranteed due process, which means he was entitled to a judicial hearing and an opportunity to defend himself in a court of law. These guarantees of due process have their roots in the Magna Carta and have long been considered procedural safeguards against tyranny and the abuse of presidential power.[38] In discussing the impact of *Boumediene v. Bush* (2008),[39] Michael Chertoff, the secretary of homeland security, has questioned the "very puzzling situation for al-Awlaki. Because, if you need court permission to detain somebody, and if you need court permission to wiretap somebody, how can you kill that person without court permission?"[40]

While some scholars argue that the US Constitution prohibited the Obama administration's extrajudicial killing of al-Awlaki, others have argued that the killing was justified under the president's commander in chief powers, which allow the president to take actions to protect the nation from attack by an imminent threat for self-defense purposes.[41] The justification for the targeted killing of al-Awlaki was provided by a number of government officials, including Attorney General Holder.

In a March 2012 speech given at Northwestern Law School, Holder explained the legal reasoning behind the administration's decision to kill al-Awlaki. First, Holder stated, the government used a three-part test for determining the legality of killing an American citizen who is beyond the immediate reach of US courts. "The government must determine after careful review," he said, "that the citizen poses an imminent threat of violent attack against the US, capture is not feasible, and the killing would be consistent with laws of war." But to date, the Obama administration has not released any legal memo or brief explaining what is meant by "careful review," what the review consists of, who conducts the review, and on what legal standards such a review is based. Further, according to Holder, "the government may not use this authority [standing statutory law] intentionally to target a US person, here or abroad, or anyone known to be in the United States." Though at odds with the policy of the Obama administration, this comment seems to prohibit the targeted killing of al-Awlaki. Holder continued by providing several examples of terrorists who had been prosecuted in a court. He then moved away from courts by noting that military commissions also provide viable alternatives to federal courts. Lastly, Holder stated that "the government must take into account all relevant constitutional considerations with respect to United States citizens—even those who are leading efforts to kill innocent Americans. Of these, the most relevant is the Fifth Amendment's Due Process Clause, which says that the government may not deprive a citizen of his or her life without due process of law."[42] This claim is despite the fact that lawyers have been prohibited since 2003, by the national government, from taking some suspected terrorists as pro bono clients without explicit permission . . . from the national government.[43]

Perhaps the most controversial portion of the speech came when, in an effort to clarify the administration's official reasoning for killing al-Awlaki, Holder stated: "Where national security operations are at stake, due process takes into account the realities of combat. . . . 'Due process' and 'judicial process' are not one and the same, particularly when it comes to national security. The Constitution guarantees due process, not judicial process."[44] Another concern related to due process was raised by David Cole, professor of law at Georgetown University, who questioned why Holder "opposes any judicial process, even where there is time to provide it."[45] After all, al-Awlaki had been on the kill list for months, if not years. Is the threat imminent if that much time has gone by? Holder, in a prescient move, addressed his future critic in his speech, noting that:

> The evaluation of whether an individual presents an "imminent threat" incorporates considerations of the relevant window of opportunity to act, the possible harm that missing the window would cause to civilians, and the likelihood of heading off future disastrous attacks against the United States. As we learned on 9/11, al-Qaeda has demonstrated the ability to strike with little or no notice—and to cause devastating casualties. Its leaders are continually planning attacks against the United States. . . . Given these facts, the Constitution does not require the President to delay action until some theoretical end-stage of planning—when the precise time, place, and manner of an attack become clear. Such a requirement would create an unacceptably high risk that our efforts would fail, and that Americans would be killed.[46]

In this speech, Holder failed to explain how the administration determined that al-Awlaki was an imminent threat and under what legal standards this was determined. Perhaps the most troubling aspect of this decision was that it was conducted in secret without oversight by US courts. According to the *Washington Post,* in or around January 2010, the Obama administration added al-Awlaki's name to a "shortlist of US citizens" containing the names of individuals whom the CIA was specifically authorized to kill on sight.[47] The "kill list" was drawn up as part of a closed executive process involving secret criteria. This process was explained in the *New York Times:*

> It is the strangest of bureaucratic rituals: Every week or so, more than 100 members of the government's sprawling national security apparatus gather, by secure video teleconference, to pore over terrorist suspects' biographies and recommend to the president who should be the next to die. This secret "nominations" process is an invention of the Obama administration, a grim debating society that vets the PowerPoint slides bearing the names, aliases and life stories of suspected members of Al Qaeda's branch in Yemen or its allies in Somalia's Shabab militia.[48]

The Obama administration officially has refused even to confirm or deny that such a list exists or to provide details on these processes.

Benjamin Farley of Emory Law School makes the argument that al-Awlaki and AQAP presented a threat such that placing al-Awlaki on a kill list was justified, because the United States was in an armed conflict with AQAP. However, because of the continuous targeting of al-Awlaki, the immediacy of the US self-defense claim is "troubling. . . . On its face, such continuous targetability seems to violate self-defense's fundamental principle relating a particular use of force to a particular armed attack and not merely the desire or hope of a state or armed group to launch an attack in the future."[49] Besides the question of the extent to which al-Awlaki was an imminent threat, we must also ask whether his status as a US citizen should matter given that he was an enemy combatant against the United States and also a Yemeni citizen.

Abraham U. Kannof believes that al-Awlaki's US citizenship should not be of legal concern. Kannof makes the argument that al-Awlaki had dual Yemeni and American citizenship, but that the cleric had established his Yemeni citizenship as the dominant of the two, according to customary international law. He did so in many ways, such as living in Yemen, where he felt comfortable and safe, by taking a Yemeni bride, and by keeping a website dedicated to jihad against the United States. Although he would not completely strip al-Awlaki of his citizenship rights, Kannof wonders why al-Awlaki, having established his Yemeni citizenship as dominant, "should even be entitled to the full Constitutional protections afforded to US citizens?"[50] This point, arguably, is supported by the Supreme Court, which recognized in *Ex Parte Quirin* (1942) that an American citizen is subject to the laws of war when acting as an enemy of the state.[51]

The Obama administration argues that the laws of war, coupled with the force authorized by Congress under the Authorization to Use Military Force (AUMF) in September 2001, provide the legal justification for using lethal force against those whom the administration designates as terrorists—namely, Al-Qaeda and its affiliates around the world. The AUMF authorized the president "to use all necessary and appropriate force against those nations, organizations, or persons he determines planned, authorized, committed or aided in the terrorist attacks that occurred on September 11, 2001 . . . in order to prevent any future acts of international terrorism against the US by such nations, organizations or persons."[52] The AUMF is the legal basis by which the United States has justified its military action in Afghanistan and other counterterrorism operations, such as the use of drones to target Al-Qaeda terrorists, including al-Awlaki, regardless of their citizenship status. Under the AUMF, according to the Obama administration, al-Awlaki was a lawful target in an armed conflict.[53]

There is also debate about the legality of the targeted killing of al-Awlaki because of the location where he was killed. Despite the *Quirin* opinion, the opinion in a more recent Supreme Court case, *Hamdi v. Rumsfeld* (2004), suggests that there may be limitations on the ability of the United States to kill in places such as Yemen. In *Hamdi v. Rumsfeld,* the Court reversed the dismissal of a habeas corpus petition brought on behalf of Yaser Esam Hamdi, a US citizen being detained indefinitely as an "illegal enemy combatant." The Court recognized the power of the government to detain enemy combatants, but ruled that detainees who are US citizens must have the ability to challenge their enemy combatant status before an impartial judge. In *Hamdi,* the Supreme Court held that a US citizen is entitled to the full measure of constitutional protections; thus, if al-Awlaki is considered a US citizen, then he is entitled to the same constitutional rights. Also in *Hamdi,* the Supreme Court limited the Authorization to Use Military Force by noting that Hamdi was in fact captured in a war zone. Yemen, in contrast, probably does not meet that requirement of being a war zone. The Obama administration has argued that al-Awlaki's location outside of a so-called hot battlefield such as Afghanistan did not preclude him from the armed conflict given his association with Al-Qaeda in the Arabian Peninsula.[54] The United States, according to this argument, still had a right to use force to defend itself against him.

Leading experts on international law have not accepted the Obama administration's rationale. Most importantly, the concept of an "armed conflict" has historically been understood to mean an openly declared military conflict between two countries. The vague and unending "war on terror" that the United States has declared on the entire world does not suffice to meet this standard. Mary Ellen O'Connell, a professor of law at Notre Dame, argues that drone strikes are not legal. Central, in O'Connell's opinion, is the meaning of a nation's self-defense, which she describes in this way: "the right to use military force for self-defense means using force on the territory of a state responsible for an armed attack." This condition is not met in either Pakistan or Yemen.[55]

In contrast to these legal analysts, Kenneth Anderson, a professor of law at Washington College, finds strong legal support for the Obama administration's use of targeted drone killings in Pakistan. Anderson notes that humanitarian advocates have long sought more precise means of killing hostiles in war, and drones are such a weapon. Moreover, senior administration lawyers, including Harold Koh, the State Department's legal adviser, despite O'Connell's claims, have said that drone attacks are justified owing to US rights of self-defense.[56]

Finally, although al-Awlaki was probably the first American citizen to be placed on the list of approved targeted killings, there is general consensus that other Americans are on the list. Some experts believe that al-Awlaki's addition to the list may serve as precedent for the targeting of Americans within the United States.[57]

The Hypothetical Case:
The Nexus of Drug Smugglers and Al-Qaeda

Following the successes of the border surveillance UAVs, manufacturers begin a vast lobbying effort with Congress.[58] Members of Congress from most of the border states and from several large cities, especially those with large Latino and Muslim communities, form the Drone Caucus in Congress.[59] UAV production companies spend millions of dollars to lobby the national government to purchase more drones. This leads to the increased use of surveillance and armed drone technologies by federal border patrols and law enforcement agencies.[60] In turn, many large cities also use drones for surveillance purposes, and a few cities, typically those with high levels of gang activity, even use armed drones during firefights between police and civilians, to disperse violent crowds, and as backup during large festivals or sporting events in which the threat of violence is elevated.

By 2017, drug cartels from Mexico, Colombia, and Venezuela have begun to cooperate with known Al-Qaeda in Latin America (AQLA) terrorists to disperse and sell drugs throughout the United States.[61] Muhammed Akbar, leader of AQLA, has released several videos in which he notes that there are at least three reasons why AQLA has begun this relationship. First, the infestation of drugs leads to the addiction and death of many Americans and weakens the country from within. Second, ties to drug cartels have shown AQLA where and how the cartels enter the United States and thus have given the group easy points of access. Akbar recently claimed that AQLA operatives have established "strongholds" in at least ten major US cities.[62] Finally, according to Akbar, the money made in shipping opiates and other types of drugs has provided AQLA with nearly $80 million in revenue in recent years.[63] This number is substantiated by estimates from the Department of Justice and the Department of Homeland Security.

The Plot: A Worst-Case Scenario

A joint investigation by the Federal Bureau of Investigation (FBI), Coast Guard intelligence units, Immigration and Customs Enforcement (ICE), and the Bureau of Alcohol, Tobacco, and Firearms (ATF) has led to evidence of a training operation, on US soil, by AQLA. The evidence suggests that AQLA has purchased a great deal of property, in obscure, remote, and/or isolated places throughout the United States, that it is using as training grounds for a terrorist attack in the late summer or perhaps early fall. Suspected AQLA members have recently purchased weapons, including explosive components, high-powered rifles, and machine guns, but following these purchases the suspects have disappeared.

Perhaps even more distressing is the Internet chatter, picked up by the National Security Agency (NSA) over a period of several months, which may indicate that AQLA is entering the country at alarming rates, with falsified passports. The chatter indicates that many of these AQLA terrorists are entering the United States through international airports in the South and the Southwest. The chatter suggests that one suspected terrorist in particular, known only by his alias, Alif, has covertly entered the United States. No government agency can confirm or deny this.[64]

On August 10, a Yemeni man, Sharif al-Aqad, is detained during a routine traffic stop just outside of Phoenix, Arizona. When asked for identification after being pulled over for speeding and failure to yield, the local officer notices some discrepancies between al-Aqad's license and passport. After a search of the car, the police department finds several names and flight arrival times in cities in the South and, perhaps surprisingly, in some northern states as well, including Michigan, New York, Massachusetts, and Pennsylvania.

When the FBI learns of al-Aqad's arrest, agents take him into custody and begin to question him. After nearly ten days of being questioned, he begins to talk. He tells the FBI about sleeper cells in Phoenix, Dallas, and Houston. He also indicates that these cells are most likely "under the radar" of most local law enforcement, suggesting that the cells are tightly bound groups that have entered communities within the larger cities. On the eleventh day of his detention, al-Aqad dies in custody. The cause of death is not released.

On August 28, Akbar of the AQLA releases a video. The chilling message is one of imminent destruction within the United States. Akbar states, with a slight grin interpreted by law enforcement officials as egotistical and sure, that AQLA plans to explode multiple bombs, which will be unleashed "where the gladiators play." Local and national law enforcement agencies, having connected the dots within days, believe the signs point to a massive siege of professional football stadiums on opening day of the football season.[65] Opening day is slated for September 7, one week away.

The president addresses the American public about the dire straits facing the nation and promises that "every available officer and resource, military and otherwise," will be used to prevent the bombings of the stadiums, including military aircraft patrolling the skies and the crowds. The football league asks the government if the games should be canceled. The government responds by telling the league that postponing the games might only lead to a retrenchment of AQLA resources. The games will go on!

Based on its intelligence, the national government focuses on protecting stadiums and locating terrorists in the following cities: Phoenix, Dallas, Houston, New Orleans, Detroit, and Buffalo. As a result, local and federal law enforcement agencies launch domestic surveillance drones in record numbers. Because some AQLA members are Middle Easterners, Middle East communities, mosques, and other common gathering areas such as ethnic restaurants and grocery stores in the six cities and surrounding areas are targeted by these drones. For example, drones are used to hover at mosques and Middle Eastern or Mediterranean restaurants and collect the pictures and identities of worshipers and patrons. Moreover, all conversations taking place within the buildings or surrounding grounds are recorded.[66]

Because AQLA has ties to African Muslims, such as members of Al-Shabaab, and also to the Latino drug cartels, historically African American and Latino neighborhoods, places of worship, and common gathering spots also come under widespread surveillance. Moreover, any gathering of more than three males believed to be African American, Latino, of Arab descent, or of the Islamic faith, between the ages of sixteen and fifty (estimated), is subject to surveillance. Vehicles with more than three passengers meeting this demographic profile are subject to being followed by a drone.[67]

In addition to drone surveillance, all local and national law enforcement and intelligence agencies are on high alert. Wiretaps are implemented with the permission of the FISA (Foreign Intelligence Surveillance Act) court. Social media monitoring has increased. Satellite technology has been used to intercept all forms of communications and, based on profiling of suspected groups, to cut off some types of electronic communication.[68]

Importantly, owing to the high threat risk, the Department of Homeland Security, its various agencies, and the CIA, with emergency presidential and congressional approval, begin to use armed drones above the borders and in the cities under intensified surveillance. These drones are outfitted with at least two Hellfire missiles designed for targeted strikes against homes, vehicles, and a variety of other targets. These missiles are extremely accurate and are thought to minimize collateral damage.

The American Civil Liberties Union (ACLU) and the Center for Constitutional Rights (CCR), two civil liberties organizations, sue all of the government agencies over the widespread surveillance and deployment of weaponized drones across the cities thought to be used to target AQLA terrorists. There are two fundamental issues these organizations are suing to have resolved. Their hope is to get some judicial answer as to "whether the entire world is a battlefield for legal purposes, or whether terrorism suspects who are found away from combat zones must, in the absence of an imminent threat, instead be treated as criminals and given trials."[69]

The lawsuits are dismissed, for lack of justiciability. In other words, according to the court, the legal system is not the right place for the dispute to be resolved. There are two more reasons why the lawsuits are dismissed. First, the ACLU and the CCR lack standing, meaning that they lack "a concrete and particularized injury resulting from a defendant's allegedly illegal activity."[70] In other words, neither organization is actually harmed by the deployment of drones.

More importantly, even if the plaintiffs could have shown that they had standing, the case presents a classic "political question," or an issue that is best resolved by the two elected branches and from which the courts remove themselves. Indeed, "the quintessential political question case is one challenging a military or foreign policy decision," and federal courts refuse to answer many such issues.[71]

Sweet Success

As a result of the dedicated surveillance across wide portions of the cities of Houston, New Orleans, and Buffalo, the local and federal law enforcement agencies have made several arrests. After arresting ten men between the ages of nineteen and thirty-five, authorities in Houston have determined that they have prevented the planned attack from occurring. Law enforcement agencies have found a great deal of incriminating evidence, including explosives, weapons, drug money, and computers with names in incriminating information for more than forty suspects across the Americas and North Africa. The president and the Director of National Intelligence (DNI) jointly make an appearance at the Pentagon, with the DNI stating that at least one entire cell of AQLA and its allies have been set back by "years" and that "the good people of Houston, Texas, and the United States can sleep better tonight knowing that their government is securing their lives and continued well-being."

Federal law enforcement, after three days of constant and detailed surveillance, detain nine Arab and Latino men in New Orleans and more than a dozen Arab, Latino, and African American men in Buffalo. Many firearms, some legally registered, are found and confiscated, as are phones and computers. No bomb-making materials or drugs are found. Although money is found, it does not appear to be an amount that would meet the financial needs of a large, concerted terrorist effort in either city.

The local FBI in each city releases the statement that, although investigations continue, it is believed that the plots to blow up the football stadiums, filled with thousands of fans, have been thwarted in both New Orleans and Buffalo. Two days later, the FBI offices in those cities announce that, despite the mass arrests and searches of the information on the phones and computers of those detained, no evidence has been found that any of the detainees are part of a terrorist plot of any type, and certainly not one to blow up stadiums. Despite the lack of evidence, the men will be detained until the day after the football season opens, to ensure the safety of the public.[72]

Surveillance efforts in Phoenix also pay off. Drones track two men who are gathering munitions from stash sites around the city and the surrounding desert to a water treatment plant in the desert that had previously been thought to be abandoned, about ten miles from the city limits. Terrain issues at the former water treatment site combine with the discovery of about twenty armed men already entrenched there to lead the federal government—after consultations between the president, the secretaries of defense and homeland security, the National Security Council, and the DNI—to decide to send in an air force drone strike team to eliminate the threat posed by the terrorists at the former water treatment site. The air force sends five weaponized UAVs to rain Hellfire missiles on the site.

After the attack is over and the fires are put out, the remains of thirty people are found at the site. After the bodies are identified, it is discovered that ten of them were American citizens. Although three of them were adult males who match the descriptions of suspected terrorists, three of them were adult women and four were children. The women and children were not suspected of terrorist activities, and none of them had appeared on terrorist watch lists or "no-fly" lists. All of the American citizens were born in the United States, and only two had spent more than a year abroad. Nonetheless, it is clear that the site was a staging and training facility for terrorists. The military, local and federal law enforcement, and the president all deem the strike a success, as it prevented an attack on thousands of football fans.

Meanwhile, efforts in Buffalo are stymied, until Saturday night before Sunday's kickoff. Finally able to tie several leads together, federal law enforcement agencies discover that the cell in Buffalo is much smaller than originally thought based on the predicted size and sheer number of terrorists killed in the Phoenix strike. In fact, only four terrorists are now thought to be involved in the plan to attack the Buffalo stadium by detonating an enormous car bomb outside the stadium gate just before kickoff. This plan could result in a sizable death toll immediately, as thousands of fans will be entering the stadium right at that time. Moreover, because they have to wait in line to have their tickets processed and pass through security, the irony of killing so many fans at the security checkpoint is not lost on the bombers.

The CIA and NSA discover that the terrorists plan to use one SUV as the bombing vehicle and three identical decoy SUVs, because of the increased surveillance by local police and federal intelligence agencies in the area. At 11:30 PM, a local police surveillance drone begins to follow a black, late-model GMC Yukon in Fredonia, New York, a city about an hour southwest of Buffalo. Pictures of the driver indicate that it is "Alif," the terrorist who disappeared at New York's JFK Airport. Video shows that the SUV is weighted down; it seems sluggish and lower to the ground than an empty vehicle would be. By 11:40, local police are scrambled to intercept the SUV. The president orders a DHS Predator drone to monitor the SUV and to attack it if the police are unable to stop it. Alif does pull over when the power to the vehicle is remotely killed by the manufacturer. After engaging with the police in a brief but fierce struggle in which two officers are injured, Alif is taken alive.

Efforts to prevent terrorist attacks at the Dallas stadium are successful, but the terror caused by such a threat significantly impacts the community. The game kicks off at noon, as scheduled. Only twenty thousand fans arrive, but many of them do so, according to local news outlets with reporters in the parking areas prior to the game, because they "aren't going to let any terrorists dictate how they're going to live" and because they "consider it un-American to kowtow to terrorists." Indeed, despite the suspicion permeating the city, the logging of thousands of hours of drone time in the air, and the electronic surveillance of a sizable percentage of the city's citizens, no one has been arrested. Moreover, despite the feeling of dread in the stadium during the game and the fear as the fans exit the building after a hometown loss to their big East Coast rival, there is no attack on the Dallas stadium.

DISCUSSION QUESTIONS

1. How comfortable are you with the US government killing American citizens, even if they are suspected terrorists and are living abroad?
2. What are the political and policy implications of the US policy as presented by Attorney General Eric Holder?
3. Are you comfortable with domestic uses of drones? Is domestic drone surveillance legally and morally sound?
4. What amount of collateral damage is acceptable? Is your opinion affected by the age or citizenship of the innocents killed?
5. How should the president balance the security of the nation and its citizens against the rights of suspected terrorists?
6. Present an argument for or against the domestic use of drones.

NOTES

1. National Commission on Terrorist Attacks Upon the United States, "The 9/11 Commission Report: Final Report of the National Commission on Terrorist Attacks Upon the United States: Executive Summary," http://www.c-span.org/pdf/911finalreportexecsum .pdf (accessed September 22, 2012).

2. "Afghanistan Profile," *BBC News,* http://www.bbc.co.uk/news/world-south-asia -12024253 (accessed September 22, 2012; last updated June 19, 2013); "Operation Iraqi Freedom," *PBS Frontline,* http://www.pbs.org/wgbh/pages/frontline/shows/invasion/cron / (posted February 26, 2004; accessed September 22, 2012).

3. Susan Breau, Marie Aronsson, and Rachel Joyce, "Drone Attacks, International Law, and the Recording of Civilian Casualties of Armed Conflict," Oxford Research Group Discussion Paper 2, June 2011, http://www.oxfordresearchgroup.org.uk/sites /default/files/ORG%20Drone%20Attacks%20and%20International%20Law%20Report .pdf (accessed September 10, 2012).

4. A figure can only be estimated, not confirmed, because the CIA and other federal agencies have not officially recognized the use of drones, though several individuals within the government have done so; see Carlos Muñoz, "ACLU Demands Disclosure of Details on CIA Drone Strikes," *The Hill,* September 20, 2012; see also Simon Rogers,

"US Drone Strikes Listed and Detailed in Pakistan, Somalia, and Yemen," *The Guardian,* August 2, 2012.

5. Avery Plaw, Matthew S. Fricker, and Brian Glyn Williams, "Practice Makes Perfect? The Changing Civilian Toll of CIA Drone Strikes in Pakistan," *Perspectives on Terrorism* 5, nos. 5–6 (2011), http://www.terrorismanalysts.com/pt/index.php/pot/article/view/practice-makes-perfect/html (accessed September 13, 2012).

6. Daniel Klaidman, "Drones: How Obama Learned to Kill," *Newsweek,* May 28, 2012, http://www.thedailybeast.com/newsweek/2012/05/27/drones-the-silent-killers.html (accessed September 6, 2012).

7. "At Least One Arrest in Killings of Americans in Libya," CNN, September 13, 2012, http://www.cnn.com/2012/09/13/world/africa/libya-us-ambassador-killed/index.html (accessed September 13, 2012). The Obama administration also used armed Predator drones in Libya during the "Arab Spring" standoffs against longtime Libyan strongman Muammar Qaddafi; Elisabeth Bumiller and Thom Shanker, "War Evolves with Drones, Some Tiny as Bugs," *New York Times,* June 19, 2011.

8. See discussion in Jack Goldsmith, *Power and Constraint: The Accountable Presidency After 9/11* (New York: W. W. Norton, 2012), esp. 199–200.

9. This debate is most famously whittled down to a quote from Benjamin Franklin, who said: "Those who would give up essential Liberty, to purchase a little temporary Safety, deserve neither Liberty nor Safety." Perhaps those who cite this remark to suggest that the federal government should not inconvenience citizens in order to protect them have failed to understand the context in which it was offered. Benjamin Wittes, "What Benjamin Franklin Really Said," Lawfare, July 15, 2011, http://www.lawfareblog.com/2011/07/what-ben-franklin-really-said/ (accessed September 26, 2012).

10. Rogers, "US Drone Strikes Listed and Detailed in Pakistan, Somalia, and Yemen."

11. Plaw et al., "Practice Makes Perfect?" table 1.

12. Peter Bergen and Katherine Tiedemann, "The Year of the Drone: An Analysis of US Drone Strikes in Pakistan, 2004–2010," New American Foundation, February 24, 2010, http://www.newamerica.net/publications/policy/the_year_of_the_drone (accessed September 6, 2012).

13. Scott Shane, "CIA Is Disputed on Civilian Toll in Drone Strikes," *New York Times,* August 11, 2011.

14. Joshua Faust, "US Drones Make Peace with Pakistan Less Likely," *The Atlantic,* July 12, 2012.

15. Daniel Klaidman, quoted in Rosa Brooks, "What's *Not* Wrong with Drones?" *Foreign Policy,* September 5, 2012, http://www.foreignpolicy.com/articles/2012/09/05/whats_not_wrong_with_drones (accessed September 6, 2012).

16. Kenneth Anderson, "They Also Serve Who Sit and Wait in Cubicles Far Away, or, Mark Mazzetti, 'The Drone Zone,'" Lawfare, July 8, 2012, http://www.lawfareblog.com /2012/07/mark-mazzetti-the-drone-zone-in-the-new-york-times-magazine/ (accessed September 22, 2012).

17. Brooks, "What's *Not* Wrong with Drones?" See also Bradley Strawser, "The Morality of Drone Warfare Revisited," *The Guardian*, August 6, 2012.

18. Scott Shane and Thom Shanker, "Strike Reflects US Shift to Drones in Terror Fight," *New York Times*, October 1, 2011.

19. Jonathan Dienst, "Al-Qaida Leader Killed in Drone Strike Played Role in NYC Terror Plots," *NBC New York*, June 6, 2012, http://www.nbcnewyork.com/news/local/al -Qaida-Killed-Drone-Strike-New-York-City-Terror-Plots-Abu-Yahya-al-Libi -157345505.html (accessed September 22, 2012).

20. "Yemeni Al-Qaeda Leader 'Killed in Drone Strike,'" *BBC News*, May 7, 2012, http://www.bbc.co.uk/news/world-middle-east-17979424 (accessed September 22, 2012).

21. Micah Zenko, "Drone, Sweet Drone," *Foreign Policy*, June 21, 2012, http://www .foreignpolicy.com/articles/2012/06/21/drone_sweet_drone (accessed September 6, 2012).

22. Ibid.; see also Lorenzo Franceschi-Biccierai, "Revealed: 64 Drone Bases on American Soil," *Wired*, June 13, 2012, http://www.wired.com/dangerroom/2012/06/64-drone -bases-on-us-soil/ (accessed September 22, 2012).

23. Zenko, "Drone, Sweet Drone."

24. Jennifer Lynch, "FAA Releases Lists of Drone Certificates—Many Questions Left Unanswered," Electronic Frontier Foundation, April 19, 2012, https://www.eff.org /deeplinks/2012/04/faa-releases-its-list-drone-certificates-leaves-many-questions -unanswered (accessed October 1, 2012).

25. Thomas J. Billitteri, "Drone Warfare: Are Strikes by Unarmed Aircraft Ethical?" *CQ Researcher*, August 6, 2010 (updated April 27, 2012), 677.

26. Lisa Hajjar, "Anatomy of the US Targeted Killing Policy," Middle East Research and Information Project, http://www.merip.org/mer/mer264/anatomy-us-targeted-killing -policy (accessed September 13, 2012).

27. Craig Whitlock, "US Airstrike That Killed American Teen in Yemen Raises Legal, Ethical Questions," *Washington Post*, October 22, 2011; see also Nathan Goetting, "The National Defense Authorization Act for Fiscal Year 2012: Battlefield Earth," *National Lawyers Guild Review* 68, no. 4 (2011): 247–255.

28. Billitteri, "Drone Warfare."

29. Whitlock, "US Airstrike That Killed American Teen in Yemen."

30. Peter Katel, "Eloquent US-Born Cleric Linked to 9/11 Attacks," in Peter Katel, "Homegrown Jihadists: Can Muslim Terrorists in the US Mount Serious Attacks?" *CQ Researcher*, September 3, 2010, 712–713.

31. Michael Epstein, "The Curious Case of Anwar al-Aulaqi: Is Targeting a Terrorist for Execution by Drone Strike a Due Process Violation When the Terrorist Is a United States Citizen?" http://apps.law.georgetown.edu/state-secrets-archive/resourcedocuments /Epsteinnote_161.pdf (accessed September 6, 2012).

32. Katel, "Homegrown Jihadists," 707.

33. Ibid.

34. *New York Times* reporter Charlie Savage reports that by June 2010 the Office of Legal Counsel had penned a fifty-page legal opinion explaining the legal reasoning for killing an American citizen; Charlie Savage, "Secret US Memo Made Legal Case to Kill a Citizen," *New York Times,* October 8, 2011. Benjamin R. Farley suggests the earlier date in "Targeting Anwar al-Aulaqi: A Case Study in the US Drone Strikes and Targeted Killing," *National Security Law Brief* 2 (2012): 57–88.

35. Quoted in Katel, "Homegrown Jihadists."

36. Klaidman, "Drones: How Obama Learned to Kill."

37. *Black's Law Dictionary,* 6th ed. (St. Paul, MN: West Group, 1990), 500.

38. Ryan Alford, "The Rule of Law at the Crossroads: Consequences of Targeted Killing of Citizens," *Utah Law Review* (2011): 1203–1274.

39. In *Boumediene v. Bush* 553 US 723 (2008), the US Supreme Court ruled that the Military Commissions Act of 2006 was an unconstitutional suspension of the writ of habeas corpus and that foreign nationals held at the US detention center in Guantanamo Bay, Cuba, had the right to trial.

40. Michael Chertoff, "The Decline of Judicial Deference on National Security," *Rutgers Law Review* 63 (2011): 1117–1134.

41. See Philip Dore, "Greenlighting American Citizens: Proceed with Caution," *Louisiana Law Review* 7, no. 1 (2011): 1–5; Michael Ramsden, "Targeted Killings and International Human Rights Law: The Case of Anwar al-Awlaki," *Journal of Security Law* 16, no. 2 (2011): 385–406; Jamelle Nelson, "The al-Awlaki Assassination and Due Process," *Law and Liberty Bulletin* 6, no. 2 (2011): 1–3.

42. US Department of Justice, "Attorney General Eric Holder Speaks at Northwestern University School of Law, March 5, 2012," http://www.justice.gov/iso/opa/ag /speeches/2012/ag-speech-1203051.html (accessed September 25, 2012).

43. Lesley Wexler, "Litigating the Long War on Terror: The Role of al-Aulaqi v. Obama," *Loyola University Chicago International Law Review* 9: 159–176, esp. 163, where it is noted that the Office of Foreign Assets Control, located in the Treasury Department, issued the order.

44. US Department of Justice, "Attorney General Eric Holder Speaks."

45. David Cole, "An Executive Power to Kill?" *New York Review of Books,* March 6, 2012.

46. US Department of Justice, "Attorney General Eric Holder Speaks."

47. Greg Miller, "Muslim Cleric Aulaqui Is First US Citizen on List of Those CIA Is Allowed to Kill," *Washington Post,* April 7, 2010.

48. Jo Becker and Scott Shane, "Secret 'Kill List' Proves a Test of Obama's Principles and Will," *New York Times,* May 29, 2012.

49. Farley, "Targeting Anwar al-Aulaqi," 85.

50. Abraham U. Kannof, "Dueling Nationalities: Dual Citizenship, Dominant and Effective Nationality, and the Case of Anwar al-Aulaqi," *Emory International Law Review* (2011): 1371–1430, 1414.

51. As noted in Lindsay Kwoka, "Trial by Sniper: The Legality of Targeted Killing in the War on Terror," *Journal of Constitutional Law* 14 (2011): 301–326, 310.

52. Pub. L. No. 107-40, 115 Stat. 224 (2001).

53. Charlie Savage, "Secret US Memo Made Legal Case to Kill a Citizen," *New York Times,* October 9, 2011.

54. Ibid.

55. Mary Ellen O'Connell, "Are Drone Strikes in Pakistan Legal? No," in Billitteri, "Drone Warfare," 669.

56. Kenneth Anderson, "Are Drone Strikes in Pakistan Legal? Yes," in Billitteri, "Drone Warfare."

57. Wexler, "Litigating the Long War on Terror," 162.

58. This is not simply a hypothetical situation. In fact, Lockheed Martin, a major drone manufacturer, spent $190 million on lobbying efforts in 2009 alone. Erik Chait, "Unmanned Aerial Vehicles for Civilian Use: Violating Rights, Privacy, and Safety?" *The Triple Helix* (Fall 2010).

59. The "Drone Caucus" also is not simply a hypothetical creation: in reality, Congress now has the Unmanned Systems Caucus, co-chaired by members of Congress from Texas and California—two border states—and comprising about sixty members. See the Congressional Unmanned Systems Caucus website at: http://unmannedsystemscaucus .mckeon.house.gov/ (accessed September 24, 2012).

60. "With law enforcement budgets shrinking, technology is playing a greater role in policing. And for agencies that want air coverage, a camera-equipped drone, at a cost of around $50,000, can be a cheaper alternative to owning and operating a piloted airplane or helicopter." Jennifer Vogel, "Police See Drones as Cheap Eye in the Sky," *Minnesota Public Radio News,* August 13, 2012, http://minnesota.publicradio.org/display/web /2012/08/02/ground-level-price-of-safety-drones (accessed September 20, 2012).

61. Hugh Bronstein, "Colombia Rebels, al Qaeda in 'Unholy' Drug Alliance," *Reuters,* January 4, 2010.

62. Islamic terrorists have acted within the United States with increased frequency in recent years. Katel ("Homegrown Jihadists") notes that several domestic attacks (only some of which were successful) have been planned or carried out by Muslims.

63. If anything, this estimate may be too low; see Patrick Radden Keefe, "Cocaine Incorporated," *New York Times,* June 15, 2012.

64. For more on the ability of intelligence agencies to gather and access information from the Internet, and the difficulties in doing so, see generally Justin D. Bañez, "The Internet and Homegrown Jihadist Terrorism: Assessing US Detection Techniques," master's thesis, Naval Postgraduate School, December 2010, http://www.dtic.mil/cgi-bin /GetTRDoc?AD=ADA536371 (accessed October 2, 2012).

65. The plot of a major Hollywood blockbuster includes the destruction of a stadium with a nuclear weapon. Although a plot with a nuclear weapon is, at this point in time, farcical, there have been a number of suspected terrorist plots to attack heavily attended stadiums worldwide, including a plot to attack South Africa during the 2010 World Cup and a plot to fire a rocket into an Israeli sports stadium. Rumored threats have also been made against NFL stadiums in the United States. "Feds: Threat Against NFL Stadiums Not Credible," CNN, October 18, 2006, http://articles.cnn.com/2006–10–18/us/football .threats_1_comprehensive-security-procedures-threat-dirty-bomb?_s=PM:US (accessed September 24, 2012).

66. Major police departments, such as New York's, have been focused on Muslim communities for years; Joseph Ax, "NYPD Surveillance of Muslims Popular, but Is It Legal?" *Reuters,* March 13, 2012. AP reporters Adam Goldman and Matt Apuzzo report that "in more than six years of spying on Muslim neighborhoods, eavesdropping on conversations and cataloguing mosques, the New York Police Department's secret Demographics Unit never generated a lead or triggered a terrorism investigation"; "NYPD: Muslim Spying Led to No Leads, Terror Cases," *Associated Press,* August 21, 2012.

67. Chicago had an anti-loitering law that was designed to cut down on gang violence until it was struck down by the US Supreme Court as unconstitutional in 1999 (*Chicago v. Morales,* 527 US 41 [1999]). If a police officer observed two or more people who he "reasonably believed" were gang members, he could order them to disperse, and the officer could arrest them if they ignored the order and continued to loiter.

68. In the recent Arab Spring tumult in Egypt, the government shut down the Internet in the hope of preventing a successful revolution; James Glanz and John Markoff, "Egypt Leaders Found 'Off' Switch for Internet," *New York Times,* February 16, 2011. For a discussion of recent proposals in Congress to allow the president to shut down Internet activity in the wake of a cyber-emergency, which would be declared by the president, see David W. Opderbeck, "Cybersecurity and Executive Power," *Washington University Law*

Review 89 (2012): 795–845. Additionally, Bay Area Rapid Transit (BART) police have shut down cell-phone service when detecting attempts to "interfere with and impede against BART police"; Jennifer Spencer, "No Service: Free Speech, the Communications Act, and BART's Cell Phone Network Shutdown," *Berkeley Technology Law Journal* 27 (2012): 767.

69. Charlie Savage, "Rule Limiting Legal Services in Terror Cases Is Challenged," *New York Times,* August 3, 2010. The answer to this question has broad implications, including but not limited to the legality of the targeted killing of American citizens who are accused of terrorism and the use and recognition of due process, discussed at length in this chapter. Determining that the entire world is in fact a battleground would have dramatic implications for the use of drones domestically, the decrease in citizenship and other rights, and potentially the suspension of habeas corpus.

70. Richard D. Rosen, "Drones and the US Courts," *William Mitchell Law Review* (2011): 5282.

71. Ibid., 5284. A lawsuit offered by the ACLU and CCR on behalf of al-Awlaki's father (*Al-Aulaqi v. Obama* 727 F. Supp. 2d 1 [2010]) was similarly dismissed in 2010.

72. From a constitutional perspective, the US Supreme Court decided in 1972 that a person cannot be detained based on future dangers to himself or others that he may pose (*Foucha v. Louisiana* 504 US 71 [1992]). More recently, liberal and conservative lawmakers have been discussing whether a law passed in 2011 allows the president to indefinitely detain suspected terrorists, including American citizens; John M. Donnelly, "Detainee Provisions Could Snag House Panel's Defense Authorization Bill," *CQ Today,* May 7, 2012, http://public.cq.com/docs/news/news-000004076587.html?ref=corg (accessed September 26, 2012).

Presidential Declaration of Disaster Decisions

The Case of Turndowns

RICHARD T. SYLVES

Introduction

When a US state or trust territory experiences what its governor considers a disaster, that governor may decide to ask the president for either a declaration of major disaster (authorized in federal law since 1950) or a declaration of emergency (law since 1971).[1] From May 1953 through December 2011, governors requested 2,760 major disaster declarations, and since 1971 they have petitioned for 466 emergency declarations.[2] Many may be surprised to learn that presidents have turned down a sizable share of these requests.

"Turndown" refers to the action authorized by the president, and signed by the Federal Emergency Management Agency (FEMA) director, that denies a governor's request for a major disaster or emergency declaration. It is noteworthy that the White House announces presidential approvals of governors' requests for declarations, while it is left to FEMA—from 1979 to 2003, and to FEMA within the Department of Homeland Security (DHS) since

2003—to announce turndowns. FEMA's turndown announcements deflect away from the president the negativity of a turndown, but make no mistake: a turndown means a governor's request for a declaration has been denied by the president.[3]

All presidents from Harry Truman to Barack Obama have sometimes turned down governor requests for major disaster declarations. All presidents from Richard Nixon to Obama have turned down a fraction of governor requests for emergency declarations. Why would any president turn down a governor's request for a major disaster or emergency declaration?

This study explores this question in seven parts, beginning with a theoretical discussion. Several contrasting normative theories are put forward. These theories posit the principles underlying presidential judgments regarding governor requests for major disaster and emergency declarations. Second, the study summarizes the process by which governors seek a presidential declaration, including a brief description of some of the law and policy of presidential disaster declarations. Third is an examination of how criteria are used by FEMA to offer presidents guidance on the worthiness and necessity of a declaration. The president is free to consider FEMA's criteria, data, and professional advice. However, each president since 1950 has been authorized by law to make an independent determination. In other words, modern presidents are not legally obligated to follow FEMA's recommendations regarding approvals or turndowns.

Fourth is the issue of how governors win or lose in the competition to win presidential declarations. The study considers what an approval or a turndown generally means for governors and their states—the stakes, if you will. It describes the benefits generally conferred by an approved major disaster or emergency declaration. Conversely, the section elucidates what the denial of federal disaster assistance generally means for states, counties, cities, and disaster victims of all types. Fifth is an overview of official turndown justifications. Included in this section is a short case study of one governor's turndown experience.

Sixth is a data and findings section. Here three tables of declaration totals are introduced and analyzed. The section also includes a table listing President George W. Bush's turndowns, case by case, during his first three years of office, and another listing President Barack Obama's turndowns in his first three years in office. Finally, observations are made on the possible motivations of both presidents and governors in disaster declaration decision-making.

Theories of Presidential Motivation

Can all presidential decisions on governor requests for disaster declarations be explained in terms of presidential politics? To what extent do a president's personal, political, partisan, and perhaps selfish motives come into play? Perhaps we could boil the issue down to a multiple-choice question: presidential decisions about whether to approve or deny governor requests are (a) always political, (b) usually political, (c) rarely political, or (d) never political.

There are a great many factors at work when a governor asks the president for a declaration. It would be both wrong and foolish, however, to assume that only choice (a) is true—that all such presidential decisions are purely political in nature. Conversely, it would be both incorrect and naive to assume that all such presidential decisions are never political in nature (d).

If such decisions could be depoliticized and made administratively routine, Congress, perhaps with presidential assent, would have long ago delegated them to federal executive branch officials, as has been the case in so many other realms of federal law and policy. In fact, Congress "wants" the president to hold and exercise authority and responsibility for declaration decision-making. Moreover, Congress insists that the president have largely unfettered discretion in deciding what is, or what is not, a federally declarable disaster. This is quite extraordinary given US separation of powers and long-standing congressional reluctance to cede power to the president. Since the years of President Ronald Reagan's new federalism, in which more federal authority would devolve to, or be delegated to, the states, trends have been away from centralization of power at the federal level in most policy domains.[4] Not so in the domain of disaster policy and emergency management. From 1979 to 2001, disaster management grew as a federal concern, sometimes at the expense of states and localities. Moreover, in this period FEMA helped build up and enhance state and local emergency management capacity and capabilities. The terror attacks of September 11, 2001, further accelerated disaster policy and emergency management centralization. FEMA was recruited into the "war on terrorism." The agency was folded into the new Department of Homeland Security in 2003, and a proliferation of generously funded federal laws and programs greatly increased FEMA's impact at the state and local levels.

Using three simple normative theories, this case study posits that presidential decisions regarding governor requests for declarations of major disaster or emergency manifest either Hamiltonian principles or Jeffersonian/Jacksonian principles.

Hamiltonian theory posits that presidential behavior is professional, largely apolitical, and often policy-technical; that it is based on scrupulous judgments of need, is responsible in federal budgetary terms, and is anchored in meeting the president's constitutional and legal obligations to the people of the nation. Hamiltonians are practical problem-solvers largely unswayed by often-vacillating public opinion.[5]

Jeffersonian principles espouse the benefits of placing priority at the state and local governmental levels and keeping the federal government as small and non-interfering as possible. What is important to Jeffersonians is seeking grassroots approval and consent for all laws and administrative actions. For Jeffersonians, the mark of a good policy proposal is its degree of public support more than its technical or scientific merit.[6]

Jacksonian principles maintain that presidents are elected to serve the people. For Jacksonians, to the victor go the spoils: the president's political partisans both expect and deserve preferential presidential treatment where possible. In addition, Jacksonian motives are geared toward winning reelection, punishing competitors, currying favor with key legislators, and rewarding supporters. Jacksonian presidents seek to do what is politically popular, and they are expected to be highly responsive to public needs. Not to be overlooked is the Jacksonian value of treating people equitably and fairly.

Do modern presidents exhibit Hamiltonian principles or some combination of Jeffersonian and Jacksonian principles in their judgments about the worthiness of governor requests for major disaster or emergency declarations?[7]

This study posits that for presidents politically subjective determinations—when political motives trump objective administrative motives—play a role in the case of marginal disasters.[8] Marginal disasters are those events that are far less than catastrophic, that do not pose a national security concern, and that are within—or close to within—the recovery capacity of the state or states in which they occur.[9] From my own analysis of nearly sixty years of presidential disaster declarations, I find that among hundreds of "marginal" disasters, some were granted a presidential declaration and some were denied approval.[10] Turndowns can be appealed and if successful be converted into approvals, but the record shows that such reversals are rare.

The Process, the Law, and the Presidential Decision Point

Presidents need help in determining if and when to bring the federal government into a disaster or emergency. They need help in judging the worthiness of the governor declaration requests they receive. From 1950 to 1979, before the creation of FEMA, presidents were advised about disaster declarations by their staffs and by the relevant federal agency officials. Since 1979, each president has been advised by the FEMA director or administrator about whether to approve or reject governor-requested declarations of major disaster.[11] FEMA directors may well have advised various presidents about governor requests for emergency declarations, but because governors are not required to document need in their emergency declaration requests (as they are expected to do when they ask for major disaster declarations), presidents and their White House staffs, perhaps in consultation with the FEMA director, often make "emergency declaration" decisions quickly and on the basis of life and safety considerations.[12]

The Administrative Process for Requesting a Declaration
Some of the common factors that FEMA officials consider before they make their recommendation to the president include:

- The number of homes that were destroyed or sustained major damage
- The extent to which the damage was concentrated or dispersed
- The estimated cost of repairing the damage
- The demographics of the affected area
- State and local governments' capabilities.

The Robert T. Stafford Disaster Relief and Emergency Relief Act of 1988 does not prescribe exact criteria to guide FEMA's recommendations or the president's decision. As a prerequisite to federal disaster assistance under the act, however, a governor must take "appropriate action" and provide information on the nature and amount of the state and local resources committed to alleviating the disaster's impacts. Other relevant considerations are:

- What are the demographics of the affected areas with regard to income levels, unemployment, concentrations of senior citizens, numbers of special needs individuals, and so on?

- To what degree does insurance cover the damage?
- To what degree have people in the disaster area been "traumatized"?
- How much disaster-related unemployment has the event produced?
- How much assistance is available from other federal agencies, such as the Small Business Administration (SBA) and its disaster loans to homeowners and businesses, or from FEMA's National Flood Insurance Program?
- Are state and local governments capable of dealing with the disaster on their own?
- How much disaster assistance is coming from volunteer organizations, and how adequate is that assistance given the magnitude of the disaster?
- How much rental housing is available for emergency occupancy?
- What is the nature and degree of the health and safety problems posed by the disaster and its effects?
- What is the extent of the damage to essential public services, such as utilities, medical, police, and fire?[13]

Noting that this rule does not affect presidential discretion in declaring disasters and does not change published regulations and policies established under the Stafford Act of 1988, the agency has announced that the 1999 rule will be used by the agency to evaluate requests as they apply to its Public Assistance Program and its Individual Assistance Program.[14] Under the Public Assistance Program (the government-to-government aid program that pays for infrastructure repair and reimburses certain nonprofit organization disaster expenses), FEMA examines the estimated cost of the assistance, using such factors as the cost per capita impact within the state. FEMA initially used a figure of $1 per capita as an indicator that the disaster was of sufficient magnitude to warrant federal assistance. This figure has been adjusted annually based on the Consumer Price Index (CPI). In addition, FEMA has established for each county a price-indexed threshold of $2.50 per capita.[15]

In addition, FEMA evaluates the impact of a disaster at the local and tribal level, particularly if critical facilities are involved; the amount of insurance coverage in force; the degree of hazard mitigation undertaken prior to the disaster; the recent disaster history of the applicants; and the availability of other federal assistance.

FEMA relies most heavily on how the assessment of a state's capability compares with the costs imposed by the disaster. Each governor requesting a declaration is expected to demonstrate to FEMA and the president that the state's ability to respond to the disaster or emergency, of whatever nature, is inadequate, so that federal assistance is needed.

If the president issues a disaster declaration, FEMA is authorized to coordinate federal disaster assistance. However, it is difficult and sometimes impossible for FEMA officials to ascertain that an event warrants a presidential declaration unless Preliminary Damage Assessments (PDAs) are first conducted and analyzed (often through photographs or video recording) or unless media coverage of the event makes it obvious that a major disaster has occurred. Moreover, it is difficult to judge whether state and local areas are capable of recovering on their own if disaster damage has not been assessed beforehand. Consequently, the president sometimes issues declarations of major disaster or emergency without documentary evidence that the disasters have met FEMA's criteria.

A key step in the process involves the "White House Package," which refers to the documents prepared for the president's action regarding a governor's request for a major disaster or emergency declaration. The package includes the governor's request and contains a memorandum from the FEMA administrator (director) to the president that summarizes significant aspects of the event; presents statistics on damage and losses; outlines the contributions made by federal, state, local, and private agencies; highlights the unmet needs for which the governor seeks federal assistance; and presents a recommended course of action for the president.[16] Based on the recommendation, the package also contains appropriate letters and announcements related to the action to be taken (either a declaration or a turndown).

There is an assumed serial path and hierarchy of public and private emergency response and recovery. Presidents understand that federal disaster and emergency aid involves federal, state, and local relations. Local authorities usually ask their governor for state assistance first. When a governor judges that the state and its impacted localities are unable to appropriately mobilize for, respond to, or recover from a disaster or emergency without federal disaster assistance, that governor formulates a request to the president and FEMA. Governors make formal requests for declarations to the regional FEMA office first, and after an official review the request is sent on with regional office comments to FEMA headquarters and the agency's administrator. From there a FEMA official sends the request package on to the White House, where the ultimate decision is made.

However, mass media coverage of local calamities broadcast on the national level, the lack of precision in declaration eligibility conditions, and pressures on governors and other state and local authorities to respond to the disaster, all come to bear on modern presidents. The strong disaster video that television presents, sometimes in live broadcasts, is not ignored in the White House. Occasionally, a combination of these imperatives invites presidents to short-circuit the formal FEMA review process and quickly issue declarations of major disaster or emergency.

Since the enactment of the Disaster Relief Act of 1970, the definition of disaster has been expanded to include not only major disasters but also emergencies. Then, in 1988, new categories of emergency were approved in law. Today the term "emergency" is used to define any event determined by the president to require federal assistance as stipulated by the Disaster Relief and Emergency Assistance Amendments of 1988. As noted previously, emergencies are usually of lesser magnitude and scope than major disasters, and federal aid is capped at $5 million.[17] Emergency designations, more than major disaster designations, are likely to stretch the rule that states must lack the capacity to recover on their own to qualify for a presidential declaration. If an incident occurs at a time when state and local budgets are tight or in deficit, the emergency designation offers a flexible category for help. FEMA records disclose that snowstorms, windstorms, minor flooding, and drought are the most common types of emergency declarations. Emergencies sometimes also allow politically subjective determinations to come into play, because need does not have to be proven by factual documentation or as a general condition of deservedness.

However, calamities of relatively small scale that have been judged by federal disaster authorities not to have sufficiently met declaration criteria are often vulnerable to presidential turndowns. For example, a tornado that damages only a small number of predominantly privately insured structures may be a candidate for a presidential turndown. A severe storm causing minor losses and little infrastructure damage in a single county may also draw a turndown. A problem arises when a governor judges his or her state's scale of disaster damage or loss to be worthy of a presidential declaration but the president disagrees. Perhaps the president's top disaster manager told him that the scale of damage was insufficient to justify issuing a declaration. This official may have determined that the state in question had the capacity to respond to, or recover from, the disaster using its own resources. In such a case, this decision would be consistent with "functional federalism"—the president's turndown is Jeffersonian in the sense that he is limiting the involvement of the federal government in what is more appropriately a state and local issue—and yet also "functional" from a Hamiltonian perspective because the president is judging the governor's request on the basis of need and deservedness.

Criteria in Presidential Decision-Making

In examining the issue of presidential declarations, it is important to recognize that the federal government has never developed or employed a set of objective criteria by which to approve or deny the requests of governors for presidential declarations of major disaster or emergency.

The record of approvals and turndowns raises questions about how any governor's request for a presidential declaration is considered, particularly for marginal disaster denials. Since there are no mandatory objective criteria in law or policy for making approval or turndown decisions, only the president who received the request knows the reasoning in each case. The written record about what FEMA advised the president to do and what the president actually did is closely protected by executive privilege nondisclosure restrictions.[18] Governors may choose to reveal to the public the content of the letter they received from the president (an approval) or from FEMA (a turndown). However, most information about the details of a president's declaration decisions is not released until decades after a president has left office, if at all, and usually only through permissions obtained by the presidential library for that president or other bodies.[19]

One might assume that the number of deaths and injuries in a disaster makes a difference in judging a request's worthiness. Though it may certainly make a difference in the Oval Office, strangely, FEMA does not keep records of fatalities in disaster incidents.[20] Consequently, it is not possible to ascertain from FEMA's public records whether or not fatalities played a role in the president's decision. Sometimes the FEMA director recommends to the president that a request be turned down because it does not fit within the Stafford Act of 1988 general criteria of eligibility, yet the ultimate decision resides with the president.

All this invites political subjectivity into presidential decision-making. But remember, there are two sides in this game. Governors play the game by seeking presidential declarations for temporary drought, crop failures, minor wildfires, small floods, beach erosion, and a wide range of other calamities that cannot be considered "beyond the capability of the State and local government to adequately respond." The records of approvals and turndowns contain many possible candidates for marginal disaster declarations. Moreover, many governors are astutely aware of the strategic political importance of their state to a president. This is especially so when an incumbent president seeks reelection and the state in question is considered a "swing" state or a battleground state in the forthcoming general election.[21] Usually such states hold a substantial number of electoral votes and are nearly evenly divided between Republicans and Democrats or they have a sizable pool of independent voters whose vote is difficult to predict.

Over the years, federal disaster officials have attempted to establish definitive and quantitative requirements for disaster declaration eligibility.[22] One such effort would have tied declarations to damage translated in dollars per capita. These efforts proposed rigorous declaration criteria, but presidents have resisted and Congress has vehemently opposed such measures. Presidents do not want their range of declaration discretion further circumscribed or ceded to federal disaster officials. Legislators want reassurance that they may use their legitimate political authority to seek declarations directly from the president when their home states and districts experience incidents or events they consider emergencies or disasters.

According to former FEMA director James Lee Witt, each event or incident is evaluated individually on its own merits. The criteria set forth in the Stafford Act include:

1. The severity and magnitude of the incident;
2. The impact of the event; and
3. Whether the incident is beyond the capabilities of the State and affected local governments.[23]

For many years, the process and criteria have been purposely subjective to allow the president discretion to address a wide range of events and circumstances. Director Witt once remarked that there are no definitive objective evaluators that can be used in the declaration process, although he recommended that FEMA endeavor to establish some.[24] Without such objective criteria, governors and their state disaster officials have little to guide them in estimating whether to go ahead with a request for a presidential declaration of major disaster or emergency. They have little basis for concluding in advance whether their petition for a presidential declaration will be approved or denied.

The Consequences of Winning or Losing a Petition for a Presidential Declaration

The modern federal disaster assistance program was enacted into law in 1950. Its benefits and coverage expanded slowly over the years. There were major expansions of benefits in 1970, 1988, and 1993. Today the program provides grants to states and local governments to pay for emergency costs and repairs to public facilities—usually funded at the 75 percent level. Minimal repairs and temporary housing are furnished by the federal government directly to individuals. The federal government relief program under a major disaster declaration funds 75 percent of small grants through the states to help disaster victims replace housing and furnishings. In cases of destroyed homes, the grants usually provide only a share of the total assistance needed. The remainder may be borrowed from the Small Business Administration at a low interest. For businesses in damage zones, the only form of disaster assistance is an SBA loan. Federal assistance for agricultural damage is handled through US Department of Agriculture programs and consists mainly of crop insurance and farm loans, with some cost-share grants. Certain types of nonprofit organizations are offered grant assistance at the 75-percent-of-cost level, although some are required first to apply for a loan through the SBA. The grant assistance is available for them only if the SBA denies their disaster loan application.

While almost every governor can issue declarations and proclamations of state-level disaster, states often cannot provide substantial disaster recovery aid without securing a special spending measure from the state legislature, drawing down contingency funds or raising taxes. Moreover, absent federal inducements like 75/25 federal subsidies of state spending that enable states to collect sizable sums of federal money, many state governments have done little to provide help to their resident citizens or businesses in disasters. Many state officials routinely expect that the post-disaster help for their citizens will come from the federal government, from private donations, or from voluntary relief organizations, such as the American Red Cross. Led by their governors, state governments do sometimes come to the aid of their disaster-stricken local governments, even occasionally when the governor has had a request for a presidential declaration turned down or elected not to apply for a presidential declaration at all.

Justifications Given for Turndowns

There may be administrative reasons why a governor's request is denied by a president, including:

1. The governor's request was not filed in a timely fashion and/or the request lacked essential information about the event.
2. The governor's request did not prove convincingly to FEMA and the president that the state was unable to respond to, and recover

from, the incident without the help provided by a declaration of major disaster or emergency. This is a complicated issue because the assessment may rest on the state's population and area as well as its financial condition. For example, the turndown may hold that the geographic area covered by the incident was too small or covered too few counties to warrant a declaration. FEMA employs a threshold of qualification under which total damage is divided by state population, yielding a state per capita damage cost total. Sometimes state per capita damage totals may fall below FEMA's threshold of eligibility. (But remember, presidents are not bound by this criterion and may grant a declaration even if state per capita damage is below FEMA's threshold at the time and even if FEMA therefore advises the president to turn down the declaration request.) Embedded in the administrative judgment of deservedness is also the question of the amount of disaster economic loss covered by public and private insurance. Incidents with little public infrastructure damage and with substantial insurance coverage for disaster-victim losses run a relatively high risk of presidential turndown. In other words, if most disaster victims own various forms of public and private insurance, and if this insurance is sufficient to cover the bulk of their disaster losses, the worthiness of a declaration request diminishes. Federal law and policy is not designed to cover the same loss that is also covered by an insurance claim. Moreover, a governor's request for a declaration may not be defensible if she or he is asking for help to address an incident that the state and its localities have long been able to address on their own (for example, heavy snow in northern states accustomed to winter snowstorms, minor earthquakes in Pacific region states, and so on).

3. The governor asked for a declaration to address an incident better addressed by one or more other federal programs outside of a presidential declaration. Remember, a presidential declaration of major disaster or emergency mobilizes a host of federal agencies and programs under the federal plans and incident management systems in place during the era when the request is filed. Sometimes governors press ahead with their requests despite official advice from FEMA or the White House not to request federal assistance through a presidential declaration.

4. Related to (3), sometimes the nature of the incident is anomalous and risks creating a new category of federally declarable incident. History shows that certain types of incidents (such as terrorist acts, hazardous material incidents, certain insect-borne diseases, and wildfire threat) were declared for the first time by various presidents and so opened up a precedent that encouraged governors to ask for declarations for these types of events. However, presidents are often reluctant to invite new categories of declarable incidents because they fear that governors will exploit these incidents to draw excessive federal agency resources as well as undeserved federal funding to their states. Some of these dubious types of incident requests have included bridge collapses, uncremated bodies, red tide, and fisheries closures. Categories that governors deem exploitable hold out the danger of running up federal spending unnecessarily.[25]

Turndowns, Federally Unaided Recovery, and a Turndown Case

The Case of a Turndown in Alabama

Let us consider an actual turndown example:

MONTGOMERY, ALABAMA—The federal government turned down Gov. Bob Riley's request for disaster aid for three north Alabama counties hit by killer tornadoes on Feb. 6 (2008). While the governor considers whether to appeal that decision, the state Emergency Management Agency is trying to determine the financial impact of a tornado that hit Prattville on Sunday and whether Alabama should apply for federal assistance.

Riley had sought a federal disaster declaration for Jackson, Lawrence and Walker counties after tornadoes claimed six lives. Riley's press secretary, Tara Hutchison, said Tuesday the Federal Emergency Management Agency denied the request on Friday because there was not enough uninsured damage in the counties to meet federal requirements. Victor Manning, emergency management director for Jackson County, said Tuesday he was disappointed it took so long to get a response. Hutchison said the governor has 30 days to decide whether to appeal the decision. A federal disaster declaration provides federal funding for cleanup, housing and other assistance.[26]

This case conveys certain pieces of essential information. First three northern Alabama counties were struck by a so-called killer tornado that took six lives and damaged homes in the path it took across these counties. The governor of Alabama asked FEMA and the president for a major disaster declaration for his state that would direct federal disaster aid to eligible victims in these counties. The ruling to approve or deny the governor's request always resides in the White House, but since the standard practice is that FEMA announce the president's turndowns while the White House customarily announces approvals. President George W. Bush turned down the request and FEMA made the announcement. It is perfectly reasonable to assume that FEMA recommended to the president that he turn down the request, for the reasons given in the AP article. Finally, governor appeals of turndowns are sometimes won, but much more often lost.

Data, Analysis, and Simple Statistical Findings

The data files used for this study were provided to the author by FEMA and the Congressional Research Service in August 2012.[27] Table 1.2.1 reveals that from May 1953, when the first serially numbered major disaster declaration was issued, through December 31, 2011, governors asked presidents for a total of 2,760 major disaster declarations. Beginning in 1971 and through the end of 2011, they asked presidents for another 466 emergency declarations. The grand total of all governor requests, for both types of declarations, was 3,226.

As Table 1.2.1 depicts, from Eisenhower (beginning in May 1953) through Obama (ending January 31, 2011), presidents approved 2,050 major disaster declaration requests, which is 74.28 percent of requests for all such declarations. Conversely, over the same period, presidents denied 710 governor requests for a major disaster declaration (25.72 percent). In other words, over the fifty-nine-year period, governors as a group stood a three-in-four chance that their request for a major disaster declaration would be approved, but also a one-in-four chance that they would be denied.

Over the same period, presidents approved 344 emergency declaration requests, or 73.82 percent of all such requests. Conversely, governors experienced 122 turndowns of their requests for an emergency declaration (26.18 percent). Over the fifty-nine-year period, governors as a group stood about a three-in-four chance that their request for an emergency disaster declaration would be approved—only slightly less than their chances of receiving a major disaster declaration.

TABLE 1.2.1: Presidential Turndowns for Major Disaster and Emergency Declarations, May 1953 to January 31, 2011

	Major Disaster Declaration Requests	Emergency Declaration Requests	Combined Major Disaster and Emergency Requests
Presidential approvals	2,050 (74.28% of major disaster requests)	344 (73.82% of emergency requests)	2,394 (74.21% approved)
Presidential turndowns (denials)	710 (25.72% of major disaster requests)	122 (26.18% of emergency requests)	832 (25.79% denied)
Total	2,760 (85.56% of all requests)	466 (14.44% of all requests)	3,226

Source: Assembled from Federal Emergency Management Agency (FEMA), "Major Disaster, Emergency, and Turndowns," Microsoft Excel file, obtained August, 12, 2012 (34 pages); and FEMA, Disaster Financial Status Report (DFSR), projections summary, grouped by event and calendar year, Microsoft Excel file, obtained August 14, 2012.

What kind of governor declaration requests have been turned down by Presidents George W. Bush and Barack Obama? We turn next to an examination of these presidents' approval and turndown records.

Table 1.2.2 depicts the same type of information as Table 1.2.1, but is restricted to the two terms, or eight years, in which President George W. Bush held office. President Bush's record shows an 84.93 percent approval rate when governors requested major disaster declarations—about a 15 percent turndown rate. Bush approved over 82.74 percent of all requests he received—a 17.26 percent turndown rate. When Bush is compared to the total pool (which began with Eisenhower and included Bush as well as President Obama), governors had a 10.65 percent higher chance with him that their major disaster declaration request would be approved. In terms of odds, governors for the entire period 1953–2011 had a three-in-four (or fifteen-in-twenty) chance of approval, but for the Bush administration they enjoyed a seventeen-in-twenty chance of approval.

TABLE 1.2.2: President George W. Bush's Major Disaster and Emergency Declaration Decisions, January 20, 2001, to January 20, 2009

	Major Disaster Declaration Requests	Emergency Declaration Requests	Combined Major Disaster and Emergency Requests
Presidential approvals	513 (84.93% of major disaster requests)	139 (82.74% of emergency requests)	652 (84.46% approved)
Presidential turndowns (denials)	91 (15.07% of major disaster requests)	29 (17.26% of emergency requests)	120 (15.54% denied)
Total	604 (78.24% of all requests)	168 (21.76% of all requests)	772

Source: Assembled from Federal Emergency Management Agency (FEMA), "Major Disaster, Emergency, and Turndowns," Microsoft Excel file, obtained August, 12, 2012 (34 pages); and FEMA, Disaster Financial Status Report (DFSR), projections summary, grouped by event and calendar year, Microsoft Excel file, obtained August 14, 2012.

President Barack Obama's totals deviate only modestly from those of President George W. Bush. Table 1.2.3 shows that Obama approved 88 percent of governor requests for a major disaster declaration, which compares to about 85 percent for Bush. For the first three years of the Obama administration, governors faced odds of approval for major disaster declaration requests that were only slightly less than eighteen out of twenty. Obama approved over 89 percent of all emergency declaration requests—or about a 10 percent turndown rate. This represents a slightly more generous emergency approval rate than that of Bush, who approved about 83 percent of all emergency requests.

Further research beyond the scope of this study is needed to further partition the data and conduct tests of statistical significance for differences. However, some general conclusions are in order. The odds that governors will win approval of both their major disaster and emergency declaration requests have improved significantly since 1953. President George W. Bush was only 4 percent less generous in issuing declarations of major disaster when compared with President Obama. Yet Obama was about 6 percent more generous than Bush in approving emergency declaration requests.

TABLE 1.2.3: President Barack Obama's Major Disaster and Emergency Declaration Decisions, January 20, 2009, to December 31, 2011

	Major Disaster Declaration Requests	Emergency Declaration Requests	Combined Major Disaster and Emergency Requests
Presidential approvals	234 (87.97% of major disaster requests)	43 (89.58% of emergency requests)	277 (88.22% approved)
Presidential turndowns (denials)	32 (12.03% of major disaster requests)	5 (10.42% of emergency requests)	37 (11.78% denied)
Total	266 (84.71% of all requests)	48 (15.29% of all requests)	314

Source: Assembled from Federal Emergency Management Agency (FEMA), "Major Disaster, Emergency, and Turndowns," Microsoft Excel file, obtained August, 12, 2012 (34 pages); and FEMA, Disaster Financial Status Report (DFSR), projections summary, grouped by event and calendar year, Microsoft Excel file, obtained August 14, 2012.

Another noteworthy observation is the increase in governor requests and total declarations, of both types, since 1953. For Bush's eight years in office, major disaster and emergency declaration requests totaled 772 (or an average of 96.5 per year). For the first three years of the Obama administration, declaration requests totaled 314 (an average of nearly 105 per year). The average number of both types of requests submitted per year from 1953 through 2011 was 54. The total pool of major disaster declarations from 1953 up to President Bush's inauguration on January 20, 2001, totaled 1,358, and emergency declarations from 1971 to the same point in time totaled 183. In other words, it took forty-seven years to generate 1,358 major disaster declarations and thirty years to produce 162 emergency declarations (Eisenhower through Clinton), but only eleven years (2001 through 2011) for Bush and Obama to generate 747 major disaster declarations and 182 emergency declarations. Together Bush and Obama issued more than 33 percent of the total number of major disaster declarations over the entire fifty-nine-year period and 53 percent of the total number of emergency declarations issued since 1971.

Given the great number of presidential turndowns from Eisenhower to Obama, it is impossible to show a complete list of raw case-by-case turndowns from 1953 through 2011. However, in order to provide a sense of what composes turndown decisions in official terms, the case turndowns issued by President Bush can be seen in Table 1.2.4, and those by President Obama in Table 1.2.5. In each case, the first two years and a few months of the Bush and Obama administrations are depicted.

The factors presented in the next section seem to be evident in many of the cases. Neither the magnitude nor the extent of the turndown has been officially reported by FEMA or its predecessor agencies. In the absence of this information, it may well be that a vast majority of turndowns in the FEMA era stem from the failure of the requesting state and its counties to meet or exceed the eligibility thresholds that FEMA uses in advising each president. Also, anomalous cases appear in the list (bridge collapse, red tide, uncremated bodies, single-structure fires, and so on). Some turndown events may seem anomalous but have been granted to other governors before: for instance, the turndowns for the 9/11 attacks issued to Massachusetts and Florida, when New York, New Jersey, and Virginia won declarations for the same attacks.[28]

Speculation on the Factors in a Presidential Turndown Decision

Presidents, in considering governors' requests for presidential declarations of major disaster or emergency, decide which events qualify and which events do not. Sometimes presidents have approved requests for major disasters and emergencies when the incidents affected very few people or very few organizations. These "judgment calls" had to take a host of factors into consideration, such as: the national interests at stake; the media news coverage of the event; the political costs to the president in approving or rejecting the request; the need for the president to exhibit compassion and responsiveness; the precedents set by approval or rejection; the effect of the decision on the image of the president as a person and on the presidency as an institution; and the president's relations with various governors, mayors, lawmakers, and interest groups.

Factor 1: Magnitude and Extent

The degree or scale of human suffering produced by a disaster or emergency is a factor—arguably a paramount factor—in a president's decision to approve a governor's request for a declaration. Presidents, their advisers, and emergency management leaders take into account both the number of people affected and the severity of the suffering they have experienced or continue to experience. The magnitude and extent of a disaster also encompass infrastructure loss, economic loss, loss of housing stock, degree of disruption, and the size of the land area impacted by a disaster.

Yet presidents and governors sometimes disagree over what is declarable as a major disaster or emergency and what is not. These disagreements often run along two dimensions: the magnitude, or scale, of the disaster, which includes the ability of states and localities to recover from the disaster given its magnitude; and the nature of the incident or the type of disaster at issue.

Expansive, deadly, costly, catastrophic disasters easily qualify as being of sufficient magnitude to win almost immediate presidential declaration approvals. Large-scale disasters usually embody great human suffering. Presidents approve routinely most earthquake and hurricane requests and the vast majority of flood requests, especially floods with large-scale loss and damage. However, other types of disasters, particularly those of relatively small scale or loss, are considered "marginal" and are susceptible to presidential turndown—especially disasters that states and localities might recover from on their own without federal relief.

Sometimes governors request presidential declarations for incidents that have produced very few victims and little human suffering, most often when their state has suffered economic calamities in the wake of natural or human-caused disasters. Governors have asked for presidential declarations, for instance, to cover damaging citrus crop freezes, fishing losses or fisheries closures, toxic substance spills, urban structure fires, barge accidents, and slow-moving landslides or mudslides. Presidents sometimes grant these requests, and sometimes they deny them.

Although the top federal disaster agency leader may recommend that the president turn down a particular marginal request, the president may choose to disregard this advice and approve it anyway, for a variety of reasons: he does not want to appear unresponsive or unsympathetic; he seeks to maintain support or curry favor with the requesting governor, members of the requesting state's congressional delegation, and the disaster-affected mayors or county leaders; he is taking into account the state's strategic political importance; or perhaps the state has previously suffered other misfortunes. The president may also choose to deny a marginal request for political reasons, public management reasons, or both.

TABLE 1.2.4: President George W. Bush's Turndowns by Case, October 24, 2001, to December 22, 2003

State	Incident Name	Date Governor Made Request	Incident Begin Date
MD	Tornadoes and severe storms	10/2/01	9/24/01
FM	Micronesia-toxic substance 8/20/01	9/10/01	7/1/01
MA	Fires and explosions	10/2/01	9/11/01
FL	Fires and explosions (terrorist investigation)	10/17/01	9/11/01
TX	Severe storms and tornadoes 10/12/01	10/25/01	10/12/01
TX	Queen Isabel bridge collapse 9/15/01	10/3/01	9/15/01
AZ	Wildfire 5/27/03	6/12/03	4/1/02
TX	Severe storms and flooding 11/15/01	11/30/01	11/15/01
TN	Severe weather system with flooding	2/6/02	1/23/02
GA	Unburied and uncremated bodies	2/21/02	2/15/02
FL	Red tide (microalgae Karenia brevis)	12/4/01	10/16/01
IL	Tornado 4/21/02	4/25/02	4/21/02
NM	Wildfire threat 3/24/02	6/3/02	3/24/02
ME	Drought	4/9/02	6/1/01
IL	Flooding 6/3/02 to 6/5/02	7/1/02	6/3/02
NE	Severe storms	7/15/02	7/6/02
AZ	Monsoon 7/9/02	8/6/02	7/9/02
ND	Wildfire threat	8/1/02	2/22/02
WY	Flooding 8/27/02	8/30/02	8/27/02
FL	Hurricane Isidore 9/23/02	10/8/02	9/26/02
CT	Winter storm: freezing rain, sleet, and snow	12/11/02	11/16/02
NJ	Severe storm power outage 8/2/02	8/14/02	8/2/02
VA	Orange County drought	8/23/02	8/26/02
MS	Severe storms and tornado	12/23/02	12/18/02
RI	Nightclub fire	2/24/03	2/20/03
MS	West Nile virus 8/16/02	8/16/02	7/19/02
LA	West Nile virus 8/5/02	8/5/02	6/1/02
FL	Sustained severe freeze events	3/20/03	11/1/02
NH	Mt. Washington structural fire	4/9/03	2/9/03
MS	Flooding and damaging winds	6/12/03	5/17/03
FL	Severe storms and tornadoes	8/13/03	8/7/03
LA	Tropical Storm Bill	7/9/03	6/30/03
MI	Dam failure 5/14/03	6/4/03	5/10/03
KY	Severe storms and flooding	8/29/03	8/22/03
TX	Severe storms 10/12/03	10/21/03	9/18/03
NJ	Hurricane Isabel	10/3/03	9/18/03
TX	Severe storms and tornadoes 11/17/03	11/21/03	11/17/03
CA	Severe fire threat	4/16/03	3/1/02

Source: Assembled from Federal Emergency Management Agency (FEMA), "Major Disaster, Emergency, and Turndowns," Microsoft Excel file, obtained August 12, 2012 (34 pages); and FEMA, Disaster Financial Status Report (DFSR), projections summary, grouped by event and calendar year, Microsoft Excel file, obtained August 14, 2012.

Incident End Date (Some incidents lack clear end date and are left blank)	Request Type DR=Major Disaster EM=Emergency	Action by President	Date of President's Turndown
9/24/01	DR	Turndown	10/24/01
8/26/01	DR	Turndown	10/29/01
	EM	Turndown	10/31/01
	EM	Turndown	11/7/01
10/13/01	DR	Turndown	11/27/01
	DR	Turndown	12/21/01
	EM	Turndown	1/8/02
11/18/01	DR	Turndown	1/9/02
	DR	Turndown	2/19/02
	EM	Turndown	2/26/02
	DR	Turndown	3/13/02
4/21/02	DR	Turndown	5/7/02
7/19/02	EM	Turndown	6/17/02
	DR	Turndown	7/19/02
6/5/02	DR	Turndown	7/19/02
7/6/02	DR	Turndown	7/29/02
7/15/02	DR	Turndown	8/30/02
	EM	Turndown	9/5/02
8/28/02	DR	Turndown	9/18/02
9/27/02	EM	Turndown	11/18/02
11/18/02	DR	Turndown	1/8/03
	EM	Turndown	1/8/03
	DR	Turndown	1/21/03
12/19/02	DR	Turndown	2/14/03
	DR	Turndown	4/23/03
	EM	Turndown	4/25/03
	EM	Turndown	4/25/03
2/28/03	DR	Turndown	4/28/03
2/9/03	DR	Turndown	6/20/03
	DR	Turndown	8/28/03
8/8/03	DR	Turndown	8/29/03
	DR	Turndown	9/12/03
5/26/03	DR	Turndown	9/24/03
8/22/03	DR	Turndown	10/7/03
10/20/03	DR	Turndown	11/6/03
	DR	Turndown	11/6/03
11/18/03	DR	Turndown	12/4/03
	EM	Turndown	12/22/03

TABLE 1.2.5: President Barack Obama's Turndowns by Case, May 6, 2009, to November 30, 2011

State	Incident Name	Date Governor Made Request	Incident Begin Date
TX	Extreme fire hazard	2/25/09	1/16/09
TX	Wildfires	4/16/09	4/7/09
ND	Snow	2/19/09	11/4/08
OK	Severe storms, tornadoes, and flooding	5/21/09	4/25/09
PA	Severe storms and flooding	6/29/09	5/28/09
TX	Extreme fire hazard	8/18/09	7/15/09
CA	Drought	6/19/09	4/14/09
IN	Severe storms and flooding	9/9/09	8/4/09
AZ	Havasupai flood 8/17/08	10/6/08	8/17/08
AL	Subfreezing temperatures	2/1/10	1/7/10
FL	Subfreezing temperatures	3/18/10	1/2/10
NY	Snowstorm	2/2/10	12/18/09
AR	Severe storms, tornadoes, and flooding	5/10/10	4/30/10
OH	Tornado 6/6/10	6/9/10	6/5/10
IL	Severe storms and tornadoes	6/18/10	6/5/10
LA	Tornado	5/7/10	4/24/10
OK	Tornadoes, severe storms, and flooding	7/19/10	7/6/10
CT	Severe storm and tornado	8/20/10	6/24/10
CA	Explosions and fires	9/5/10	9/9/10
RI	Hurricane Earl	9/2/10	8/30/10
TX	Tropical Storm Hermine	9/20/10	9/6/10
MO	Severe storms and tornadoes	1/14/11	12/30/10
MS	Severe storms and flooding	3/31/11	3/8/11
IN	Severe winter storm	3/14/11	1/31/11
AL	Severe storms, tornadoes, and flooding	4/19/11	4/15/11
LA	Tornado	3/18/11	3/5/11
WA	Severe winter storm, flooding, landslides, and mud	2/14/11	12/8/10
NJ	Severe storms and flooding	3/31/11	3/10/11
VA	Severe storms, tornadoes, and flooding	4/18/11	4/8/11
WA	White Swan fire 2/12/11	3/25/11	2/12/11
CA	Severe storms, flooding, debris, and mud flows	4/22/11	3/15/11
IL	Severe storms and flooding	8/26/11	7/27/11
VA	Remnants of Tropical Storm Lee	10/8/11	9/8/11
NE	Severe storms and flooding	9/15/11	8/18/11
MD	Remnants of Tropical Storm Lee	9/8/11	9/3/11
NY	Severe storms and flooding	7/13/11	5/13/11
OK	Earthquakes	11/21/11	11/5/11

Source: Assembled from Federal Emergency Management Agency (FEMA), "Major Disaster, Emergency, and Turndowns," Microsoft Excel file, obtained August 12, 2012 (34 pages); and FEMA, Disaster Financial Status Report (DFSR), projections summary, grouped by event and calendar year, Microsoft Excel file, obtained August 14, 2012.

Incident End Date	Request Type	Action by President	Date of President's Turndown
(Some incidents lack clear end date and are left blank)	DR=Major Disaster EM=Emergency		
	EM	Turndown	5/6/09
	DR	Turndown	5/8/09
	EM	Turndown	5/20/09
5/16/09	DR	Turndown	9/2/09
	DR	Turndown	9/3/09
	EM	Turndown	9/16/09
	DR	Turndown	10/19/09
8/9/09	DR	Turndown	11/3/09
	DR	Turndown	12/4/09
1/12/10	DR	Turndown	3/2/10
2/1/10	DR	Turndown	4/16/10
12/20/09	DR	Turndown	5/10/10
	DR	Turndown	5/20/10
6/6/10	DR	Turndown	6/24/10
6/5/10	DR	Turndown	6/29/10
4/24/10	DR	Turndown	7/23/10
7/12/10	DR	Turndown	7/28/10
6/24/10	DR	Turndown	10/8/10
9/11/10	DR	Turndown	10/28/10
	EM	Turndown	11/3/10
9/10/10	DR	Turndown	11/5/10
12/31/10	DR	Turndown	1/26/11
3/9/11	DR	Turndown	4/8/11
2/4/11	DR	Turndown	4/20/11
4/16/11	DR	Turndown	4/22/11
3/5/11	DR	Turndown	5/10/11
12/18/10	DR	Turndown	5/17/11
3/17/11	DR	Turndown	5/31/11
4/8/11	DR	Turndown	6/23/11
2/13/11	DR	Turndown	7/1/11
3/27/11	DR	Turndown	8/4/11
7/28/11	DR	Turndown	9/9/11
9/9/11	DR	Turndown	11/4/11
8/22/11	DR	Turndown	11/10/11
	EM	Turndown	11/10/11
5/31/11	DR	Turndown	11/23/11
	DR	Turndown	11/30/11

Factor 2: Speed of Onset

How rapidly has a disaster transpired? Almost inherent in the definition of disaster is that it hits with little or no notice. There is no time to mitigate its effects or to seek special legislation to address its consequences. Disasters such as earthquakes, flash floods, tornadoes, and hurricanes are readily seen as the types of disasters that should be the subject of a presidential disaster declaration. Slow-developing events, such as the gradual reduction in fish available for commercial catches or drought generally have not been the types of events that warrant a declaration, although declarations have occasionally been triggered by these types of events. For example, global warming is a slow-developing disaster whose effects cannot be adapted to or mitigated without decades of study and planning. As such, global warming is not likely to be declared a disaster by the president. Another example is the AIDS epidemic. Although it has killed millions and made millions more very ill, it is not seen as a disaster amenable to a presidential declaration. The spread of West Nile virus, on the other hand, was declared an emergency in several states by the president. It was a problem that developed suddenly and could be mitigated by existing public health measures that did not require years of study and scientific research.

Disasters with a slow speed of onset have had a difficult path to a presidential declaration. Droughts and fishing losses are often in this category. As mentioned earlier, suddenness of onset seems essential to the definition of disaster: if emergency managers can anticipate untoward results of an event before it transpires, then they should also be able to take steps to protect life and property as well as prevent significant damage. Sometimes presidents approach Congress. Governors may go to their state legislature to secure specific remedies to problems like failing dams, malfunctioning infrastructure, inadequate flood works, land subsidence, slope failure, and coastal erosion. Consequently, slow-speed-of-onset hazards and obvious disaster vulnerabilities are commonly addressed during regular policymaking periods, not as if they were transpiring disasters.

Factor 3: Program Fit

When a governor requests a presidential declaration, is the event suited in nature to assistance through the basket of federal programs made available under a presidential declaration of major disaster or emergency? A problem may be serious, even life-threatening, but the presidential declaration issued to address the problem may do little good if the federal program tools activated by a declaration are inappropriate given the nature of the problem. One example is structural fire damage. For most homeowners and businesses, fire losses are well covered under privately purchased insurance policies. Those who devised federal disaster law expected homeowners and businesses to be indemnified against possible fire loss. Therefore, federal relief rules stipulate that insurance proceeds must be applied to recovery before any federal aid is given. Consequently, unless fire damage is far beyond what insurance could be reasonably expected to cover, and unless a greater public interest is at stake, governor requests for presidential declarations to cover structure fire loss stand little chance of presidential approval. It is up to the president to decide when a "greater public interest" is at stake.

Oil spills represent another example. A variety of federal programs are available to help states and localities handle minor to major oil spills. These programs do not require a presidential declaration of major disaster or emergency in order to take effect. In the aftermath of the *Exxon Valdez* oil tanker spill in 1989, White House and FEMA officials pondered whether the president should approve the Alaska governor's request for a declaration of major disaster. That request ultimately was turned down, largely because the availability of other federal programs to address the problem made a presidential declaration unnecessary. In the aftermath of the 2011 BP Deepwater Horizon oil spill in the Gulf of Mexico, the White House discouraged Gulf Coast governors from even making such requests because White House officials did not want American taxpayers to fund the response and recovery with the possibility that they might not be reimbursed by the responsible party, BP.

Factor 4: Legal Fit

When a governor requests a presidential declaration, is the nature of the event compatible with the body of federal law that generally authorizes the president to declare a disaster?

Most natural disasters qualify if they are of sufficiently destructive magnitude and expansiveness. However, certain calamities do not. For example, forest fires that do not threaten to burn into towns or cities are customarily addressed by state forestry or land management agencies and federal agencies (the US Forest Service, the Bureau of Land Management, the US National

Park Service, and so on). Such conflagrations, as awful as they may appear on television news, do not ordinarily warrant a presidential declaration.

In addition, various types of human-caused disasters have not fit the general legal requirements or precedents necessary to earn presidential approval of governor requests for declarations of major disaster or emergency. Over the years, various governors have sought presidential declarations for hay shortages, crop freezes and crop insect infestation, drought, slow-moving mudslides, aviation disasters (for example, the crash of TWA Flight 800 off Long Island, New York), beach erosion, and so on. Sometimes governors making these requests have been steered to federal programs in the US Department of Agriculture (USDA), the Small Business Administration (SBA), the US Army Corps of Engineers (USACE), or other agencies that can provide much of the help they seek and can obtain without a presidential declaration.

The legal authority under the Stafford Act of 1988 is indeed broad, and the president has considerably more authority to act in a disaster than do most governors. Since 1950, the US chief executive has been able to spend from the President's Disaster Relief Fund. Congress has kept the fund well capitalized and has infused it with emergency supplemental appropriations funding whenever it was heavily depleted or when money was needed to address extremely expensive disasters. Most governors and other local government executives do not have such ready access to funding. Most must get by with modest "rainy day" funds or limited state agency emergency accounts, or they must approach their state legislature to secure additional disaster funding.

However, federal disaster statutes regarding presidential declarations of disaster have never been open-ended with respect to what presidents can choose to declare a disaster. Measures in 1950, 1970, 1974, and 1988 stipulated a range of acceptable types of disasters and commensurate types of assistance that declarations could confer. The Federal Disaster Act of 1970 created "emergency" declaration authority, but the president must report back to Congress as soon as the expenditures under an emergency declaration exceed $5 million.

Sometimes federal lawmakers have raised questions or challenges, particularly when they believed that a president crossed a "statutory line" in issuing declarations of major disaster or emergency for certain events.

In 1980, President Carter's major disaster declaration for the Mariel "boatlift" raised congressional eyebrows. The president declared a major disaster for Florida and used presidential disaster relief money to support the management of several thousand refugees who had fled to the United States from Cuba. The declaration included the construction and administration of refugee camps. Congress criticized Carter for his creative interpretation of disaster declaration authority.

In 1988, Stafford Act amendments to the disaster program deleted the generic cause for a disaster ("and other catastrophes") and provided that the cause must be "natural," except for fire or explosion.

Factor 5: Congressional Interest

Governors do not ordinarily request presidential declarations of major disaster or emergency in a political vacuum. Members of Congress often play a key role in pressing the president to approve governor requests for declarations. The president, guided by White House staff, considers how many states and congressional districts have been affected by the disaster or emergency. Sometimes various legislators request face-to-face meetings with a president to argue their case directly. The senators and representatives serving these states and districts often telephone, write, or email the president to endorse a governor's request. In the Eisenhower era, these requests often came to the White House as telegraphs. Today they may come as emails or faxes.

Presidents, as political officials who must regularly interact with Congress and its individual members, cannot afford to ignore these petitions or requests. A president may discern that the requests of certain state delegations are more important than others. Moreover, lawmakers who serve in certain congressional leadership posts or chair or serve on certain committees that the president deems important may tip the balance, leading the president to conclude that a declaration is warranted. Presidents, as ostensive leaders of their political parties, must be sensitive to the political party of those who press them to issue declarations. This is to be expected in an America where vestiges of Jacksonian democracy can still be found.

Congressional interest may influence how quickly a president decides on a governor's request for a declaration. Normally, the federal disaster agency makes a detailed damage assessment and analysis either before or after a governor requests a presidential declaration. However, a congressional interest may sometimes trump considerations of need based on damage assessments and analysis. For example, a fire affecting an area near Anchorage, Alaska, won a presidential declaration within hours because of the strong intervention of the late senator Ted Stevens, who was a key committee chairman and a senator with a strong interest in FEMA. The event probably would have received a declaration if the normal process had been followed, but it certainly would have come several days later. It is common knowledge among disaster workers that any natural event affecting Los Angeles will be declared—because the city has seventeen representatives in the House.

Factor 6: Interest Groups

Disasters or emergencies affect people and organizations. Sometimes people with common interests organize and form groups to achieve their political purposes. A great many people belong to organized interest groups.

There are few standing organized interest groups that have a long-term concern with federal disaster declarations. Among the few are county governments, as represented by the National Association of Counties and the National Association of County Engineers, which are specifically interested in those programs that address the costs of restoring county facilities after a disaster. More people-oriented nonprofit and business interest groups generally do not show much interest in declarations. However, disasters that have a serious impact on a particular interest group or community, with specific social interests, sometimes mobilize corresponding national interest groups.

Interests vary with respect to how well they are organized and funded and how much political influence they have on a presidential level. Organized farming interests, the US Chamber of Commerce, the National Association of Manufacturers, the American Bankers Association, and other interest groups often know how to lobby the president and have the political resources to succeed in convincing the president and other federal officials to act. Groups like major labor unions, the NAACP, and the National League of Cities may also enjoy considerable political influence that can be brought to bear on a president pondering governor requests for declarations.

However, weak political interests may be less successful in their attempts to influence the president. American fishing interests, for example, have a mixed record of success in pressing various presidents to approve declarations to cover losses stemming from the closure of fisheries. Some local governments—and even some state governments—that seldom experience disasters or lack disaster management capacity are often poor declaration lobbyists.

Interest groups often exercise influence indirectly, that is, through their relationships with members of Congress. If a disaster affects people with little organized political power, gubernatorial requests for declarations may be handled along a public administrative path exclusively. Gubernatorial requests may include supporting letters sent to the president by elected officials or sent to FEMA directly. If powerful groups are involved, members of Congress may call the president and the FEMA director. Legislators may tour the area with the press, and they may publicly criticize the president for being too slow to help. By contrast, when one disaster in Alaska took ten days to declare, although the disaster was devastating to two small native villages, no one from Alaska's congressional delegation pressed the president to issue a declaration.

Factor 7: Federal Interest

Often presidents, their staffs, and their senior disaster managers consider whether the event in question has significant federal interest. Did the event take place on or encompass federal property or structures? Events affecting military bases, federally managed lands or facilities, airports, railroads, highways, or ports that are of strategic national importance may add weight and great national significance to a governor's request for a declaration.

A request with national security implications is likely to draw presidential interest and potentially quick approval, as may occur in incidents that involve bioterror or weapons of mass destruction. If the president believes that the event may produce civil disorder, as in the case of the Los Angeles riots triggered by the outcome of the Rodney King trial in 1992, the president may quickly approve a governor's request for a declaration. If the president believes that the public thinks the federal government itself was a party to causing a disaster or emergency, or was directly responsible for it, the president may quickly conclude that the governor's request warrants a declaration. This was the case when the Teton Dam failed in 1976, and when a "controlled burn" forest fire initiated in the Cerro Grande National Forest in 2000 got out of control and burned into major portions of Los Alamos, New Mexico. In some cases, the president may conclude that an event requires deployment of active military forces to supplement the National Guard units mobilized by a state's governor.

Factor 8: Multi-State Events

If several states have suffered damage from the same event, the states suffering damage of great magnitude or extent usually win presidential declarations of major disaster quite easily. However, a question sometimes arises as to whether other states that have experienced relatively light damage in the disaster, or damage that may be localized along their borders, deserve a presidential declaration of major disaster. Observation of pools of presidential declaration approvals for multi-state disaster events reveals that presidents are inclined to look favorably on gubernatorial requests even if such disasters fail most of the tests for a declaration. Here an equity issue, as well as a political issue, is involved: is it fair to deny a governor's request for federal assistance just because only a small fraction of his or her state was damaged by a disaster when governors of adjacent states have won presidential disaster declarations for the same disaster? When one state is blanketed with disaster-ravaged areas and clearly deserves a presidential declaration, how can a president deny a declaration, and its commensurate federal relief, to areas of an adjacent state affected by the same disaster? In such cases, the standard that holds that states should be denied a declaration if they are able to recover from a disaster on their own is dismissed on equity grounds.

The political component is obvious, and it is strong regardless of the party of the state's governor. If the governor is not in the president's party, the president stands to be accused publicly of discriminating against the state for that reason. If the governor is of the same party, he or she is likely to make a personal appeal to the president. The adjacent-state factor is strengthened if major disaster is declared in several states in the region as a result of the same event.

Factor 9: News Coverage

Disasters of late have become nationally salient because they are covered much more intensely by the news media. This focus on disasters was pioneered by CNN but characterizes all major media organizations today.[29] There is even a race to place reporters in the paths of hurricanes so that the reporting will be immediate and firsthand. The Weather Channel has brought national weather awareness to the country. With national awareness of weather events comes a national expectation that the federal government will be involved. Yet some events are more newsworthy than others and may be more likely to be affected by news coverage.

Conclusions

Any examination of presidential decision-making with regard to declarations of major disaster or emergency should take into account the factors outlined here. Declaration decision-making involves consideration of law, policy, and politics—as required by the American political system. Those who ignore these factors or who attribute too much influence to any one factor must be cautious lest they be guilty of oversimplifying or of disregarding some of the components of a presidential declaration decision.

However, as long as a governor and other state officials know that the state can afford to shoulder the 25 percent share of the 75/25 federal aid formula contained in a presidential disaster declaration, they have an incentive to request a federal declaration. State officials logically minimize their own capacity to address disaster in petitioning for federal help by crying poor. James Miskel provides a strong case for reducing presidential discretion in reviewing governor requests for disaster declarations. He maintains that the United States should examine the disaster declaration systems used by Canada and Australia. In short, Miskel favors making declaration judgments more of an administrative judgment under which states would have to experience preset thresholds of damage to qualify, and even then each state would be expected to pay an up-front deductible sum of money and pay a much larger share of the federal/state match than is now the case in the United States.[30]

Many more emergency declarations than major disaster declarations are likely to stretch the rule that states must lack the capacity to recover on their own to qualify for a presidential declaration. When state and local budgets are tight or in deficit, emergency declarations offer governors a flexible path for securing federal help after an incident. FEMA records disclose that snowstorms, windstorms, minor flooding, and drought are the most common types of emergency declarations.[31] Emergencies also allow politically subjective determinations to come into play, in part because governors do not have to document losses or need when they seek such declarations.

Presidential decisions to approve or deny governor requests for declarations embody distributive and electoral politics as well as the exercise of chief executive authority based on law and sound public management.[32] However, differentiating these elements of presidential declaration decisions is no simple task. Sometimes incidents affecting only a small number of people, such as tornadoes, win declarations, owing to the level of suffering caused by the incidents.

Since the official basis upon which presidents have made approval and turndown decisions is not open to the public, we are left to make educated guesses about why some gubernatorial requests have been approved and others have been turned down. However, we are not left helpless. The record of turndowns is becoming more public, just as the record of approvals has long been shared with the public. This study has sought to shed more light on the case of presidential turndowns, which are almost always controversial and disputed.

However, one may ask, what would happen if there were no turndowns? What would disaster management and the federal disaster budget look like if governors were always granted their disaster declaration requests? How would America's definition of disasters requiring a federal presence and federal assistance change? Conversely, how many injustices and inequities have been propounded by presidential turndowns? Is it fair when neighbors separated by a state line and suffering the same damage from the same severe storm discover that one of them got federal disaster assistance and the other did not, owing to an approval and a turndown? How many counties failed to receive disaster assistance they deserved because their state or their governor bungled the request to the president?

Turndowns are a necessary evil. Without them, governors by default would be able to define what is or is not a presidential declaration of major disaster or emergency. Yet it might be fair to speculate that turndowns are becoming a rare endangered species. In one respect this may be happening because governors, aided by their state emergency management agencies, are learning how to file worthy and fact-based requests in a rapid manner (a Hamiltonian trait). In another respect it may be that presidents are increasingly reluctant to take the political and media heat for denying requests to states and localities for even the most minor of incidents, regardless of whether the requesting state has any electoral importance to them (Jeffersonian and Jacksonian tendencies). It also might be that the answer lies somewhere between these two assumptions.

DISCUSSION QUESTIONS

1. Does it make sense to entrust the president with the authority to determine what is or is not a declarable disaster? Why not leave this determination to the secretary of homeland security or the FEMA administrator rather than the president?

2. Why have the types of hazards causing damaging incidents and subsequently earning presidential disaster declarations grown into new categories of possibly eligible disaster incidents over time? Have presidents expanded the types and range of hazards eligible for their federal declarations, or has this been caused by new federal laws passed by Congress and the president?

3. Are presidential disaster declarations ever geographically unfair or geopolitically discriminatory? Consider this: Your house and mine are located a mile apart, but your house is in state X and my house is in state Y. Both of our states lack FEMA-like state disaster relief programs that could be launched if no presidential disaster declaration is issued for an incident. State X, including your house, sustains major damage from a tornado outbreak, and your state, including the county where your house is located, wins a presidential major disaster declaration soon after your governor asks for one. My house in state Y suffers just as much tornado damage as your house does, but the only tornado damage in my state is in a small corner of one county (mine). The governor of my state asks FEMA and the president for a major disaster declaration, but she is turned down because her state is judged to be able to recover from the disaster on its own. So unlike you in state X, I get no government help, yet we both experienced home damage from the same tornado outbreak. How common do you think this situation is? Consider the northern Alabama disaster declaration turndown in this study.

4. Why has the number of presidential turndowns of governor requests for major disaster and emergency declarations shrunk so much since 1988? What do you think is the most important reason for the growth in percentage approvals and in the total number of major disaster declarations issued over time?

5. Is the federal government too generous in offering disaster assistance money to states, their localities, and their disaster victims? Does FEMA need to set the threshold of state per-capita loss at a higher level, thus inducing states and localities to pay more of the cost of their own disaster recovery? Should states and localities have to pay disaster deductibles up-front (as you do when you settle an auto accident insurance claim that was your fault) as a condition of federal disaster declaration eligibility?

ADDITIONAL WORKS

Beauchesne, Ann M. 1998. *A Governor's Guide to Emergency Management.* Washington, DC: National Governor's Association, Association Center for Best Practices, Resources Policy Studies Division.

Birkland, Thomas A. 1997. *After Disaster: Agenda Setting, Public Policy, and Focusing Events*. Washington, DC: Georgetown University Press.

Bullock, Jane A., George D. Haddow, Damon Coppola, Erdem Ergin, Lissa Westerman, and Sarp Yeletaysi. 2005. *Introduction to Homeland Security*. Boston: Elsevier Butterworth-Heinemann.

Dymon, Ude J., and Rutherford H. Platt. 1999. "US Federal Disaster Declarations: A Geographical Analysis." In *Disasters and Democracy: The Politics of Extreme Natural Events*, ed. Rutherford H. Platt, 47–67. Washington, DC: Island Press.

Haddow, George D., and Jane A. Bullock. 2006. *Introduction to Emergency Management*. 2nd ed. Boston: Butterworth-Heinemann.

Heclo, Hugh. 1977. *A Government of Strangers*. Washington, DC: Brookings Institution.

Joyce, Philip G., and Amy E. Kneedler. 1999. "Emergency Management Competencies and Incentives and Implications for Funding in the Intergovernmental Context." Paper presented at the Sixtieth National Conference of the American Society for Public Administration. April 15, 1999, Orlando, FL.

Kettl, Donald F. 2004. *System Under Stress: Homeland Security and American Politics*. Washington, DC: Congressional Quarterly Press.

May, Peter J. 1985. *Recovering from Catastrophes: Federal Disaster Relief Policy and Politics*. Westport, CT: Greenwood Press.

May, Peter J., and Walter Williams. 1986. *Disaster Policy Implementation: Managing Programs Under Shared Governance*. New York: Plenum Press.

National Commission on Terrorist Attacks upon the United States. 2004. *9/11 Commission Report: Final Report of the National Commission on Terrorist Attacks upon the United States*. New York: W. W. Norton.

Peterson, Paul E. 1995. *The Price of Federalism*. Washington, DC: Brookings Institution/Twentieth Century Fund.

Pika, Joseph A., and John Anthony Maltese. 2004. *The Politics of the Presidency*. 6th ed. Washington, DC: Congressional Quarterly Press.

Platt, Rutherford H., and Claire B. Rubin. 1999. "Stemming the Losses: The Quest for Hazard Mitigation." In *Disasters and Democracy: The Politics of Extreme Natural Events*, ed. Rutherford H. Platt, 69–107. Washington, DC: Island Press.

Public Entity Risk Institute (PERI). "All About Presidential Disaster Declarations." Available at: www.peripresdecusa.org (accessed August 15, 2012).

Relyea, Harold C. 2003. "Organizing for Homeland Security." *Presidential Studies Quarterly* 33, no. 3: 602–624.

Schneider, Saundra K. 1995. *Flirting with Disaster: Public Management in Crisis Situations*. Armonk, NY: M. E. Sharpe.

Simendinger, Alexis. 2005. "Disaster Response Threatens to Swamp Bush Administration." *National Journal*, September 5.

Sylves, Richard T. 2006. "President Bush and Hurricane Katrina: A Presidential Leadership Study." *Annals of the American Academy of Political and Social Science* 604 (March): 26–56.

Tarcey, Brian. 2004. "Flooding the Ballot Box: The Politics of Disaster." *Harvard Magazine* (March-April).

US General Accounting Office (GAO). 2001. "Disaster Assistance: Improvement Needed in Disaster Declaration Criteria and Eligibility Assurance Procedures." GAO-01–837. Washington, DC: GAO (August 31).

US House of Representatives 2006. "A Failure of Initiative: Select Bipartisan Committee to Investigate Preparation for and Response to Hurricane Katrina." 109th Cong., 2nd sess., February 16. Washington, DC: US Government Printing Office.

US Senate Committee on Governmental Affairs. 1993. "Hearing on Rebuilding FEMA: Preparing for the Next Disaster." 103rd Cong., 1st sess., May 18.

Walker, David B. 1995. *The Rebirth of Federalism: Slouching Toward Washington*. Chatham, NJ: Chatham House Publishers.

Waugh, William L., Jr. 2000. *Living with Hazards, Dealing with Disasters*. Armonk, NY: M.E. Sharpe.

———. 2003. "Terrorism, Homeland Security, and the National Emergency Management Network." *Public Organization Review* 3: 373–385.

Waugh, William L., Jr., and Richard T. Sylves. 2002. "Organizing the War on Terrorism." *Public Administration Review* 62: 145–153.

Waugh, William L., Jr., and Ronald John Hy. 1990. *Handbook of Emergency Management*. Westport, CT: Greenwood Press.

Wise, Charles R. 2002. "Organizing for Homeland Security." *Public Administration Review* 62, no. 2: 131–144.

Witt, James L., and James Morgan. 2002. *Stronger in the Broken Places: Nine Lessons for Turning Crisis into Triumph*. New York: Times Books.

NOTES

1. The author would like to gratefully acknowledge the help of Richard Buck, a former employee of the Federal Emergency Management Agency (FEMA), who provided invaluable help in developing the sets of factors that are assumed to be considered by presidents when they turn down governor requests for declarations of major disaster and emergency. See Richard Buck (FEMA retired), interview with this author, April 4, 2004.

2. Compiled from FEMA, "Resource Record Details: FEMA Disaster Declarations Summary—Open Government Dataset," http://www.fema.gov/library/viewRecord.do; jsessionid=FF24414B7F0B4BF5E5BD18852DC161F5.WorkerLibrary?action=back &id=6292 (accessed October 3, 2012).

3. The Disaster Relief Act of 1950 authorized the president to issue federal declarations of major disaster and established a framework through which governors could ask the president to issue major disaster declarations to their states and localities. The law also granted the president discretion to decide when federal assistance was justified and necessary, and conversely, when it was not justified or necessary. See Richard Sylves, *Disaster Policy and Politics* (Washington, DC: Congressional Quarterly Press, 2008), 49.

4. President Ronald Reagan, a Republican whose two terms ran from January 1981 through January 1989, came to office promising a "new federalism" in which states would be delegated more responsibility for the implementation of various federal programs in their jurisdictions. Reagan, who assumed the presidency after he had served two terms as governor of California, believed that too many federal programs that involved state grant applications or conformity to federal rules tended to distort state government even as they moved more power to Washington, DC, and away from state capitals. See Demetrios Caraley and Yvette R. Schlussel, "Congress and Reagan's New Federalism," *Publius: The Journal of Federalism* 16, no. 1 (Winter 1986): 49–79.

5. Sylves, *Disaster Policy and Politics,* 27–31.

6. Ibid.

7. Richard T. Sylves, "A Précis on Political Theory and Emergency Management," *Journal of Emergency Management* 2, no. 8 (Summer 2004): 1–6.

8. Gary L. Wamsley, Aaron D. Schroeder, and Larry M. Lane, "To Politicize is *Not* to Control: The Pathologies of Control in Federal Emergency Management," *American Review of Public Administration* 26, no. 3 (1996): 263–285.

9. Sylves, *Disaster Policy and Politics,* 103.

10. Richard Sylves, "The Politics and Budgeting of Federal Emergency Management," in *Disaster Management in the United States and Canada,* ed. Richard Sylves and William L. Waugh Jr. (Springfield, IL: Charles C. Thomas Publishers, 1996).

11. Richard T. Sylves and William C. Cumming, "FEMA's Place in Policy, Law, and Management: A Hazardous Materials Perspective, 1979–2003," in *Homeland Security Law and Policy,* ed. William Nicholson (Springfield, IL: Charles C. Thomas Publishers, 2004), 23–55.

12. Sylves, "A Précis on Political Theory and Emergency Management."

13. *Federal Register* 64, no. 169 (September 1, 1999): 47697–47699; see also Sylves, *Disaster Policy and Politics,* 90.

14. *Federal Register* 64, no. 169 (September 1, 1999): 47697–47699.

15. Richard Buck (FEMA retired), email correspondence with this author, February 8, 2007.

16. Sylves, *Disaster Policy and Politics,* 98.

17. The president may obtain permission to exceed the $5 million spending cap merely by notifying Congress that federal spending on an emergency declaration will exceed the cap. The cap is therefore more symbolic than real.

18. Sylves, *Disaster Policy and Politics,* 94.

19. See R. Steven Daniels and Carolyn L. Clark-Daniels, *Transforming Government: The Renewal and Revitalization of the Federal Emergency Management Agency,* 2000 Presidential Transition Series (Arlington, VA: PricewaterhouseCoopers Endowment for the Business of Government, April 2000).

20. Richard Buck (FEMA retired), email correspondence with this author, February 8, 2007; see also Richard Buck (FEMA retired), interview with the author, April 4, 2004.

21. Andrew Reeves, "Political Disaster: Unilateral Powers, Electoral Incentives, and Presidential Disaster Declarations," *Journal of Politics* 73, no. 4 (October 2011): 1142–1151; see also Richard T. Sylves and Zoltan I. Buzas, "Presidential Disaster Declaration Decisions, 1953–2003: What Influences Odds of Approval?" *State and Local Government Review* 39, no. 1 (2007): 3–15.

22. Allen K. Settle, "Disaster Assistance: Securing Presidential Declarations," in *Cities and Disaster: North American Studies in Emergency Management,* ed. Richard T. Sylves and William L. Waugh Jr. (Springfield, IL: Charles C. Thomas Publishers, 1990), 33–57.

23. James L. Witt, testimony before the House Subcommittee on National Security, Emerging Threats, and International Relations and the Subcommittee on Energy Policy, "Natural Resources and Regulatory Affairs," 108th Cong., 2nd sess., March 24, 2004.

24. Ibid.

25. Thomas A. Garrett and Russell S. Sobel, "The Political Economy of FEMA Disaster Payments," *Economic Inquiry* 41, no. 3 (2003): 496–509; see also Rutherford H. Platt, "Shouldering the Burden: Federal Assumption of Disaster Costs," in *Disasters and Democracy: The Politics of Extreme Natural Events,* ed. Rutherford H. Platt (Washington, DC: Island Press, 1999), 11–46; and Sylves, *Disaster Policy and Politics.*

26. "Feds Turn Down Request for Northern Alabama Disaster Declaration," *Associated Press,* February 19, 2008.

27. See FEMA, Disaster Financial Status Report (DFSR), December 2011.

28. The governor of Massachusetts believed that a major disaster declaration was warranted because the two planes flown by terrorists into the World Trade Center towers had taken off from Boston's Logan Airport. There would most certainly have been costs from

the loss of Massachusetts victims, airport security investigations, and more. The Florida 9/11-related turndown may have stemmed from the costs of investigating the residence of 9/11 terrorists in Florida before the attacks and their presumed association with an anthrax release at a Florida publishing firm. Interestingly, post-9/11 laws later opened a path for governors to request presidential declaration help in cases of suspected biological or chemical terrorism.

29. See National Academy of Public Administration (NAPA), *Coping with Catastrophe: Building an Emergency Management System to Meet People's Needs in Natural and Manmade Disasters* (Washington, DC: NAPA, 1993).

30. James F. Miskel, *Disaster Response and Homeland Security* (Westport, CT: Praeger Security International, 2006).

31. Mary W. Downton and Roger A. Pielke, "Discretion Without Accountability: Politics, Flood, Damage, and Climate," *Natural Hazards Review* 2, no. 4 (2001): 157–166.

32. Sylves, *Disaster Policy and Politics,* 100–106. Distributive politics involves allocating benefits, sometimes in excess of need, to an interested pool of applicants such that benefits are geographically concentrated while the costs to the funding source are absorbed extremely broadly. Under disaster's distributive politics, costs are covered by the national taxpayer, but at the rate of pennies per taxpayer. The benefits are the large sums of federal money going to states and localities that experience disasters or emergencies of even modest scale.

CHAPTER 2

Terrorism

The shock of the terrorist attacks on September 11, 2001, transformed how we as a nation perceive terrorism and homeland security. Prior to 9/11, terrorism was primarily seen as a crime to be addressed by law enforcement agencies and the criminal justice system. For example, throughout his administration President Clinton often referred to international terrorism as global crime.[1] This focus on terrorism as a crime is clearly demonstrated in our nation's response to the 1993 World Trade Center bombing. The first case in this chapter, "The 1993 World Trade Center Bombing: A Success or a Failure for the FBI?" shows how successful the FBI was in investigating this crime, gathering evidence, and prosecuting the perpetrators. However, this singular perspective of terrorism as a crime significantly limited the view of both policymakers and law enforcement professionals on the larger transnational terror network that was involved and would be involved again in the 2001 attacks. The *9/11 Commission Report* criticized this criminal justice frame by arguing that the law enforcement process "was meant, by its nature to mark for the public the events as finished—case solved, justice done. It was not designed to ask if the events might be harbingers of things to come. Nor did it allow for aggregating and analyzing facts to see if they could provide clues to terrorist tactics more generally—methods of entry and finance, and mode of operation in the United States."[2] Nevertheless, while there are clear weaknesses in an approach that focuses on terrorism from a crime perspective only, too strong a focus on war as a response to terrorism has also been criticized.

In the aftermath of 9/11, the deadliest terror attack on US soil in the history of the nation, the Bush administration not only created a new Department of Homeland Security to coordinate the nation's efforts against the threat of terrorism but also changed the paradigm of how we as a nation perceive international terrorism—what once was seen as a criminal act is now seen as an act of war. In an address to Congress nine days after the attacks, President George W. Bush said, "Our war on terror will not end until every terrorist group of global reach has been found, stopped and defeated."[3] Thus, within a month of the 9/11 attacks the United States launched a large-scale military operation in Afghanistan to overthrow the Taliban regime harboring Al-Qaeda, to find Osama bin Laden, and to defeat terrorist elements in the country. The war focus has raised concerns about the civil rights of alleged terrorists as well as the labeling of people as terrorists.[4]

The Bush administration created a new standard for qualifying as a terrorist actor: in addition to those who committed the acts themselves, agents of terror now included "any nation, group, entity, or individual that harbored, housed, supported, facilitated, financed, succored, tolerated or conducted business with terrorists."[5] The Bush administration fueled public fears by employing the terrorist label without hesitation and by broadening the label's usage to apply to all these various actors associated with anyone who perpetrated acts of terrorism. The second case, "Terrorist or Ecosaboteur? The Case of Briana Waters," raises questions about how terrorism is defined and labeled within a culture and about the possible consequences. This case highlights the subjectivity of the terrorism label, whose use often seems to depend largely on whether the group, person, or cause in question elicits one's sympathies or opposition.

NOTES

1. US Government Printing Office, *Preparing for the 21st Century,* March 1, 1996, www.gpoaccess.gov/int/report.html (accessed October 5, 2012).

2. National Commission on Terrorist Attacks upon the United States, *The 9/11 Commission Report: Final Report of the National Commission on Terrorist Attacks upon the United States* (New York: W. W. Norton, 2004), 73.

3. Scott Wilson and Al Kamen, "Global War on Terror Is Given a New Name," *Washington Post,* March 25, 2009.

4. Carol Winkler, *In the Name of Terrorism* (Albany: State University of New York Press, 2006), 201.

5. Ibid., 163.

The 1993 World Trade Center Bombing

A Success or a Failure for the FBI?

LINDA KILTZ

Introduction

Despite the successful investigation and prosecution of the 1993 World Trade Center (WTC) conspirators, the United States was not able to prevent future attacks against the homeland, in part because of a failure to see the extent of the new threat facing the nation at the time of the 1993 bombing. Terrorism in the United States was seen primarily as a crime, and homeland security was perceived as a problem to be addressed by law enforcement agencies and the criminal justice system. Lindsay Clutterbuck writes, "Since the resurgence of terrorism in the late 1960s, it is this conception of 'terror as crime' and not 'terror as war' that has primarily driven the response to terrorism of the liberal democratic nations."[1] For example, throughout his administration President Clinton often referred to international terrorism as global crime.[2] Carol Winkler writes, "Before leaving office the Clinton administration institutionalized terrorists as non-state, criminal actors."[3] This case presents the story of the 1993 World Trade Center bombing from this law enforcement perspective.

The 1993 World Trade Center Bombing: The Crime

In the early morning hours of February 26, 1993, a convoy of three vehicles left Jersey City headed for the World Trade Center complex in New York City. Four conspirators, Mohammad Salameh, Mahmud Abouhalima, Eyad Ismoil, and Ramzi Yousef, had been plotting for months to build the most deadly improvised explosive device (IED) ever constructed on US soil.[4] Among the vehicles in the convoy was a rented Ryder Ford Econoline van that was carrying the 1,500-pound urea-nitrate bomb.[5]

The bomb-maker and mastermind of this plot, Ramzi Yousef, had purchased 1,000 pounds of technical-grade urea and 105 gallons of nitric acid for the bomb's main charge in the months before the attack. Yousef also purchased 60 gallons of sulfuric acid in 15-gallon carboys to make nitroglycerin boosters. The conspirators had spent the previous three months mixing the chemicals for the explosives in their apartment at 40 Pamrapo Avenue in Jersey City and storing the bomb components and finished products at a rented storage shed at the Space Station Storage Company in Jersey City.[6] The bomb that was loaded into the van consisted of four cardboard boxes filled with a slurry of urea-nitrate and fuel oil, with waste paper as a binder; upon detonation it would have a velocity of 15,000 feet per second.[7]

Upon arrival at the World Trade Center complex, Ismoil and Yousef drove the van filled with explosives into the red parking lot on the B-2 level, parked along the load-bearing south wall of the North Tower, and lit the fuses. It was Yousef's hope that when the bomb detonated the force would blow laterally, cracking the supports at the skyscraper's base and causing it to topple down and kill the tens of thousands within the building.[8] The WTC complex was a prime target because it was estimated that 60,000 employees worked there and 90,000 additional visitors or commuters came to the World Trade Center each day.[9]

Yousef and Ismoil escaped in a car driven by Salameh. Yousef's escape continued that evening on a flight from New York City to Karachi, connecting to Quetta in West Pakistan.[10] Ismoil would take a flight from Kennedy Airport to Amman, Jordan, on March 2, 1993. Following Yousef's and Ismoil's lead, Abouhalima would escape by flying from New York to Sudan via Jeddah, Saudi Arabia, on March 2, 1993.[11]

At approximately 12:18 PM, the bomb exploded, killing six people, injuring more than 1,000,[12] and causing nearly $3 million in property damage.[13] The massive blast created a cavernous crater 200 feet by 100 feet wide and

Ramzi Yousef	Mohammad Salameh	Abdul Yasin	
Mahmoud Abouhalima	Ahmed Ajaj	Nidal Ayyad	Eyad Ismoil

PHOTO 2.1.1: Suspects in the 1993 World Trade Center bombing.
Source: FBI website at www.fbi.gov/news/stories/2008/february/trade
bom_022608/tradebom_022608

seven stories deep in the basement levels of the World Trade Center, causing extensive damage on several basement levels and disabling fire protection as well as electrical, water, and emergency communications systems. The explosion also ignited intense fires that quickly distributed black smoke to the upper levels of the complex's seven buildings, requiring a massive evacuation.[14]

Within minutes of the blast, first responders from the New York Police Department (NYPD) and the New York Fire Department (FDNY) arrived at the scene. For the FDNY it was the largest incident in its 128-year history (before 9/11)—equivalent to a sixteen-alarm fire involving hundreds of firefighters, representing nearly 45 percent of the on-duty staff.[15] While the fire department focused on fighting fires, evacuating people, and rescuing those trapped in the World Trade Center, the responding police units established a perimeter around the crime scene, directed traffic, helped to rescue those trapped in the building, and established a command post to coordinate the law enforcement investigation to follow.

The FBI's Joint Terrorism Task Force in New York City, headed by Neil Herman, assumed the lead role in this investigation, which was labeled TRADEBOM. Herman had a domestic terrorism unit comprising about fifty agents and New York City police detectives. These individuals, plus an additional one hundred

FBI agents, would join the investigation in New York City. Also, seven hundred FBI agents nationwide were tasked to follow up on leads in TRADEBOM.[16] To most of those involved in the investigation, this was a major criminal matter to be solved by finding, arresting, prosecuting, and punishing the perpetrators.

The Investigation of the World Trade Center Bombing

For the FBI, the TRADEBOM investigation would be one of the largest terrorism investigations in its history. In the days following the bomb explosion, a team of thirty bomb technicians from the FBI, the NYPD, and the Bureau of Alcohol, Tobacco, and Firearms (ATF) worked in shifts at the blast site looking for clues. Approximately two hundred law enforcement officers from at least eight different agencies assisted in the monumental task of collecting evidence. For David Williams, the FBI's top bomb expert, this was the biggest "post-blast" scene he or any other team had ever processed in the United States.[17] All items of potential evidence were documented on the sites to preserve the chain of evidence and chain of custody.

PHOTO 2.1.2: Investigators going through the rubble at WTC.
Source: FBI website at www.fbi.gov/news/stories/2008/february/tradebom _022608

In less than one month, the crime scene investigations were completed and approximately three thousand pounds of debris were removed from the site and transported to the FBI laboratory in Washington, DC (although the FBI was only one of several criminal investigative organizations collecting evidence at the crime scene).[18] Among the most critical pieces of evidence collected just two days after the explosion was a fragment of the Ryder van.

On Sunday, February 28, 1993, teams of investigators from the NYPD bomb squad, the ATF's explosives team, and the FBI's explosives team were sent into the bomb crater of the World Trade Center to search for additional evidence. Joseph Hanlin, a senior ATF explosives enforcement officer, was partnered with Donald Sadowy, a detective from the NYPD bomb squad. Their team also included a chemist, a photographer, a sketch artist, and several technicians. As Hanlin's team searched the edge of the crater near the bomb's center on the B-2 level, Hanlin spotted vehicle parts that looked out of place. On closer inspection, Hanlin determined that these were parts of the gear assembly that had made up the differential assembly that was ripped apart from the vehicle that had exploded.

On one of the pieces was a series of dots and digits that made up the vehicle identification number (VIN). This one piece of evidence, found in the six thousand tons of rubble that would be removed in the weeks ahead, was the proverbial needle in the haystack and led to the arrest of the first suspect in this case, Mohammed Salameh.[19] A VIN history check by the FBI revealed that the suspect parts were from an E-350 yellow Ford Econoline van with an Alabama license plate. This plate was traced to the Ryder Truck Rental Company and then to the Ryder dealership at 1558 John F. Kennedy Boulevard in Jersey City.

When FBI agents interviewed the owner of the business, Paul Mascitelli, he recounted that on Tuesday, February 23, 1993, a man with dark hair and a trimmed dark beard—who would be identified as Salameh—had rented a yellow Ford Econoline van.[20] Salameh had made it easy for the FBI to locate him because he had rented the vehicle using his real name, his own driver's license, and an address at a local Islamic cultural center.[21] The phone number on the rental agreement was traced to his apartment at 34 Kensington Avenue. Also, a chemical analysis of the rental agreement later showed traces of nitrates, a chemical associated with the explosives.

Mascitelli further reported that on Friday, February 26, 1993, about three hours after the bombing, Salameh had returned to the dealership to report that the van had been stolen the night before from the parking lot of a Shop

Rite supermarket in Jersey City and to obtain his $400 rental deposit.[22] Salameh needed the money from the deposit to upgrade his airplane ticket from a child's ticket on Royal Jordanian Airlines to an adult fare to escape.[23] Mascitelli told Salameh that he would have to obtain a police report on the stolen van before the agency would accept his account of the loss.[24] Salameh filed a police report on the stolen van with the Jersey City Police on Tuesday, March 2, 1993, and returned to the Ryder agency for his deposit, where the FBI was waiting to arrest him on Thursday, March 4.

Hours after Salameh's arrest, the FBI searched his apartment at 34 Kensington Avenue and seized a great deal of evidence. Agents interviewed Salameh's roommate, Abdul Yasin, who provided them with a great deal of information, including the location of the bomb factory at 40 Pamrapo Avenue. Seeing Yasin as a cooperative witness, the FBI did not consider him a suspect and released him. However, he fled the country on March 4, 1993, to Amman, Jordan.[25] Later Yasin was indicted as a conspirator for his role in the plot. Yasin helped to obtain and mix the chemicals for the bomb and taught Salameh how to drive the rental van that had carried the bomb to the World Trade Center parking garage.[26] He is still at large today, and the United States continues to offer a reward of up to $5 million for information leading directly to his apprehension or conviction through the US State Department's Rewards for Justice Program.[27]

The ground-floor apartment at 40 Pamrapo was used by the conspirators to mix the chemicals that they had obtained from City Chemical Corporation and stored at a rented storage shed at the Space Station Storage Company. Salameh had rented a ten-by-ten-foot room at Space Station Storage on November 30, 1992, for $90 a month.[28] In December 1992, Yousef went to City Chemical, where he purchased 1,000 pounds of technical-grade urea and 105 gallons of nitric acid to make urea-nitrate for the bomb's main charge, as prescribed in the bomb-making manuals brought into the country by Ahmed Ajaj and Ramzi Yousef on August 31, 1992.[29]

Ajaj was arrested by agents of the Immigration and Naturalization Service (INS) at Kennedy Airport on August 31 because he had a fraudulent Swedish passport. On inspection of Ajaj's luggage, INS agents found videos, bomb books, and fake passports from Jordan. Yousef also raised the suspicion of INS agents when he failed to show a US visa and presented an identification card with a name that was different from what was on his passport. Yousef, too, was detained and questioned by INS agents, whereupon he asked for political asylum. Unlike Ajaj, Yousef was not subsequently detained, because there was no room at the INS Varick Street detention facility.[30] Once in New York, Yousef put together the personnel (Salameh, Ayyad, Abouhalima, Yasin, and Ismoil) and supplies he would need to carry out his plan to bomb the World Trade Center.

Among the key items that Ajaj brought into the country were two notebooks with handwritten notes on explosives, six printed bomb-making manuals, two instructional videotapes on making explosives, and anti-American and anti-Israeli materials.[31] Ajaj's bomb-making manuals were identical to those found in the London apartment of Khalid al-Fawa, who would be indicted in 1998 for the US embassy bombings in Nairobi, Kenya, and Dar es Salaam, Tanzania.[32] From January to February 1993, the conspirators mixed the chemicals they had obtained from City Chemical in a manner consistent with the formulas and other specifications in Ajaj's materials. In the course of the mixing process, the conspirators spilled chemicals on the floors and walls of the apartment at 40 Pamrapo, on their clothing, and on other items, thereby leaving telltale traces of their illegal activities.[33] The process of mixing these chemicals created harsh fumes, which required the conspirators to wear surgical masks during the mixing process, caused some of the paint on the walls to change from white to blue, and resulted in corrosion on the inside of the back bedroom's doorknob and door hinges.[34]

Another explosive mixed in the Pamrapo Avenue apartment was nitroglycerin, which the conspirators used to make boosters for the World Trade Center bomb. Nidal Ayyad, one of the convicted conspirators, was able to obtain "restricted" chemicals to make these boosters because of his status as a chemical company employee at Allied Signal.[35] During the mixing process, the conspirators spilled nitroglycerin in the apartment and on their clothing, again leaving revealing traces of the explosive.[36] The evidence collected at this apartment and at Salameh's apartment on Kensington Avenue would be presented during the trials of these individuals.

At Salameh's apartment, the FBI found more evidence of the World Trade Center conspiracy. Salameh's briefcase contained bank records of accounts he had set up for Ramzi Yousef. A phone record search on a telephone that agents also found in Salameh's apartment led to more phone numbers and addresses of the suspects and revealed their activities prior to the bombing. These telephone records were a gold mine of information for the FBI because from them agents were able to obtain other possible contacts and suspects. Neil Herman described the telephone database created during this investigation as so massive that managing it required four agents working full-time—

uploading numbers into computers, identifying whom the calls went to, and running their names through a criminal database.[37]

Ramzi Yousef spent thousands of dollars on phone calls while in the United States, calling terrorist contacts in Pakistan, the Middle East, and the Philippines.[38] Among the terrorist contacts Yousef was calling was his uncle, Khalid Sheikh Mohammed (KSM)—later identified as the architect of the terrorist attacks of September 11, 2001. On November 3, 1992, KSM wired $600 from Qatar to the bank account of Salameh. KSM was inspired by Yousef's instant notoriety in 1993, and he, too, became involved in planning attacks against the United States. In 1994, KSM and Yousef went to the Philippines and began planning "Project Bojinka"—a plot to bomb twelve US commercial jets over the Pacific Ocean.[39] In September 1996, Yousef and two other defendants, Abdul Hakim Murad and Wali Khan Amin Shah, were convicted of crimes related to the Bojinka plot.

Another critical piece of information was a photo of Salameh standing next to El Sayyid Nosair, the "lone deranged gunman" accused of assassinating Zionist rabbi Meir Kahane in 1991.[40] The Nosair case is important because many of the individuals who were friends of Nosair's, and who were known by the FBI as early as 1989, later became the conspirators in the 1993 WTC bombing.

As investigators developed leads, evidence, and suspects, the investigation seemed increasingly to be just a matter of good police work involving a variety of expert professionals from several agencies. And as sometimes happens in such investigations, the evidence and suspects led the investigators to other cases with linkages that became clear as the cases unfolded. The linkage of the 1993 WTC case with the assassination of Meir Kahane is important in showing how long these conspirators had been in the United States planning terrorist activities prior to the 1993 attack. These linkages had gone largely unnoticed by law enforcement because each criminal event was perceived as an isolated activity instead of being linked to a broader criminal conspiracy or terrorist operation.

The Assassination of Meir Kahane: The First Blow in a Terrorist Campaign

On November 5, 1990, El Sayyid Nosair, a thirty-four-year-old immigrant from Egypt, shot and killed Meir Kahane, the founder of the Jewish Defense League, after Kahane had finished a fund-raising speech at the New York Marriott East Side Motel. In attempting to flee the murder scene, Nosair shot and wounded a bystander, Irving Berlin.[41] Three blocks from the hotel, US Postal police officer Carlos Acosta was shot and wounded by Nosair. Upon being hit, Acosta drew his own .357 Magnum and fired once, hitting Nosair in the chin.[42] Nosair was forced to flee on foot from the scene because his getaway car, driven by Mahmud Abouhalima (a WTC conspirator), had been parked in the wrong location.

When police arrived at the scene, they found a .357 Ruger in Nosair's hand, and in his pockets were bullets that fit the gun. Given the number of witnesses at the scene of the crime and a clear murder weapon, this appeared to be an open-and-shut case for the New York Police Department and the district attorney. Although the evidence gathered at Nosair's home in Cliffside Park, New Jersey, by the FBI's New York Joint Terrorism Task Force (NYJTTF) clearly showed that this was not a simple murder case—the work of a lone gunman—but rather a larger terrorist conspiracy, the implication of this evidence was largely ignored by investigators at the time.

When NYJTTF detectives arrived at Nosair's home following the shooting, they found Mahmud Abouhalima and Mohammed Salameh, two of the WTC bombers, and took them in for questioning. In addition, the detectives found evidence that included formulas for bomb-making. One of these formulas was for a device constructed of fuel oil and urea-nitrate, the same combination that would be used by Ramzi Yousef twenty-five months later in the World Trade Center bomb.[43] Nosair's home also contained "literature relating to guns, weapons, and combat, including subjects such as bomb making, hand grenades, security and listening devices, 'Arms in Afghanistan,' 'Explosive Traps,' 'How to Teach Yourself to Shoot like an Expert,' and a guide to buying guns and ammunition."[44]

Among the most critical pieces of evidence collected at Nosair's home clearly showing that a conspiracy was being developed by a terrorist cell were audio sermons by Sheikh Omar Abdel-Rahman, Nosair's notebooks containing parts of Rahman's speeches, and maps and drawings of New York City landmarks, such as the Statue of Liberty and the World Trade Center complex.[45] Rahman was one of the spiritual leaders of the international terrorist organization, the Egyptian Al-Gama'a al-Islamiyya, or Islamic Group (IG), from at least the early 1990s and was known throughout the world by Islamic fundamentalists through his recorded sermons and writings. Islamic Group was Egypt's largest militant group and was an offshoot of the Muslim Brotherhood.[46] IG's goals included overthrowing Egypt's secular regime and creating an Islamic state, as well as waging jihad against Americans. When Rahman entered the United States in 1990, he recruited persons to IG and solicited them to commit violent jihad actions through his sermons at the Farouq Mosque in Brooklyn, New York.[47] Among the people who attended those sermons were Nosair, Salameh, and Abouhalima.

Rahman played a key role in defining IG's goals and provided guidance to followers on whether particular jihad actions, including acts of terrorism, were permissible under his extremist interpretations of Islamic law. For example, written in one of Nosair's notebooks was the future vision of jihad in the United States that Rahman called for: "[the] breaking and destruction of the enemies of Allah. And this by means of destroying by exploding, the structure of their civilized pillars such as touristic infrastructure which they are proud and of their statues which they endear and the buildings which gather their heads, their leaders, and without any announcement for our responsibility of Muslims for what had been done."[48]

In August 1992, Rahman would begin planning for the destruction of the "civilized pillars" by telephoning Ramzi Yousef in Pakistan; Yousef would become the bomb builder and mastermind of the WTC bombing.[49] Upon arrival in the United States, Yousef called Mahmud Abouhalima, who was Rahman's chauffeur and assistant. Yousef began gathering his cell members, who were all followers of Rahman. Yousef also kept in close contact with Rahman in the weeks leading up to the WTC bombing, as evidenced by repeated phone calls to Rahman's home.[50]

In October 1995, Sheikh Abdel-Rahman would be convicted of engaging in seditious conspiracy to wage a war of urban terrorism against the United States, which included the 1993 bombing of the World Trade Center and a plot to bomb New York landmarks, including the United Nations, the FBI building in New York, and the Lincoln and Holland Tunnels.[51]

At the time of Nosair's arrest, the FBI did not recognize the larger conspiracy and the link to Middle Eastern terrorist organizations because many of the materials in Nosair's apartment were not translated until after the 1993 WTC bombing.[52] The primary task of the FBI was to gather the evidence needed to obtain a conviction for the homicide committed by Nosair; thus, many of these materials were not needed in the prosecution of this case. In addition, the FBI lacked Arabic translators to translate and analyze Nosair's documents. Joseph Borelli, chief of detectives for the NYPD, saw the Kahane murder as a clear-cut homicide committed by a "lone deranged gunman" with no ties to known terrorists or Middle East conspiracies, and thus the official stance of the NYPD was that Nosair acted alone.[53]

When the Nosair case went to trial, there was a great deal of media attention because of the large number of protesters from the Kahane and Nosair camps who picketed in front of the courthouse. Among the protesters were Mahmud Abouhalima and Mohammad Salameh. The leader of the Brooklyn mosque, Mustafa Shalabi, helped raise funds for Nosair's legal fees. Some of these funds came from the wealthy Saudi Osama bin Laden.[54] It was during the Nosair case that the FBI's New York office first heard bin Laden's name.[55] Nosair was acquitted of murder, but received a seven- to twenty-two-year sentence for a weapons charge.

The Arrest, Prosecution, and Conviction of the World Trade Center Conspirators

After arresting Mohammad Salameh on March 4, 1993, as he tried to secure his deposit for the Ryder van that was used to carry the WTC bomb, FBI agents were able to obtain and execute a series of search warrants for various locations linked to the conspirators. As a result, they were able to uncover the identities of Salameh's accomplices, Mahmud Abouhalima, Ibrahim El-Gabrowny, and Nidal Ayyad.[56] The day Salameh was arrested, the manager at the Space Station Storage Company in Jersey City opened the locker rented by Salameh because his employees had witnessed Salameh and Yousef delivering and storing suspicious-looking containers at the shed.[57] He called the FBI and reported his suspicions. The search of the storage locker at Space Station revealed evidence of cans of chemicals that were identified as urea and sulfuric acid like that used in the bomb, as well as bottles, beakers, funnels, tubing, and a fuse.[58] In addition, the identification that Salameh had used to rent the van bore his name, but the address was that of Ibrahim El-Gabrowny, cousin of Nosair.[59]

While searching Salameh's apartment on Kensington Avenue on March 4, 1993, agents found receipts for airplane tickets for Ahmed Ajaj, who had just been released from prison for attempting to enter the United States on a fraudulent Swedish passport. Agents found Ajaj on March 9, 1993, at an INS center and arrested him. Nidal Ayyad, was arrested on March 10 at his New Jersey home. Phone records showing calls from the Space Station Storage Company in Jersey City to Ayyad's business office, joint bank accounts with Salameh, and his inquiries into buying explosives provided enough probable cause for the FBI to secure his arrest.[60] On Ayyad's computer, FBI agents found the WTC bombing letter in which Yousef's cell, named the Fifth Battalion in the Liberation Army, claimed credit for the bombing and listed their grievances.[61]

Besides claiming responsibility for the bombing and listing certain political demands, the letter also threatened future acts of terrorism. When the *New York Times* received this letter four days after the WTC attack, the newspaper turned it over to the FBI.[62]

After Salameh's arrest, one of the first names that surfaced as a co-conspirator was Mahmud Abouhalima. Within a week of the WTC bombing, the FBI had traced Abouhalima's flight to Saudi Arabia and then to Egypt, using ticket manifests and information from its Egyptian informant, Emad Salem.[63]

The FBI informed the Egyptian government, and soon Abouhalima was taken into custody by the Egyptian authorities and viciously tortured because of his connections to Islamic militants campaigning against the Egyptian government.[64] Abouhalima was linked to the bombing through his close association with Ayyad and Salameh. The FBI stated that Abouhalima was seen on the morning of the WTC attack riding in the Ryder van with Salameh and was also seen near the Jersey City storage lockers where explosive materials similar to those at the bomb site were found.[65]

As FBI agents made arrests and interviewed witnesses, they became aware of a mysterious young "Iraqi" man called "Rashid" who appeared to be the mastermind of the plot. Rashid would be later identified as Ramzi Yousef. The NYJTTF gathered enough evidence in the months following the bombing to charge him with the bombing and circulated details of his aliases and crimes around the world.[66] Investigators stated that not only was Yousef spotted by witnesses at the Pamrapo Avenue apartment where the bomb was made, but his fingerprints were found at this apartment, in the storage shed where the chemicals were kept, and on the bomb manuals carried into the country by Ajaj.[67]

On April 2, 1993, Yousef was listed as one of the FBI's ten most wanted terrorists, and a worldwide manhunt for him began. Half a dozen agents were assigned to Yousef's case and tasked with building up the evidence against Yousef, finding him, capturing him, arranging his extradition, and securing a conviction in a US court.[68] The State Department offered a $2 million reward through its Rewards for Justice Program for information that would lead to the arrest of Yousef.[69]

While a fugitive from justice, Yousef continued his militant activities, including an attempt to assassinate Prime Minister Benazir Bhutto of Pakistan in September 1994 and the detonation of liquid bombs on twelve jumbo jets headed to the United States, the Project Bojinka plot.[70] While Yousef was mixing the chemicals for his bomb plot in his apartment in Manila on January 6, 1995, a fire broke out, forcing him to flee and prompting fire and police to respond. When police arrived, they found cartons of chemicals, Casio timers, watches with wires attached, components for nitroglycerin, and Yousef's laptop.[71] This laptop contained a great deal of incriminating evidence against Yousef, such as information relating to flight numbers and departure times of commercial airlines, including civilian commercial aircraft to the United States, and times for the detonation of bombs aboard such airliners. It also contained a letter in which the "Fifth Battalion of the Liberation Army under the leadership of Lt. General Abu Baker Almaki" threatened to attack American targets "in response to the financial, political, and military assistance given to the Jewish State in the occupied land of Palestine by the American Government."[72] The use of airplanes as tools of terror to kill hundreds of civilians was initially conceived by Yousef and fine-tuned by Khalid Sheikh Mohammed in the attack on 9/11.

While Yousef eluded police, a great deal of evidence was gathered against him. Yousef was finally captured on February 7, 1995, when the United States embassy in Islamabad, Pakistan, acted on a tip from Istiaque Parker, who stated that Yousef was at the Su Casa Guesthouse on the outskirts of Islamabad. Pakistani officials, together with a special agent from the US Department of State, arrested Yousef. The next day agents from the FBI and Secret Service arrived to take Yousef into custody and transport him back to the United States.

According to US Secret Service agent Brian Parr, who escorted Yousef from Pakistan to the United States, Yousef gave him a detailed account of his role in the bomb plot, even bragging about it.[73] In fact, Yousef not only drew a rough sketch of the crime scene and the path he had taken into the World Trade Center but also explained the methods and tactics he had used. For example, Yousef told Agent Parr that he received money for the bombing from friends and family members and that had he had more money, he would have made "a more efficient bomb." Yousef also reported to Parr that he had hoped the explosion would cause one tower to fall into the other and kill 250,000 civilians because if they suffered those types of casualties Americans would realize they were at war.[74]

On August 3, 1995, Eyad Ismoil was the final conspirator to be arrested in the WTC bombing. Ismoil had driven the van filled with explosives into the garage of the World Trade Center on February 26, 1993, and escaped on a plane to Amman, Jordan, the night of the bombing. Telephone records indicated that Ismoil was in constant contact with other conspirators, including

Yousef, in the Jersey City apartment where the bomb was constructed in the months before the explosion. In 1995, FBI agents located Ismoil in Jordan, and Jordanian police arrested him on July 30, 1995.[75] Ismoil told authorities after his arrest that he believed he was transporting boxes of soap into the World Trade Center garage as part of a business deal.[76]

Although there had been a global manhunt to apprehend and arrest some of the WTC perpetrators, as the defendants went to trial it appeared to law enforcement officials that the case was nearly over. From a law enforcement perspective, a case is closed once a perpetrator is tried and convicted. As a result, there was no follow-up on the linkages of these perpetrators to other possible terror plots or suspects.

In September 1993, Ayyad, Abouhalima, Ajaj, Salameh, Yousef, and Yasin were indicted in the US District Court for the Southern District of New York on a number of charges relating to their participation in the WTC bombing. The trial of Ayyad, Abouhalima, Ajaj, and Salameh lasted from September 1993 to March 1994. During the trial, the prosecution called 207 witnesses and presented 1,003 exhibits in an effort to present an avalanche of circumstantial evidence with which to bury the four defendants.[77] Since there were no witnesses who actually saw the defendants at or near the World Trade Center on the day of the blast, the government had to build its case on myriad small details such as the telephone records showing that the men were in constant touch with each other, computer files, DNA tests, fingerprint analyses, reports on chemical traces found on articles of clothing, rental contracts, and bomb-making manuals.[78]

On March 4, 1994, the jury found Ayyad, Abouhalima, Ajaj, and Salameh guilty of all charges, including conspiracy to damage buildings by use of an explosive device, damaging or destroying the WTC complex by explosive, causing injury or death, explosive destruction of property, explosive destruction of government property, and interstate transportation of explosives.[79]

Mahmud Abouhalima was convicted on 9 counts and sentenced to 240 years' imprisonment. Mohammed Salameh was convicted on 10 counts and sentenced to 117 years' imprisonment. Nidal Ayyad was convicted on 9 counts and sentenced to 117 years in prison. Ahmed Ajaj was convicted on 9 counts and sentenced to 115 years. All four of these conspirators were also fined $250,000 and ordered to pay $250 million in restitution.[80]

On May 29, 1996, Yousef went to trial in US Federal Court in Manhattan for the Bojinka plot. In September 1996, he was convicted of conspiracy to damage or destroy aircraft by planning to bomb eleven US jumbo jets over the Pacific Ocean. A year later, in August 1997, Yousef and Ismoil went on trial for their participation in the 1993 WTC bombing. As in the first WTC trial, a great deal of forensic evidence and expert testimony was presented on chemicals, fingerprints, and explosive residue.[81] The most compelling evidence against Yousef was his own admissions on his role, motivations, and goals to Secret Service agent Brian Parr.[82]

Ismoil and Yousef were found guilty of all charges, which included conspiracy to destroy by explosives buildings, vehicles, and property, damaging or destroying the World Trade Center complex by means of an explosive, causing injury or death, and transporting explosive materials in interstate commerce with the intent to destroy buildings or vehicles.[83] Yousef received a sentence of 240 years in prison without the possibility of parole, was fined $4.5 million, and was ordered to pay $250 million in restitution.[84] Eyad Ismoil was convicted on 10 counts, sentenced to 240 years' imprisonment, and fined $250,000.

In sentencing the terrorists convicted in this trial, the judge computed the actuarial life spans of the six victims and added them together to arrive at a sentence of 240 years.[85] It is particularly interesting to note that at the time of the 1993 bombing there was no crime in the federal statutes specifically addressing terrorism. Rather, the practice was to charge defendants with a broad range of criminal statutes, which in this case included conspiracy to damage buildings by use of an explosive device, explosive destruction of property, and interstate transportation of explosives, to name a few.[86] The conspiracy charge was based on the letter sent to the *New York Times* four days after the bombing by Nidal Ayyad claiming responsibility for the bombing.[87]

The 1993 terrorist attack against the World Trade Center complex was largely perceived by policymakers and the public as a crime, and as such, law enforcement agencies were given responsibility for investigating the crime, gathering evidence, apprehending suspects, and successfully prosecuting the perpetrators. Handled as a singular criminal incident, the WTC bombing was not seen as part of a larger terrorist conspiracy that needed to be addressed through new counterterrorism programs and policies. The FBI's success in this case highlighted the effectiveness of the criminal justice system in coping with the threat of terrorism in the United States at that time. Despite the successful investigation and prosecution of the 1993 WTC conspirators, the United States was not able to prevent future attacks against the homeland because law enforcement agencies failed to recognize the larger transnational terror network that was involved. The larger organization with which the Liberation Army was associated, Islamic Jihad, was not examined, and future plans and plots were not investigated by the FBI, though evidence gathered during the 1993 WTC investigation showed a much larger transnational conspiracy than the crimes committed in New York on February 26, 1993.

DISCUSSION QUESTIONS

1. What was the motivation of the conspirators in the 1993 World Trade Center bombing? Was it similar to jihadist ideology today? Explain.

2. What was the method of attack and type of weapon used in this attack? Who were the intended victims? Compare and contrast the tactics and strategy of the perpetrators with those involved in the 9/11 attacks against the World Trade Center.

3. What was the role of the FBI in the 1993 WTC case? Explain how the agency was involved in responding to and investigating this attack. Did the FBI make any attempts to prevent the attack from occurring?

4. In this case, the FBI successfully investigated and prosecuted the perpetrators, yet failed to see the larger transnational network. Was this oversight due to failures of the FBI or to the limited law enforcement perspective that was in play at that time?

NOTES

1. Lindsay Clutterbuck, "Law Enforcement," in *Attacking Terrorism,* ed. Audrey Kurth Cronin and James Ludes (Washington, DC: Georgetown University Press, 2004), 141.

2. US Government Printing Office, *Preparing for the 21st Century,* March 1, 1996, www.gpoaccess.gov/int/report.html (accessed October 5, 2007).

3. Carol Winkler, *In the Name of Terrorism* (Albany: State University of New York Press, 2006), 135.

4. The FBI concluded during the investigation that this was the "largest by weight and by damage of any improvised explosive device since the inception of forensic explosion identification in 1925." Simon Reeve, *The New Jackals: Ramzi Yousef, Osama bin Laden, and the Future of Terrorism* (Boston: Northeastern University Press, 2002), 154.

5. Jim Dwyer et al., *Two Seconds Under the World* (New York: Crown, 1994), 50.

6. *United States of America v. Mohammed A. Salameh et al.,* S593 Cr. 180 (KTD).

7. Peter Lance, *1,000 Years for Revenge* (New York: Regan Books, 2003), 116.

8. Ibid., 118.

9. US Fire Administration, *The World Trade Center Bombing: Report and Analysis,* Technical Report Series USFA-TR-076, February 1993, 1, http://www.usfa.fema.gov /downloads/pdf/publications/tr-076.pdf (accessed July 15, 2007).

10. Laurie Myloie, "Iraqi Complicity in the World Trade Center Bombing and Beyond," *Middle East Intelligence Bulletin* 3, no. 6 (June 2001), http://www.meib.org /articles/0106_ir1.htm (accessed August 20, 2007).

11. J. Gilmore Childers and Henry DePippo, statement before the Senate Judiciary Committee, "Hearing on Foreign Terrorists in America: Five Years After the World Trade Center," February 24, 1998, http://www.fas.org/irp/congress/1998_hr/s980.

12. There were 1,042 people injured, mostly from smoke inhalation. In addition, 88 firefighters, 35 police officers, and one EMS worker sustained injuries in the rescue efforts. See US Fire Administration, *The World Trade Center Bombing.*

13. Childers and DePippo, statement before the Senate Judiciary Committee.

14. Ibid. For more details on the experience of victims, see N. R. Kleinfield, "First Darkness, Then Came the Smoke," *New York Times,* February 27, 1993, 1.

15. US Fire Administration, *The World Trade Center Bombing.*

16. John Miller and Michael Stone, *The Cell* (New York: Hyperion, 2002), 103.

17. Ibid., 101.

18. Dave Williams, "The Bombing of the World Trade Center in New York," *International Criminal Police Review* 4 (1998): 469–471.

19. Reeve, *The New Jackals,* 31; Dwyer et al., *Two Seconds Under the World,* 86.

20. Ralph Blumenthal, "Insistence on Refund for a Truck Results in an Arrest in Explosion," *New York Times,* March 5, 1993, A1; see also *United States v. Ramzi Ahmed Yousef,* Indictment S10 93 Cr. 180 (KTD).

21. Dwyer et al., *Two Seconds Under the World,* 91.

22. Ibid.

23. Lance, *1,000 Years for Revenge,* 138.

24. Blumenthal, "Insistence on Refund for a Truck Results in an Arrest in Explosion."

25. Dwyer et al., *Two Seconds Under the World,* 189; see also *United States v. Ramzi Ahmed Yousef,* Indictment S10 93 Cr. 180 (KTD).

26. David Kocieniewski, "Suspect Still Sought in Trade Center Bomb Case," *New York Times,* November 14, 1997.

27. Ibid.; see also US State Department, Rewards for Justice, "Wanted: Information Leading to the Location of Abdul Rahman Yasin: Up to $5 Million Reward," http://www .rewardsforjustice.net/index.cfm?page=Yasin&language=pashtu. Yasin remains one of the FBI's most wanted terrorists: see FBI, "Most Wanted Terrorists: Abdul Rahman Yasin," http://www.fbi.gov/wanted/wanted_terrorists/abdul-rahman-yasin/view (accessed July 15, 2012).

28. Reeve, *The New Jackals,* 146.

29. Childers and DePippo, statement before the Senate Judiciary Committee.

30. Dwyer et al., *Two Seconds Under the World,* 162–163.

31. Childers and DePippo, statement before the Senate Judiciary Committee.

32. Miller and Stone, *The Cell,* 82.

33. Ibid., 83.

34. Ibid., 85; see also Dwyer et al., *Two Seconds Under the World,* 104.

35. Dwyer et al., *Two Seconds Under the World;* see also Miller and Stone, *The Cell,* 91.

36. Miller and Stone, *The Cell,* 91.

37. Reeve, *The New Jackals,* 39.

38. Ibid.

39. National Commission on Terrorist Attacks upon the United States, *The 9/11 Commission Report: Final Report of the National Commission on Terrorist Attacks upon the United States* (New York: W. W. Norton, 2004), 147.

40. NYPD detective Joseph Borelli declared Nosair a lone gunman in a news conference and stated that he did not believe Nosair was part of a conspiracy or terrorist organization. Karen Freifeld and David Kocieniewski, "The Fateful Hours," *Newsday,* November 8, 1990.

41. *United States of America v. Omar Ahmad Abdel Rahman,* Indictment S3 93 Cr. 181 (MBM).

42. Dwyer et al., *Two Seconds Under the World,* 113.

43. Lance, *1,000 Years for Revenge,* 36.

44. John Kifner, "Kahane Suspect Said to Have Arms Cache," *New York Times,* December 11, 1990, B1.

45. Lance, *1,000 Years for Revenge,* 35.

46. Peter Lance, "The Blind Sheikh: A Flashpoint for Terror 20 Years After the World Trade Center Bombing," *The Public Record,* February 17, 2013, http://pubrecord.org /nation/10726/blind-sheikh; Center for Defense Information, "Al-Gama'a al-Islamiyya— Islamic Group," December 2, 2002, http://www.cdi.org/terrorism/algamaa.cfm.

47. See *United States v. Ahmed Abdel Sattar,* Indictment 02 Cr. 395.

48. Daniel Benjamin and Steven Simon, *The Age of Sacred Terror* (New York: Random House, 2002), 6.

49. Ibid., 7.

50. *United States of America v. Omar Ahmed Ali Abdel Rahman,* August 1997, US Court of Appeals for the Second Circuit, http://openjurist.org/189/f39/88/united-states -of-america-v-omar-ahmad-ali-abdel-rahman.www.mipt.org/usvrahman2cir081997.asp (accessed August 8, 2007).

51. See *United States v. Ahmed Abdel Sattar,* Indictment 02 Cr. 395.

52. Miller and Stone, *The Cell*, 6; see also Bill Gertz, *Breakdown: How America's Intelligence Failures Led to September 11* (Washington, DC: Regnery Publishing, 2002).

53. In a press conference Borelli said, "What we have and all we know is that we have a lone gunman who committed a homicide in New York City"; John Kifner, "Kahane Suspect Is a Muslim with a Series of Addresses," *New York Times,* November 7, 1990, A1. See also note 40.

54. "Bin Laden Helped Fund Defense of Meir Kahane's Killer, Officials Say," *New York Daily News,* October 9, 2002.

55. Eleanor Hill, *"Joint Inquiry Staff Statement*: Hearing on the Intelligence Community's Response to Past Terrorist Attacks Against the United States from February 1993 to September 2001," October 8, 2002, http://www.fas.org/irp/congress/2002_hr/100802hill .html (accessed December 12, 2007).

56. Ibid.

57. Dwyer et al., *Two Seconds Under the World,* 181.

58. Ibid., 182.

59. Ibid.

60. Ibid., 190.

61. Lance, *1,000 Years for Revenge,* 130–131; see also Alison Mitchell, "Letter Explained Motive in Bombing, Officials Now Say," *New York Times,* March 28, 1993, A2.

62. Mitchell, "Letter Explained Motive in Bombing, Officials Now Say."

63. Lance, *1,000 Years for Revenge,* 148; see also Reeve, *The New Jackals,* 40.

64. Reeve, *The New Jackals,* 40.

65. Richard Lyons, "Fourth Arrest Made in Bombing at Trade Center," *New York Times,* March 23, 1993, A1.

66. Reeve, *The New Jackals,* 97.

67. James McKinley, "Bomb Plot, Chapter 3: Enter an Accused Master of Terrorism," *New York Times,* October 3, 1995.

68. Reeve, *The New Jackals,* 98.

69. Lance, *1,000 Years for Revenge,* 213.

70. Ibid.; see also Reeve, *The New Jackals,* 101; *United States v. Ramzi Ahmed Yousef,* S10 93 Cr. 180 (KTD).

71. Miller and Stone, *The Cell,* 104; *United States v. Ramzi Ahmed Yousef,* S10 93 Cr. 180 (KTD).

72. *United States v. Ramzi Ahmed Yousef,* S10 93 Cr. 180 (KTD).

73. Benjamin Weiser, "The Trade Center Verdict: The Overview," *New York Times,* November 13, 1997, A1.

74. Benjamin Weiser, "As Trade Center Smoldered, Suspect Watched, Jury Hears," *New York Times,* October 23, 1997, A1.

75. James C. McKinley, "Suspect Said to Be a Longtime Friend of Bombing Mastermind," *New York Times,* August 4, 1995.

76. Benjamin Weiser, "Driver Gets 240 Years in Prison for Bombing of Trade Center," *New York Times,* April 4, 1998.

77. Richard Bernstein, "In Bomb Plot Trial: A Blizzard of Evidence," *New York Times,* February 9, 1994, A1.

78. Richard Bernstein, "Four Are Convicted in Bombing at World Trade Center," *New York Times,* March 5, 1994, A1; see also Robert Precht, *Defending Mohammad* (Ithaca, NY: Cornell University Press, 2003).

79. Judgment in a criminal case: *United States of America v. Mahmud Abouhalima* S5 93 Cr. 180-03 (KTD); *United States of America v. Mohammed A. Salameh et al.,* S5 93 Cr. 180-000; *United States of America v. Nidal Ayyad,* S5 93 Cr. 180-002; *United States of America v. Ahmad Mohammad Ajaj,* S5 93 Cr. 180-006.

80. *United States of America v. Eyad Ismoil et al.,* 93 Cr. 180 (KTD).

81. Weiser, "As Trade Center Smoldered, Suspect Watched, Jury Hears."

82. Ibid.; see also Lance, *1,000 Years for Revenge.*

83. Judgment in a criminal case: *United States of America v. Eyad Ismoil,* S12 93 Cr. 180-009; *United States of America v. Ramzi Ahmed Yousef,* S12 93 Cr. 180-004.

84. Benjamin Weiser, "Mastermind Gets Life for Bombing of Trade Center," *New York Times,* January 9, 1998.

85. Richard Bernstein, "Trade Center Bombers Get Prison Terms of 240 Years," *New York Times,* May 25, 1994, A1, B4.

86. Title 18, USC 844(i); Title 18, USC 844(d); Title 18 USC 844(f).

87. *United States v. Ramzi Ahmed Yousef,* S10 93 Cr. 180 (KTD).

Terrorist or Ecosaboteur?

The Case of Briana Waters

LINDA KILTZ

Introduction

The study of terrorism is first and foremost a study in human behavior, which is highly volatile and constantly changing. Texts on terrorism focus on terrorist events, ideas, motivations, theories, and histories that result in terrorist violence.[1] In any study of terrorism, one finds a plethora of definitions, yet no one agreed-upon definition.[2] In fact, some scholars, such as Walter Laqueur, discourage attempts to define terrorism. Laqueur argues that "many terrorisms exist, and their character has changed over time and from country to country. The endeavor to find a general theory of terrorism, one overall explanation of its roots, is a futile and misguided exercise."[3] While other scholars argue that a general definition of terrorism is possible, they are aware of the difficulty of such an endeavor given the nature of terrorism research and the challenges of implementing policy solutions to a broad range of threats labeled as "terrorism."[4]

Elected officials, security experts, journalists, and academics all use a variety of definitions of terrorism. Some definitions emphasize the characteristics and motivations of individual terrorists, while others focus on terrorist organizations' mode of operation. This is highlighted by Alex Schmid and Albert Jongman in their book *Political Terrorism*, in which they cite 109 different definitions of terrorism that they obtained in a survey of leading academics in the field. From these definitions, the authors isolated the following recurring elements, in order of their statistical appearance in the definitions: violence, force (appeared in 83.5 percent of the definitions); political (65 percent); fear, emphasis on terror (51 percent); threats (47 percent); psychological effects and anticipated reactions (41.5 percent); discrepancy between the targets and the victims (37.5 percent); intentional, planned, systematic, organized action (32 percent); and methods of combat, strategy, tactics (30.5 percent).[5] In most definitions of terrorism there are common elements that include the illegal use of violence or force by subnational actors in a planned and systematic way in order to achieve political objectives and instill fear in a population.[6] While there are hundreds of definitions of terrorism, what most can agree on is that applying the label of terrorism to individuals or organizations elicits a strong negative reaction by the public because their acts are seen as morally impermissible and perpetrated by evil people.[7]

Defining socially important concepts such as terrorism is an important activity because definitions, particularly those found in legal statutes, serve as powerful tools of persuasion. Labeling a person or act as terroristic is a powerful rhetorical technique that carries a strong normative connection.[8] Such labeling frames how we perceive an act—as good or bad, as right or wrong. Brian Jenkins has written, "What is called terrorism seems to depend on one's point of view. Use of the term implies a moral judgment; and if one party can successfully attach the label 'terrorist' to its opponent, then it has indirectly persuaded others to adopt its moral viewpoint."[9] Thus, the terrorism label can be very subjective depending largely on whether one sympathizes with or opposes the group, person, or cause concerned. While most Americans would label the perpetrators of the 9/11 attacks as terrorists owing to the large number of people who were indiscriminately killed in the attacks, how would they label environmental activists' acts of arson or tree-spiking that cause property damage but do not physically harm persons? Are these acts of "ecotage" (ecosabotage) or ecoterrorism?

This case study will describe the arson attack on the Center for Urban Horticulture at the University of Washington on May 21, 2001, by Briana Waters and four other members of the Earth Liberation Front (ELF) and detail the investigation and prosecution of Waters. For the FBI and federal prosecutors, an act of arson by ELF adds up to terrorism, yet others have argued that these are not acts of terrorism because they are not directed at people but at property; further, they argue, the acts of ELF are not calculated to influence the government but are meant only to intimidate industries or businesses involved in the exploitation of the environment.[10] This case will first provide an overview of the legal definitions of terrorism used by the FBI, as well as the definition and characteristics of ecosabotage. Next is a description of the perpetrators, motive, and method of attack. The case will then follow the investigation of the FBI and conclude by discussing some of the problems that occurred in the prosecution of Waters.

Defining Ecotage and Ecoterrorism

Ecosabotage, or "ecotage," has been defined as the "practice of damaging property to prevent ecological damage,"[11] or similarly, as acts of "sabotage carried out by environmental activists that are intended to cause material damage to their opponents."[12] Ecotage includes acts of sabotage and property destruction, acts such as tree-spiking, "monkeywrenching," fence-cutting, arson of buildings and vehicles, and other acts carried out in a way so as to avoid harm to humans.[13] The term "monkeywrenching," drawn from Edward Abbey's *The Monkey Wrench Gang* (1990), originally included only sabotage to industrial machinery but has since come to be used interchangeably with "ecotage."[14]

Fundamental to the philosophy of direct action as espoused by environmental extremists, particularly members of ELF, is the determination to do whatever is necessary to disrupt, not merely oppose, any activity they consider detrimental to the environment. While the broader objective of militant environmentalists is to draw attention to and sway legislation on behalf of environmental protection, acts of sabotage have a twofold purpose: to prevent or delay activities, such as logging, from going ahead by destroying equipment and infrastructure, and to force companies to halt and perhaps reconsider their operations.[15] Although most companies have not stopped their operations after being attacked, they have been hampered by the resulting damage.

Over the past several decades, ecotage has caused millions of dollars in damage to businesses, individuals, and government organizations. In fact, it is estimated that between 1997 and 2006 the Earth Liberation Front was responsible for over $100 million in property damage.[16] Two such acts were among the most destructive: the arson at a Colorado ski resort in 1998 that destroyed buildings and equipment worth an estimated $2 million, and another arson in 2003 at a California housing development that resulted in roughly $22 million in reconstruction costs and lost revenues.[17] Members of ELF and other supporters of ecosabotage see these acts as a form of "civil disobedience," while the FBI and many Americans clearly see such acts as eco-terrorism, a category of domestic terrorism.

The question remains: does ecotage actually constitute terrorism? To help answer this question it is useful to turn to the various definitions found in federal statutes and regulations and in the FBI's definitions. The federal regulations that outline the scope of the FBI's investigative and enforcement duties define terrorism as "the unlawful use of force and violence against persons or property to intimidate or coerce a government, the civilian population, or any segment thereof, in furtherance of political or social objectives."[18] The FBI's definition is quite broad and encompasses the ecosabotage activities of ELF members. In fact, the FBI has not only defined such conduct as terrorism but has described groups such as ELF as one of the greatest domestic terrorism threats facing the United States today.[19]

The USA PATRIOT Act of 2001 expanded this definition to include domestic acts within the definition of terrorism. Section 802 of the act modified the legal definition of terrorism to include a category of "domestic terrorism," which is defined by acts that are "dangerous to human life that are a violation of the criminal laws of the United States or of any State," are conducted primarily within the jurisdiction of the United States, and are intended to "intimidate or coerce a civilian population," "influence the policy of a government by intimidation or coercion," or "affect the conduct of a government by mass destruction, assassination, or kidnapping."[20]

Further, the FBI defines eco-terrorism as "the use or threatened use of violence of a criminal nature against innocent victims or property by an environmentally-oriented, subnational group for environmental-political reasons, or aimed at an audience beyond the target, often of a symbolic nature."[21] Under this definition, ELF's acts of ecotage would constitute ecoterrorism.

Despite how the FBI defines terrorism or eco-terrorism, the ambiguity in the definition of terrorism across federal agencies, statutes, and regulations can create confusion "in the investigative process regarding exactly what becomes domestic terrorism."[22] A 2009 study from Syracuse University found that US federal district courts, the Department of Justice's National Security Division, and federal prosecutors all rely on different criteria to determine whether or not specific cases involve terrorist acts. This lack of agreement has led to widespread failures to obtain prosecutions of the suspects recommended for charges by investigative agencies. In fact, the study found that from 2004 to 2009, "assistant United States attorneys all over the country declined to bring any charges against two out of every three (67%) of the thousands of terrorism matters that the investigative agencies had recommended for criminal prosecution." The Syracuse study ends with a warning about the ambiguity surrounding the definition of terrorism: "The strong evidence that various parts of the government do not share a common understanding about terrorism has important consequences for all Americans. Those most immediately affected are the thousands of people whom the investigative agencies each year incorrectly recommend for prosecution in federal court. But to the extent that the investigators systematically waste their time targeting the wrong suspects, the chances increase that they will fail to identify the real terrorists who right now may be seeking to plant bombs, spread poisons or otherwise harm a much larger number of innocent people."[23] Given this ambiguity in the definition of terrorism, is Briana Waters a terrorist?

The Attack

In the early morning hours of May 21, 2001, a group of five men and women associated with the Earth Liberation Front broke into the Center for Urban Horticulture on the University of Washington campus in Seattle and set the building ablaze with a homemade, timed incendiary device. While one of the intruders served as a lookout, the other three broke into the building and set up the bombs in the office of Toby Bradshaw, an associate professor and poplar-tree geneticist at the center.[24] The incendiary devices were composed of several gallons of fuel, a container or bucket filled with road flares that served as an igniter, batteries, and a cheap digital timer.[25] When the timer went off, the igniter clicked and the gasoline blew. The result was a small, yet fierce explosion that spread through the offices, labs, and libraries of the Center for Urban Horticulture, causing over $6 million in losses.[26]

Arson was immediately suspected by law enforcement and fire investigators because the homemade incendiary device that was used to torch the UW building was similar to a device used in another fire that same morning that destroyed the Jefferson Poplar Farm, hundreds of miles away in Clatskanie, Oregon.[27] At the site of the Oregon fire, the words YOU CANNOT CONTROL

WHAT IS WILD and ELF were spray-painted on one of the surviving buildings.[28] In the wake of both fires, investigators found no real evidence that would link specific individuals to either of these crimes. Five days after the attacks, investigators received their first confirmation on who was responsible in the form of a press release, dispatched by Craig Rosebraugh, ELF spokesman in Portland, Oregon, in which it was claimed that ELF was behind the attack (see the appendix for the communiqué).[29] As a spokesperson for ELF, Craig Rosebraugh was provided information about these "direct actions" after they occurred through encrypted email. Rosebraugh said he was not surprised that ELF had set the fires in Washington and Oregon, since the group had targeted genetic engineering in the past. As Rosebraugh also pointed out, however, these attacks were unique because it was the first time ELF had targeted sites in multiple states at the same time.[30]

The target at the University of Washington was Professor Toby Bradshaw, who received funding from the timber industry to develop fast-growing, cross-pollinated poplar trees, which are used to produce paper and lumber products. The ELF cell's communiqué explained that it had targeted Bradshaw's office because they believed he was genetically engineering trees for the benefit of the timber industry. They said that his research would "unleash mutant genes into the environment" and "cause irreversible harm to forest ecosystems."[31] However, Bradshaw was not doing research in genetic engineering: he was involved in basic research to identify genes in poplars that were resistant to cold temperatures and disease.[32] Despite ELF having targeted a scientist who was not involved in genetic engineering, spokesman Rosebraugh openly supported the attacks, stating, "The only way to fight the profit-driven environmental and humanitarian offenses of capitalistic society is through economic sabotage by any means necessary." Further, Rosebraugh stated that ELF actions were driven by four guidelines: (1) cause immediate economic damage; (2) educate the public; (3) take all necessary precautions to ensure no life forms are injured; and (4) instill a fear of sabotage in similar businesses.[33]

The Family

At the center of this case was a radical environmental group known as "the Family." An ecoterrorist cell, the Family comprised over a dozen Animal Liberation Front (ALF) and ELF members.[34] Most members of the Family were white, middle-class, young adults with an "anarchist-hippies attitude reflective of the late 1960s leftist extremism." Almost all of its members (about twenty) lived in the Pacific Northwest and became acquainted through the anarchist-environmental movement in and around Eugene, Oregon. Between 1996 and 2001, the group was responsible for twenty-one ecotage and arson attacks that targeted US Forest Service ranger stations, wild horse facilities, lumber companies, the Vail ski resort, and the simultaneous attacks on the UW Horticulture Center and the Jefferson Poplar Farm on May 21, 2001.[35] It is estimated that $80 million in damages resulted from these strings of arsons and other acts of sabotage by the Family across the states of Washington, Oregon, California, and Colorado.[36]

Prior to the attack on the UW Center for Urban Horticulture, four members of the Family—Bill Rodgers, Lacey Phillabaum, Jennifer Kolar, and Justin Solondz—met in Oregon, Arizona, and California for what they called "Book Club" meetings to plan their attacks and to receive training in lock-picking, computer security, target reconnaissance, and bomb-making. (Waters denied ever attending any of these meetings.) At one of these meetings, Jennifer Kolar (who was a software designer for AOL) shared "her extensive expertise in computers by providing encryption diskettes and instructing members in their use, so the group could communicate secretly."[37] An analysis of the Family revealed extensive planning activities prior to an attack by knowledgeable and well-trained individuals:

> Members of the Family engaged in significant Internet research on potential targets as much as three to four months in advance of target selection. . . . Others had similar in-depth knowledge of potential environmental targets in the region because of their extensive earlier participation in the environmental movement. Most members of the Family were not novices; they were knowledgeable about environmental issues, the corporations and facilities to be targeted, and basic monkey wrenching tactics.[38]

In this case, all of the individuals involved had in fact been environmental activists and had participated in direct actions in the past.

The leader and mastermind of the attack on the UW Center for Urban Horticulture was William Rodgers (aka Avalon), who was a forty-year-old bookstore operator in Prescott, Arizona, and one of the top organizers and participants in ELF. Rodgers was implicated in at least nine attacks, including the arson at UW and in Vail, Colorado, at the time of his arrest by the

FBI in December 2005.[39] Before being involved in ELF, Rodgers was an environmental activist who had participated in the Warner Creek blockade and the vandalism during the World Trade Organization (WTO) meeting in Seattle.[40] Rodgers was also known for the several manuals he wrote for would-be saboteurs that had become Internet classics, including "Setting Fires with Electrical Timers: An Earth Liberation Front Guide."[41]

Like Rodgers, Lacey Phillabaum, Jennifer Kolar, Justin Solondz, and Briana Waters had been environmental activists in the late 1990s and participated in numerous protests as animal rights and environmental activists. For example, Phillabaum was a former *Earth First! Journal* editor who participated in the Warner Creek blockade in 1996 and the WTO protests in Seattle in 1999.[42] Solondz and Waters met while attending Evergreen State College in Olympia, Washington, in the late 1990s and participated as protesters and tree-sitters with the Cascadia Defense Network to prevent the logging in Gifford Pinchot National Forest and other old-growth forests in the region.[43] Waters and her boyfriend, Solondz, met Rodgers through their involvement with various environmental organizations such as Earth First! and Forest Defense.[44] According to Waters, Rodgers first recruited her to assist him in small tasks such as obtaining a cell phone for him in her name, but she had never attended "Book Club" meetings.[45] In 2001 Waters and Solondz were recruited by Rodgers to be involved in the action against the UW Center for Urban Horticulture.[46] According to terrorism scholar Brent Smith, recruitment into the Family was unique because unlike the practice common among other terrorist groups of inducting people with little or no experience in violent extremism, the Family recruited new members for specific terrorist attacks and allowed them to participate in Book Club meetings. Most of these new additions were seasoned environmental extremists who had been arrested numerous times as demonstrators in other direct actions and were viewed as "true believers" in the cause.[47]

Once all of the members were recruited for the action against the UW Center for Urban Horticulture, the cell began to make logistical plans in Waters's house in Olympia, Washington.[48] First, Kolar and Solondz performed reconnaissance of the UW Center and Dr. Bradshaw's office.[49] Second, they turned Waters's garage into a "clean room" to construct incendiary devices. This room was lined with plastic sheeting that was thrown away so that no DNA evidence or elements of the incendiary devices would be found. These firebombs were primarily designed and constructed by Rodgers and Solondz, but Waters and Phillabaum also participated in their construction. Lastly, Waters obtained the car that would be used for the arson attack at UW. Waters had her cousin,

Robert Corrina, obtain a rental car for her on May 19, 2001, so that the vehicle could not be traced back to her or the other cell members.[50] Records obtained from the car rental company by the FBI indicated that the car was rented sometime before 6:30 AM on May 21, 2001, and was driven 237 miles, a distance sufficient to cover a round-trip between Olympia and Seattle.[51]

On the evening of May 20, 2001, Waters complained to her cousin, Corrina, that she was having abdominal pains and left in the rental car with Solondz, purportedly to go to the hospital. Waters did not return until Monday, May 21, 2001, when she told Corrina that she had been unable to find an emergency room in Olympia and had driven to Seattle. In fact, Waters and Solondz had picked up Rodgers and Phillabaum and driven to Seattle with the incendiary devices. The foursome met with Kolar at the Greenlake Bar and Grill in Seattle, and after midnight they traveled to the Center for Urban Horticulture. Waters acted as a lookout, hiding in nearby bushes with a police scanner and walkie-talkie.[52] Solondz served as the getaway driver and a lookout.[53] Rodgers, Kolar, and Phillabaum carried the firebombs to the Center for Urban Horticulture, where they broke into the building through a window and set up the devices. Sometime after 3:00 AM, the incendiary devices ignited, starting a fire that would destroy the building. Though federal, state, and local officials converged on the scene after this attack, sifting through the wreckage for evidence—just as they had done in other major arson attacks around the West claimed by the ELF—they were unable to gather enough evidence to charge anyone with a crime.

The Investigation—Operation Backfire

The attack on the UW Center for Urban Horticulture was just one of a string of attacks by the Family or ELF, and as a result, in 2004, the FBI merged seven of its ongoing investigations into the animal rights and environmental movements into Major Case 220, called "Operation Backfire." The primary purpose of this operation was to find and prosecute those members of the Family who had committed crimes, including arson, vandalism, property damage, and animal releases. According to Michael Ward, deputy assistant director of the FBI's Counterterrorism Division, these individuals were terrorists: "regardless of their political or social message, their actions were criminal and violated federal laws." As part of this effort, the FBI offered a reward of up to $50,000 each for information leading to the capture and arrest of these criminals.[54] This new focus on ecoterrorism was largely due to the shifting priorities of the FBI in the wake of the terror attack on the World Trade Center on September 11, 2001. After 9/11, FBI director Robert Mueller decided to restructure the FBI as a terrorism prevention organization rather than just a crime-fighting organization.[55] Mueller stated, "Investigating and preventing animal rights and environmental extremism is one of the FBI's highest domestic terrorism priorities. We are committed to working with our partners to disrupt and dismantle these movements, to protect our fellow citizens, and to bring to justice those who commit crime and terrorism in the name of animal rights or environmental issues."[56] Until the FBI coordinated its efforts with local law enforcement and other agencies, it did not have much to work with in regard to the UW arson.

Since no real evidence was left behind, the best hope for the FBI was someone coming forward as an informant. The FBI found its informant in the spring of 2003 when Jake Ferguson, a heavy metal guitarist and heroin addict from Eugene, Oregon, agreed to cooperate with the FBI so that he would not have to go to prison for the dozens of arsons he had participated in while a member of ELF. Ferguson was a radical environmentalist who was well known in the activist community for his participation in the Warner Creek blockade with William Rodgers. Ferguson claimed to know almost every member of ELF and agreed to wear a recording wire to gather evidence against his former friends and accomplices and provide testimony against them. Those recordings included conversations with Rodgers on his how-to manual, "Setting Fires with Electrical Timers," and details on the arson attacks on May 21, 2001, at the poplar farm in Oregon and the UW Center for Urban Horticulture.[57]

With the information provided by Ferguson, the FBI was soon knocking on doors across the country. Most of the suspected arsonists, if convicted, would face at least thirty years in prison. Lured with promises of reduced sentences, friends turned in friends, girlfriends offered up the names of boyfriends, and boyfriends handed over the names of girlfriends. Recriminations flew. Those who named names "have dishonored themselves . . . by becoming vicious traitors and tools of the state," wrote two noncooperators in the *Earth First! Journal.*[58] In 2006 the trail of accusations led the FBI to the door of a quiet thirty-two-year-old violin teacher in Berkeley, California, named Briana Waters.

In early 2002, Waters left Olympia, Washington, and moved to the San Francisco Bay Area of California, where she started a new life away from her associates in ELF/ALF. In California, Waters worked as a nanny, music teacher, and musician. She was a talented violinist who taught children and adults to play the violin and regularly performed at charitable events. While living in the Bay Area, Waters had a relationship with a carpenter named John Landgraf, and in 2005 their baby daughter was born. Waters lived a modest life at that point, with no ties to the radical environmental movement.[59]

In February 2006, the FBI knocked on Waters's door in Oakland, California, and informed her that she was the target of an investigation into ELF/ALF activities. Waters declined to cooperate and declined to plead guilty, instead choosing to go to trial and risk being sentenced to a thirty-five-year mandatory minimum sentence. In her trial in 2008, Waters testified that she was not guilty because "her motivation was that she would do anything to avoid prison so she could be with her young daughter who was still a baby and completely dependent on her in every way."[60]

Despite her pleas of not guilty, the government was able to present an effective case against Waters because of the information they had gathered from informants.

The Trials of Briana Waters

The following section describes the investigation that took place in Briana Waters's case. These details were written in the decision of Judge A. Wallace Tashima when Waters's case went before the US Court of Appeals for the Ninth Circuit on March 5, 2010.[61]

The investigation into these fires had seen little progress until 2004, when a man suspected of participating in the Oregon arson agreed to cooperate. With the help of this witness, the case broke wide open. With this new information, the FBI came to believe that the UW arson had been the work of five individuals, although which five was a matter of debate. Authorities were certain of the identities of three participants. Lacey Phillabaum and Jennifer Kolar, both seasoned ELF members, admitted to participating in the arson. William Rodgers, the man the government described as the head of the ELF cell that committed many of the arsons across the West, was identified by both Phillabaum and Kolar as a third member. Rodgers committed suicide while in jail shortly after he was arrested. The identities of the final two participants were less clear. Kolar was the first to give a statement to the FBI, but her memory was hazy.

A few weeks after making her initial statement, Kolar returned to the FBI and told them that she had remembered Briana Waters's involvement in the crime. Kolar claimed that she had remembered Waters's involvement after coming across Waters's name in her telephone contact list. Kolar never identified the remaining two arsonists, and she never named Phillabaum as a participant, despite the fact that the two had a long acquaintanceship, during which they had attended various small meetings together where they discussed environmental sabotage.

Two months after Kolar's proffer, Phillabaum met with the FBI. She confessed to her participation in the UW arson and told investigators that the remaining four participants were Rodgers, Kolar, Waters, and Waters's boyfriend, Justin Solondz.[62] A search of Solondz's residence soon thereafter uncovered evidence that he had been involved in the arson. He fled the country before police could find him.

Based on this information, a grand jury indicted Waters and Solondz, along with three individuals who had been involved in the Jefferson Poplar Farm arson. Phillabaum and Kolar pled guilty to separate charges and were sentenced to three and five years' imprisonment, respectively. Phillabaum and Kolar were key witnesses in Waters's trial, both giving detailed accounts of her role in the arson. Both agreed that Waters was not significantly involved with ELF and did not attend the initial meetings in which the UW and Jefferson Poplar arsons were planned. In May 2001, however, close to two weeks before the UW arson was to take place, Waters joined the plot to destroy the UW Center for Urban Horticulture. Kolar and Phillabaum also gave similar descriptions of the night the arson occurred. The government was able to corroborate some of this testimony through another witness, Robert Corrina.

Waters's defense was that she was being set up by Phillabaum and Kolar, both of whom she claimed held grudges against her. She offered little in the way of an alibi and was unable directly to contradict much of the testimony against her. Instead, she focused on highlighting discrepancies in the government's case and attacking the FBI's investigation. Much of Waters's defense was spent trying to convince the jury that she did not agree with ELF's tactics. She testified that she was "absolutely not" involved in the UW arson because it was "very dangerous to human lives," and she felt "very strongly about not hurting people in any way."[63]

Waters also called a number of character witnesses in her defense. These witnesses generally agreed that Waters was kind, peaceful, and responsible. They included an assistant attorney general for the State of Washington, Waters's former college professors, a mother whose children Waters had babysat, and some who had worked with Waters during the making of a documentary film. They testified that Waters was not violent and never advocated violence, that she was full of "integrity" and "peacefulness," and that she was "extremely ethical."[64] After hearing the above testimony, the jury returned a verdict finding Waters guilty of two counts of arson and deadlocked on five other charges.

On June 19, 2008, Briana Waters was sentenced to six years in federal prison and ordered to pay $6 million in restitution for her role in the 2001 arson at the UW Center for Urban Horticulture.[65] She was convicted of two counts of arson but not on the charge of the use of a destructive device in a crime of violence, which carries a thirty-year mandatory minimum sentence.

Waters served two and a half years in prison following her conviction, but this was overturned in October 2010 after the Ninth Circuit Court of Appeals held that a folder of documents containing anarchist materials was improperly admitted into evidence at her trial.[66]

The FBI had obtained a folder of documents from Kolar, who claimed that Waters gave it to her sometime after the UW arson. The folder, but none of the contents, had Waters's fingerprints. Waters admitted giving the folder to Kolar, but believed that the articles were about women and activism, not anarchist political theory. The government argued that the articles were properly admitted and were relevant to the case because they established an association between Waters and Kolar, contained one article on the UW arson, and were needed to rebut the character evidence that Waters had introduced in her defense. The court did not support these government claims, stating: "We do not find the articles to be particularly probative of any of these theories. The folder, which was found in Kolar's possession and bore Waters' handwritten note and fingerprints, established that Kolar and Waters were friends; the articles were unnecessary for that purpose. And, while one article mentioned the UW arson, it did so in a brief blurb that occupied less than one-tenth of one page, out of a total of 212 pages of articles."[67]

In addition, the court was highly critical of the government for focusing on the content of the articles that were highly prejudicial and likely to have swayed jurors' emotions in this case.

In this decision, Judge Tashima wrote the following, which highlights the reasoning of the court:

> We believe that an appropriately skeptical eye would have excluded the articles from Waters' trial, or at least limited the articles that were provided to the jury. In contrast to the article's slight probative value, their content

was problematic on many levels. To begin with, the foundation for their admission was weak. Kolar could not positively state that the articles in the folder were the articles that Waters had provided her; instead, she testified that, after glancing at the folder, she placed it in a box and never looked at it again before producing it to her lawyer. Waters testified that the articles introduced into evidence were not the articles she gave Kolar. In addition, there was no evidence that Waters ever read the articles. In fact, the lack of her fingerprints on the articles suggests that she did not.

More importantly, however, the articles were highly prejudicial. While most espoused anarchist political theory, a number advocated violence in no uncertain terms. Many of the articles referred to deriving a disturbing joyfulness from acts of destruction, glorifying actions such as rioting and looting. Other articles explicitly advocated the destruction of society, encouraging readers to "com[e] together to destroy all domination," and advocating for a "strong-willed revolt aimed at developing a revolutionary project that can destroy this society and its institutions." Perhaps the most problematic article was entitled "Beyond the ELF." It condemned the "westernized way of life," and emphasized the need for "guerrilla tactics in the form of economic sabotage and beyond." It suggested that anarchists "choos[e] targets that have the most impact," such as "symbolic targets that if destroyed would place a major blow to the false reality [of US society]." It concluded: "Think big. Wall Street, the stock market, Statue of Liberty, US Capitol, . . . Disneyland, . . . government agencies. . . . Realize the difference between pulling up an acre of [genetically engineered] crops and destroying Monsanto. The difference between spray paint and fire."

These passages are highly prejudicial, and even if the record demonstrated an adequate analysis by the district court, we would be inclined to hold that admitting them was an abuse of discretion. Their repugnant and self-absorbed embrace of destruction is likely to have swayed jurors' emotions, leading them to convict Waters not because of the facts before them but because she represented a threat to their own values. We need not reach this question, however, because the district court did not properly exercise its discretion. The district court admitted the articles without ever reviewing them. Our case law establishes that this was error.

The district court had the responsibility to read every page of the articles in order properly to understand their contents before ruling on their admissibility. Its failure to do so means that it could not have properly weighed the impact of the articles under Rule 403. Accordingly, we hold that the district court's admitting the folder of anarchist literature constituted an abuse of discretion.[68]

In this case, not only did the district court make a number of erroneous evidentiary rulings, but these rulings clearly caused harm to the defendant, Briana Waters. In such cases, the government bears the burden of proving harmlessness; that is, it must demonstrate that it is more probable than not that the errors it made do not materially affect the verdict. Judge Tashima wrote that the evidentiary errors were sufficiently prejudicial to require a reversal of Waters's conviction:

> The government has not carried its burden of convincing us that the admission of the anarchist literature was harmless. As we have already described, the anarchist literature was highly prejudicial. It contained a number of inflammatory statements glorifying violence, advocating destruction, and calling for an end to society. It endorsed attacks on symbols of American culture—symbols that many jurors likely held dear—such as the Capitol Building, the Statue of Liberty, and Disneyland. Rather than contributing to any issue in the case, it played to the jury's emotions, encouraging it to convict because it believed Waters held loathsome views that threatened the jurors' way of life.
>
> No doubt recognizing the impact these articles would have on the jury, the prosecutor emphasized this prejudicial interpretation of the articles during his closing argument. Importantly, the prosecutor did not emphasize the government's theory that the articles showed a connection between Waters and Kolar, nor did he argue that the articles demonstrated a shared conspiratorial objective. Rather, the prosecutor argued that the articles represented Waters' values: "[c]learly she thinks these [articles] are important." He highlighted the fact that she had selected the specific articles that were in the folder, inviting the jury to convict not because of the articles' existence, but because of their content: "I didn't choose these articles to put in here. She did. What are these articles about? They are anarchist articles. The only way to really save the earth is to destroy capitalism. The Defendant chooses to select these articles and send them to her co-conspirator and say let's talk about them. . . . "
>
> We find it probable that the district court's evidentiary errors had a material effect on Waters' verdict. Accordingly, her conviction must be reversed.[69]

After her release from prison in 2010, Waters decided to come forward and tell the truth about what took place in 2001 instead of going back to trial after reaching a plea agreement with the government. In June 2011, Waters entered a guilty plea for her involvement in the arson that destroyed the UW Center for Urban Horticulture. A year later, in June 2012, Waters was found guilty of conspiracy, arson, and using a destructive device during a crime of violence. She was sentenced to four years in prison.[70] However, she would return to prison for only eleven months because she had already served about thirty-seven months.

In this plea agreement, prosecutors agreed to the reduced sentence provided that Waters cooperate with the government's ongoing domestic terrorism investigation into the Animal Liberation Front and Earth Liberation Front.[71] In fact, one of the first people Waters agreed to testify against was Justin Solondz, her former boyfriend and co-conspirator. During sentencing, Waters admitted that she had lied under oath when she testified to her innocence during her 2008 trial and that she had participated in a second fire in October 2001 at the federal Bureau of Land Management's Litchfield Wild Horse and Burro Facility in California. On the day of Waters's sentencing, US Attorney Jenny Durkan stated, "Today's sentencing closes a chapter on one of the most dangerous and damaging acts of domestic terrorism in our community. The $6 million Ms. Waters and the rest of the defendants owe in restitution will never compensate the researchers who lost their life's work, their sense of security and the endangered plants they were trying to propagate."[72]

Today Waters is a thirty-six-year-old single mother and former violin teacher who is in prison for her involvement in the 2001 arson at the University of Washington. Her sentencing memorandum says that she looks "back at her life in 2001 with shame" and describes what she did as "motivated by peer pressure and youthful misguided idealism."[73]

The other conspirators involved in this case were also prosecuted and sentenced for the UW arson. Phillabaum pled guilty to participating in the arson in exchange for assisting the prosecution of others involved, including Waters, and was sentenced to three years in prison. Kolar also pled guilty to arson and agreed to assist the government's prosecution and was sentenced to five years in prison for the UW fire and other arsons. Solondz entered a guilty plea to conspiracy and arson in 2011 and was sentenced to seven years in prison.[74] William Rodgers was indicted by a federal grand jury in Seattle, Washington, in connection with this case. From his jail cell in Flagstaff, Arizona, two weeks after his arrest in December 2005, Rodgers wrote, "I chose to fight on the side of the bears, mountain lions, skunks, bats, saguaros, cliff roses and all things wild. But tonight . . . I am returning home, to the Earth, the place of my origins."[75] He placed a plastic bag over his head and suffocated himself. According to medical records, Rodgers was found with his right arm raised, his hand held tight in a fist—the Earth First! symbol of resistance.

Appendix: ELF Communiqué, Part 1

Craig Rosebraugh issued the following communiqué on behalf of ELF on May 27, 2001:

"At 3:15 AM on Monday, May 21, 2001, the research of Toby Bradshaw was reduced to smoke and ashes. We attacked his office at the University of Washington while at the same time another group set fire to a related target in Clatskanie, Oregon, 150 miles away.[76]

"Bradshaw, the driving force in GE tree research, continues to unleash mutant genes into the environment that is certain to cause irreversible harm to forest ecosystems.

"After breaking into Bradshaw's office at the Center for Urban Horticulture, we inspected the building for occupants and set up incendiary devices with a modest amount of accelerant. Although we placed these devices specifically to target his office, a large portion of the building was damaged. This extensive damage was due to the surprisingly slow and poorly coordinated response from the fire department, which was evident by their radio transmissions.

"As long as universities continue to pursue this reckless 'science,' they run the risk of suffering severe losses. Our message remains clear: we are determined to stop genetic engineering.

"From the torching of Catherine Ive's office at Michigan State University to the total incineration of GE seeds at the D & PL warehouse in Visalia, CA, the Earth Liberation Front is growing and spreading. As the culture of domination forces itself onto our very genes, wild fires of outrage will continue to blaze."

DISCUSSION QUESTIONS

1. Was Briana Waters a terrorist? Make an argument using various definitions of terrorism.

2. When you think of the term "terrorism," what label or pictures come to mind? Can Briana Waters be characterized in ways similar to how the typical terrorist is portrayed in the media today?
3. The FBI's investigation in this case took many years. Was the agency successful in this case in bringing the perpetrators to justice? Why or why not?

NOTES

1. Gus Martin, *Understanding Terrorism,* 2nd ed. (Thousand Oaks, CA: Sage, 2006); Clifford Simonsen and Jeremy Spindlove, *Terrorism Today,* 3rd ed. (Upper Saddle River, NJ: Prentice-Hall, 2007); Jonathan White, *Terrorism and Homeland Security,* 5th ed. (Belmont, CA: Thomson-Wadsworth, 2006); Jonathan White, *Terrorism: An Introduction*, 3rd ed. (Belmont, CA: Thomson-Wadsworth, 2002).

2. Texts with multidisciplinary perspectives include: Martin, *Understanding Terrorism*; Ekkart Zimmermann, *Political Violence, Crises, and Revolutions: Theories and Research* (Cambridge, MA: Schenkman Publishing, 1983); and Yonah Alexander, ed., *Terrorism: Interdisciplinary Perspectives* (New York: John Jay Press, 1977).

3. Walter Laqueur, *No End to War* (New York: Continuum, 2003), 22.

4. Audrey Kurth Cronin, *Attacking Terrorism* (Washington, DC: Georgetown University Press, 2005); Alex Schmid, *Political Terrorism* (New Brunswick, NJ: Transaction Books, 1984).

5. Alex Schmid and Albert Jongman, eds., *Political Terrorism* (Amsterdam and New Brunswick, NJ: SWIDOC and Transaction Books, 1988), 5.

6. Ibid., 6.

7. Timothy Shanahan, "Betraying a Certain Corruption of the Mind: How (and Why Not) to Define 'Terrorism,'" *Critical Studies on Terrorism* 3, no. 2 (August 2010): 173–190.

8. Pippa Norris, Montague Kern, and Marion Just, "Framing Terrorism," in *Framing Terrorism: The News Media, the Government, and the Public,* ed. Pippa Norris and Kern Montague (New York: Routledge, 2003).

9. Brian Jenkins, *The Study of Terrorism: Definitional Problems* (Santa Monica, CA: RAND, 1980), 10.

10. Kevin Grubs, "Saving Lives or Spreading Fear: The Terrorist Nature of Eco-extremism," *Animal Law* 16, no. 351 (2010): 6.

11. Christopher Manes, *Green Rage: Radical Environmentalism and the Unmaking of Civilization* (Boston: Little, Brown, 1990), 175.

12. Steve Vanderheiden, "Eco-terrorism or Justified Resistance? Radical Environmentalism and the 'War on Terror,'" *Politics and Society* 33, no. 3 (September 2005): 440–441.

13. Dave Foreman and Bill Haywood, eds., *Ecodefense: A Field Guide to Monkeywrenching,* 3rd ed. (Chico, CA: Abbzug Press, 1993).

14. Edward Abbey, *The Monkey Wrench Gang* (Salt Lake City, UT: Dream Garden Press, 1990).

15. Jonathan Lange, "Refusal to Compromise: The Case of Earth First!" *Western Journal of Speech Communication* 54 (Fall 1990): 473.

16. Donald Liddick, *Eco-terrorism: Radical Environmental and Animal Liberation Movements* (Westport, CT: Praeger Publishers, 2006), 4.

17. James Jarboe, FBI Domestic Terrorism Section Chief, testimony before the US House Resources Committee, Subcommittee on Forests and Forest Health, "Hearing on the Threat of Eco-terrorism," February 12, 2002, http://web.archive.org/web/20080311231725/http://www.fbi.gov/congress/congress02/jarboe021202.htm (accessed July 30, 2012).

18. 28 CFR § 0.85; see also Kevin Grubs, "Saving Lives or Spreading Fear," 5.

19. Grubs, "Saving Lives or Spreading Fear."

20. Legal Information Institute, "18 USC 2331—Definitions," http://www.law.cornell.edu/uscode/text/18/2331 (accessed July 15, 2012).

21. Jarboe, testimony before the House Resources Committee.

22. Jerome Bjelopera, *The Domestic Terrorist Threat: Background Issues for Congress* (Washington, DC: Congressional Research Service, May 15, 2012), 6.

23. TRACReport, "Who Is a Terrorist? Government Failure to Define Terrorism Undermines Enforcement, Puts Civil Liberties at Risk," September 8, 2009, http://trac.syr.edu/tracreports/terrorism/215/ (accessed August 1, 2012).

24. *United States v. Briana Waters,* CR05-5828 FDB (9th Cir., March 5, 2010), 14102.

25. Paul Shukovsky and Angela Galloway, "UW Arson May Mean Escalation by Ecoterrorists; Attack Apparently Coordinated with Blaze at Oregon Tree Farm," *Seattle Post Intelligencer,* May 24, 2001; see also ELF, "Setting Fires with Electrical Timers: An Earth Liberation Front Guide," May 2001, http://media.portland.indymedia.org/media/2003/09/271507.pdf.

26. *United States v. Briana Waters,* CR05-5828 FDB (9th Cir., March 5, 2010).

27. Shukovsky and Galloway, "UW Arson May Mean Escalation by Ecoterrorists."

28. *United States v. Briana Waters,* CR05-5828 FDB (9th Cir., March 5, 2010), 14105.

29. Craig Rosebraugh, *Burning Rage of a Dying Planet: Speaking for the Earth Liberation Front* (New York: Lantern Books, 2004), 201; see also "Radical Group Claims It Set

Arson Fires," KOMO News Network, June 1, 2001, last updated July 24, 2009, http://www.komonews.com/news/archive/4007616.html (accessed August 1, 2012).

30. Shukovsky and Galloway, "UW Arson May Mean Escalation by Ecoterrorists."

31. Rosebraugh, *Burning Rage of a Dying Planet,* 201–202.

32. Robert Service, "Arson Strikes Research Labs and Tree Farm in Pacific Northwest," *Science* 292, no. 5522 (June 1, 2001): 1622.

33. Shukovsky and Galloway, "UW Arson May Mean Escalation by Ecoterrorists."

34. Anti-Defamation League, "Seattle Woman Sentenced for Washington ELF Arson," July 24, 2008, http://www.adl.org/learn/extremism_in_america_updates/movements/ecoterrorism/jennifer_kolar_sentenced.htm (accessed July 30, 2012).

35. Brent Smith and Kelly Damphousse, "Patterns of Precursor Behaviors in the Life Span of a US Environmental Terrorist Group," *American Society of Criminology,* 8, no. 3 (2009): 483–484.

36. Jenny Durkan, "Oakland Woman Sentenced for Role in 2001 Arson at UW Center for Urban Horticulture," press release, US Attorney's Office, Western District of Washington, Seattle, June 22, 2012.

37. Smith and Damphousse, "Patterns of Precursor Behaviors in the Life Span of a US Environmental Terrorist Group," 486.

38. Ibid., 489.

39. Hal Bernton and Christine Clarridge, "Earth Liberation Front Members Plead Guilty in 2001 Firebombing," *Seattle Times,* October 5, 2006.

40. Information on the Warner Creek blockade in Oregon and other actions by Earth First! members can be found at: Kera Abraham, "Flames of Dissent: Eco-Anarchy Rising: Part 11.09.06," *Eugene Weekly,* November 9, 2006, http://www.eugeneweekly.com/2006/11/09/news1.html (accessed August 1, 2012). For information on ELF involvement at the WTO protests in Seattle see the DVD, *If a Tree Falls: A Story of the Earth Liberation Front,* Oscilliscope Laboratories, 2011.

41. Hal Bernton, "Prosecutors Portray Close-Knit Arson Team," *Seattle Times,* January 21, 2006.

42. Kera Abraham, "Flames of Dissent: The Local Spark That Ignited an Eco-Sabotage Boom—and Bust," *Eugene Weekly,* November–December 2006, http://www.brontaylor.com/courses/pdf/EugeneWeekly(Nov-Dec06).pdf (accessed August 2, 2012).

43. *United States of America v. Briana Waters,* CR 05-5828 RBL, Defendant's Sentencing Memorandum and Motion for Downward Departure, June 18, 2012, 3.

44. Ibid., 4.

45. Ibid.; see also *United States of America v. Justin Solondz,* CR05-5828 RBL, Plea Agreement, December 20, 2011, 5.

46. Ibid.

47. Smith and Damphousse, "Patterns of Precursor Behaviors in the Life Span of a US Environmental Terrorist Group," 491.

48. *United States v. Briana Waters,* CR05-5828 FDB (9th Cir., March 5, 2010), 14107.

49. Nina Shapiro, "Justin Solondz Torches a Movement," *Seattle Weekly,* June 20, 2012, 6.

50. *United States v. Briana Waters,* CR05-5828 FDB (9th Cir., March 5, 2010), 14107.

51. Ibid., 14108.

52. Ibid., 14107.

53. *United States of America v. Justin Solondz,* CR05-5828 RBL, Plea Agreement, December 20, 2011, 6.

54. Federal Bureau of Investigation, "Operation Backfire: Help Find Four Eco-terrorists," November 19, 2008, http://www.fbi.gov/news/stories/2008/november/backfire_11908 (accessed August 12, 2012), 1.

55. Pierre Thomas, "FBI Shifting Main Focus to Terrorism," *ABC News,* May 28, 2002, http://abcnews.go.com/WNT/story?id=130320&page=1#.UDH2p78jd4s (accessed August 1, 2012).

56. US Department of Justice, "Eleven Defendants Indicted on Domestic Terrorism Charges," press release, January 21, 2006.

57. Hal Bernton, "An Activist Turned Informant," *Seattle Times,* May 7, 2006.

58. Tracy Tullis, "Is Briana Waters a Terrorist?" *Salon,* March 27, 2008, 3.

59. *United States v. Briana Waters,* Cause No. CR 05-5828 RBL, Defendant's Sentencing Memorandum and Motion for Downward Departure, June 18, 2012, 5.

60. Ibid., 6.

61. *United States v. Briana Waters,* CR05-5828 FDB (9th Cir., March 5, 2010), 14105–14108.

62. Solondz was discovered in China in November 2009. He is currently serving a three-year term of imprisonment and will be extradited to the United States when that sentence is completed.

63. *United States v. Briana Waters,* CR05-5828 FDB (9th Cir., March 5, 2010), 14108.

64. Ibid.

65. Nancy Bartley and Mike Carter, "UW Arsonist, Briana Waters, Sentenced to 6 Years," *Seattle Times,* June 20, 2008, L1.

66. Durkan, "Oakland Woman Sentenced for Role in 2001 Arson at UW Center for Urban Horticulture."

67. *United States v. Briana Waters,* CR05-5828 FDB (9th Cir., March 5, 2010), 14113–14114.

68. Ibid., 14115–14117.

69. Ibid., 14121–14122.

70. Ibid.

71. Christine Clarridge, "Last Ecoterrorist Sentenced for UW Horticulture Arson," *Seattle Times,* June 22, 2012.

72. Durkan, "Oakland Woman Sentenced for Role in 2001 Arson at UW Center for Urban Horticulture."

73. Nina Shapiro, "Briana Waters Says She Lied About Arson for Her Child; Feds Call Her Vicious," *Seattle Weekly,* June 22, 2012.

74. Ibid.

75. Tullis, "Is Briana Waters a Terrorist?"

76. Reprinted in Rosebraugh, *Burning Rage of a Dying Planet,* 201–202.

CHAPTER 3

Environmental Security

Environmental security is a relatively new concern in the homeland security community. As recently as five years ago, it might have been difficult to find mention of it in any of the nation's security strategic plans, much less in homeland security plans. Now, however, environmental security can be found in significant ways in many of today's strategic plans. For example, environmental security is discussed in the 2010 *Quadrennial Defense Review (QDR)*, the US military's overarching strategic planning document, where it is mentioned prominently in the context of the security implications of global climate change. Similarly, environmental security is discussed in the 2010 *Quadrennial Homeland Security Review (QHSR)* and the 2010 *Quadrennial Diplomacy and Development Review (QDDR)*, which are, respectively, the strategic planning documents for the US Department of Homeland Security and the US State Department. It takes only a moment's thought to realize that the concerns expressed by the greater homeland security community over global environmental change make sense. "Global environmental change" is a term that includes global warming, but also includes the larger impacts on weather and climate from anthropomorphic (human-caused) activities.

Students of homeland security can define environmental security in the following way: as an interdisciplinary study of the effects of extreme environmental or climatic events that can act locally or transnationally to destabilize countries or regions of the world, resulting in geopolitical instability, resource conflicts, vulnerabilities in critical infrastructure, or some combination of these impacts.

Environmental security theory holds that natural phenomena can significantly impact man-made activities (such as food and energy production) and population dynamics in such a way that the combination of these factors exacerbates an already tenuous geopolitical situation, in turn creating security challenges. Let us look briefly at an example of how this interaction works. The "greenhouse effect" is a naturally occurring warming of Earth's surface due to the radiation of specific gases in the lower atmosphere. For the most part, today's lifestyles, growth, and economic development in many parts of the world are tied to the use of fossil fuels. However, the use of fossil fuels releases greenhouse gases, which exacerbate the greenhouse effect, which subsequently perturbs the present climate, resulting in changes to occurrence frequencies and locations of extreme weather events and changes in regional climates. The weather and climatic changes engender security concerns by disrupting the social, political, or economic stability of nations. In turn, such disruptions can lead to enhanced opportunities for transnational asymmetric terrorism, which challenges the stability of fragile nation-states, or they might lead to major economic threats to otherwise stable and well-established nations owing to the degradation or destruction of critical infrastructure. In the developing world, examples would include the activities of Al-Shabaab in Somalia or the Islamic Courts Union in Ethiopia. These nations are already vulnerable economically, socially, and politically, and their populations are particularly vulnerable to environmental catastrophes. In the developed world, environmental security is manifest through the enormous economic and infrastructure consequences of the Japanese earthquake in 2011 and of Hurricane Katrina in 2005 and Hurricane Sandy in 2012 in the United States.

The two cases in this chapter represent real-life applications of both sides of the environmental security definition: how climate change is motivating security concerns in an undeveloped region of the world, and how extreme events cause security challenges in a developed nation. In the first case, we see how persistent warming in the Arctic as a result of global climate change is motivating several security challenges for the United States, ranging from access to resources like fish and oil to questions about territorial ownership, which came to light when the Russian Federation planted its flag at the bottom of the Arctic Ocean. Each case represents a different set of critical consequences due to extreme weather events and climatic changes, and both illustrate vividly why US national security strategy needs to better incorporate the principles of environmental security in order to mitigate those consequences.

In the second case, we see how environmental security concepts can be applied to a developed nation—namely, the United States. Hurricane Katrina provides an example of how one extreme weather event damaged or destroyed so much critical infrastructure that an entire region became economically unstable and the result was a mass migration on a scale that had not been seen since the Dust Bowl of the 1930s.

Arctic Security

Oil, Polar Bears, Melting Ice Caps, and US National Security

JAMES D. RAMSAY AND JOHN LANICCI

Anthropogenic climate change can reasonably be expected to increase the frequency and intensity of a variety of potentially disruptive environmental events—slowly at first, but then more quickly. Some of this change is already discernible. Many of these events will stress communities, societies, governments, and the globally integrated systems that support human well-being. Science is unlikely ever to be able to predict the timing, magnitude, and precise location of these events a decade in advance, but much is already known that can inform security analysis, including details about the character of events that are becoming more likely and about the general trajectory of increasing risk.

—National Academy of Sciences (2012)[1]

For the average human being, the Arctic is an inaccessible region inhabited mainly by walruses, polar bears, Santa Claus, Eskimos, and Survivorman.[2] And this has been true for all of recorded history (with the possible exception of Survivorman). To most people, few places on Earth seem as mysterious or as rugged or as uninhabitable. Over the last century, however, climate trends have shifted from their historical norms all over the world. Nowhere is this more evident than in the polar regions of our planet. While it may be difficult for the average person or region to appreciate or to see changes in average temperature of 5 degrees Celsius (9 degrees Fahrenheit), to the polar regions such a change has been traumatic indeed. A major consequence of this climatic shift to the Arctic is an immense change in its geopolitical importance to US national security.

Attributing such climate shifts to human activities (referred to as "anthropomorphic changes") has clearly been one of the most politicized and controversial issues of our age. This is easily understood when we consider the deeper implications of how our society and our economy function. Fossil fuels account for about 86 percent of the current sources of energy that power the US economy.[3] Hence, our political economy is substantially dependent on the use of fossil fuels. Other than the need for a constant supply, this fact would not be important were it not for the inescapable fact that fossil fuel combustion produces carbon dioxide (CO_2), with troublesome consequences. Consider that the US Energy Information Administration (EIA) estimates that about 19.64 pounds of CO_2 are released for each non-ethanol gallon of gas burned, and that for diesel the figure is actually closer to 22.38 pounds of CO_2 released per gallon of gas burned.[4] Ultimately, the main environmental challenge presented by the continuous production of CO_2 is that it functions as a greenhouse gas: over time, since CO_2 is the Earth's key temperature regulator, it will drive changes in temperature patterns, weather patterns, food production, and water access across the planet as it accumulates in the lower atmosphere. Changing our emission patterns has been the subject of much research and debate, but as Professor Joseph Kalt reminds us, although we have become much more energy-efficient in our building and transportation systems, we continue to use more and more energy.[5] The only way to avert such globally important consequences seems to be changing the very fabric of society. But changing (or even challenging) systems, structures, and lifestyles that make this problem worse is proving to be neither easy, convenient, nor politically popular.

The purpose of this case study is to understand more about the Arctic, the impact of changes in its ecology and climate on US national security, and the security challenges that such ecological changes pose for the United States and the world. To better understand how and why the Arctic has become such a

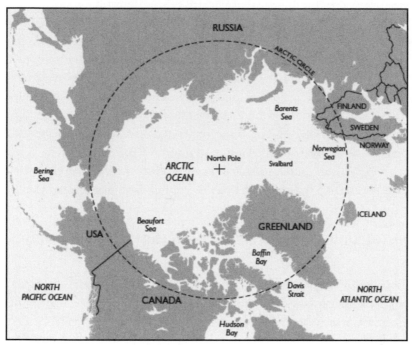

FIGURE 3.1.1: The Arctic Region

Source: Annika Rosamund, "Perspectives on Security in the Arctic Region," (Copenhagen: Danish Institute for International Studies, 2011), http://www.diis.dk/graphics/Publications/Reports2011/RP2011-09-Arctic-security_web.pdf.

significant security issue, we begin with a brief description of arctic ecology and the environmental changes believed to be motivated and fueled by anthropomorphic events and activities. This is followed by a discussion of the security challenges that arise because of these environmental changes, including a brief discussion of the implications of those challenges if solutions are not found and implemented immediately.

What Is the Arctic?

Named for the bear, *arktos* in Greek, the Arctic is a large region that represents an interestingly variable expanse of Earth's surface. Figure 3.1.1 shows that the Arctic Circle is set at 66°32'N latitude and is the common delimiter of the region, which borders eight nations. In total, the Arctic occupies roughly 13,400,000 km².[6] This is equivalent to one-sixth of the Earth's landmass or, alternatively, a region so large that it spans twenty-four time zones.[7] The Arctic is characterized by persistent stratus cloud cover, low temperatures, a polar maritime climate along its coastal perimeter, and a more continental climate in the interior. Whereas the coastal perimeter tends to average greater precipitation and warmer temperatures, the interior on average displays a harsher reality. Coastal Arctic regions tend toward weather patterns similar to those of Anchorage, Alaska. Average high temperatures range from 5 degrees Celsius (23 degrees Fahrenheit) in the winter to 10 degrees Celsius (50 degrees Fahrenheit) in the summer, and precipitation ranges up to approximately 500 millimeters (20 inches) in the coastal areas and usually much less in the interior.[8]

The next section begins to describe the scope of the climate change challenge.

Anthropomorphic Climate Change and Economics

National security strategists and environmental security scholars are concerned about both human-based and natural processes and phenomena that can pose threats to US security and prosperity. As highlighted in several US security strategic planning documents, climate change is increasingly understood to be such a threat.[9] Understanding climate change drivers requires one to realize that temperature and precipitation are the primary factors that determine climate.[10] To better understand what security strategists mean when they discuss human (or societal) factors that affect the climate, we need to distinguish between the commonly understood term "weather" and what scientists refer to as "climate." The National Snow and Ice Data Center, for instance, characterizes the difference between "weather" and "climate" very pragmatically:

> Weather is the day-to-day state of the atmosphere, and its short-term (minutes to weeks) variation. Popularly, weather is thought of as the combination of temperature, humidity, precipitation, cloudiness, visibility, and wind. We talk about the weather in terms of "What will it be like today?," "How hot is it right now?," and "When will that storm hit our section of the country?"
>
> In contrast, climate is defined as statistical weather information that describes the variation of weather at a given place for a specified interval. In popular usage, it represents the synthesis of weather; more formally it is the weather of a locality averaged over some period (usually 30 years) plus statistics of weather extremes.

We talk about climate change in terms of years, decades or even centuries. Scientists study climate to look for trends or cycles of variability (such as the changes in wind patterns, ocean surface temperatures, and precipitation over the equatorial Pacific that result in El Niño and La Niña), and also to place cycles or other phenomena into the bigger picture of possible longer term or more permanent climate changes.[11]

The Intergovernmental Panel on Climate Change (IPCC) defines climate change as "a change in the mean or variability of any of the properties of climate that persists for an extended period, typically decades or longer."[12] The quote above suggests that it is not easy to know when, or the degree to which, the climate has "changed." In addition to natural cycles and long time frames, natural phenomena often complicate the picture as well. For example, the greenhouse effect is a natural phenomenon that heats the Earth's surface owing to the emission of infrared radiation by certain types of gases (water, carbon dioxide, and so on) in the lower atmosphere. Though the greenhouse effect is a natural phenomenon, scientists have known for some time that human activities that produce carbon dioxide, such as combusting fossil fuels, exacerbate it.[13] Indeed, it may be hard to believe that it was in 1988 that a NASA scientist, James Hansen, testified to Congress that the science of the greenhouse effect was clear, solid, and believable.[14] Ultimately, the Earth's climate is the result of a balancing act between competing and reinforcing factors. That is, while it is well known that carbon dioxide and other greenhouse gases tend to warm the Earth's surface, atmospheric aerosols such as sea salt, dust, and sulfates from pollution are known to cool the Earth.[15] The balancing act occurs when these two sets of components vary in their relative concentrations. The anthropogenic contribution to CO_2 and the resulting changes in globally averaged surface temperature are highlighted in Figures 3.1.2 and 3.1.3, which show that CO_2 concentrations are becoming primarily the result of anthropomorphic sources and that there is a significant and persistent correlation between the level of CO_2 in the atmosphere and mean surface temperature such that, as CO_2 concentrations rise, so does mean surface temperature. This correlation becomes problematic when we consider that economic development is largely tied to the use of fossil fuels. As nations develop economically, they tend to emulate Western-style industry and lifestyles—that is, the connection between development and fossil fuel use becomes more pronounced. We should recall that the US economy can be considered an exemplar for more developed nations. That is, just as upwards of 86 percent of the US economy is directly dependent on oil,[16] and most of the greenhouse gas generation in the United States is from lifestyles (transportation, electricity and heat),[17] such is the case for *all* more developed nations. A difference lies in the US population. The United States is by far the largest consumer of oil, consuming over 52 percent of the world's oil even though the country constitutes roughly only 5 percent of Earth's total population.[18] Given that the majority of people live in less developed nations, the problem of anthropomorphic climate change is vexing: as the lifestyles and economies of less developed nations mature, they will begin to more deeply emulate those of the more developed nations and naturally use more fossil fuels. As a consequence, the persistent reliance on fossil fuels to power the national economic engines of the world makes it inevitable that the Earth's climate will continue to warm.

The essential question for this case is to ask how anthropomorphic climate change has begun to change the Arctic region and how those changes may be creating security challenges for the United States. The next section begins a discussion on the effect of climate change processes on the Arctic region.

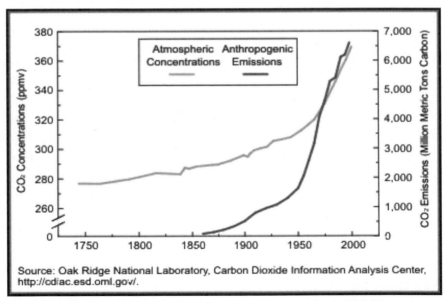

Source: Oak Ridge National Laboratory, Carbon Dioxide Information Analysis Center, http://cdiac.esd.oml.gov/.

FIGURE 3.1.2: Greenhouse Gas Emissions vs. Concentrations (PPMV= parts per million by volume).

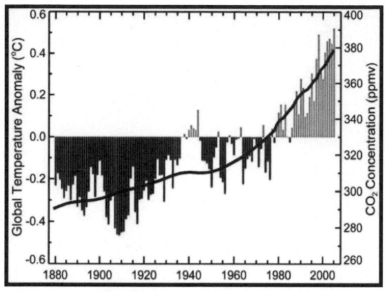

FIGURE 3.1.3: Global Average of Surface Air Temperature and Carbon Dioxide Emissions Since 1880 (PPMV= parts per million by volume)

Source: Karl Thomas, NOAA, "A Written Statement to the US House of Representatives Committee on Government Reform," July 20, 2006, http://www.legislative .noaa.gov/Testimony/Karl072006.pdf.

The Impact of Climate Change on the Arctic

To better understand the threat posed to US national security by the recent changes in the Arctic, it is important to understand how the Arctic has changed over the last twenty years. By exacerbating the greenhouse effect, anthropomorphic climate change has gradually warmed the air and water in the Arctic. As a result, several significant physical changes have occurred. These can be categorized as changes to Arctic sea ice, changes to wildlife and ecosystems, and changes to the perceived economic and strategic value of the Arctic by not only the eight Arctic nations but also by a host of other nations around the world.

Changes to Arctic Sea Ice

Since 1955, there has been a tremendous loss of sea ice (aka ice pack, or ice volume) in the Arctic. Figure 3.1.4 illustrates the significant diminishment of Arctic sea ice over the last sixty years, and specifically over the last twenty years.

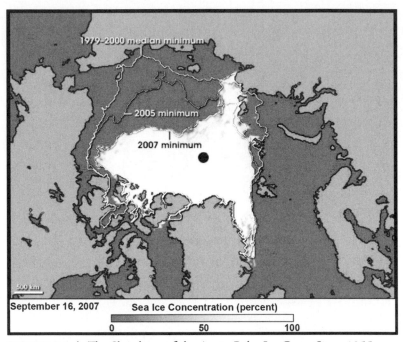

FIGURE 3.1.4: The Shrinkage of the Arctic Polar Ice Cover Since 1955
Source: NASA's Earth Observatory, http://earthobservatory.nasa.gov/Newsroom/New Images/images.php3?img_id=17800.

Specifically, the Committee on Future Arctic Sea Ice Research claims that "the last six summers (2007–2012) have experienced the six lowest sea ice extent minima over three decades of satellite record, and the past decade (2003–2012) has exhibited 9 of the 10 lowest minima. This trend is predicted to continue, and many climate models predict a total loss of Arctic sea ice before the year 2100."[19]

Changes to Arctic Wildlife

Since a comprehensive discussion of the ecological perturbations in the Arctic region is beyond the scope of this case study, the following abbreviated discussion is limited to changes observed in selected species of wildlife. Generally, climate change has produced shorter winter seasons, less ice cover, and warmer temperatures in the Arctic. As a consequence of these changes in traditional climate patterns, many species of animals have experienced stresses. For example, diminishment of sea ice has caused polar bears to deal with restricted migration patterns and restricted food supplies. In turn, reproductive rates are declining, and the polar bear population is showing signs of stress. In addition to polar bears, ice seals (including bearded, ringed, ribbon, and harp seals), which tend to use the sea ice for raising their young, are also demonstrating signs of stress. With rapid and dramatic changes to sea ice cover, seal species are now considered at risk of becoming endangered. For both polar bears and ice seals, changes in the physical parameters of their climate and loss and fragmentation of habitat have combined to force more frequent exposures with human environments. And at the current rate of disruption to the Arctic, the US Geological Survey has estimated that two-thirds of the polar bear population could vanish by 2050.[20] Further, David Johnston and his colleagues have estimated that along the Gulf of St. Lawrence, harp seals are much less able to breed successfully, owing to thinning (or no) sea ice in their traditional habitats, and that in 2007 up to 75 percent of ice seal pups died because of inadequate habitat.[21]

Walruses have migrated with ice flows, traveling southward each year as the sea ice expands in winter. Over the last decade, large sections of the Chukchi Sea Shelf were devoid of ice from as little as one week to as much as two and a half months. Previously, this region had perpetual ice cover during the winter. As a result, walruses were forced to either migrate into deeper water, where there is comparatively less food, or move to land locations, where they have never been observed before. For example, in 2001 Arctic walruses were added to the candidate list for the Endangered Species Act.[22] This level of habitation relocation tends to rapidly exhaust available food and foster confrontations with humans; ultimately, it could cause a reduction in population. Subsequently, according to Greenpeace, "in 2007, there was no ice for about 80 days and several thousand walruses moved to shores in northwest Alaska that had never been used by walruses before."[23] There are similar accounts of habitat fragmentation, breeding pattern disruptions, and food supply shortages forcing overpopulation of specific areas for both the Arctic fox and the bowhead whale.[24]

Changes in the Perceived Economic Value of the Arctic

When the Arctic was perpetually frozen and there was no standing water for large portions of the year, most of the Arctic nations did not expend much effort in attempting to exploit—or occupy—the Arctic. Rather, and much like the Antarctic (as discussed later), the Arctic was a region reserved for exploration, research, and discovery. Today the Arctic represents vastly different sorts of opportunities. For some, the Arctic is a largely untapped environmental resource. For others, it represents access to billions of gallons of oil and a potential economic boom. In fact, making a point not overlooked by those who seek such access—and one particularly vexing given the recent extent of Arctic thawing—Philip Budzik of the US Energy Information Administration said, "According to the USGS mean estimate, the Arctic holds about 22 percent of the world's undiscovered conventional oil and natural gas resource base, about 30 percent of the world's undiscovered natural gas resources, about 13 percent of the world's undiscovered oil resources, and about 20 percent of the world NGL resources."[25] Put differently, according to the US EIA website, "The region north of the Arctic Circle has an estimated 90 billion barrels of undiscovered, technically recoverable oil, 1,670 trillion cubic feet of technically recoverable natural gas, and 44 billion barrels of technically recoverable natural gas liquids in 25 geologically defined areas thought to have potential for petroleum."[26] Still, for other nations, the Arctic is becoming either a reliably navigable shipping lane or a geopolitically strategic military location, or both.[27] With oil, natural gas, and other resources in mind, Russian president Vladimir Putin recently said, "Not one industrial project in the Russian Arctic will be undertaken without consideration for the strictest ecological demands. This is a key position of the Russian Federation." Putin was also quick to claim the environmental resources on the floor of the Arctic as distinctly Russia's owing to the geological characteristics of the Lomonosov Ridge.[28] In addition to these "new" opportunities to extract valuable resources like oil, natural gas, and fish and the advantages of the geological location and shipping rights of way, the fact that eight nations each lay claim to some portion of the Arctic region makes the development of appropriate governance structures a particularly difficult challenge for international diplomacy.

As we have seen thus far, global climate change is altering the traditional ecology of the Arctic. While there are political difficulties that complicate a comprehensive international governance system, the fact remains that resources and capabilities that have heretofore been inaccessible to many of the developed economies of the world are now suddenly available. Warmer average temperatures and thinning ice have combined to allow shipping and maritime exploration at unprecedented rates. Through the use of the Northeast Passage and travel along the Russian coast, Luke Coffey estimates that this shortened route would reduce a trip from Hamburg to Shanghai by almost 6,740 kilometers (4,000 miles), reduce delivery times by one week, and reduce fuel costs by approximately $650,000 per trip.[29] In a related way, commercial fishing stands to be affected as well, given the suspected disruptions and alterations to traditional migration patterns of native fish as the oceans warm.

As has been discussed thus far, the Arctic represents a highly unregulated and contentious region to many of the world's nations. Issues for diplomatic negotiations include not only access to vital economic resources but the location of military installations and details of maritime navigation. Clearly, there is a lot to be gained by extraction and ownership of Arctic resources and control of the Arctic Ocean. To better understand the security implications of these newly navigable seaways and the now-accessible natural resources in the Arctic, the next section briefly discusses how access to and use of the Antarctic was determined and then describes some of the politics associated with developing similar international accords in the Arctic.

Politics, International Accords, and the Arctic Region

Though it is on the opposite end of the planet, a brief history of international diplomacy and treaties that govern use of the Antarctic provides insights into the unique challenges posed by the recently enhanced access to the Arctic. To start, it is important to note that the Antarctic is quite different than the Arctic. Among those differences is the fact that the Antarctic is a continent as opposed to a geographic region. The Antarctic is also not surrounded by a set of nations that claim a perimeter with it, as is the case with the Arctic. And the Antarctic has no Cold War history. In contrast, although there are known reserves of oil and coal and several significant stores of minerals in the Antarctic, neither extraction nor mining of them has occurred because both are totally banned by the Antarctic Treaty (discussed later).[30]

While the Cold War raged, twelve nations ratified the original Antarctic Peace Treaty (APT) of 1961. Designed to foster cooperation, peace, and research, and perhaps consistent with the "Cold War" politics to the north, both the United States and the Soviet Union were original signatories. (Note that China did not sign the treaty until 1985.) The APT applies to the landmass south of 60°S latitude and contains fourteen main articles, espoused generically by the following three main concepts:

1. To demilitarize Antarctica, to establish it as a zone free of nuclear tests and the disposal of radioactive waste, and to ensure that it is used for peaceful purposes only;

2. To promote international scientific cooperation in Antarctica;

3. To set aside disputes over territorial sovereignty.[31]

Today, forty-six nations representing about 80 percent of the Earth's population have signed on to the Antarctic Peace Treaty, making it a notably comprehensive international peace effort. Since the APT originated, there have been many subsequent treaties and cooperative efforts based mainly in conservation and research. For example, each year the signatories meet at the Antarctic Treaty Consultative Meeting to negotiate use of the Antarctic. This process has resulted in over three hundred recommendations that are still in use today.[32]

It is odd, then, that so much time elapsed between the development and successful dissemination of the APT and the first nascent efforts to similarly structure and manage the Arctic. Indeed, although the United States had enacted the Arctic Research Policy Act (ARPA) in 1984 to govern research activities in the Arctic region, ARPA was not an international accord.[33] It was not until 1991 that negotiations began in earnest to develop an analogous peace structure for the Arctic region. Referred to by the Canadian government as the "Arctic Council," the initial effort involved all eight "Arctic nations" (Canada, Denmark [Greenland], Finland, Sweden, Norway, Iceland, the United States, and the Soviet Union).[34] The Arctic Council is an international organization consisting of the eight Arctic states, six "participating parties" (indigenous peoples' organizations) that have permanent representation on the Council, and a handful of self-defined "observers." The Arctic Council and its members play an important role by focusing international attention on environmental and climate-related issues; sadly, however, the Council has no law enforcement mechanism or capability, and (technically) neither security nor political issues are within its mission set.

A major international agreement governing the Arctic and the surrounding seas, the United Nations Convention on the Law of the Sea (UNCLOS), resulted in the third United Nations Conference on the Law of the Sea (UNCLOS III). The result of conferences and negotiations that took place from 1973 through 1982, UNCLOS defines the rights and responsibilities of signatory nations in their use of the world's oceans and establishes guidelines that regulate the activities of businesses, protections for the environment, and the management of marine natural resources. As of October 2012, 163 nations have signed UNCLOS, with the notable exception of the United States.[35] Though the United States was originally a significant player in the development of the Arctic Council and the early draft of the UNCLOS, it remains the only developed nation to not sign the UNCLOS treaty.[36] However, policy, security, and Arctic scholars—notably those at the Carnegie Endowment for International Peace—have called on the United States to sign the UNCLOS treaty.[37]

However, it is not simply that the United States is not interested in Arctic security or international cooperation. The real story is much more complex and probably highly political. For example, in July 2012, and along party lines, thirty-four Republican US senators indicated their intention to vote against ratification of the UNCLOS treaty if it came to a vote. Since ratification requires at least two-thirds of the one-hundred-member Senate (at least sixty-seven senators), the issue was dead before it was introduced. Across the aisle, and in stark contrast to the Republican position, Secretary of Defense Leon Panetta (a Democrat appointed by President Barack Obama) stated at a conference earlier this year, in urging support for ratification, "Not since we acquired the lands of the American West and Alaska have we had such a great opportunity to expand US sovereignty."[38] Interestingly, as stated in a recent assessment by the Center for Naval Operations regarding security issues in the Arctic, essentially the entire US military is in favor of ratifying the UNCLOS, from the perspective of US national security.[39]

More recently, two significant national security–oriented legislative actions have been undertaken that further define the US security concerns about the Arctic. In January 2009, President George W. Bush signed National Security Presidential Directive 66 (NSPD 66)—also known as Homeland Security Presidential Directive 25 (HSPD 25)—which specifically addressed Arctic security policy for the United States. In section III, on policy, HSPD 25 states:

It is the policy of the United States to:
• Meet national security and homeland security needs relevant to the Arctic region;
• Protect the Arctic environment and conserve its biological resources;
• Ensure that natural resource management and economic development in the region are environmentally sustainable;

• Strengthen institutions for cooperation among the eight Arctic nations (the United States, Canada, Denmark, Finland, Iceland, Norway, the Russian Federation, and Sweden);

• Involve the Arctic's indigenous communities in decisions that affect them; and

• Enhance scientific monitoring and research into local, regional, and global environmental issues.[40]

Following suit in support of HSPD 25, the Obama administration stated in the 2010 *National Security Strategy:* "The United States is an Arctic Nation with broad and fundamental interests in the Arctic region, where we seek to meet our national security needs, protect the environment, responsibly manage resources, account for indigenous communities, support scientific research, and strengthen international cooperation on a wide range of issues."[41]

Clearly, despite the ostensible US position on the UNCLOS treaty, one can see that although the United States intends to cooperate on a global basis in this vital region, strengthen existing governance bodies, and preserve and protect the Arctic's natural resources, it is not ready to ratify UNCLOS. Inasmuch as all nations work to protect their strategic security interests, for some in the United States there seem to be several unresolved, complex issues. For example, given an expected increase in maritime activity and possible fossil fuel extraction, storage, and distribution, there remains the risk of oil pollution preparedness and spill remediation.[42] Further, HSPD 25 spells out US interests in the Arctic as follows:

National Security and Homeland Security Interests in the Arctic

1. The United States has broad and fundamental national security interests in the Arctic region and is prepared to operate either independently or in conjunction with other states to safeguard these interests. These interests include such matters as missile defense and early warning; deployment of sea and air systems for strategic sealift, strategic deterrence, maritime presence, and maritime security operations; and ensuring freedom of navigation and over flight.

2. The United States also has fundamental homeland security interests in preventing terrorist attacks and mitigating those criminal or hostile acts that could increase the United States' vulnerability to terrorism in the Arctic region.

3. The Arctic region is primarily a maritime domain; as such, existing policies and authorities relating to maritime areas continue to apply, including those relating to law enforcement.[43]

Some maintain that it is essential that the United States ratify UNCLOS. For example, in addition to the Center for Naval Operations' assessment cited earlier, among the fourteen key findings at the 2008 Arctic Climate Change and Security Conference were the following:

1. As a major Arctic power, the US has responsibility for stewardship and protection of vital environmental, security, economic, and political interests in the Arctic region.
2. The failure of the US to ratify UNCLOS weakens the ability of all institutions in the international system, as well as the American government, to advance US interests in developing stronger regional governance.
3. Global warming is accelerating the pace at which climate change is affecting the Arctic region as well as climatic and environmental conditions in the US.[44]

Complicating the political nature of the Arctic region is the fact that nations disagree on what the Arctic region represents geopolitically. How does such a region best fit into the complex dynamic of international diplomacy and the international governance structures that need to be developed? For example, Canada, Russia, Norway, and Denmark are all extending their territorial claims in the Arctic region.[45] As a result of expanding their exclusive economic zones, they are able to extend their reach into the Arctic region for the purposes of extracting resources. As a nonparty to UNCLOS, the United States cannot participate in the UNCLOS Commission on the Limits of the Continental Shelf and submit a claim against nations that it feels are illegitimately extracting resources (fish, fossil fuel, and so on).

Also, regarding the question of how best to manage the immigration of people into the Arctic as well as those peoples native to the area, the Heritage Foundation published an issue brief in August 2012 recommending five principles to guide US Arctic policy. The first principle states that "National Sovereignty (of the indigenous population) is the highest priority." This principle really is intended to suggest that only indigenous peoples and "purely intergovernmental organizations such as the North Atlantic Treaty Organization (NATO) or the Arctic Council" should have a role in Arctic matters—

an observation that is clearly debatable, as evidenced by Canada's objection to NATO's involvement in managing Arctic affairs. Canada, for example, is seeking the formation of a stable, rule-based organization (possibly a more robust version of the Arctic Council) whose function it would be to protect the environment, improve governance of the region, and promote economic and social development.[46] Further complicating diplomatic efforts to manage the Arctic's resources and to understand the strategic importance of the region, there is wide disagreement between members of the Arctic nations. For example, Norway favors a strong NATO presence and proactive NATO posture in defense of the Arctic, and itself has positioned at least one full-time military installation north of the Arctic Circle. Canada, however, appears not to want any NATO involvement in the Arctic. This concern stems from the widely held belief in Canada that were NATO to play a more prominent role in Arctic security, NATO member nations that are not Arctic nations would stand to gain some measure of strategic advantage or access to resources by virtue of their position within NATO.[47]

The ability to place military assets in key locations for much of the year has intensified the geopolitical and geostrategic meaning of the Arctic region. Indeed, even nations that do not border the Arctic region are developing a keen interest in establishing a presence there. For example, China has petitioned the Arctic Council for "permanent observer" status in the Arctic. Although NATO's recent strategic update included renewed interest in cyber-security and energy policy, Arctic security was not included.[48] This seems to be an odd exclusion given that the United States, Norway, and Russia have planned joint military exercises and search-and-rescue training in the Arctic, while at the same time there is mounting evidence that Russia is militarizing its region of the Arctic. Russian air and sea patrol activity has steadily increased, and the North Fleet is now the largest in the Russian Navy. Moreover, Russia recently announced that not only would it reopen airbases on selected island chains above the Arctic—bases that it had closed after the end of the Cold War—but it will also stand up two new Arctic brigades to be specifically deployed as rapid response forces in the region.[49]

While such international political discussions continue, recent years have witnessed calls to structure both Arctic occupation and resource management along the lines of how the Antarctic region has been developed. For example, in 2008 the Arctic Climate Change and Security Policy Conference (ACCSP) was held at Dartmouth College and was jointly sponsored by the Carnegie Endowment for International Peace, Dartmouth College, and the University of the Arctic Institute for Applied Circumpolar Policy.[50]

Among the conference's many key findings, it is noteworthy that shortly following the conference the Presidential Directive on Arctic Regional Policy was released (in January 2009) and that much of the PD was in line and consistent with the findings of the conference. Furthermore, the US National Research Council in the National Academies developed a standing Committee on Climate, Energy, and National Security (CENS).[51] CENS was designed to foster collaboration across nations and among scientists focused on addressing and answering questions related to climate and environmental change, energy, natural disasters, and security. CENS specifically aims to bring scientific expertise to bear on questions of importance to the intelligence community related to climate and environmental change. Ultimately, CENS activities led to a request in 2010 for a study that would "identify ways to increase the ability of the intelligence community to take climate change into account in assessing political and social stresses with implications for US national security."[52] Still, what remains is some challenging interplay between policy and science. Indeed, the ACCSP reminds us that although the scientific community has solid consensus that climate change is real, that global warming due to anthropomorphic factors is increasing the rate of climate change, and that evidence of its negative impact on the Arctic region (as well as the global environment) is incontrovertible, policymakers could still benefit from more data on which to base policy decisions and structures in response to these global climatic changes.

The next section more thoroughly describes climate-change-based concerns in the Arctic, and the section following will present tools that policymakers can use to better execute governance and diplomatic efforts to manage the Arctic securely and sustainably. In addition, the next section presents recent and salient security concerns that the United States is advised to consider given the changing nature of the Arctic region.

Anticipated Climate Change–Based Security Concerns

While climate change alone does not cause conflict, it may act as an accelerant of instability or conflict, placing a burden to respond on civilian institutions and militaries around the world. In addition, extreme weather events may lead to increased demands for defense support to civil authorities for humanitarian assistance or disaster response both within the United States and overseas.[53]

Several recent publications identify and discuss a variety of emergent security concerns emanating from global warming's impact on the Arctic.[54] Though these and other sources discuss in detail a wide spectrum of security concerns, it is helpful to group these concerns into three categories: homeland security operations and diplomatic concerns, economic and infrastructure concerns, and research-based concerns. Students should keep in mind that there is significant overlap between types of security concerns and that the suggested categorizations are not mutually exclusive.

Homeland Security and Diplomatic Security Concerns

Homeland security and diplomatic security concerns involve aspects of Arctic security that will require a wide variety of agencies and organizations in the homeland security enterprise to develop new policy, strategy, and partnerships. In addition, these concerns require that the United States continue to work with its partner Arctic nations on international accords and treaties to manage the natural resources in the region. For example, the 1982 UNCLOS treaty defined three zones above the continental shelf extending from the coast into the open sea. From the shore to twelve nautical miles is referred to as a nation's territorial waters; twelve to twenty-four nautical miles is referred to as a nation's contiguous zone; and from the boundary of the contiguous zone to two hundred nautical miles offshore is the exclusive economic zone (EEZ) of a given nation. Part of what UNCLOS attempts to do is to preserve and protect a nation's rights within its own EEZ. However, global warming in the Arctic is challenging this understanding. With increasingly accessible oil, gas, and other resources (fishing, maritime navigation), the United States, Canada, Russia, and Denmark are extending their territorial claims and expanding their EEZs into the Arctic.[55] In his comments to the US Senate Subcommittee on Homeland Security, Mead Treadwell, chair of the Arctic National Research Commission, cited the need for more research into how the United States and other nations might legitimately extend their EEZ. He cited other homeland security–oriented concerns as well, including the need for better use of space imaging and coastal radar in ship detection and tracking, and threats to critical infrastructure from electromagnetic pulse attacks or even from solar flares of sufficient magnitude, such as the Carrington Event.[56] Last, although the National Research Council deems the probability of armed conflict in the Arctic to be low, it also warns the United States to be prepared for such conflict. As a result, it recommends the following security measures for the US Navy: (1) investigate and form new force structure capabilities; (2) prepare for more frequent deployments of humanitarian assistance and disaster relief operations in the Arctic region; (3) review combatant commanders' responsibilities to ensure smooth integration of effort across the services; (4) ensure that the efforts of the chief of naval operations to increase Arctic operations are well funded; and (5) develop and share lessons learned with the US Coast Guard (USCG), the Marines, and US allies.[57]

Economic and Infrastructure Security Concerns

Economic and infrastructure security concerns are related to the types and conditions of existing infrastructure affected by a warming Arctic region. For example, cited earlier as one reason why the United States may not have signed the UNCLOS accord to date is concern over oil pollution remediation and mitigation. The USCG remains concerned about not only its role in cleanup operations but its role in search-and-rescue operations. To the USCG, melting Arctic sea ice means increased shipping traffic, oil exploration, and recovery activities. Together, these activities signal an increased strategic interest in the Arctic for the United States and other Arctic nations, which in turn signals increased responsibilities for the USCG in the Arctic. The US Government Accountability Office examined the Coast Guard's current state of readiness to respond to these increased responsibilities and found that it lacks adequate information about the Arctic, lacks an adequate supply of personnel who are properly trained to work in this environment, and lacks sufficient infrastructure, such as icebreakers, to navigate in the ice-ridden seas. Moreover, owing to the inherent uncertainty of operating conditions in the Arctic, the USCG, the GAO concluded, needs to develop more detailed plans for operating in the harsh Arctic environment. Finally, the GAO determined that although the USCG is aggressively investigating how best to incorporate so many new resource requirements, it currently lacks adequate funding to develop, test, and acquire the required new resources.[58]

In addition to the concerns raised by the GAO, Treadwell raised concern about the US need for better surveillance, imaging, and communications infrastructures if intelligence and defense operations, shipping, and emergency response activities are to function more effectively in the Arctic.[59] The security community will need a common telecommunications, imaging, and sensing infrastructure to better understand and communicate weather conditions and to continue to monitor environmental changes in the Arctic brought on by global warming.

Research-Based Security Concerns

Research-based concerns are rooted in the realization that the Arctic is a complex and rapidly evolving environment that we do not know as much about as we would like to know. For example, increased oil and gas exploration and recovery, fishing, transportation, and tourism through the Bering Sea and the Arctic Ocean are rapidly enhancing the risk of significant oil spills. Perhaps one of the most publicized oil spills in recent times was the *Exxon Valdez* spill in Prince William Sound in 1989. The *Valdez* spill led to passage of the Oil Pollution Act (OPA) of 1990. The OPA produced several powerful outcomes, including a well-funded research program, an oil spill trust fund, and better extraction, transportation, and cleanup technologies. Given the uniquely challenging physical characteristics of the Arctic region, Treadwell recommended that Congress fund the development of similar research capabilities through the OPA.[60] Last, inasmuch as energy represents critical infrastructure, more research is needed to help diversify the US energy supply and promote movement away from fossil fuels. Such movement would reduce the risk of catastrophic oil spills and enhance the economic sustainability of local Alaskan communities. In addition, since the USCG oversees the environmental health of bulk fuel storage sites in Alaska, adoption of alternative energy supplies would help to reduce the USCG's budget by reducing the need for oversight of so many facilities.[61]

As mentioned earlier, threats to critical infrastructure arise from a variety of sources. Treadwell recommended that a homeland security research agenda be formed whose aim would be to identify threats to critical infrastructures specific to the Arctic, such as electromagnetic pulses and solar flares. Further, since the Department of Homeland Security plays a major role in pandemic response, it should learn more about the development and spread of bird-based disease epidemics by studying the migration patterns of birds in the Arctic.[62]

The next section introduces an intellectual framework for examining how the security and policy community might evaluate the impacts of climate change and be better positioned to avoid or mitigate impacts before they become challenges to US national security.

Arctic Security and Risk Analysis Tools

Risk management tools and principles are just as appropriate for use in environmental security as they are in any other sort of security, such as homeland security or emergency management. The notion of "risk" is often characterized as the product of "likelihood" and "consequence," or "impact." Risk management is central to modern homeland security since no nation can afford to protect itself all the time from all risks—hence, in trying to decide how best to secure the nation, policymakers need to be able to prioritize what to do and in what order. Managing emergent security risks is particularly difficult precisely because good, solid estimates of likelihood or impacts are not easy. Further, the emergent nature of climate-driven risks has given us few opportunities to learn lessons we could apply. As such, the sorts of threats to security that a warming Arctic region seems to be presenting will require that the security community develop new frameworks and tools in order to better anticipate, understand, characterize, and manage threats in a timely fashion.

For example, in its most recent report, the Intergovernmental Panel on Climate Change describes how climate change forces may end up leading to national security challenges. The IPCC suggests that security challenges occur when climate change forces (global warming, weather extremes, and so on) directly collide with vulnerable social assets (people, property, the environment). The IPCC refers to this confluence as the EEV (exposure, event, and vulnerability) model of climate-driven social impacts. In the EEV model, a climate event

is any event that is directly connected to the properties of climate through deterministic physical or biological mechanisms. Such events might be acute (e.g., a storm or heat wave), slowly developing (e.g., a drought or a change in the ecological range of a crop pest), or a combination of the two (e.g., wildfires in a drought-stricken forest). The behavior of climate includes the full range of climate events; the term *weather* normally is applied to short-term climate events.

An "exposure" is "the presence of people, livelihoods, environmental services and resources, infrastructure, or economic, social, or cultural assets in places that could be adversely affected." And "vulnerability" refers to "the propensity or predisposition to be adversely affected. Aspects of vulnerability include the susceptibility to being harmed and the likelihood of effective coping or response in the event of harm."[63]

In turn, and from a security management perspective, vulnerability can also be seen as having two embedded characteristics. First is susceptibility, which refers to the degree to which the social, economic, or political systems impacted by external threats such as climate events are able to recover. The second embedded characteristic of vulnerability is the ability of the political system to respond to and recover from the threat.[64] Finally, we should keep in mind that climate change may also cause disruptions via second- or third-order events—that is, by causing adverse interactions in biological systems when human structures or systems are directly involved, with the potential to lead eventually to disruption in human systems indirectly.

The EEV model and the possibility of second- or third-order consequences raise an important question: do security and policy experts have the tools they need to identify and mitigate disruptions to society from climate-driven events? Students should note that current science is relatively unlikely to be able to make specific predictions of exactly where and when certain climatic anomalies will occur and the disruptions they may cause. The analogy is that before events arise it is difficult to separate signal from noise; after events have occurred, however, it becomes clearer what led to what and what caused what to happen.

What are the best ways for security and policy experts to think about anthropomorphic changes in the Arctic region? There are at least four approaches that could be used to examine changes to the Arctic and how the United States might better manage the coming impacts: forecasting, the use of advanced warning systems, system vulnerability analysis, and policy vulnerability analysis. Each has limitations, and in real life a mix of approaches is indicated.

Forecasting involves detailed understanding of key variables and the ability to mathematically characterize each variable with some level of precision.[65] Regarding the Arctic region, forecasting would incorporate an understanding of the anthropomorphic activities that are directly tied to changes in the Arctic climate, the susceptibility of the Arctic region to those activities, and the consequences that arise from those susceptibilities. In addition, a sense of the timeline involved would be critical to a policymaker's ability to respond to both changes that have already happened and those that have yet to arrive. Forecasting allows policymakers to consider high-likelihood/low-impact events as well as low-likelihood/high-impact events as they decide how many social resources they will allocate to each risk and in what order they will allocate them.

The second approach, building systems of early warning of potentially catastrophic events, requires detailed knowledge of indicators that portend a coming condition, such as species of animals or other natural or biological systems. When such indicators are animals, biologists refer to such species as "indicator species." Such early warning systems might also consist, however, of social or economic conditions. For example, the inability of the Inuit to find polar bears for hunting may indicate other, deeper problems with the Arctic region climate that, in turn, may indicate a coming security challenge.

The third approach is a detailed assessment of the system vulnerabilities of existing systems or structures and the existing capability to respond to or recover from a climatic event.[66] For example, how capable was the government in responding to a traumatic climatic event such as Hurricane Sandy? Could the Canadian government have responded as the US government did? Or could the Sri Lankan government respond adequately if a Sandy-like storm made landfall there? This approach includes detailed consideration of worst-case scenarios as well as examination of the existing capability to harden infrastructure, the national-level response capability, or the government's ability to work with large numbers of unhappy or displaced citizens. This approach might adapt and use existing security and policy management tools—such as the intelligence community's use of "stress tests" to better characterize the likelihood that a nation, or its political economy, will fail, in order either to help position the United States to benefit from such a failure or to help the United States understand how to prevent it.

Similar in concept to the third approach, the final approach is a policy vulnerability analysis, which involves a detailed look at the political capability and governmental structures needed to anticipate, identify, characterize, and defeat threats.[67] Policy vulnerability analysis asks at what point might a government fail owing to high-impact events. In this sense, this analysis is related to the principles of risk management. Policy vulnerability analysis, then, is an analytical method that could provide policymakers with the tools and thresholds they need to understand relative risks and alternatives and thereby be better positioned to make policy that helps the nation to offset and survive large-scale, high-impact events.

Conclusions

This case has presented details about the Arctic region and an account of how anthropomorphic perturbations in the climate may be producing security challenges there for the United States. Unlike the Antarctic, which has been managed by a consortium of over one hundred nations for the past forty years, the Arctic region has not benefited as much, for a variety of reasons, from a long-term, robust international peace accord that would preclude the extraction of minerals and resources and thereby preserve it as a bastion of only international research. As Arctic sea ice melts and nations maneuver to create greater footholds in the region, enlarge their respective EEZs and lay claim to resources and shipping lanes, and even enhance their military installations, security concerns begin to manifest themselves. Such concerns pose major international governance, diplomatic, and scientific challenges to the United States and its allies.

The case has also pointed out a major underlying theme that links homeland security to national security. Among all developed nations—and increasingly so among less-developed nations—it is clear that fossil fuels are the primary energy source that powers economic development and supports lifestyles. The catch with using fossil fuels to power economic opportunity and development is the inescapable generation of CO_2 and other greenhouse gases, which in turn exacerbate the rate and intensity of global warming. Hence, almost ironically, as more developed nations continue to predominantly rely on fossil fuels to drive and support their economies, their militaries, and their lifestyles, scientists, diplomats, and military strategists around the world have noticed security challenges that are directly attributable to anthropomorphic climate change. Such climate change has thoroughly altered what the Arctic region means to the nations of the world. Geopolitically, the Arctic is rich in oil, natural gases, and other resources, offers a semi-reliable navigational pathway from the Atlantic to the Pacific, and represents a strategic military vantage point, as it borders eight Arctic nations. In combination, this makes for a complex mix of tensions and economic opportunities that will require the development of new governance structures, international policy, and international accords to sort out.

DISCUSSION QUESTIONS

1. Explain how global climate change poses a security challenge to the US homeland and to US national security.
2. Describe four approaches to examining environmental change in the Arctic and determining how the United States might better manage such change.
3. What US policies and strategies have been implemented that address the issue of Arctic security? What seems to be lacking?

4. Why is understanding Arctic security important to homeland security professionals?

NOTES

1. Board of Environmental Change and Society, Division of Behavioral and Social Sciences and Education, National Research Council, National Academy of Sciences, *Climate and Social Stress: Implications for Security* (Washington, DC: National Academies Press, 2012), S-2.

2. *Survivorman* is a television series produced by the Discovery Channel.

3. Joseph Kalt, "Coping with the Hard Truth of Energy Economics," Analysis Online, http://analysisonline.org/site/aoarticle_display.asp?article_id=140001490&sec_id =140002434&news_id=140001490&issue_id=3 (accessed October 12, 2012).

4. US Energy Information Administration (EIA), "Frequently Asked Questions: How much carbon dioxide is produced by burning gasoline and diesel fuel?" http://www.eia .gov/tools/faqs/faq.cfm?id=307&t=11 (accessed October 20, 2012).

5. Kalt, "Coping with the Hard Truth of Energy Economics."

6. Adapted from International Waters Learning Exchange and Resource Network, "Physical and Geographical Characteristics of the Arctic," http://iwlearn.net/iw-projects /807/reports/amap-assessment-report-arctic-pollution-issues-1998/physical-geographical -characteristics-of-the-arctic/view (accessed October 20, 2012).

7. National Geographic Society: The Arctic, http://arctic.ru/arctic-facts (accessed November 1, 2012).

8. Ibid.; see also Task Force Climate Change and Oceanographer of the Navy, "Arctic Environmental Assessment and Outlook Report: In Support of the Navy Arctic Roadmap," action item 5.7. (August 2011), http://greenfleet.dodlive.mil/files/2011 /08/U.S.-Navy-Arctic-Environmental-Assessment.pdf.

9. See, for example, US Department of Defense, *Quadrennial Defense Review Report,* February 2010; US Department of Homeland Security, *Quadrennial Homeland Security Review Report: A Strategic Framework for a Secure Homeland,* February 2010; and US Department of State, *Leading Through Civilian Power: The First Quadrennial Diplomacy and Development Review,* 2010.

10. Intergovernmental Panel on Climate Change (IPCC), *Climate Change 2007: The Physical Science Basis: Contribution of Working Group I to the Fourth Assessment Report of the Intergovernmental Panel on Climate Change,* ed. S. Solomon, D. Qin, M. Manning, Z. Chen, M. Marquis, K. B. Averyt, M. Tignor, and H. L. Miller (Cambridge: Cambridge University Press, 2007).

11. National Snow and Ice Data Center, "All About Arctic Climatology and Meteorology," http://nsidc.org/arcticmet/basics/weather_vs_climate.html (accessed November 1, 2012).

12. Intergovernmental Panel on Climate Change, *Managing the Risks of Extreme Events and Disasters to Advance Climate Change Adaptation: Special Report of Working Groups I and II of the Intergovernmental Panel on Climate Change,* ed. C. B. Field, V. Barros, T. F. Stocker, D. Qin, D. J. Dokken, K. L. Ebi, M. D. Mastrandrea, K. J. Mach, G.-K. Plattner, S. K. Allen, M. Tignor, and P. M. Midgley (Cambridge: Cambridge University Press, 2012).

13. See US Environmental Protection Agency (EPA), "Sources of Greenhouse Gas Emissions: Overview," http://epa.gov/climatechange/ghgemissions/sources.html (accessed November 20, 2012).

14. James Hansen, testimony before the Senate Committee on Energy and Natural Resources, June 23, 1988, http://image.guardian.co.uk/sys-files/Environment/documents /2008/06/23/ClimateChangeHearing1988.pdf (accessed October 10, 2012).

15. American Meteorological Society, "Climate Change: An Information Statement of the American Meteorological Society," adopted August 2012.

16. Kalt, "Coping with the Hard Truth of Energy Economics."

17. EPA, "Sources of Greenhouse Gas Emissions: Overview."

18. Oil: US and the World, "US Oil Consumption," http://roopak330.wikidot.com /stats:u-s-oil-consumption (accessed November 11, 2012); see also Central Intelligence Agency (CIA), *The World Factbook,* https://www.cia.gov/library/publications/the-world -factbook/rankorder/2119rank.html (accessed November 11, 2012).

19. Committee on the Future of Arctic Sea Ice Research in Support of Seasonal-to-Decadal Predictions, Polar Research Board, Division on Earth and Life Studies, National Research Council, *Seasonal-to-Decadal Predictions of Arctic Sea Ice: Challenges and Strategies* (Washington, DC: National Academies Press, 2012).

20. Michelle Allsopp, David Santillo, and Paul Johnston, "Climate Change Impacts on Arctic Wildlife," Greenpeace Technical Report 04-2012, http://www.greenpeace .org/international/Global/international/publications/climate/2012/Arctic/420-Arctic Wildlife.pdf (accessed October 20, 2012).

21. David W. Johnston, Matthew T. Bowers, Ari S. Friedlaender, and David M. Lavigne, "The Effects of Climate Change on Harp Seals (*Pagophilus groenlandicus*)," *PLoS/ONE* 7, no. 1 (2002): e29158, Doi: 10.1371/journal.pone.0029158.

22. Ibid.

23. Ibid., 10.

24. Ibid.

25. Philip Budzik, "Arctic Oil and Natural Gas Potential," US Energy Information Administration, Office of Integrated Analysis and Forecasting, Oil and Gas Division, October 2009.

26. US Geological Survey, "90 Billion Barrels of Oil and 1,670 Trillion Cubic Feet of Natural Gas Assessed in the Arctic," July 23, 2008, http://www.usgs.gov/newsroom/article.asp?ID=1980&from=rss_home (accessed November 20, 2012).

27. See Committee on National Security Implications of Climate Change for US Naval Forces, National Research Council, *National Security Implications of Climate Change for US Naval Forces* (Washington, DC: National Academies Press, 2011); and Board of Environmental Change and Society, *Climate and Social Stress.*

28. "Putin Says Arctic Must Remain 'Zone of Peace,'" TerraDaily.com, September 23, 2010, http://www.terradaily.com/reports/Putin_says_Arctic_must_remain_zone_of_peace_999.html (accessed November 3, 2012).

29. Luke Coffey, "NATO in the Arctic: Challenges and Opportunities," Heritage Foundation Issue Brief 3646, June 22, 2012.

30. Cool Antarctica, "Human Impacts on Antarctica and Threats to the Environment: Mining and Oil," http://www.coolantarctica.com/Antarctica%20fact%20file/science/threats_mining_oil.htm (accessed November 24, 2012).

31. British Antarctic Survey, "The Antarctic Treaty: Background Information," http://www.antarctica.ac.uk/about_antarctica/geopolitical/treaty/index.php (accessed November 2, 2012).

32. Ibid.

33. Ronald O'Rourke, "Changes in the Arctic: Background and Issues for Congress," Congressional Research Service Report, 7-5700, July 5, 2013, http://www.fas.org/sgp/crs/misc/R41153.pdf (accessed November 20, 2012).

34. Donat Pharand, "A Draft Arctic Treaty: An Arctic Region Council," University of Ottawa, Canadian Arctic Resources Committee, 1991, http://www.carc.org/pubs/v19no2/5.htm (accessed November 2, 2012).

35. "United Nations Convention on the Law of the Sea," Wikipedia, http://en.wikipedia.org/wiki/United_Nations_Convention_on_the_Law_of_the_Sea (accessed November 3, 2012).

36. Roger Rufe, president of the Ocean Conservancy, statement before the Senate Committee on Foreign Relations, October 21, 2003. The discussion on UNCLOS and the US involvement in it is complex and ongoing. For more information, see O'Rourke, "Changes in the Arctic."

37. Kenneth S. Yalowitz, James F. Collins, and Ross A. Virginia, "The Arctic Climate Change and Security Policy Conference: Final Report and Findings," December 2008,

http://www.carnegieendowment.org/files/arctic_climate_change.pdf (accessed November 5, 2012).

38. Keith Johnson, "GOP Scuttles Law-of-Sea Treaty," *Wall Street Journal,* July 16, 2012.

39. Committee on National Security Implications of Climate Change for US Naval Forces, *National Security Implications of Climate Change for US Naval Forces.*

40. The White House, Office of the Press Secretary, "National Security Presidential Directive/NSPD 66 [and] Homeland Security Presidential Directive/HSPD 25," January 9, 2009, p. 2, http://www.nsf.gov/od/opp/opp_advisory/briefings/may2009/nspd66 _hspd25.pdf (accessed November 5, 2012).

41. The White House, *National Security Strategy* (Washington, DC: The White House, May 2010), 50. The quoted sentence constitutes the entirety of the document's comments specifically on the Arctic. It is the final sentence of a section on "sustain[ing] broad cooperation on key global challenges" that includes longer discussions on climate change, peacekeeping and armed conflict, pandemics and infectious disease, transnational criminal threats and threats to governance, and safeguarding the global commons.

42. Mia Bennett, "Arctic Council Close to Reaching Agreement on Marine Oil Pollution Preparedness," Foreign Policy Association, October 12, 2012, http://foreignpolicyblogs .com/2012/10/12/arctic-council-close-to-reaching-agreement-on-marine-oil -pollution-preparedness.

43. The White House, Office of the Press Secretary, "NSPD 66 [and] HSPD 25."

44. Yalowitz, Collins, and Virginia, "The Arctic Climate Change and Security Policy Conference."

45. O'Rourke, "Changes in the Arctic."

46. Luke Coffey, "Arctic Security: Five Principles That Should Guide US Policy," Heritage Foundation Issue Brief 3700, August 15, 2012.

47. Coffey, "NATO in the Arctic."

48. Ibid.

49. Ibid.; see also Thomas Grove, "Russia Creates Two Brigades of Arctic Troops," *Reuters,* July 1, 2011.

50. Yalowitz, Collins, and Virginia, "The Arctic Climate Change and Security Policy Conference."

51. Board of Environmental Change and Society, *Climate and Social Stress.*

52. Ibid.

53. US Department of Defense, *Quadrennial Defense Review Report,* February 2010, 85, http://www.defense.gov/qdr/images/QDR_as_of_12Feb10_1000.pdf (accessed November 15, 2012).

54. Task Force Climate Change and Oceanographer of the Navy, "Arctic Environmental Assessment and Outlook Report"; Mead Treadwell, Chair, Arctic National Research

Commission, comments to the field hearing of the US Senate Appropriations Committee, Homeland Security Subcommittee, University of Alaska, Anchorage, August 20, 2009; Board of Environmental Change and Society, *Climate and Social Stress;* Yalowitz, Collins, and Virginia, "The Arctic Climate Change and Security Policy Conference"; O'Rourke, "Changes in the Arctic."

55. O'Rourke, "Changes in the Arctic."

56. Treadwell, comments to the field hearing of the US Senate Appropriations Committee. The Carrington Event was a solar superstorm that occurred in 1859.

57. Committee on National Security Implications of Climate Change for US Naval Forces, *National Security Implications of Climate Change for US Naval Forces.*

58. US Government Accountability Office (GAO), "Coast Guard: Efforts to Identify Arctic Requirements Are Ongoing, but More Communication About Agency Planning Efforts Would Be Beneficial," GAO-10-870, September 2010, http://www.gao.gov/assets /320/311302.pdf (accessed November 22, 2012).

59. Treadwell, comments to the field hearing of the US Senate Appropriations Committee.

60. Ibid.

61. Ibid.

62. Ibid.

63. IPCC, *Managing the Risks of Extreme Events and Disasters to Advance Climate Change Adaptation.*

64. Board of Environmental Change and Society, *Climate and Social Stress.*

65. Ibid.

66. Ibid.

67. Ibid.

The Impact of Hurricane Katrina on the Environmental Security of the US Gulf Coast Region and Beyond

JOHN M. LANICCI AND JAMES D. RAMSAY

Introduction

On the morning of Monday, August 29, 2005, Hurricane Katrina made landfall in southeast Louisiana as a large Saffir-Simpson Scale Category 3 hurricane, with winds of 110 knots and a central pressure of 920 hectopascals. The center of the storm moved north and maintained hurricane intensity for nearly another one hundred miles after landfall. Katrina subsequently moved through Mississippi and the lower Mississippi River Valley and into the Ohio River Valley, causing destruction from straight-line winds and dozens of tornadoes spawned from the storm.[1] All told, the geographic area of the United States affected by Katrina spanned some 93,000 square miles, a region the size of Great Britain.[2] Katrina ranks fourth or fifth on the list of deadliest hurricanes in US history, with 1,833 known fatalities, according to state and local officials in Louisiana, Mississippi, Florida, Georgia, and Alabama.[3] Several sources have estimated damage costs from the storm in excess of $100 billion, making it the costliest natural disaster in US history.[4]

While these numbers may seem staggering, there is another aspect of this storm worth examining—the impact of Hurricane Katrina on the *environmental security* of the Gulf Coast region and the entire United States. We begin with a definition of environmental security that accounts for the impacts of extreme weather events and climatic anomalies on the ability of a nation or region to maintain the security of its inhabitants. From there, this case study will go on to examine the impacts of this particular extreme weather event on a significant portion of the US population in the Gulf Coast region and the substantial security challenges presented to state and local governments by these impacts, not only in the affected areas but well beyond. The framework for the environmental security case-study analysis is a "cascading effects model" (hereafter referred to as the "cascade model") developed by the authors, who based it on the findings of a 2007 report by the CNA Corporation on the national security implications of global climate change.[5]

We will employ the cascade model in this case study to examine the following questions:

1. How did Hurricane Katrina destabilize the natural and physical environments of the Gulf Coast region?
2. How did Hurricane Katrina affect critical infrastructure in Louisiana and Mississippi?
3. How did the aftermath of Hurricane Katrina impact the physical and economic security of New Orleans and the Gulf Coast region in the weeks immediately following the storm?
4. How did the physical and economic security impacts spread from the Gulf Coast region into other areas of the United States?
5. How would a Katrina-like storm impact a less developed nation with less mature infrastructure, economy, and means to respond? How would these impacts be different from what happened in New Orleans and on the Gulf Coast?

A Brief History of Environmental Security and Introduction to the Cascade Model

Although environmental security as a field of study has been around since the 1970s,[6] there are many definitions of the term itself, ranging from those based on remediation or compliance to those oriented toward restoration or safety.[7] Therefore, it is important to define the term as it will be used in this case-study analysis. Here, we are more interested in the ways in which environmental issues can affect the physical and economic security of a nation or region. Thus, we define environmental security as "an interdisciplinary study of extreme environmental events and climatic anomalies, the destabilizing effects of these events and anomalies on a country or region of the world, and the potential security implications of the resulting geopolitical instability."[8]

Early environmental security studies focused on the causes of the famine in the Sahel region of sub-Saharan Africa. A multi-decadal drought combined with poor land-use management by the region's inhabitants to create a humanitarian catastrophe that resulted in an estimated 100,000 deaths and significantly affected a majority of the region's 50 million inhabitants. These studies were interested in the interactions between the climate, geography, and people and the implications of these changes on the security of the individuals and tribal groups living in the region. Environmental security first caught the attention of the US policymaking community during the 1990s, when a debate emerged within that community as to whether the definition of national security should be expanded to include more than just military hardware, personnel under arms, and other nation-centric considerations.[9] One side of the debate argued that an increasingly complex, multipolar world could only be understood by incorporating environmental issues and other nontraditional issue areas (such as social and economic issues) into a *redefined* concept of security. However, traditional security experts countered that while environmental, health, and socioeconomic concerns had important *connections* to security, these issues were not properly characterized as security concerns.

During this same period, there was a great deal of research interest in exploring the links between the natural environment and national/international security issues. The idea was to examine potential linkages between sustainability issues, resource contention, geopolitical instability, and environmental issues—from single-event disasters, such as tropical cyclones, to the cumulative changes wrought by climatic anomalies, such as drought. The body of work took the

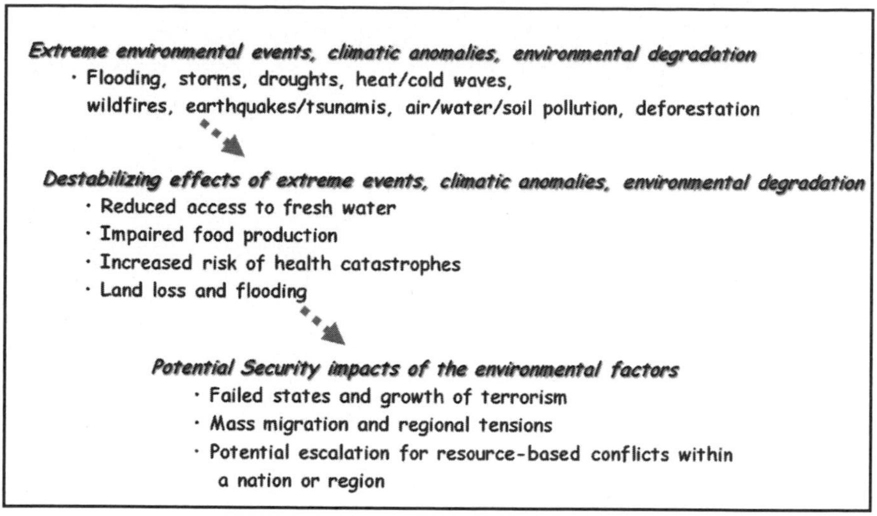

FIGURE 3.2.1: The Environmental Security Cascade Model

Source: John M. Lanicci and James Ramsay, "Environmental Security: Exploring Relationships Between the Natural Environment, National Security, and Homeland Security," Fifth Symposium on Policy and Socioeconomic Research, American Meteorological Society, Atlanta, January 18–21, 2010.

form of a number of research and pilot programs conducted by a combination of academic institutions, nongovernmental organizations, and the US federal government (primarily the departments of state and defense). During this period, seminal works on environmental security began to explore the complex linkages between environmental degradation, resource scarcity, and conflict in many regions of the world.[10]

In the aftermath of the September 11, 2001, terrorist attacks, US foreign policy was redirected toward the Global War on Terrorism (GWOT). During the first ten years of this conflict, the military instrument of national power was used more than other means, such as diplomatic, informational, or economic approaches. As a result, environmental security was not given the same level of emphasis by the US policymaking community. Beginning around 2007, however, concerns within the civilian, military, and diplomatic communities about the potential security implications of global climate change rekindled an interest in environmental security.[11]

Of particular interest was the 2007 CNA report. Developed by a panel of retired US generals and admirals after extensive interviews with scientific and business leaders, the report describes a series of potentially destabilizing impacts from climate change, including reduced access to fresh water, impaired food production, health catastrophes, and population displacements from land loss. It then lists the geostrategic implications of these climate change impacts: greater potential for failed states and the growth of terrorism, mass migrations, and potential escalation of resource-based conflict. We have summarized these effects and impacts diagrammatically through a three-tiered cascade model (Figure 3.2.1). The model represents the escalation of geopolitical instability that might be instigated from a single severe environmental event, a series of such events, a prolonged period of climatic anomaly, or a combination of these. In the following sections, we present a step-by-step application of the cascade model as it played out during Hurricane Katrina's evolution, with special emphasis on analyzing the storm's aftermath.

Cascade Model Preconditions:
The Geography, Demographics, Key Infrastructure, and Industries of the Gulf Coast Region

In order to apply the cascade model to this case, it is important to understand the preexisting conditions in the region affected by Hurricane Katrina. This section describes the natural and physical environments of the US Gulf coast, paying special attention to Louisiana, Mississippi, and the city of New Orleans.

Geographically, Louisiana can be divided into the upland region of the north and the alluvial region along the Gulf coast. The alluvial region has low swamplands, coastal marshlands, beaches, and barrier islands. The Mississippi River defines the border between Louisiana and Mississippi until it reaches the alluvial region and empties into the Gulf of Mexico. The alluvial region along the Mississippi River ranges from ten to sixty miles and averages about ten miles along the other rivers in the state. Mississippi consists entirely of lowlands, as most of the state is part of the East Gulf Coastal Plain, which is generally composed of low hills. The Gulf coast includes large bays at Bay St. Louis, Biloxi, and Pascagoula, which are separated from the Gulf of Mexico by the Mississippi Sound. The northwest portion of the state consists of the Mississippi Delta, which is a section of the Mississippi alluvial region.[12] A topographic map of Louisiana, Mississippi, and the surrounding states is shown in Figure 3.2.2 (left panel).

New Orleans is located on the east and west banks of the Mississippi River, and south of Lake Pontchartrain, a little over one hundred miles from

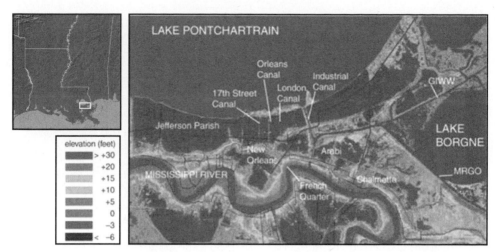

FIGURE 3.2.2: Topographic Map of Louisiana, Mississippi, and Surrounding States, with Detailed Topographic Map of New Orleans

Source: "Understanding Katrina," from the Teaching with Hurricane Katrina: The Physiography, Climate, Storm and Impact website, http://serc.carleton.edu/research_education/katrina/understanding.html.

the Gulf of Mexico. As seen in the right panel of Figure 3.2.2, a considerable fraction of the city and surrounding area lies below sea level. Because of its geography, the city and surrounding areas are protected by a network of levees, a very important point that we return to later.

Demographically, Louisiana and Mississippi do not resemble the United States as a whole in either racial/ethnic makeup or level of poverty. A comparison of the racial/ethnic profiles of these two states compared to the entire United States, using figures from the 2000 US Census, reveals some interesting facts. The data show that the poverty rate in Louisiana and Mississippi was over 7 percent higher than the national rate of 12.4 percent. These two states also had a percentage black population that was 20 percent higher than the national average of 12.1 percent.[13] The racial demographics represent historical trends that date back to the nineteenth century, when thousands of black slaves were imported into the Southern states to support the growing agriculture-based economy there. We used these data, combined with other information about infrastructure and economics, to determine the "pre-Katrina" conditions necessary for the cascade model analysis.

The Louisiana State Division of Administration contains a great deal of information about the state's industrial capacity, which is also necessary to define the pre-Katrina physical and natural environments. Louisiana has the greatest concentration of crude oil refineries, natural gas processing plants, and petrochemical production facilities in the Western Hemisphere.[14] Louisiana is the nation's third-largest producer of petroleum and third nationally in petroleum refining, and the state is the second-largest producer of natural gas, supplying slightly more than 25 percent of US total production. According to the American Society of Civil Engineers, Louisiana is fifth nationally in domestic oil production, is home to a network of pipelines, storage facilities, and seventeen refineries, and has two of the nation's four Strategic Petroleum Reserves, making it the largest center of emergency crude oil supply in the world. New Orleans is also a business center for energy companies such as BP, Shell, Chevron, and ConocoPhillips.[15]

Louisiana is a top agricultural state; its featured crops are sugar cane, sweet potatoes, rice, cotton, and pecans. Louisiana's commercial fishing industry produces 25 percent of the nation's seafood. The state is very important to US shipping: it has the nation's farthest inland port for seagoing ships (Baton Rouge) and the nation's only port capable of handling superships. More than 25 percent of the nation's waterborne exports are shipped through the state's five major ports. The total value of Louisiana's chemical shipments is more than $14 billion a year, and the state is the nation's largest handler of US grain exports to international markets, with more than 40 percent of exports moving through the state's ports.[16]

Mississippi is one of the most rural states in the country and has the distinction of being the poorest in terms of income. Mainly an agricultural state, it is a major producer of cotton, along with rice, soybeans, chickens, catfish, and dairy products. As in Louisiana, the petroleum industry has grown with the development of oil resources, and industrial products such as chemicals, plastics, furniture, lumber, and other wood products have recently become more profitable than agricultural products.[17]

Because of its many bays and sounds, Louisiana has the longest coastline (15,000 miles) of any state and 41 percent of the nation's wetlands.[18] However, because of the need to divert floodwaters away from New Orleans and the importance of the Mississippi River channel to the lucrative shipping industry, the river has had flood control levees built along its lower extent for more than two hundred years. Within the last eighty years, the US Army Corps of Engineers has built a comprehensive flood control and navigation program for the Mississippi River. However, one of the consequences of this program has been to sever the river from its delta, causing the bulk of its sediments to be diverted to the mouth of the river instead of into the delta.

As a result, the delta's wetlands—which are an important asset to the fishing industry and also act as a buffer against land-falling tropical cyclones—have been disappearing.[19]

Tier 1 of the Cascade Model: The Evolution of the Storm and the Quality of Storm Forecasts

August 23–25, 2005

The analyzed "best track" of the center of Hurricane Katrina's path is displayed in Figure 3.2.3. Katrina began as a tropical depression that became organized over the central Bahamas during the evening of August 23. The depression was upgraded to tropical storm status and named Katrina on August 24, based on aircraft reconnaissance flight-level wind data.[20] Katrina initially moved northwestward, but as it strengthened on the 24th, it came

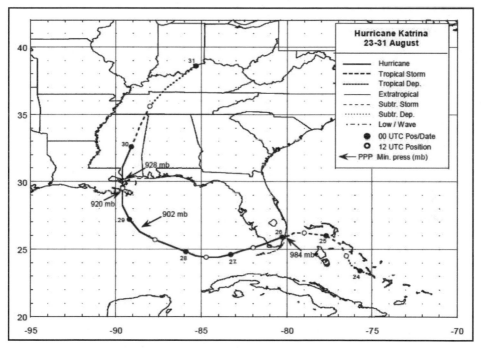

FIGURE 3.2.3: Hurricane Katrina Storm Center Track: National Weather Service
Source: Richard D. Knabb, Jamie R. Rhome, and Daniel P. Brown, "Tropical Cyclone Report: Hurricane Katrina, August 23–30, 2005" (Miami: National Hurricane Center, 2005).

under the influence of a strengthening middle-to-upper tropospheric ridge over the northern Gulf of Mexico and southern United States, which turned the storm westward toward south Florida on August 25. Katrina is estimated to have reached hurricane status during the afternoon of the 25th, less than two hours before its first landfall between North Miami Beach and Hallandale Beach in southeast Florida as a Category 1 storm. The storm is blamed for two fatalities in south Florida.[21]

August 26–28, 2005

Katrina tracked west-southwestward overnight into August 26, having spent a relatively short time over land before moving into the southeastern Gulf of Mexico as a tropical storm. Once Katrina entered the Gulf, it restrengthened to a hurricane early on the 26th. At this stage, the National Hurricane Center (NHC) reported winds of 85 to 90 knots. Owing to a favorable upper tropospheric environment, Katrina rapidly intensified between August 26 and 28. On the 27th, the storm reached Category 3 status with sustained maximum winds of 100 knots. Katrina's circulation covered the entire Gulf of Mexico. Category 4 status was reached later that day, with sustained maximum winds over 125 knots. At this point, the eye was about 310 miles from the mouth of the Mississippi River. By the 28th, Katrina had nearly doubled in size and become a Category 5 storm with maximum sustained winds of 150 knots. The amplification of an upper-tropospheric trough over the northern United States began to affect Katrina's movement, and the storm track turned to the northwest (over the warm Loop Current), and then to the north on the 29th. By midafternoon on August 28, the storm center was located about 200 miles southeast of the mouth of the Mississippi River, and later that day tropical storm–force winds had extended to about 230 miles from the center, with hurricane-force winds out to about 100 miles from the center. At this point, Hurricane Katrina was an extremely intense *and* large tropical cyclone.[22]

August 29–30, 2005

After Katrina turned northward early on August 29, it began to lose some intensity, but it was still a large Category 3 system. A weather buoy about fifty miles east of the mouth of the Mississippi River reported waves at least forty feet high. The hurricane made its second landfall as a strong Category 3 storm with estimated maximum sustained winds of 110 knots near Buras, Louisiana, early on the morning of the 29th. Katrina continued its northward track and made its final landfall near the mouth of the Pearl River at the

Louisiana-Mississippi border as a Category 3 hurricane with estimated maximum sustained winds of 105 knots. Katrina weakened rapidly after moving inland over southern and central Mississippi, weakening to a Category 1 hurricane by midafternoon on the 29th. It subsequently diminished to a tropical storm about six hours later just northwest of Meridian, Mississippi.[23]

According to a poststorm service assessment conducted on Katrina by the National Weather Service (NWS), the timeliness and accuracy of the forecast products and warnings issued by the NHC were well above average. The storm forecast track error was considerably better than average for up to five days in advance. Lead times on hurricane watches and warnings for Louisiana, Mississippi, Alabama, and the Florida Panhandle were eight hours above average. Although the intensity forecast error for Katrina was worse than average, the intensity forecasts within forty-eight to seventy-two hours of landfall in Louisiana correctly predicted that Katrina would be a major hurricane (defined as Category 3 or higher). Of particular note was the forecast statement issued by the NWS Forecast Office in New Orleans–Baton Rouge one day prior to Katrina's landfall, which strongly emphasized the likely impacts of the hurricane on southeast Louisiana and coastal Mississippi in language never used before. As a result, the statement helped reinforce the actions of emergency managers coordinating one of the largest evacuations in US history.[24] This is an important point that we come back to later in this case study.

The Storm's Aftermath: Applying the Cascade Model

Tier 1 and Tier 2 of the Model: Effects and Impacts of the Extreme Event

In this section, we provide a summary of the human, environmental, and economic toll from Hurricane Katrina. We discuss the storm's direct impacts on the physical and economic security of New Orleans and the eventual ripple effects across the entire United States from the poststorm events in Louisiana and Mississippi, but do not delve into the decisions made by local, state, and federal officials in preparation for the storm and in its immediate aftermath. There is a wealth of information on this topic, and a discussion of this aspect of the storm is beyond the scope of this case-study analysis, which we wish to confine to the realm of environmental security versus emergency management, freely acknowledging that these two disciplines are related.

On August 26, Governors Kathleen Blanco of Louisiana and Haley Barbour of Mississippi declared states of emergency. The National Hurricane

Center predicted that Katrina would become a major hurricane by the time it reached the central Gulf of Mexico. New Orleans mayor Ray Nagin called for a voluntary evacuation of the city on the afternoon of August 27. Describing Katrina as a "potentially catastrophic" hurricane, the NHC warned that levees in the New Orleans area could be overtopped and significant storm surge flooding could occur elsewhere along the central and northeastern Gulf Coast. Based partially on a phone call on the evening of the 27th from the NHC director, Max Mayfield, to the mayor, warning him of the dire consequences from the approaching hurricane, Mayor Nagin ordered an unprecedented mandatory evacuation of New Orleans on the morning of August 28, less than twenty-four hours before Hurricane Katrina's landfall.[25]

Recall that earlier we mentioned the importance of the levee system used to protect the New Orleans area, nearly half of which is under sea level, from flooding. There were over fifty levee and floodwall failures in the New Orleans area following Hurricane Katrina's passage, with two direct causes, according to the American Society of Civil Engineers. The first was a design flaw in several levees with concrete floodwalls that caused them to collapse, and the second was overtopping: water pouring over the tops of the levees and floodwalls eroded the structures away. A contributing but not direct reason for the flooding was that the many pump stations that might have helped remove floodwaters were inoperable during and after the storm.[26]

It is estimated that between 80 and 90 percent of New Orleans residents evacuated in advance of the storm's landfall; for those who did not evacuate, conditions quickly became desperate. Thousands of people were without food or potable water, and as the floodwaters rose, they needed to be rescued from certain death. According to figures from the US Coast Guard, search-and-rescue operations alone saved the lives of 24,135 people, many of whom were pulled from rooftops. An additional 9,409 patients were evacuated from local hospitals. To put these numbers in perspective, the total number of people rescued and evacuated by the Coast Guard in the aftermath of Hurricane Katrina nearly equaled the number of people the Coast Guard saves in an entire year![27] In addition to the Coast Guard, 10,000 US Army and Air National Guardsmen and 7,200 active-duty troops were subsequently deployed to the Gulf Coast region to assist with hurricane relief operations.

Approximately 80 percent of New Orleans, primarily residential neighborhoods, flooded during the storm's aftermath. Floodwater depth ranged from one foot to well over ten feet, with some areas approaching twenty feet.[28] Keep in mind that our description of the demographics of Louisiana and Mississippi earlier in our analysis revealed that the poverty rates in these states were over one and a half times larger than the national average, based on the 2000 census data. Many of the areas in New Orleans that suffered the worst effects of the levee failures and flooding were also the poorest neighborhoods, containing the city's most vulnerable residents.

In Louisiana, the death toll from Hurricane Katrina and the levee failures was at least 986. The major causes of death included drowning (40 percent), injury and trauma (25 percent), and heart conditions (11 percent). Nearly half of the Louisiana victims were older than age seventy-four. Katrina damaged more than a million housing units in the Gulf Coast region, about half of them in Louisiana. In New Orleans, 134,000 housing units, about 70 percent of all occupied units, suffered damage from Hurricane Katrina and the subsequent flooding.[29]

While the human toll from the storm was awful, the infrastructure and economic tolls were just as staggering. According to testimony from the director of the Congressional Budget Office (CBO) in late 2005, estimates were that about 25 percent of the total damages occurred in housing, more than 45 percent in business structures and equipment (with half of these being in the energy industry), nearly 20 percent in public infrastructure such as roads, bridges, and sewer systems, and nearly 10 percent in consumer durable goods. The CBO director further reported that the storm destroyed or extensively damaged sixty-six oil-producing structures in the Gulf. All told, Hurricane Katrina and Hurricane Rita (which hit about a month later to the west of the Katrina impact area) disrupted nearly 20 percent of US refining capacity (equivalent to losing 3 million barrels of refining capability per day).[30] Additionally, the extensive oil and gas pipeline network was shut down by the loss of electrical power, producing shortages of natural gas and petroleum products.

Another important part of the economic impact from Hurricane Katrina was the damage to the Gulf region's transportation infrastructure. The storm caused $260 million in damage to the Port of New Orleans, although it was open to ships just a week later.[31] The storm damaged or destroyed key area highway and railroad bridges, resulting in traffic being rerouted and putting increased strain on other routes, particularly other rail lines. Replacement of major infrastructure took from months to years. The CSX Gulf Coast Line was reopened after five months at a cost of $250 million, while the Biloxi–Ocean Springs Bridge took more than two years to reopen. Barge shipping was halted, as was grain export out of the Port of New Orleans. Total recovery

costs for the roads, bridges, and utilities as well as for debris removal was estimated at $15 billion to $17 billion.[32]

Two good-news stories could be found amid all of the infrastructure damage: the redundancy in the region's transportation system, and the storm's timing and track, which helped keep the storm from having major or long-lasting
impacts on national-level freight flows. According to a report from the US
Global Climate Change Research Program, truck traffic was diverted from
the collapsed bridge that carries Interstate 10 over Lake Pontchartrain to Interstate 12, which parallels Interstate 10 well north of the Gulf Coast. The
primary north-south highways that connect the Gulf Coast with major inland
transportation hubs were not damaged, and they had opened for nearly full
commercial freight transportation within days after Katrina hit. The railroads
were able to route some traffic not bound directly for New Orleans through
Memphis and other rail hubs in the Midwest.[33]

Tier 3 of the Model: Security Implications of the Extreme Events for the Gulf Coast

Recall that despite the calls for evacuation, tens of thousands of people stayed
in their residences and heroic rescue efforts were required to save them. As
a result of these rescues and the devastation caused by the levee failures and
flooding in New Orleans, many of these people sought shelter at the Ernest
N. Morial Convention Center and Louisiana Superdome. Evacuees poured
in by the tens of thousands and quickly overwhelmed the facilities' capacity
to support them. By September 1, both facilities were declared unusable as
shelters owing to a lack of adequate sanitary facilities. The same day, Mayor
Nagin issued a "desperate SOS" on national TV for help from the federal
government, saying that there was no food for those who took shelter at the
Superdome and Convention Center, and Governor Blanco ordered a mandatory evacuation of New Orleans.[34]

By the next day (September 2), a convoy of US National Guard troops
and supply trucks arrived in New Orleans and began distributing food and
water to residents stranded at the Superdome and Convention Center. Congress approved $10.5 billion in aid for Hurricane Katrina rescue and relief,
and President Bush signed the bill. The work of repairing the city's levees,
pumping out the floodwaters, and finding homes for tens of thousands of
displaced residents began.[35]

Consider the security implications of having such a large crowd of displaced people confined to such a small area where most of the comforts we

take for granted (food, clean water, sanitary facilities, communications, and accessible medical care) were no longer available. Many media reports circulated in the days following Katrina's landfall about shootings, looting, rapes in the Superdome, and general lawlessness in New Orleans. Some of these stories were true, but most were not. The problem was that Mayor Nagin and Police Superintendent Eddie Compass were telling some of the same stories to the mainstream media, who believed that these public officials had reliable sources.

During the first weeks following Katrina's passage, many media outlets, trying to report from a location that had just been thrown back into the mid-nineteenth century, reported stories that had been transferred multiple times by word of mouth. As it turned out, many of the "sources" for these stories did not witness firsthand the events they described. Eventually, many of these same media outlets recanted these early exaggerated reports. However, amid the rumors and urban legends swirling around the city during this time were some facts: police officers left their jobs without permission, and there was looting, including the acts of desperate people breaking into stores to take whatever food and water they could get for survival.[36]

Tier 3 of the Model: Security Implications of the Extreme Events Beyond the Gulf Coast

By September 2, buses began arriving in New Orleans to take evacuees to other locations in Louisiana and beyond, where adequate shelter could be obtained. Most estimates are that as many as 800,000 people evacuated from the path of Hurricane Katrina. However, in the largest US mass migration since the 1930s Dust Bowl, a significant fraction of that number (between 100,000 and 300,000 Louisianans alone) resettled in other parts of the country and never returned to their original homes. As in other mass migrations, the areas receiving these people had significant challenges in being able to accommodate such a massive influx of people over such a short period of time.

Figure 3.2.4 displays the "Louisiana Diaspora," which shows the locations of displaced residents who applied for federal assistance in the aftermath of Hurricane Katrina. Now consider the regional security implications of having a large number of displaced people dispersed to shelters across the country.

In the months following the Katrina mass migration, stories began to surface about evacuees causing a spike in the crime rate in several cities that took in a large number of people who fled New Orleans after the storm. A case study conducted in 2010 examined crime rates in three cities with a

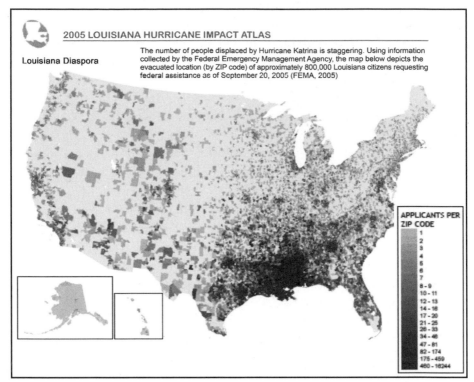

FIGURE 3.2.4: Geographic Depiction of Louisiana Residents Displaced by Hurricane Katrina
Source: "2005 Louisiana Hurricane Impact Atlas," available at: Louisiana Geographic Information Center, http://lagic.lsu.edu/. Data from FEMA (2005).

large number of former New Orleans residents: Houston (whose population increased by 10 percent immediately following Katrina), San Antonio, and Phoenix. Contrary to what had been reported in the media, this study found only modest effects on crime in these three cities. The study acknowledged that communities across the country were faced with substantial challenges associated with absorbing such large numbers of displaced persons. The study showed that while Katrina evacuees had some effect on serious crime in at least two of the three cities examined, those effects were neither widespread (across all crime categories) nor pervasive (across the three cities).[37]

Recalling the demographic data presented in the pre-Katrina portion of the case study gives an indication of the other challenges faced by the communities that took in the large number of evacuees, especially those from New Orleans.

In Houston especially it was noted that because the city took in so many evacuees directly from the Superdome and Convention Center, its population of New Orleans evacuees was more heavily underclass than had been the case in New Orleans itself. This fact was underscored by the extreme financial needs of this displaced population and their attendant physical and mental health problems. Although the Houston experience may not have been typical (and the situation there has actually turned out so well that many individuals have decided to settle there permanently), the human services and public safety sectors of many host communities were simply overwhelmed by the numbers and the rapidity with which they saw their populations change literally overnight.[38]

Conclusions

This case introduced the concept of environmental security and presented a brief history of this multidisciplinary area. We then introduced the cascade model, which describes the sequence following an extreme environmental event, a series of extreme events, a period of anomalous climatic conditions, or a combination of these. The cascade model allows us to analyze the impacts on US security when the natural state of a region is seriously perturbed and to study more than just the natural environmental changes that result. In the Katrina case study presented here, we described the preexisting conditions in the US Gulf Coast region prior to the storm's landfall, including the natural environment, key demographics, industries, and infrastructure that were important in understanding the effects that Katrina had on the region, and especially on the city of New Orleans.

A brief summary of the storm's evolution and discussion of the quality of the forecasts from the National Weather Service was also important in placing the events surrounding Katrina in their proper context. Although the storm predictions were more accurate than average, the urgency of the situation did not become apparent to the most vulnerable residents and local and state officials in the affected region until the storm was twenty-four hours away from making landfall in southeastern Louisiana, at which time tens of thousands of people either were no longer able to evacuate or had never had the means to do so owing to their socioeconomic conditions.

The storm's toll in human, infrastructure, and economic costs was incredible. The US death toll was the largest from a hurricane in seventy-seven years, and the direct economic costs made it the costliest natural disaster in

US history (pending final costs from Hurricane Sandy in 2012). In many respects, the region has still not completely recovered from the damages. The storm displaced more than a million people in the Gulf Coast region. Although many returned home within days, up to 600,000 households were still displaced a month later. At the peak, 273,000 people were housed in hurricane evacuee shelters; later on, FEMA trailers housed at least 114,000 households. In New Orleans, the population fell from an estimated 484,674 (based on April 2000 numbers) to 208,548 (based on a July 2006 estimate), which was a loss of over half the city's population. By July 2011, the population was back up to 360,740, which is still only 74 percent of the 2000 number.[39]

Now consider the national implications of this disaster. Federal spending on the region's recovery has been well over $100 billion, the vast majority of which went toward emergency relief versus rebuilding (see Figure 3.2.4). Some experts believe that the indirect costs top $250 billion when Katrina's impacts on the US petroleum industry are factored into the calculations. This event occurred during a period of relative economic prosperity in the United States and around the world. In the fourth quarter of 2005, gross domestic product (GDP) growth dropped to 1.3 percent, down 2.5 percent from the previous quarter, owing to the losses from petroleum production impacts. By early 2006, however, these numbers had rebounded. The combined damage to petroleum processing from Hurricanes Katrina and Rita caused oil prices to increase by $3 a barrel, and gas prices reached nearly $5 a gallon in some parts of the United States. To stop the escalation in gas prices, the US government released oil from the Strategic Petroleum Reserves.[40] While these national-level impacts were significant, imagine how differently they would have played out if this tragedy had occurred in the midst of the 2008 recession. Would Houston have been able to absorb a 10 percent increase in population consisting of mainly poor and undereducated evacuees in less than a month, during a peak period of unprecedented unemployment and a major housing crisis?

Like the preceding case study on Arctic security, this case points out the major importance of natural environmental considerations for policymakers and planners, whether their strategy concern is homeland security or international security. As we saw with Hurricane Katrina, the environmental consideration can affect many different dimensions of the national picture, from demographics to the economic dimension to infrastructure. For these and many other reasons, planners in the departments of defense, state, and homeland security have included consideration of environmental consequences of global climate change in their long-range planning documents.[41] Indeed, today's strategists, whether they are in the military or work for large companies that deal with risk and uncertainty, such as Lloyd's of London or Munich Re, understand that those who ignore the potential impacts of extreme environmental events or climate change do so at their peril. In the words of former US Army chief of staff General (Ret.) Gordon Sullivan: "We seem to be standing by and, frankly, asking for perfectness in science. . . . We never have 100 percent certainty. We never have it. If you wait until you have 100 percent certainty, something bad is going to happen on the battlefield. That's something we know. You have to act with incomplete information. You have to act based on the trend line. You have to act on your intuition sometimes."[42]

DISCUSSION QUESTIONS

1. How did Hurricane Katrina impact the environmental security of the Gulf Coast region of the United States?
2. What is environmental security, and why is understanding this concept important for homeland security professionals?
3. What are the elements of the cascade model? Do you think this model is an effective tool in analyzing the impacts of extreme environmental events on US security? Why or why not?

NOTES

1. David L. Johnson, "Service Assessment: Hurricane Katrina, August 23–31, 2005" (Washington, DC: National Oceanic and Atmospheric Administration [NOAA], National Weather Service [NWS], June 2006).

2. "The Federal Response to Hurricane Katrina: Lessons Learned" (Washington, DC: The White House, 2006); see also US Senate Committee on Homeland Security and Governmental Affairs, "Hurricane Katrina: A Nation Still Unprepared: Special Report" (Washington, DC: US Senate Committee on Homeland Security and Governmental Affairs, 2006).

3. Richard D. Knabb, Jamie R. Rhome, and Daniel P. Brown, "Tropical Cyclone Report: Hurricane Katrina, August 23–30, 2005" (Miami: National Hurricane Center, 2005).

4. US Senate Committee on Homeland Security and Governmental Affairs, "Hurricane Katrina"; Knabb, Rhome, and Brown, "Tropical Cyclone Report." It is not known at present whether the total costs of Hurricane/"Superstorm" Sandy will exceed those of Katrina, but it is possible.

5. CNA Corporation, "National Security and the Threat of Climate Change" (Alexandria, VA: CNA Corporation, 2007).

6. Norman Myers, "Environmental Security: What's New and Different?" paper presented at The Hague Conference on Environment, Security, and Sustainable Development, The Peace Palace, The Hague, the Netherlands, May 9–12, 2004.

7. W. Chris King, "Understanding International Environmental Security: A Strategic Military Perspective," AEPI-IFP-1100A (Atlanta: Army Environmental Policy Institute, November 2000).

8. John M. Lanicci and James Ramsay, "Environmental Security: Exploring Relationships Between the Natural Environment, National Security, and Homeland Security," Fifth Symposium on Policy and Socioeconomic Research, American Meteorological Society, Atlanta, January 18–21, 2010.

9. Geoffrey D. Dabelko and P. J. Simmons, "Environment and Security: Core Ideas and US Government Initiatives," *SAIS Review* (Winter–Spring 1997): 127–146; see also William H. Mansfield, "The Evolution of Environmental Security in a North American Policy Context," *The Environment Times,* September 2, 2004, United Nations Environmental Program, Grid-Arendal, Arendal, Norway.

10. See, for example, Thomas E. Homer-Dixon, *Environment, Scarcity, and Violence* (Princeton, NJ: Princeton University Press, 1999).

11. CNA Corporation, "National Security and the Threat of Climate Change"; Kurt M. Campbell, Jay Gulledge, J. R. McNeill, John Podesta, Peter Odgen, Leon Fuerth, R. James Woolsey, Alexander T. J. Lennon, Julianne Smith, Richard Weitz, and Derek Mix, *The Age of Consequences: The Foreign Policy and National Security Implications of Global Climate Change* (Washington, DC: Center for Strategic and International Studies and Center for a New American Security, November 2007); Joshua W. Busby, "Climate Change and National Security: An Agenda for Action," Council Special Report 32 (New York: Council on Foreign Relations, November 2007); The High Representative and the European Commission, "Climate Change and International Security," S113/08, paper presented to the European Council, Brussels, Belgium, March 14, 2008.

12. Zhu H. Ning, R. Eugene Turner, Thomas Doyle, and Kamran Abdollahi, "Integrated Assessment of the Climate Change Impacts on the Gulf Coast Region: Findings of the Gulf Coast Regional Assessment" (Baton Rouge, LA: GCRCC, June 2003), 9–13.

13. "CensusScope: Your Portal to Census Data," http://www.censusscope.org/.

14. Louisiana Department of Administration (Louisiana DOA), http://doa.louisiana.gov/doa/ (accessed December 1, 2012).

15. American Society of Civil Engineers, "The New Orleans Hurricane Protection System: What Went Wrong and Why: A Report by the American Society of Civil En-

gineers Hurricane Katrina External Review Panel" (Reston, VA: American Society of Civil Engineers, 2007).

16. Louisiana DOA website.

17. Agricultural and industrial information from e-ReferenceDesk, "Mississippi Economy: Agriculture and Industry in Mississippi," http://www.e-referencedesk.com /resources/state-economy/mississippi.html (accessed December 1, 2012).

18. Louisiana DOA website.

19. James T. B. Tripp, Senior Counsel, Environmental Defense Fund, background statement to the meeting of the Gulf Coast Restoration Task Force, Galveston, TX, June 27, 2011.

20. Knabb, Rhome, and Brown, "Tropical Cyclone Report."

21. Ibid.; see also Willie Drye, "Hurricane Katrina: The Essential Timeline," *National Geographic News,* August 23, 2005, http://news.nationalgeographic.com/news/2005 /09/0914_050914_katrina_timeline.html (accessed December 1, 2012).

22. Knabb, Rhome, and Brown, "Tropical Cyclone Report."

23. Ibid.

24. Johnson, "Service Assessment: Hurricane Katrina, August 23–31, 2005."

25. C. H. Hauser and T. J. Lueck, "Mandatory Evacuation Ordered for New Orleans as Storm Nears," *New York Times,* August 28, 2005.

26. American Society of Civil Engineers, "The New Orleans Hurricane Protection System."

27. Scott Price, "The US Coast Guard and Hurricane Katrina: The Coast Guard's Katrina Documentation Project," http://www.uscg.mil/history/katrina/docs/karthistory .asp (accessed December 2, 2012).

28. Allison Plyer, "News Release—Facts for Features: Hurricane Katrina Impact," Greater New Orleans Community Data Center, August 10, 2012.

29. Ibid.

30. Douglas Holtz-Eakin, "Macroeconomic and Budgetary Effects of Hurricanes Katrina and Rita," testimony of the director of the Congressional Budget Office before the House Committee on the Budget, October 6, 2005.

31. Kimberly Amadeo, "About.com: How Much Did Hurricane Katrina Damage the US Economy?" http://useconomy.about.com/od/grossdomesticproduct/f/katrina _damage.htm (accessed December 2, 2012). Note that her report includes the impacts from Hurricane Rita, which also affected US petroleum production owing to where it hit.

32. Thomas R. Karl, Jerry M. Melillo, and Thomas C. Peterson, eds., *Global Climate Change Impacts in the United States* (Cambridge: Cambridge University Press, 2009).

33. Ibid.

34. Drye, "Hurricane Katrina: The Essential Timeline."

35. Ibid.

36. Henry W. Fischer, Kathryn Gregoire, John Scala, Lynn Letukas, Joseph Mellon, Scott Romine, and Danielle Turner, "Quick Response Report: The Emergency Management Response to Hurricane Katrina: As Told by the First Responders—A Case Study of What Went Wrong and Recommendations for the Future" (Millersville: Millersville University of Pennsylvania, Center for Disaster Research and Education, 2006); see also Brian Thevenot, "Myth-making in New Orleans," *American Journalism Review* (December–January 2006), http://www.ajr.org/article.asp?id=3998 (accessed December 2, 2012).

37. S. P. Varano, J. A. Schafer, J. M. Cancino, S. H. Decker, and J. R. Greene, "A Tale of Three Cities: Crime and Displacement After Hurricane Katrina," *Journal of Criminal Justice* 38 (2010): 42–50.

38. N. Gelinas, "Houston's Noble Experiment," *City Journal* (Spring 2006).

39. Plyer, "News Release—Facts for Features."

40. Amadeo, "How Much Did Hurricane Katrina Damage the US Economy?"

41. See, for example, the 2010 *Quadrennial Defense Review,* the 2010 *Quadrennial Homeland Security Review,* and the 2010 *Quadrennial Diplomacy and Development Review.*

42. CNA Corporation, "National Security and the Threat of Climate Change."

PART II

Operational Challenges in Homeland Security

Following the terrorist attacks on the United States on September 11, 2001, President George W. Bush began to mobilize and organize the federal government as well as the nation to secure the homeland from future terrorist attacks. Organizing and leading a national effort in homeland security is an exceedingly complex mission that requires coordinated and focused effort from the entire society—state and local governments, the federal government, the private sector, and the American people. The first *National Strategy for Homeland Security* (2002) served as the first strategic document after 9/11 that not only provided direction to federal government departments and agencies with a role in homeland security but also suggested steps that state and local governments, businesses, and individuals could take to improve our security.

Although not intended to be a roadmap, the *National Strategy for Homeland Security* gave academic homeland security its first hints of what to teach by identifying six critical mission areas: intelligence and warning, border and transportation security, domestic counterterrorism, defending against catastrophic terrorism, protecting critical infrastructure, and emergency preparedness and response. Extending earlier work and definitions, the 2010

Quadrennial Homeland Security Review highlights the need for continued vigilance in these same mission areas while also placing new focus on complex and emergent threats emanating from climate change, resource conflicts, mass migration, etc., and a renewed sense of emphasis on preparedness, resilience, and environmental security.

Part II includes four chapters on these initial mission areas: intelligence (Chapter 4), critical infrastructure protection (Chapter 5), transportation security (Chapter 6), and emergency management (Chapter 7). The cases in these chapters highlight the vast domain and complexity of the homeland security enterprise. The sheer number of agencies and organizations, stakeholders, policies, and conceptual issues to consider in each of these mission areas may be overwhelming. We offer a broad range of cases in the chapters ahead as a means of providing a holistic review of some of the more operational aspects of the growing homeland security enterprise. For homeland security students and faculty, taking note of a more holistic perspective and its interconnected mission areas allows better recognition of the inherent relationships and possible synergies between the public and private sectors, as well as the dependencies between them. Part II also addresses the implications for policy and operations.

Taken as a whole, Parts I and II of this casebook cover many practical examples of what the homeland security enterprise is maturing into, and where it is likely to be going.

CHAPTER 4

Intelligence

The Central Intelligence Agency (CIA) has primary responsibility for intelligence collection and analysis, which is critical for providing information on asymmetric threats (terrorists) to US national security. The process of collecting and analyzing information is at the heart of counterterrorist intelligence. An optimal outcome of this type of intelligence is the ability to anticipate the behavior of terrorists and thereby predict terrorist incidents. Thus, it was not a surprise that following the attacks on September 11, 2001, the intelligence community was excoriated for failing to connect the dots that could have prevented the attacks and for a lack of imagination.[1] The *9/11 Commission Report* highlights the struggles faced by the intelligence community throughout the 1990s and up to 9/11 to collect intelligence on and analyze the phenomenon of transnational terrorism. The report states, "The combination of an overwhelming number of priorities, flat budgets, an outmoded structure, and bureaucratic rivalries resulted in an insufficient response to this new challenge."[2] While the report recognizes that many dedicated intelligence officers worked day and night for years to understand the threat posed by Al-Qaeda and wrote many reports on Osama bin Laden, "there was no comprehensive review of what the intelligence community knew and what it did not know, and what that meant."[3] Furthermore, prior to 9/11 the CIA had minimal capacity to conduct paramilitary operations with its own personnel and had limited capability to collect intelligence from human agents.[4] Even with these limitations, by late 1996 bin Laden was on the CIA's radar screen as someone who could pose a serious threat to US interests and national security, and in Afghanistan he had become one of two major intelligence collection targets—the other being the Taliban.

The first case study in this chapter, "The Attack on Mumbai, India," analyzes the preparation and planning of the terrorist organization responsible for this attack, using the US Army's terrorist operational planning cycle as a guide. This case not only highlights the critical role that tactical intelligence plays in planning such an operation but also shows areas of vulnerability that can be exploited by the intelligence and law enforcement communities to prevent such attacks from occurring. Unless intelligence or security organizations have a source inside a group that is planning an attack or manage to intercept the group's communication, the only way to identify attack planners is by noting their actions before the actual attack occurs. For example, attackers may be identified by their actions during the preoperational surveillance required for target identification as well as during the surveillance they conduct at later stages. In addition, during the planning phase and as the operatives prepare to deploy, communication and movement between group members often increases in detectable ways. Group members may also engage in outside training that can attract attention, such as visiting a firing range or, as was the case with the 9/11 pilots, attending flight schools. Such increases in activity, which also might include money transfers and weapons purchases, leave signs that can tip off law enforcement agencies and provide more information for the intelligence community on a possible threat. However, it is important that this intelligence be shared between national intelligence agencies and between the CIA and FBI if they are to be truly effective in preventing attacks.

After 9/11, President Bush ordered the CIA to increase the number of human operations officers by 50 percent to meet the challenges presented by transnational terrorism.[5] However, as the second case in this chapter, "Using a Principal Agent in Intelligence Collection in Afghanistan," highlights, it is very difficult to penetrate terrorist networks. It takes time to recruit, investigate, train, and deploy new clandestine officers, particularly ones with the diverse backgrounds and language skills necessary to operate effectively in the Muslim world. Furthermore, it is riskier, more costly, and more time-consuming to put clandestine officers under the deep cover required to improve recruitment of terrorist informants and agents. The challenges of intelligence collection are highlighted in this case as it discusses the intelligence cycle and how it applies to the special circumstances in Afghanistan, the concept of intelligence collection, and where the principal agent fits into the six phases of the agent acquisition cycle, using Afghanistan as a backdrop.

NOTES

1. National Commission of the Terrorist Attack upon the United States, The 9/11 Commission Report: Executive Summary, 9, http://govinfo.library.unt.edu/911/report /911Report_Exec.pdf.

2. Ibid., 12.

3. Ibid.

4. Ibid., 10.

5. Robert Vickers, "Intelligence Reform: Problems and Prospects," Breakthroughs 14, no. 1 (2005): 6.

The Attack on Mumbai, India

STEVE YOUNG

A t approximately 8:00 PM on November 26, 2008, two motorized rubber boats containing ten men belonging to the terrorist group Lashkar-e-Taiba (LET) landed on the southern tip of the peninsula jutting into the Arabian Sea that is home to nearly 21 million citizens of the city of Mumbai, formerly known as Bombay. Armed with small arms (AK-47s and pistols), hand grenades, and improvised explosive devices (IEDs), they proceeded up the peninsula conducting their terrorist attacks. By 8:00 AM on November 29, Indian Rapid Action Force personnel, Marine commandos, and National Security Guard forces had killed nine of the attackers and captured Pakistani citizen Ajmal Kasab. However, the terrorists had succeeded in killing at least 173 persons and wounding at least another 300. It was India's worst terrorist attack in terms of casualties and is often equated by Indians with the September 11, 2001, attack suffered by the United States.

The purpose of this case study is to describe this event and examine the preparation and planning that made the attack successful. The case utilizes the US Army's "terrorist operational planning cycle" as a guide to explain how the attack was formulated and emphasizes the critical role of tactical intelligence in planning such an operation.[1]

Before describing the events of the Mumbai attack, we offer a brief discussion of intelligence, which means different things to different people depending on the context. There are many kinds of intelligence—economic intelligence, business intelligence, and cultural intelligence, to name a few—but within the US intelligence community the word "intelligence" refers simply to information that is collected by a variety of methods, including human sources, photographs taken by satellites, and electronically intercepted conversations. Each of these sources of information is turned into intelligence by analysts trained in their particular fields to put perspective on the intelligence and offer insights into the information it provides about a particular issue. Mark Lowenthal said plainly that information is anything that can be known, but intelligence refers to information that is collected in response to a particular intelligence requirement and then analyzed.[2] Succinctly put, all intelligence is information, but not all information is intelligence. Moreover, not all intelligence is classified information: a component called open source intelligence (OSINT) is available to anyone who can read a newspaper, the Internet, or a journal article.

There are different kinds of intelligence as well. Military intelligence normally focuses on matters such as troop movements, weapons capabilities, and information on an enemy's plans and intentions. Moreover, the military collects strategic intelligence, which is big-picture-type information that may be important to military strategists or planners but is not particularly useful to troops on the ground. The Pentagon's official definition of "strategic intelligence" includes intelligence that is required for the formulation of strategy, policy, and military plans and operations at the national and theater levels. "Tactical intelligence" refers to calculated moves that follow a methodical line of thinking and action that includes both offensive and defensive measures and countermeasures. Tactical intelligence encompasses every activity from the initial thoughts about a potential operation to its logical conclusion and every planning element in between.[3] Tactical intelligence is essential to the war fighter. It is also essential to a terrorist planning an operation.

The Terrorist Operational Planning Cycle

George Habash, founder of the terrorist group Popular Front for the Liberation of Palestine, once said, "The main point is to select targets where success is 100 percent assured." Truer words have never been spoken. In the Mumbai case, several targets were selected and the attack was planned based on what the US Army calls the terrorist operational planning cycle:

1. Broad target selection
2. Intelligence and surveillance
3. Specific target selection
4. Pre-attack surveillance and planning
5. Attack rehearsal
6. Actions on the objective (the attack)
7. Escape, evasion, and exploitation

Although the success of the Mumbai attack is, from a terrorist perspective, well documented, it is the operational planning that went into the operation that is most interesting from a tactician's or intelligence perspective because, as noted in the IRA handbook: "Information gathering is a continuous operation."[4] For example, planning for the September 11, 2001, attacks on the United States began in either late 1998 or early 1999 when Osama bin Laden gave Khalid Sheikh Mohammed final approval to begin planning in earnest.[5] What is unique about the Mumbai operation is that target selection and surveillance were not conducted by any of the terrorist perpetrators, but by the American citizen Daood Gilani, aka David Headley.

Terrorist Operational Planning, Phase 1: Broad Target Selection

In the broad target selection phase, potential targets are selected based on their symbolic value, their vulnerability to attack, the expected number of casualties, and their publicity value. The targets chosen in this phase may fit one or all of these criteria, and most of this initial research can be accomplished using open source information such as the Internet and various print media. In this phase, the planners become familiar with the area and the so-called soft or less protected targets within the area, such as hotels and shopping malls.

It is unclear from news reports why the terrorists chose Mumbai as the target city, but one can imagine that it was chosen because it is India's commercial, financial, and entertainment center. Moreover, it is located on the Arabian Sea and therefore provides access to invaders from the sea. A successful attack on the city by a limited number of terrorists would strike a psychological blow to the city's citizens and create a significant number of potential casualties because of the large presence of foreign and local businesses, government, and tourists.

The Perfect Terrorist

In order to analyze the Mumbai case, it is critical to understand Daood Gilani, aka David Headley, and how he came to be an almost perfect selection to conduct surveillance and select the targets for this attack. Headley was born Daood Sayed Gilani on June 30, 1960, to his American mother, Sherrill Headley, and Pakistani father, Syed Saleem Gilani, who worked in Washington, DC, as a broadcaster for the Voice of America. Gilani grew up in Karachi, Pakistan, after his parents divorced. Here he became extremely nationalistic (Pakistani) and anti-Indian. In his late teens, Gilani returned to the United States and lived with his mother in Philadelphia, where he was employed at the Khyber Pass Pub, owned by his mother. Gilani returned to Pakistan several times and delved into drugs. In 1988 German police arrested him in Frankfurt trying to smuggle two kilograms of heroin into the United States. Gilani served only four years in prison after US Drug Enforcement Agency (DEA) agents offered him a deal to cooperate against his two partners, who received heavier sentences.[6]

In 1997 DEA agents again arrested Gilani, who, as a result, became a paid confidential informant. This incident is crucial to the case because the DEA then assigned him to travel to Pakistan, which gave Gilani a reason to consort with drug dealers. However, he ran afoul of the law again and served an additional eight months in prison. While in prison, Gilani allegedly became a devout Muslim and, unknown to the DEA, a radical Islamist. In 2000 Gilani again traveled to Pakistan under DEA control, but during this trip he discovered Lashkar-e-Taiba, whose radical Islamist ideology and anti-Indian manifesto appealed to him. Eventually, Gilani was introduced to LET founder Hafiz Mohammad Saeed, who recruited Gilani for the Islamist cause. Unbeknownst to the DEA, Gilani made several additional trips to Pakistan during 2000 and early 2001 to meet with LET operatives.[7]

After September 11, 2001, the DEA had Gilani travel to Pakistan several times to search out Pakistani drug dealers and also infiltrate terrorist groups. It is unclear how many of these trips were actually sanctioned or paid for by the DEA. Nevertheless, in February 2002, at the same time he was possibly working for the DEA, Gilani began attending LET training camps. According to his plea agreement, he received additional LET training in August 2002 and in April, August, and December 2003.[8] Though Gilani's activities between 2003 and 2006 are not very well documented, it is known that in January 2006 he met Major Iqbal (probably an alias), a Pakistani representative of the Inter-Services Intelligence (ISI) directorate, the Pakistani intelligence equivalent of the CIA; Iqbal recruited Gilani to spy for Pakistan and to also continue working with the terrorist group LET. In February 2006, Gilani flew to Philadelphia, where he began the process of changing his official name to David Headley (his mother's maiden name) from Daood Gilani. In terms of the spy game, this was an important event because now Headley would be able to travel on his US passport as a tourist and his Westernized name would not tend to raise any official suspicions about his international travel, especially when crossing the Pakistani border into India. When he returned to Pakistan from the United States, Major Iqbal began training Headley for his surveillance duties in Mumbai.[9]

Terrorist Operational Planning Phase 2: Intelligence Gathering and Surveillance

The second phase of the terrorist operational planning cycle following broad target selection is intelligence gathering and surveillance. In the Mumbai case, this was most likely accomplished principally by LET operatives in conjunction with Pakistani ISI. Once these initial targets were identified, Headley was sent to Mumbai to determine the feasibility of the targets in the context of the planned operational activity. This classic intelligence-gathering phase can be either short or lengthy, and it may include topics such as determining security measures at the intended target site and transportation and travel routes for the attackers. In the Mumbai case, the attackers needed to divide themselves into groups of two to three persons, travel up the Mumbai peninsula, and find their various targets. Use of GPS and video surveillance then became essential to the surveillance phase of the operation, and Headley performed this task well. In fact, when engaged in surveillance activities throughout the city, Headley stayed frequently at what was eventually a prime target, the Taj Mahal Palace Hotel, where he went on in-house tours and took photographs and shot surveillance videos. By the time he finished his surveillance at this location, he had documented almost every square inch of the hotel (See Photo 4.1.1).[10]

PHOTO 4.1.1: Taj Mahal Palace Hotel.
Source: Ashok Duraphe, Final Report Mumbai Cases, 26 November, 2008, February 2, 2009, www.hindu.com/nic/mumbai-terror-attack-final-form.pdf.

Terrorist Operational Planning Phase 3: Specific Target Selection

According to the US Army's terrorist operational planning cycle, reviewing the broad range of targets (phase 1) and conducting the initial surveillance (phase 2) are followed by selecting specific targets for the attack (phase 3). Criteria to consider when selecting specific targets are:

1. Does success affect a larger audience than the immediate victims?
2. Will the target attract high-profile media attention?
3. Does success make the desired statement to the correct target audience?
4. Is the effect consistent with the objectives of the group?
5. Does the target provide an advantage to the group by demonstrating its capabilities?

In the Mumbai case, most if not all of the targets eventually selected fit these criteria. The final targets were the Taj Mahal Palace Hotel, the Leopold Café, Nariman House (the Mumbai Chabad House, which is a Jewish community center), the Chhatrapati Shivaji Terminus (CST) train station, and the Oberoi-Trident Hotel. The Oberoi was considered a target of opportunity because it had not been on Headley's original list of potential targets; however, he took an opportunity to videotape the hotel, and it was eventually selected for the attack.[11]

Trying to draw conclusions about how the LET and/or ISI made their final target selections is difficult at best. However, in the context of the criteria cited here, the targets seem appropriate. The fact that Mumbai, in one of the world's most populated countries, itself has nearly 22 million people guarantees immediate publicity, which is what terrorist groups like LET thrive on.[12] Without media coverage, the event would never get noticed, nor would the terrorist group's political message be conveyed to the general public. This certainly satisfies the first criterion. With respect to the second criterion, the two hotels attacked are among the largest in the city and traditionally host many foreigners. It can be assumed that these hotels were chosen for maximum casualties. The Jewish community center appears to have been a target because of the traditional animosity between Muslims and Jews. The Leopold Café is a popular restaurant and bar hangout for foreigners as well as locals. Finally, the CST train station was an excellent target because of the large number of Indian passengers present in the terminal.

Criteria three and four can be addressed by understanding LET's ideological manifesto, which states that its members' Muslim religion is overwhelmingly their ideological motivator.[13] Moreover, the individuals who founded the group were opposed to Indian sovereignty in Kashmir. In fact, Indian-held Kashmir was the primary focus of LET's attacks for the first few years after its founding sometime around 1990. In December 2001, LET conducted its first operation in India proper by attacking the Indian Parliament building in New Delhi.[14] This was followed by a bomb attack in Mumbai in August 2003, and additional bomb attacks in New Delhi in 2005.[15] The stated reason for these incursions onto Indian soil was to establish Islamic rule throughout India. Taken together, including the Mumbai attack of 2008, these attacks certainly satisfy the group's stated ideological objectives.

Criterion five is fulfilled because the attack itself demonstrated the operational reach of LET and the planning capabilities of the group as it took advantage of an apparent Western tourist (Headley) to perform the surveillance. Although nine of the ten terrorists were killed by Indian security forces, the attack itself could be seen by other terrorist groups and potential recruits as a success. It achieved the goal of taking the fight to the Indians directly, much as Al-Qaeda did to the United States on September 11, 2001. Any terror attack creates apprehension in the population, and this one reverberated throughout major Indian population centers because it clearly showed that the Indian security forces were unable to protect the general population. The Indian public became outraged when it took nearly three days for government forces to subdue ten terrorists, and the Indian minister for home affairs (responsible for border and internal Security) was forced to resign.

Terrorist Operational Planning Phase 4: Pre-attack Surveillance and Planning

Pre-attack surveillance and planning is normally accomplished by members of the attack team just prior to the attack in order to confirm previously supplied surveillance information and to make necessary adjustments to either the plan itself or even the targets. It is advantageous to have a surrogate conduct the intelligence collection and target surveillance because that reduces the operational team's exposure to possible detection by local security forces. But the operational team eventually has to become intimately familiar with the targets and gain a certain comfort level by conducting their own "eyes-on" surveillance. In this manner, team members can make planning adjustments in accordance with their individual skill sets. This is fine-tuning the operational planning. At this point, the Mumbai case deviates significantly from the textbook phase 4 planning.

As previously stated, in the Mumbai case David Headley conducted the surveillance for the ten Pakistani terrorists. In fact, Headley made trips to Mumbai to conduct surveillance in September 2006, February and September 2007, and April and June 2008. On each occasion, posing as a tourist, he took extensive videos that he delivered back to his LET and ISI handlers in Pakistan for analysis.[16] He did not learn of the planned assault from the sea until just before his April 2008 travel to Mumbai, when potential landing sites were discussed. After arriving in Mumbai in April, Headley identified the various landing sites using GPS by traveling by boat to each one so he could further describe and discuss the sites upon his return to Pakistan.

Terrorist Operational Planning Phase 5: Rehearsals

Rehearsals are crucial to the success of any military operation, and it is also true with planned terrorist attacks. Generally speaking, the more familiar the operator is with the target, the greater chance his mission will be successful. A typical rehearsal situation includes:

1. Equipment and weapons training and performance
2. General area familiarization and physical layouts of the targets and surrounding area
3. Designing and testing escape routes

Because the ten terrorists were from Pakistan, they had no opportunity to get "eyes on" the targets until they actually arrived on-site. However, with the videos supplied by Headley and Google Earth satellite overhead imagery, they were able to greatly familiarize themselves with the five targets. In addition, they were able to hone their seafaring skills while in Pakistan and familiarize themselves with the rubber boats used to transport them ashore in Mumbai.

Terrorist Operational Planning Phase 6: Actions on the Objective

Phase 6, "actions on the objective," is the kinetic or action phase of the attack. If their planning has been meticulous and detailed, the terrorists' chances of success are great. By this time terrorists are well prepared and focused on their individual tasks and have significant advantages over local security forces: the capacity to seize the initiative and the element of surprise. The actions and locations of enemy security forces have been accounted for and relatively neutralized at the initial attack phase by the plan simply to avoid them as long as possible.

At this phase, if no one expects an attack, the element of surprise is the first of several advantages of the perpetrators. In the Mumbai case, the element of surprise worked well for the attackers because they came to Mumbai in rubber dinghies after having begun their journey in Karachi, Pakistan, hijacked an Indian fishing trawler, and killed the captain. The element of surprise, besides causing significant tactical problems for the security services, also creates psychological problems for the general public following the attack. The psychological impression left by a group of terrorists on a general population cannot be overstated. The public is left with a feeling of helplessness when it seems that their government cannot provide basic security functions. If this impression remains, it can lead to a general distrust in the government and a paranoid population.

Second, terrorists have the advantage in being able to choose the time, place, and conditions of attack. If no one expects that something is coming, then there is no defensive preparation and the terrorists have the advantage of choosing the ideal conditions to complete their objectives. In this case, all of the facilities attacked were soft targets that were largely unguarded. In places where there were security forces, the terrorists' reconnaissance had informed them that those forces would be only lightly armed and easily overcome.[17]

Third, terrorists can employ diversions. Even in the case of a vehicle-borne-improvised-explosive-device (VBIED), there is usually more than one bomb that responders have to deal with. It is not uncommon to have one bomb detonate only to have a second bomb detonate minutes later in order to cause more casualties. In the Mumbai case, there were no diversions. Each terrorist had an objective, and by all accounts they located and concentrated their individual attacks on their objectives.

All things look different at night, even if one is familiar with an area in the daylight. In the Mumbai case, attacking at night created more confusion within the population and security services than a daytime attack. It also provided a degree of cover and concealment for the terrorists. Having landed their rubber boats at approximately 8:00 PM on November 26, 2008, the terrorists split up and began their attacks (see Map 4.1.1).

At approximately 9:30 PM, two members of the LET team, including Ajmal Kasab, attacked the Chhatrapati Shivaji Terminus train station. By the time this assault ended at about 10:45 PM, 58 people had been killed and 104 others wounded. Shortly after the attack, Kasab was captured alive and his co-perpetrator was killed by Indian security forces. At approximately the same time the CST was being attacked, the Leopold Café was assaulted by another two-man team. Approximately ten people were killed there while having coffee and tea. The terrorists spent little time there and sprayed the café with AK-47 automatic weapons fire before moving on to assist in the takeover of the two major hotels, the Taj Mahal and the Oberoi. Meanwhile, Nariman House, the Chabad House Jewish community center, was taken

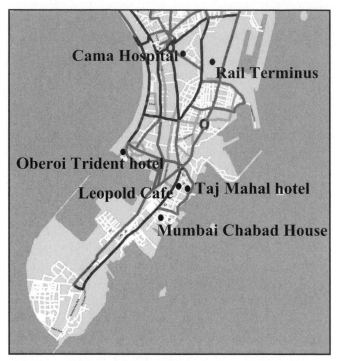

MAP 4.1.1: The Mumbai Attacks

Location of the five principal targets of the LET terrorists in Mumbai as well as the principal hospital where most of the dead and wounded were transported. Two terrorists also briefly attacked the Cama Hospital but there were no casualties there. The attacks lasted November 26–29, 2008.

Source: Creative Commons.

over by two additional terrorists, and thirteen residents of the center were held hostage, five of whom were subsequently murdered. According to transcripts of phone calls between the terrorists and their handlers during the attack, terrorists at the Chabad House were instructed to kill their Jewish hostages in order to "spoil relations between India and Israel."[18]

It is clear that this was a complicated, multipart operation. By dispersing into separate teams and moving from target to target, the terrorists were able to sow confusion and create the impression of a greater number of attackers.[19] During the second day of the attack, the five-story Nariman House was stormed by Indian commandos. By late evening of November 28, both terrorists and a commando had been killed during the assault. The terrorists also murdered Rabbi Gavriel Holtzberg and his wife Rivka Holtzberg, who was six months pregnant, along with four other hostages.[20]

The sequence of events at the Taj Mahal Palace and Oberoi-Trident Hotels is less clear than the sequence at the other attack sites, presumably because so many witnesses made for conflicting reports. Nevertheless, it can be assumed from the official record that the attacks on the two hotels were conducted nearly simultaneously and began at approximately 11:00 PM on November 26. Four terrorists assaulted the Taj Mahal, and two assaulted the Oberoi. At the Oberoi, the two-man team killed people indiscriminately as they moved from the dining room to each floor. At least thirteen diners in the Oberoi were killed, including thirteen-year-old Naomi Sherr, who was having dinner with her father, who was also killed.[21] Terrorists then made their way onto the various floors, looking for targets of opportunity. At the Taj Mahal Palace Hotel, the four terrorists walked through the grounds and first floor of the hotel, killing along the way, then moved to the upper floors, setting fires and moving constantly in order to confuse and delay government commandos.

Indian security forces arrived first at the Taj Mahal at approximately midnight on the 26th and fought with the terrorists throughout the night while evacuating as many hotel guests and staff as possible. Fighting continued throughout November 27 and 28. In the early morning hours on November 29, it was reported that the Taj Mahal Palace Hotel was under the control of Indian security forces. However, not all terrorists were accounted for, and at 7:30 AM Indian commandos discovered the last remaining terrorist and killed him in a gun battle. It was not until 8:00 AM on November 29 that the Taj Mahal Palace Hotel was secured, with 31 hotel guests and staff having been killed in the attack and approximately 250 surviving it.[22]

Security forces did not arrive at the Oberoi until approximately 6:00 AM on November 27, when they immediately began to assault the building. The terrorists retreated to the upper floors and began detonating hand grenades, which set the roof on fire and trapped a number of hotel guests. Fighting continued throughout the day and night of the 27th, but by midmorning of the 28th many hostages had been rescued. By approximately 3:00 PM, Indian security forces had killed both terrorists. Thirty hostages had been killed and 140 people rescued. Many foreigners were killed in the five attacks, including six American citizens. Of the 173 persons killed during the three-day attack, 138 were Indian citizens, most of whom were killed at the train station.[23]

Terrorist Operational Planning Phase 7: Escape, Evasion, and Exploitation

Escape plans are usually well rehearsed and executed as part of the overall operational plan. The exception to the rule is the suicide operation, which depends only on the willingness of the terrorists to die while achieving their objective. In the Mumbai case, there was no evidence that the terrorists had a planned escape route or weapons caches, so it can be concluded that they were on a suicide mission.

One of the chief objectives of the terrorist mission is exploitation: the point at which a group normally takes responsibility for an attack and makes self-serving statements about its cause. Publicity adds strategic value to the operation. All terrorist groups seek this attention for their mission and their cause in order to attract recruits and, more importantly, acquire additional funding. In the Mumbai case, however, because the terrorists were acting on behalf of LET and the group was allegedly supported by elements of ISI, the Pakistani intelligence services, it is likely that the Pakistani government was not interested in any publicity.[24] It was not until Ajmal Kasab, the lone survivor, was interrogated that LET and Pakistani involvement was determined. Presumably, the Pakistanis were not pleased that Kasab had been captured alive because Pakistani support for the operation, although suspected, was then confirmed by the Indians. Kasab was convicted of eighty-six counts of murder in an Indian court and sentenced to death on May 6, 2010. On April 25, 2012, his death sentence was upheld by the Indian Supreme Court.[25]

The Aftermath of the November 26, 2008, Mumbai Attacks

During his interrogation, Ajmal Kasab provided many of the operational details of the attacks, including the detailed operational phases described in this case. Together with information supplied by David Headley, Indian and US authorities were able to piece together a timetable of events as well as the details of Headley's surveillance. Indian citizens reacted strongly to the attacks on their city, and many Indian security officials were severely criticized. As a result, the Indian minister for home affairs (responsible for border and internal security) and two other top officials from this agency resigned, as did other officials responsible for security within the city. Further, security was increased at all hotels that catered to foreigners.

On the political level, relations between Pakistan and India, never very positive, reached new lows. Pakistan had previously outlawed LET because of the group's previous involvement in terrorist incidents, but continued to allow it to operate. In fact, in early April 2012, the US government offered a $10 million reward for the capture of Hafiz Mohammad Saeed, founder of LET. The day following the announcement, Saeed gave a press conference in Pakistan's capital, Islamabad, demonstrating his freedom of movement and quasi-official Pakistani government support.[26]

As for David Headley, in 2010 the US government accepted a plea agreement after he pled guilty to all federal terrorism-related charges. According to the terms of the plea agreement, the US attorney general agreed not to seek the death penalty against Headley as long as he continued to cooperate with federal officials. Interestingly, Headley's sentencing has been deferred until after the conclusion of his cooperation.[27] This allows Headley to remain in US custody indefinitely and avoid extradition to India, where he would be likely to face the death penalty.

DISCUSSION QUESTIONS

1. In this case, we discussed the November 26, 2008, terrorist attacks on Mumbai, India, in the context of the terrorist operational planning cycle, from broad target selection to escape and exploitation. The Mumbai operation carried out by ten terrorists from Pakistan deviated, however, in several aspects from the "textbook" application of the terrorist operational planning cycle. Describe these deviations and discuss why they were or were not necessary to the Mumbai operation's success.

2. In what ways did the operation satisfy LET's ideology?

3. Discuss the potential for long-term political animosity between Pakistan and India as a result of the 2008 Mumbai operation, and why.

4. Do you believe the operation could be considered a success? Why or why not?

NOTES

1. US Army Training and Doctrine Command, TRADOC Intelligence Support Activity–Threats, *A Military Guide to Terrorism in the Twenty-First Century*, US Army TRADOC G2 Handbook No. 1 (Fort Leavenworth, KS: US Department of the Army, August 15, 2007).

2. Mark Lowenthal, *Intelligence: From Secrets to Policy* (Los Angeles: Congressional Quarterly Press, 2012), 5.

3. Kevin Fenning, "Strategic vs. Tactical Intelligence," Hub Pages, posted December 19, 2011, http://kevinfenning.hubpages.com/hub/Strategic-vs-Tactical-Intelligence (accessed April 7, 2012).

4. *Handbook for Volunteers of the Irish Republican Army: Notes on Guerrilla Warfare* (New York: Paladin Press, 1985).

5. National Commission on Terrorist Attacks upon the United States, *The 9/11 Commission Report: Final Report of the National Commission on Terrorist Attacks upon the United States* (New York: W. W. Norton, 2004).

6. Sebastian Rotella, "The American Behind India's 9/11—And How US Botched Chances to Stop Him," ProPublica, November 22, 2011, http://www.propublica.org/article/david-headley-homegrown-terrorist (accessed April 4, 2012), 1–6.

7. "A Perfect Terrorist," Frontline/ProPublica, November 22, 2011, http://www.pbs.org/wgbh/pages/frontline/david-headley/ (accessed April 4, 2012).

8. US Department of Justice, Office of Public Affairs, "Chicago Resident David Coleman Headley Pleads Guilty to Role in India and Denmark Terrorism Conspiracies," March 18, 2010, http://www.justice.gov/opa/pr/2010/March/10-ag-277.html (accessed April 4, 2012).

9. Rotella, "The American Behind India's 9/11."

10. Ibid.

11. Ibid.

12. "Profile: Lashkar-e-Taiba," BBC News, May 30, 2010, http://news.bbc.co.uk/2/hi/south_asia/3181925.stm (accessed July 30, 2012).

13. Gus Martin, *Understanding Terrorism*, 2nd ed. (Thousand Oaks, CA: Sage, 2006), 199–201.

14. "Profile: Lashkar-e-Taiba," BBC News.

15. Kainaat Kinha, "Tracing Lashkar-e-Toiba," The Viewspaper, August 19, 2007, http://theviewspaper.net/tracing-lashkar-e-toiba/ (accessed April 7, 2012).

16. US Department of Justice, "Chicago Resident David Coleman Headley Pleads Guilty to Role in India and Denmark Terrorism Conspiracies."

17. Angel Rabasa, Robert Blackwill, and Peter Chalk, *The Lessons of Mumbai* (Santa Monica, CA: RAND, 2009), 5, http://www.rand.org/pubs/occasional_papers/2009/RAND _OP249.pdf (accessed July 30, 2012).

18. Ibid.

19. Ibid.

20. "Mumbai Attacks: Key Sites," BBC News, November 26, 2009, http://news.bbc .co.uk/2/hi/south_asia/7751876.stm (accessed April 7, 2012).

21. Rotella, "The American Behind India's 9/11."

22. "2008 Mumbai Attacks," Fantastico Journal Articles, http://www.fantastico .herobo.com/?media=2008_Mumbai_attacks (accessed April 26, 2012); "Casualties of the 2008 Mumbai Attacks," Wikipedia, http://en.wikipedia.org/wiki/Casualties_of_the_2008 _Mumbai_attacks (accessed May 1, 2012).

23. "Casualties of the 2008 Mumbai Attacks."

24. Alan Kronstadt, *Terrorist Attack in Mumbai, India, and Implications for US Interests* (Washington, DC: Congressional Research Service, December, 2008), 5.

25. "Supreme Court Reserves Verdict on Ajmal Kasab's Plea," The Times of India, April 25, 2012, http://articles.timesofindia.indiatimes.com/2012-04-25/india/31398159 _1_sabauddin-shaikh-ajmal-kasab-death-sentence (accessed May 1, 2012).

26. "Pakistani Militant Leader Defiant After US Slaps $10 Million Bounty on Him," Fox News, April 4, 2012, http://www.foxnews.com/world/2012/04/04/pakistani-militant -leader-defiant-after-us-slaps-10-million-bounty-on-him/ (accessed May 2, 2012).

27. US Department of Justice, "Chicago Resident David Coleman Headley Pleads Guilty to Role in India and Denmark Terrorism Conspiracies."

Using a Principal Agent in Intelligence Collection in Afghanistan

STEVE YOUNG

Afghanistan: A Country of Conflict

Peshawar, Pakistan, has long been known in intelligence circles as a place where almost anything goes, a sort of Wild West where guns can be bought at a convenient price or your choice of weapon can be made in Dara. Dara is located a few miles from Peshawar and just inside the border of the Khyber Agency, one of the components of the federally administered tribal areas (FATAs, or tribal areas). During its heyday from the early 1980s through 1989, many Muslim *mujahedin* (fighters in holy war) passed through Peshawar on their way into Afghanistan via the Khyber Pass to fight the invading Red Army of the Soviet Union. Abdullah Azzam and Osama bin Laden established the Islamic charity Makhtab al-Khidmat in Peshawar in order to provide social services and additional funding to mujahedin returning from and going to the front lines. The list of mujahedin assisted by bin Laden later constituted the database of names that became the basis for the founding of Al-Qaeda (The Base).[1]

The Soviet Union invaded Afghanistan in December 1979 and did not depart the country until February 1989, following ten years of intense fighting with the mujahedin backed by arms and money from the United States and Saudi Arabia. Celebration of the Soviet departure was short-lived because the country erupted once again into civil war when no credible government filled the political void following the Soviet defeat. The civil war was fought largely along ethnic lines between the Tajiks, Uzbeks, Pashtuns, and Hazaras. Tribal conflicts often erupted among these ethnic groups, corruption was rampant in the government of Afghanistan, and roadside bandits or police who wanted "tax payments" for safe passage often abused common people. The Taliban, a collection of ultra-religious students led by Mullah Omar, emerged in the southern Afghan city of Kandahar when it gained the people's trust by fighting back against government corruption and providing a measure of safety for local populations.[2] Eventually, however, the Taliban began imposing its brand of religious conservatism in areas it controlled. Especially tough were restrictions on women, including but not limited to:

1. A complete ban on women's work outside the home, which also applied to female teachers, engineers, and most professionals. Only a few female doctors and nurses were allowed to work in some hospitals in Kabul.

2. A complete ban on women's activity outside the home unless accompanied by a *mahram* (close male relative such as a father, brother, or husband).

3. A ban on women studying at schools, universities, or any other educational institution. (The Taliban converted girls' schools into religious seminaries.)

4. A requirement that women wear a *burqa,* a long veil that covered them from head to toe.

5. The whipping, beating, and verbal abuse of women not clothed in accordance with Taliban rules or of women unaccompanied by a *mahram.*[3]

There were also other very strict restrictions on men and their daily activities, including the requirement that they wear Islamic clothes and a cap and not shave or trim their beards. Also, all people were required to attend prayers in mosques five times daily and were forbidden to keep birds or play with birds or kites.[4]

Gradually, the Taliban fought successfully against the remnants of the old mujahedin coalitions and, in September 1996, captured Kabul, Afghanistan's capital city. The result was a Taliban takeover of approximately two-thirds of Afghanistan and, in the areas they controlled, imposition of Taliban rules and restrictions. This situation continued until the arrival of Central Intelligence Agency (CIA) operations officers and US special forces personnel in October 2001.

Collecting Intelligence in Afghanistan

Even after the Soviet Union departed Afghanistan in 1989, the US intelligence community, primarily the CIA, continued to collect intelligence in the area because in August 1996 bin Laden issued his infamous *fatwa,* or religious edict, declaring war on the United States.[5] Bin Laden used quotes from the Quran to justify his fatwa, for example: "O you who believe! be careful—of your duty—to Allah and speak the right word; He will put your deeds into a right state for you, and forgive you your faults; and whoever obeys Allah and his Apostle, he indeed [will] achieve a mighty success."[6] In addition, he referred to the United States and Israel as a Crusader-Zionist alliance resorting to killing and arresting members of the *Ulema* (Muslim faithful). In the fatwa, bin Laden called on Muslims throughout the world to kill Jews and Americans anywhere. After issuing his fatwa, bin Laden relocated to Afghanistan and was afforded the nominal protection of the Taliban. Thus, by late 1996 bin Laden was on the CIA's radar screen as someone who could pose a serious threat to US interests and national security. With the Taliban, he became a major intelligence collection target in Afghanistan at that time. These targets, the Taliban and Osama bin Laden, posed unique challenges because the United States had had no official or unofficial presence in Afghanistan since the Soviet Union's defeat by the mujahedin.

The purpose of this case study is to provide an example of how to collect intelligence on persons and events in a country without being in the country. First, this case briefly discusses the intelligence cycle and how it applies to the special circumstances of Afghanistan. Next is a discussion of the concept of intelligence collection, with examples of the various means by which intelligence is collected. Finally, the case discusses the agent acquisition cycle, using Afghanistan as a backdrop.

To begin we ask: How do we define intelligence? And how does it differ from information?

Intelligence and the Intelligence Cycle

The man on the street might view intelligence as secret information acquired by secret means, and he would not be far from wrong. However, intelligence differs from information, even information collected in secret, in that information cannot be termed "intelligence" until it has been sifted through (processed), reviewed, understood, and distributed by an analyst in response to the requirements of a policymaker. According to Mark Lowenthal, information is anything that can be known, whether it was originally in the public domain or not.[7] What is important to understand is that all intelligence is information, but not all information is intelligence.

Some of the terms mentioned—"processed," "collected," and "distributed"—deserve further explanation, and that is best accomplished by introducing a basic version of what is termed the "intelligence cycle." The intelligence cycle always begins with a requirement from a policymaker; otherwise, collectors (both human and electronic) would not understand where to concentrate their resources. The policymaker sets collection priorities, which are passed to collectors. Once the information is collected, it is processed further either in the field or back in a headquarters element of the collecting agency, where it is reviewed by an analyst. After evaluating the information, the analyst writes a report based on the policymaker's requirement. The product is then distributed or disseminated to the policymaker and other intelligence "customers" with an interest in the particular intelligence topic. Figure 4.2.1 provides a visualization of the intelligence cycle.

As we can see from Figure 4.2.1, intelligence is produced by analysts after information has been collected and processed. Missing from this simplified version of the intelligence cycle is the amount of feedback generated at almost any point in the cycle, from analysts' questions about the policymaker's requirements to collectors' requests for general clarification of the requirements. Analysts are always providing feedback to collectors as to whether the information they submit has value or responds appropriately to the policymaker's tasking. Even recipients of the final intelligence product may question either analysts or

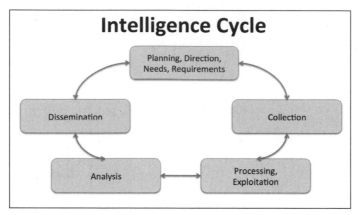

FIGURE 4.2.1: The Intelligence Cycle
Source: Created by Linda Kiltz, based on a figure at www.fbi.gov/about-us
/intelligence/intelligence-cycle.

collectors on the quality of the information provided. Thus, the intelligence or
the source of the intelligence can be questioned anywhere along the line.

Collection Platforms

During the mid to late 1990s, there were two primary intelligence collection targets in Afghanistan: the Taliban and Osama bin Laden. What
policymakers required at that time was intelligence on the plans and intentions of the Taliban and the whereabouts of bin Laden. A variety of intelligence platforms were utilized to satisfy these requirements. Among them
were human-acquired intelligence (Humint, or human intelligence) and
various forms of electronic collection, including interception of the targets'
communications (Sigint, or signals intelligence) and photographic imagery
(Imint, or imagery intelligence).

All of these techniques have their positives and negatives, but a combination of them would normally be brought to bear upon an intelligence target
according to the specific requirements levied. For example, Imint, even imagery with high resolution, only provides intelligence at one point in time and
requires multiple passes of either surveillance aircraft or spy satellites in order
to gather comparison data. However, imagery can be extremely useful when it
is necessary to determine whether a missile in North Korea is on a launch pad

or whether ongoing excavation around an Iranian mountainside may indicate Iranian attempts to conceal uranium enrichment production facilities. Today unmanned aerial vehicles (UAVs), or drones, are available to loiter in an area and provide constant data feeds. In the late 1990s, however, this tool was not yet available to the field collector. Finding bin Laden in Afghanistan with just Imint was not a very good option.

Sigint offers a more compelling tool for field collectors because once a target is identified, his communications can usually be monitored. This is when the processing part of the intelligence cycle becomes crucial because the vast majority of conversations in Afghanistan or Pakistan are conducted in either Dari, Pashto, Urdu, Tajik, or local dialects. The downside of Sigint is the need to find enough translators to process the "take." In the late 1990s, a lack of translators had created a significant bottleneck for the US intelligence community.[8] Unfortunately, this trend continues to this day. Sigint is still, however, a very useful collection platform that can be used to determine an individual's location or learn of information he is passing to a fellow Taliban or terrorist.

After processing the translated information, analysts evaluate the information and turn it into a finished intelligence product, which is then disseminated to policymakers. Now policymakers must decide what action to take, and what happens next is an ambiguous part of the intelligence cycle. Policymakers are not required to follow the recommendations or suggestions of analysts or other intelligence advisers. Some may follow their own instincts and come to a politically motivated decision not necessarily based on what could be interpreted as pragmatic or rational decision-making. For example, former senior CIA analyst Paul Pillar faulted President George W. Bush's administration for attacking Iraq based on politicized intelligence.[9] Such decisions are part of the democratic separation of powers, which is beyond the scope of this case study. It is worth mentioning, however, that policymakers make their own decisions with or without the benefit of quality intelligence.

Intelligence professionals often debate the benefits of technically collected intelligence, such as Imint or Sigint, versus human-acquired intelligence, or Humint. Both collection methods have their advantages and disadvantages, but as Loch Johnson points out, a satellite-based camera or even a drone cannot look into a tent to see who is inside or determine the plans or intentions of an adversary.[10] Moreover, one always wants to know what is going on inside the cave, not just the fact that people are in the cave. Who is there? What are they talking about? Who else are they talking to? What are their plans? What is their weaponry? In order to receive answers to these types of questions, it is necessary to have someone inside the target organization who can provide insight and context to the acquired information. This is the job of the human spy.

Humint has been a part of history since biblical times. There is the story in Joshua 2:1 about Joshua sending two spies to scout out the city of Jericho before the battle: "Then Joshua secretly sent out two spies from the Israelite camp at Acacia Grove. He instructed them, 'Scout out the land on the other side of the Jordan River, especially around Jericho.' So the two men set out and came to the house of a prostitute named Rahab and stayed there that night." Of course, at that period of history there were no technical means of collection, but the example illustrates that in order to receive good intelligence about a potential target, human "eyes on" is a necessary part of the collection process. Even in today's military, intelligence agents are often sent to verify information collected by technical means. As a point of clarification here, in CIA terminology an "agent" or "asset" is a person who has been recruited by a CIA case officer or operations officer to respond to the case officer's tasking, be it political, economic, or terrorism- or drug-related. FBI personnel are called "agents," and the people who provide information to them are called "sources," or sometimes "snitches" or "confidential informants" (CIs). Often a CI is recruited under duress. That is to say, the FBI agent has offered the source something, such as limited jail time, for his cooperation. Money also normally changes hands, and little or no personal relationship is established between the agent and the source. In this case study, we use the CIA terminology and refer to agents or assets interchangeably as employees of the CIA case officer.

The Agent Acquisition Cycle

In contrast to the FBI, CIA case officers, or operations officers, routinely compare notes and lessons learned about developing, recruiting, and handling assets—though couched so that specifics are not revealed. Operations officers' missions and their sense of accomplishment, even their professional identity, depend on the success of their assets and the intelligence they produce. Assets remain sources of information sometimes for years and sometimes, depending on the asset's goals, only a few hours. At the CIA, acquiring or recruiting the asset is normally a more involved process than simple coercion. Called the "agent acquisition cycle," this process typically involves: (1) *spotting* a potential asset based on his background or the information he may have access to; (2) *assessing* the asset over a period of time for his potential as an intelligence source; (3) forming and *developing* the bonds between the case officer and the potential asset as the case officer tries to understand the asset's motivations for cooperation well enough that the case officer can then (4) *recruit* the asset into becoming a source of information for the case officer.

When people are recruited as assets, they are made aware that they will be working for the US government and that their employment is conditional on their willingness and ability to respond to tasking based on their access to specific types of information. At this time the relationship between the asset and the case officer becomes more clandestine and the operation moves into the (5) *handling* phase, wherein the asset is tasked and clandestine meetings are held to obtain the asset's information and the case officer provides additional requirements. In return for his cooperation, the asset is provided with whatever has motivated his cooperation in the form negotiated with the case officer.

Motivations for providing information are numerous and specific to the individual. Money, though usually involved, is not always the primary motivator. What, for example, would motivate a Saudi prince who has access to all the money he would ever want? Perhaps he wants a US college education for his children, or a heart transplant at a US hospital for himself or a family member. On the other end of the scale, particularly in Afghanistan and Pakistan, a young male with access to members of a terrorist group may want to get married. But according to local cultural traditions, the males provide the dowry to the family of the potential bride. Young Afghan males out of work often cannot afford to get married and thus are vulnerable to exploitation by an astute CIA case officer. When people are recruited as assets, motivated by the desire to get married, goats and camels instead of money may be provided, with the assistance of the case officer, to the bride's unwitting family as the dowry. In this manner, the potential asset is able to get married and the case officer acquires a new reporting source.

As the saying goes, all good things must come to an end, and so it is with any operational case run by a CIA case officer. Assets are used in cases that can last from a few hours to a number of years. The short-term cases are usually based on information received from a person called a walk-in, or volunteer, who walks into an overseas US embassy and is interviewed one time by a CIA case officer, then sent on his way. Whether these individuals are contacted again depends on their willingness, an evaluation of the information they provide, and verification of their access.

Access is normally the determining factor in how long any case will be run. Humint involves people-to-people relationships, and life's circumstances change over time. This is especially true with long-term assets, who may have been recruited at a point in their professional career when they had little access to quality information but whose access to better information increased over time as they were promoted. Eventually, an asset may reach retirement age, be fired, or get transferred to another position. In this event, the asset's access to verifiable, quality information decreases to the point where he is no longer able to provide the information for which he was initially recruited. At this time the asset is (6) *terminated:* the relationship between the case officer and the asset is ended, usually with a severance package that eases the pain of the asset's reduced income, if applicable. Thus, the agent acquisition cycle is completed. The steps in the cycle have included spotting, assessing, developing, recruiting, handling, and terminating.

This description of the agent acquisition cycle has outlined the ideal situation in the relationship between a case officer and an agent. Agents may be terminated for numerous other reasons besides lack of access, such as being caught lying to the case officer, stealing money, raising the suspicion of being untruthful or fabricating reports, or even not being who they said they were. On the other hand, it is the case officer's responsibility to maintain a watchful eye on his asset's reporting and behavior so that the asset does not come to the attention of the local security service or is discovered for having penetrated a terrorist group. The old axiom "trust but verify" applies to the relationship between the case officer and the reporting source.

The Principal Agent

In most recruitment scenarios, the CIA case officer is directly involved with the person producing the information—that is, the case officer meets directly with the asset, pays the asset, debriefs the asset, and provides feedback and additional requirements to the asset. This is the ideal situation and the way the CIA usually conducts its business: with the case officer handling the asset without an intermediary. However, sometimes case officers must rely on others to act as intermediaries between themselves and their source. There may be many reasons for this, not least of which is security. Even if a case officer speaks the local language, he does not always blend in with the local population or have the cultural background to infiltrate a terrorist group. And terrorist groups are notorious for limiting their membership to family members and close friends. They, too, have their intelligence collection priorities, which often reach into the realm of counterintelligence—that is, making sure that everyone who joins the group is a trustworthy extremist.

To assist the case officer in places where he is not likely to blend in, local security services that have a formal government-to-government liaison relationship with the CIA are called upon to provide sources or act as intermediaries between the case officer and the source. Mostly these liaison relationships are very productive because of the level of trust built up over time between the two liaison officers on the ground and the US government and the government of the host country. Information is routinely shared, and occasionally sources are shared as well. However, even normally reliable liaison contacts can make mistakes. One such mistake occurred at a CIA base in Khost, Afghanistan, a town in southeast Afghanistan on the Pakistan border.

The Khost Bombing

The perpetrator of the Khost bombing, Humam Khalil Abu-Mulal al-Balawi, was an Al-Qaeda sympathizer and a doctor from the Jordanian town of Zarqa. Zarqa was also the hometown of Abu Musab al-Zarqawi, the militant Jordanian Islamist responsible for several devastating attacks in Iraq before he was killed by a US airstrike there on June 7, 2006. Al-Balawi had been arrested by Jordanian intelligence more than a year before the incident at Khost. The Jordanians subsequently used al-Balawi in several unilateral operations before offering him up to the CIA as a shared source. By this time the Jordanians believed that al-Balawi had been successfully reformed and brought over to the American and Jordanian side. The CIA and the Jordanians had cooperated for many years on various counterterrorist operations, and al-Balawi was believed to have information regarding the whereabouts of Ayman al-Zawahiri, Al-Qaeda's second in command, who was high on the US hit list. The Jordanian intelligence service, however, had not done its counterintelligence very well, because al-Balawi, using the pseudonym Abu Dujanah al-Khurasani, had posted many statements on the Internet stating his radical Islamist beliefs, with frequent posts on the Al-Qaeda propaganda website As-Sahab. Moreover, As-Sahab would release a posthumous videotape of an interview with al-Balawi in which he detailed his part in the Al-Qaeda-inspired operation not only to kill al-Balawi's Jordanian handler but also to lure CIA operatives into the trap with promises of access to al-Zawahiri.[11]

Thus, on December 30, 2009, al-Balawi was driven to the CIA base in Khost, Afghanistan, by Jordanian intelligence officers, who had not searched him and who, by this time, considered him a reliable, trustworthy asset. As al-Balawi got out of the vehicle to meet the CIA representatives and a CIA officer approached him to conduct the standard body search, al-Balawi detonated the suicide vest he was wearing under his tunic. The blast killed his Jordanian intelligence officer handler, four CIA case officers, and three CIA contractors, as well as al-Balawi himself.[12]

There are many lessons to be learned from this tragedy. First, and perhaps most obvious, is that members of the Jordanian intelligence service did not thoroughly vet their asset. The first step in the vetting of a potential new asset is conducting a full background check and confirming that the person is who he says he is. In other words, the Jordanians did not fully understand who this person really was, even though some of his radical beliefs were posted on the Internet. If an intelligence service cannot fully identify an individual through other unilateral sources, family members, or another liaison intelligence service, then his claims cannot be substantiated and he should be treated as a possible hostile penetration of the intelligence service. Al-Balawi, perhaps unwittingly and probably with Al-Qaeda assistance, proved to be proficient in conducting a deep cover operation.

The next lesson is the importance of proper security procedures, which were not followed when the meeting between al-Balawi, the CIA, and the Jordanian handler was set up. Although al-Balawi had worked with the Jordanians in the past, he had previously verbalized his radical Islamic beliefs, and therefore any task he was assigned should have been subjected to a counterintelligence review. Moreover, he was not searched by the Jordanians prior to entering the vehicle that transported him to the CIA base in Khost. He was not searched until a CIA security officer stepped up to do so, at which point he detonated his explosives.

This case also elucidates the problems of working in a foreign country with individuals whom one does not know. The CIA had to trust the Jordanian intelligence service to vet al-Balawi for them. Normally this is not too much of a problem, because these types of counterterrorist operations are most often conducted in a host country, like Jordan, where the intelligence service has a large degree of control. However, when conducting the operation in a third country (Afghanistan), the degree of control decreases substantially. In this case, it can be assumed that al-Balawi was not under Jordanian control 100 percent of the time he was in Afghanistan; otherwise, he could never have acquired a bomb.

Understanding afterwards what happened in such an incident is part of the normal process. Implementing new security procedures and reviewing those already in place are also normal reactions to such events. In this situation, however, CIA officers paid for the mistakes in security with their lives.

Working with Principal Agents

Sometimes a case officer cannot blend into the local population, or he is working in a country, such as Pakistan, whose official liaison relationship with the United States is always on shaky ground. In these cases, the case officer can recruit a person who may have only nominal access but who has trustworthy friends or relatives who have greater access to information of interest. In the late 1990s, to collect information from within Afghanistan while physically remaining in Pakistan, the CIA had to find Afghans living in Pakistan who had maintained sporadic contact with US officials since the Soviet Union's defeat but who were not members of the Taliban. Although they lived in Pakistan, relatives and friends of these Afghans were often located in Afghanistan. Normally, these individuals had a previous track record of working with the CIA, but their current access was negligible. On the other hand, they could be activated to recruit other individuals in Afghanistan who would have access to information of interest to the case officer. In this situation, the agent directly in touch with the case officer becomes a *principal agent* and eventually develops his own network of sources based on the case officer's requirements. The individuals recruited by the principal agent are called reporting *subsources,* and the numbers of these subsources associated with the principal agent and the quality of their information varies substantially.

One can imagine the positives and the negatives of working with principal agents. On the positive side, principal agents are usually known quantities: someone within the US intelligence community has worked with the principal agent and can vouch for his bona fides. In other words, a US person with some credibility can state categorically that the principal agent is trustworthy and has produced quality intelligence for the US government in the past. The principal agent is responsible directly to the case officer and is subject to all the scrutiny and counterintelligence techniques, including a polygraph, that a case officer has at his disposal to verify that the principal agent is being truthful. It is understood between the case officer and the principal agent that the case officer is the person who provides the requirements to the principal agent, and that the principal agent is responsible for recruiting and paying his subsources and for providing requirements to the subsources. The principal agent becomes, in effect, a surrogate case officer. The principal agent also understands that he will be terminated immediately if he is found stealing money or embellishing his reporting.

To a certain extent, the principal agent was assuming most of the risk in his relationship with the case officer. For example, the principal agent had to be extremely cautious and careful about whom he recruited or asked to provide information in response to the case officer's requirements. Sometimes if a close relative had access to reportable information, it was relatively easy to persuade that person to confide in the principal agent. At other times it was highly probable that the subsource did not know that the information was intended for the US government. In Afghanistan in the late 1990s, this was more likely the case than not. But it does demonstrate the dedication and adaptability of a good principal agent. It is also an example of self-preservation during this era.

There are a number of negative aspects of this type of intelligence relationship. First, there are many openings for fraud and abuse of the system. Because the case officer talks only with the principal agent, he never knows how many individuals are actually on the principal agent's source list; the agent could be fabricating his reporting and "paying" people who do not exist. In one case in Pakistan in the late 1990s, a principal agent was working with nine separate individuals as subsources. The reporting coming in from those subsources was wide-ranging, from information on Taliban activities in Afghanistan to the location of drug labs in the nearby FATAs of Pakistan. It was incumbent on the case officer to try to verify the reporting so that he and his consumers could believe the information. Again, the downside with the principal agent approach is that the case officer has difficulty verifying or confirming how many subsources the principal agent is working with, or even that he is working with any.

The one piece of leverage that the case officer has working for him is the principal agent's awareness that the case officer can confirm what is reported to him. It is understood that most secrets within Afghanistan do not normally remain secret for very long and that some information can be easily verified. For example, if the subsource is reporting on the presence of heroin labs in the FATA, eventually there will be a raid on the labs. If the raid proceeds and no lab is found, then the subsource is terminated for fabricating his reporting. Other information, such as Taliban movements of personnel, can be verified by separate reporting, since this type of information may fulfill the requirements of another agent, or by imagery verifying the presence of Taliban troops in an area.

Things of a physical nature, such as heroin labs or troop movements, can eventually be confirmed. On the other hand, plans and intentions, arguably some of the most valuable information, are the hardest to confirm or verify. This type of information is valuable because in order to acquire it, an individual must be in on the discussion or have access to the plans in some other way. But it is hard to confirm because plans often change from one day or week to the next, and if it cannot be confirmed, it is difficult to determine whether a principal agent's subsource actually had access to the information. Information of this type has to be carefully scrutinized and would probably require additional intelligence collection platforms.

Another tool for the case officer when dealing with principal officers is to request a meeting with a subsource. This became especially important in Afghanistan because it gave the case officer an opportunity to verify information allegedly supplied by the subsource. In addition, even meeting with a principal agent and a particular subsource only once a month, for example, made it possible for the case officer to spin him off of the principal agent's subsource list and meet with him directly. This ideal situation was in fact accomplished with some regularity in Pakistan in the 1990s. The benefits are obvious in that the case officer gains a greater measure of control over the case when dealing directly with the reporting source.

Conclusions

This case study, due to its sensitive nature, does not mention specific names, sources, methods and references. The reader can assume, however, that the details in the Afghanistan examples are based on a true case and the real-life experiences of CIA officers working there at that time. The principles of using a principal agent when collecting intelligence as detailed in this case study on

Afghanistan can be applied in any area where a case officer cannot be physically present.

This case discussed not only how to collect intelligence in an ideal situation, through direct contact between the case officer and the agent, but also how to acquire intelligence under less than ideal circumstances using a principal agent. This case has only scratched the surface of the range of techniques and tradecraft available to the case officer. Humint collection is especially time-consuming and intense; the people skills it requires can be learned, but most successful case officers naturally possess these skills, such as the ability to persuade a potential asset to reveal his secrets. Nevertheless, whether intelligence is collected for strategic or tactical purposes, Humint collection still remains the "eyes on" verification for boots on the ground.

DISCUSSION QUESTIONS

1. Describe how the agent acquisition cycle can or cannot be applied when recruiting a potential agent with access to a terrorist group.
2. Under what circumstances would technical forms of intelligence collection be the preferred intelligence collection platform over human intelligence?
3. Why is information not considered intelligence?
4. Why is feedback within the intelligence cycle considered essential to good intelligence collection?
5. Research the case of the killing on May 1, 2011, of Osama bin Laden. Describe which intelligence collection platforms might have been utilized during the planning of this operation and how they might have been used.

NOTES

1. National Commission on Terrorist Attacks upon the United States, *The 9/11 Commission Report: Final Report of the National Commission on Terrorist Attacks upon the United States* (New York: W. W. Norton, 2004), 56.

2. Peter Marsden, *The Taliban: War and Religion in Afghanistan* (London: Zed Books, 2002), 61.

3. "Some of the Restrictions Imposed by Taliban on Women in Afghanistan," http://www.rawa.org/rules.htm (accessed May 12, 2012); see also Ahmed Rashid, *Taliban: Militant Islam, Oil, and Fundamentalism in Central Asia* (New Haven, CT: Yale University Press, 2000), appendix 1.

4. "Taliban Restrictions," LiveLeak, last modified November 29, 2009, http://www
.liveleak.com/view?i=f3d_1259470867 (accessed May 12, 2012).

5. "Al Qaeda's Second Fatwa," PBS Newshour, February 23, 1998, http://www.pbs
.org/newshour/terrorism/international/fatwa_1998.html (accessed May 13, 2012).

6. Ibid.

7. Mark M. Lowenthal, *Intelligence: From Secrets to Policy*, 5th ed. (Los Angeles: Sage,
2012), 1.

8. Matthew M. Aid, "The Time of Troubles: The US National Security Agency in
the Twenty-first Century," in *Intelligence and National Security: The Secret World of Spies*,
ed. Loch K. Johnson and James J. Wirtz (New York: Oxford University Press, 2008), 92.

9. Paul R. Pillar, "Intelligence, Policy, and the War in Iraq," *Foreign Affairs* (March–
April 2006): 1–7.

10. Loch K. Johnson, *National Security Intelligence* (Cambridge: Polity Press, 2012), 43.

11. Bill Roggio, "CIA Agents Killed in Suicide Attack 'a Gift from Allah,'" *The
Long War Journal*, March 1, 2010, http://www.longwarjournal.org/archives/2010/03/cia
_agent_killed_in.php (accessed July 23, 2012).

12. Laura Rozen, "Jordanian Double Agent Killed CIA Officers in Khost," Polit-
ico, January 4, 2010, http://www.politico.com/blogs/laurarozen/0110/Jordanian_double
_agent_killed_CIA_officers_in_Khost.html (accessed May 18, 2012).

CHAPTER 5

Critical Infrastructure Protection

A major mission area of homeland security is protecting critical infrastructures and key assets. Critical infrastructures are the assets, systems, and networks, whether physical or virtual, so vital to the United States that their incapacitation or destruction would have a debilitating effect on the nation. These interdependent networks and systems provide an essential flow of products and services to ensure the functioning of the government and society as a whole.

The importance of critical infrastructure protection (CIP) is clearly stated in the *National Infrastructure Protection Plan* (NIPP) as:

Protecting and ensuring the resiliency of the critical infrastructure and key resources (CIKR) of the United States is essential to the Nation's security, public health and safety, economic vitality, and way of life. Attacks on CIKR significantly disrupt the functioning of government and business alike and produce cascading effects far beyond the targeted sector and physical location of the incident. Direct terrorist attacks, and natural, man-made or technical hazards could produce catastrophic losses in terms of human casualties, property destruction, and economic effects, as well as profound damage to public morale and confidence.[1]

Homeland Security Presidential Directive 7 (HSPD-7) identified seventeen critical infrastructure sectors, including: agriculture and food, the defense industrial base, energy, banking and finance, water, chemical, commercial facilities, critical manufacturing, dams, emergency services, nuclear reactors, materials and waste, postal and shipping, government facilities, transportation systems, communications, information technology, and health care and public health. This vast and diverse aggregation of highly interconnected assets, systems, and networks presents an attractive array of targets to terrorists and greatly magnifies the potential for cascading failure in the wake of natural or man-made disasters. In this chapter, the two cases focus on two of these critical sectors—health care and public health (HPH) and information technology.

The health care and public health sector provides a diverse array of goods and services that are distributed widely across the country. It includes privately owned and operated acute care hospitals and medical clinics, as well as public health agencies at the federal, state, local, tribal, and territorial levels. While the HPH sector plays a crucial role in preparedness and response for all hazards, it is the lead sector in planning for and responding to a catastrophic pandemic. However, what happens if this critical infrastructure breaks down during a pandemic? A breakdown in the health care infrastructure would result in a significant impact on the economy, a loss of human life, and breakdowns in other critical infrastructures.[2]

The first case, "Catastrophic Pandemic: Cases in Ethical Decision-Making," provides a worst-case scenario of a worldwide influenza pandemic based on planning documents prepared by the Centers for Disease Control and Prevention (CDC) and the US Department of Health and Human Services (HHS). The case shows that a severe pandemic of this magnitude would challenge almost every sector of society. In addition, this case highlights the most critical ethical issues that health care and medical professionals would most likely face in such a scenario, including: health workers' duty to provide care during a communicable disease outbreak, the allocation of scarce resources, and conceivable restrictions on individual autonomy and liberty in the interest of public health through public health management measures such as quarantine and border closures.

The second case, "The Impact of Cyber-Security on Critical Infrastructure Protection: The Advanced Persistent Threat," highlights how important the cyber-infrastructure is to critical infrastructure protection across all sectors. The advanced persistent threat (APT) highlights a new type of malicious actor that routinely conducts attacks against the cyber-infrastructure using cyber-attack tools. Because of the interconnected nature of the cyber-infrastructure, these attacks can spread quickly and have debilitating effects, as highlighted in the examples in this case. APTs represent the next escalation in cyber-warfare and present a clear threat to the nation's infrastructures, both physical (power, water, food) and systems (health care, manufacturing, banking).

NOTES

1. US Department of Homeland Security, *National Infrastructure Protection Plan* (Washington, DC: US Government Printing Office, 2009), 1.

2. US Department of Homeland Security and US Department of Health and Human Services, *Healthcare and Public Health Sector–Specific Plan* (Washington, DC: US Government Printing Office, 2010), 7.

Catastrophic Pandemic

Cases in Ethical Decision-Making

LINDA KILTZ

Introduction

Fourteen-year-old Jacob Moya was busing tables at the Texas Bible Institute in Columbus on July 8, 2009, when he felt run-down and called his dad in Pflugerville. He resisted his father's offer to come get him, saying he would tough it out, said his father, Henry Moya, later. Jacob continued to work despite feeling ill. Within a few days, Jacob had become so ill with severe flu symptoms, including fever, cough, and fatigue, that he had to be taken to the emergency room in Round Rock, Texas. In the ER, the doctor advised Jacob to see his family doctor if he did not feel better and was released. A day later, Jacob had problems breathing and was back in the ER, where he was sent to a San Antonio Hospital that had the nearest heart-lung machine. Within one month of exhibiting the first symptoms of H1N1 flu, Jacob was dead of respiratory failure and a brain hemorrhage.[1] What surprised health officials was that Jacob died from the H1N1 virus though he had no underlying health conditions. In fact, 20 to 30 percent of the children who died from H1N1 in 2009 would be like Jacob—perfectly healthy until they fell ill.[2]

The H1N1 influenza virus that killed Jacob was not the normal seasonal flu that we experience each year, but rather a new influenza flu virus of swine origin that was first detected in Mexico in April 2009, when it began infecting people throughout the world.[3] Within a few weeks, the virus had infected thousands of people around the world through person-to-person contact. The Centers for Disease Control and Prevention (CDC) estimated that from April 2009 to April 2010, between 43 million and 61 million cases of H1N1 occurred in the United States alone. Furthermore, the CDC estimated that between 195,000 and 403,000 H1N1-related hospitalizations and between 8,870 and 18,300 H1N1-related deaths occurred between April 2009 and April 2010.[4] The CDC considered the H1N1 pandemic, unlike the devastating pandemic in 1918, moderate in severity, but cautioned that we should plan for more severe pandemics in the future.

Pandemics pose unique challenges to organizations, communities, and nation-states, not only because of their capacity to cause a large number of people to become ill or die, but also because of the severe social and economic disruptions that are likely to occur. According to the US Department of Health and Human Services (HHS), it is estimated that if a pandemic influenza virus similar to the 1918 strain in virulence emerged today, in the absence of intervention, 1.9 million Americans could die and almost 10 million could be hospitalized over the course of the pandemic, which might evolve over a year or more.[5] This extraordinary number of sick people over a large geographic area, all requiring care at the same time, would overwhelm the health care system, strain local, state, and federal resources, and lead to critical shortages in vaccines, medications, medical supplies, hospital beds, and food, water, and health care workers. The economic impact on the United States of even a mild pandemic is estimated at $71.3 billion to $166.5 billion in direct health care costs, lost productivity for those affected, and lost expected future earnings for those who die, with the loss of life accounting for the majority of the economic impact.[6]

A pandemic of highly pathogenic influenza would threaten the lives of hundreds of thousands of people in the United States and confront governments and public health organizations with ethical issues that would have wide-ranging implications and consequences. Public officials and health care professionals would face difficult ethical dilemmas in trying to choose among potentially conflicting priorities, particularly if no clear ethical guidelines are developed in advance. During a severe influenza pandemic, there would not be enough time to engage in a public discussion of the ethical trade-offs in many of the critical decisions that would need to be made.

To facilitate such a discussion, this case will first provide a worst-case scenario in the United States in the near future that would be much like the 1918 pandemic. Next, three short scenarios are presented that each illustrate a particular aspect of a pandemic that is sure to challenge the ethical fitness of health care professionals, public officials, and ordinary individuals. These scenarios are based on the cases developed by the National Collaborating Centre for Healthy Public Policy in Quebec, Canada.[7] Each scenario aims to assist in the development and application of moral reasoning through concrete examples. In addition, each is meant to stimulate discussion within a group of individuals (perhaps from multiple disciplines and/or with dissimilar points of view) in order to gain a deeper understanding of the issues from different perspectives and in both general and specific contexts.

The Worst-Case Scenario: A Worldwide Outbreak of a Severe Influenza Pandemic

The pandemic catastrophe begins on January 3, 2018, after billions of people around the world have celebrated the start of the new year. That is when H5N1 (avian influenza) virus goes global, mutating so that it can be passed from one human to the next.[8] The avian influenza virus refers to influenza A virus, which was found in 2009 chiefly in birds; thus, the risk from avian influenza was believed to be generally low to most people because these viruses did not usually infect humans.[9] Nonetheless, because all influenza viruses have the ability to change, scientists have been concerned that H5N1 virus could one day infect humans and spread easily from one person to another. The Centers for Disease Control and Prevention has warned Americans, "Because these viruses do not commonly infect humans, there is little or no immune protection against them in the human population. If H5N1 virus were to gain the capacity to spread easily from person to person, an influenza pandemic (worldwide outbreak of disease) could begin."[10]

On January 10, 2018, a cluster of thirty unusual flu cases appears in the state of Perak in Malaysia. Clinical tests confirm that a new strain of the H5N1 virus has infected all thirty of these people. The population in Perak, as well as the rest of the world, has no innate immunity to this new strain. By the end of the month, at least fifteen people are dead across Malaysia, two hundred are hospitalized, and more than one thousand cases have been confirmed. Then another suspected case is discovered in Singapore.[11]

Not knowing how bad the pandemic will be, the experts at the World Health Organization (WHO) are making every effort to stop the spread of the disease and to understand how fast this new virus can spread. Teams from the WHO are deployed to Perak and elsewhere in Malaysia to issue antiviral drugs and collect samples for testing. Despite these initial efforts, within one month cases are being reported in Singapore, Hong Kong, and mainland China. Experts realize at this point that the virus's seven-day incubation period is allowing people carrying the virus to travel before they become symptomatic. With an incubation period significantly longer than that of any other flu strain, the virus has become capable of global spread.[12]

By March 2018, the flu has made its way around the world. By the middle of the month, about 700,000 people are already hospitalized in Japan, despite the distribution of four million doses of Tamiflu over the first week of the month to health care workers and those older than seventy-five and younger than fifteen. Although Tamiflu has not stopped the spread of the virus, it has lowered the death rate of severe cases significantly.[13]

In the United States, the first cases are reported in Los Angeles on March 10 and in New York on March 12, despite the nation's efforts to do health screenings of those entering the country from overseas. Despite the rapid spread of the virus, there is hope as CDC scientists in the United States isolate the H5N1 "Killer Malaysian Flu" strain that is needed to make a vaccine.[14] They also determine that the death rate is less than 5 percent of those infected.

Recently, experts have discovered that this H5N1 virus is behaving like the 1918 influenza pandemic, which killed 50 million to 100 million people around the globe.[15] One study that extrapolates from the severe 1918 pandemic finds that, in the absence of intervention, an influenza pandemic could lead to 1.9 million deaths in the United States and 180 million to 369 million deaths globally.[16] Like the 1918 virus, this new H5N1 virus is disproportionately killing healthy adults between the ages of eighteen and forty-four—not seniors or children.[17] The virus seems to cause a "cytokine storm," or an excessive amount of immune system proteins that trigger the body's inflammation response and harm the patient in the process.[18] As a result, the healthier the individual is before being infected, the worse off he or she may become when taken ill.

To better imagine the impact such a pandemic might have in today's society, consider the following hypothetical. The American people are feeling the full brunt of the pandemic by April 2018. More than 2 million people have sought hospital care.[19] In 2011 the United States had approximately 970,000 staffed hospital beds and 100,000 ventilators, with three-quarters of them in use on any given day.[20] Thus, in a pandemic most patients with influenza who need ventilation will not have access to it. In fact, according to recent pandemic planning models, it is estimated that in a pandemic the US health care system would be overwhelmed in seven to ten weeks and as such would need to turn away 3 to 4 million patients.[21] In April 2018, when many of the sick find that hospitals are crowded and unable to accommodate them, they return home to be cared for by family and friends. Many people avoid public places, quarantining themselves, and are generally unable to work. Schools and other civic buildings become infirmaries, but these too become crowded in short order. Ultimately, a depression of economic activity and general slow-down of the federal government ensue.[22]

Not only is space an issue, but supplies of the antiviral drug Tamiflu are running low after an early rush of prescriptions. Even with the stockpiling of vaccines, supplies dwindle quickly. This is problematic given that production of a new vaccine takes a minimum of six months after isolation of the circu-lating strain. In addition, given the capacity of all the current international vaccine manufacturers, supplies during those next six months are limited to fewer than 1 billion doses worldwide. Since two doses are required for protec-tion in this case, fewer than 500 million people—approximately 14 percent of the world's population—can be vaccinated.[23]

Owing to our "just-in-time delivery" economy, the United States has no surge capacity for health care, some food supplies, and many other products and services. Consequently, the global health impact of this sort of influenza pandemic can be expected to affect workforces, transportation systems, and supply chains.[24] Critical supplies such as food, water, decongestant drugs, and other cold/flu medications are scarce in some regions, particularly ur-ban areas.[25] Doctors and nurses, emergency medical personnel, teachers, and police and fire personnel are among the many who are getting sick themselves or staying home to care for sick family members. Businesses throughout the country are reporting significant increases in absenteeism, and absentee rates are expected to be between 20 and 40 percent across all sectors.[26] A CDC model has predicted that at the peak of a pandemic about 10 percent of the workforce will be absent owing to illness or the need to care for an ill family member.[27]

By the end of April 2018, about 250,000 Americans are dead from the flu. In the worst-case scenario, it is assumed that with an attack rate of 30 percent and a case fatality rate of 2.5 percent, a severe pandemic would cause the death of more than 1 million labor force participants.[28] The Killer Malaysian Flu rages on in the West through May and June. The pandemic circles the globe in three distinct waves through the winter of 2018–2019. By the end of the pandemic in June 2019, almost one-third of all Americans (about 90 million people) have been infected. Of those infected, 50 percent (about 45 million) have required outpatient medical care, 9.9 million have been hospitalized, about 1.5 million have been in an ICU, 740,000 have required mechanical ventilation, and about 2 million have died.[29]

Although a vaccine has finally been produced by the end of June 2018, it is a race at this point to produce enough vaccine to stop a second wave at the start of the traditional flu season later in the year. If all goes well, sufficient quantities of vaccine should be available by midsummer—about six months after the start of the pandemic.[30] Soon 40 million doses of the vaccine are being produced every month, but there continue to be shortages owing to the fact that more than one dose is necessary per person for adequate protection.[31]

Governments must decide who should get the vaccines first: The young? The workforce? Health care employees? In developing countries, where the vaccine is in even shorter supply, only the rich receive doses. Those who are not given first shot at the vaccines are left to rage at the inequity and fear the coming winter. Some people hunt desperately for doses of the vaccine on the black market or across international borders.

Ethical Issues to Consider in a Pandemic

In the worst-case scenario imagined above, hundreds of thousands of people in the United States could die in a period of months during a pandemic of highly pathogenic influenza. The circumstances anticipated during a severe influenza pandemic highlight the shortage of health care personnel, equipment, and vaccines necessary to meet the needs of all the critically ill patients. It is highly likely that in such a scenario the entire country would face simultaneous limitations, resulting in severe shortages of critical care resources to the point where patients could no longer receive all of the care that would usually be required and expected. As mentioned earlier, a severe pandemic will challenge almost every sector of society—the health care sector, the labor force, transportation, banking, and law enforcement, to name a few.

In addition, disasters as intense as a pandemic are sure to present many ethical dilemmas that affect decisions by federal, state, and local officials, even those who have pandemic influenza response plans and guidance documents.[32] The most critical ethical issues that will arise during a severe influenza pandemic include: health workers' duty to provide care during a communicable disease outbreak; allocation of scarce resources; and conceivable restrictions on individual autonomy and liberty in the interest of public health through public health management measures such as quarantine and border closures.[33] These issues are the subjects of the following three short scenarios.

A successful response to an influenza pandemic will depend in large part on the skills, attitudes, and efforts of health care workers. Faced with a very serious disease for which there may be no absolute protection or cure, health care workers will find themselves facing potentially overwhelming demands: that they work in a more hazardous environment with greater exposure to disease and the risk of infection; that they put in extra hours to care for the increasing number of patients; that they cover for workers who are ill; that they work outside their normal scope of practice; and that they be prepared to move their services to where they are most needed, including temporary facilities. Health care workers will be forced to weigh their duty to provide care against competing obligations, such as their duty to protect their own health and that of their families and friends. Initially, primary care and emergency service workers will take the brunt of the demands posed by a pandemic flu and therefore will bear a disproportionate risk compared to more specialized care providers. Given the high risks to which health care workers and their families are exposed, is it reasonable to demand that they put their lives on the line in the case of a pandemic, or must they provide care because they have an ethical and professional duty to care for the sick regardless of the environment or risk?

Inherent in all codes of ethics for health care professionals is the duty to provide care, to respond to suffering, and to do no harm.[34] It is assumed by society that health care professionals, because of their training, knowledge, and commitment to care for the sick and injured, have a moral and professional obligation to provide health care at all times, even during an influenza pandemic.[35] Bioethicists argue that if health care workers are expected to take on these higher risks, there is an equally strong, reciprocal obligation by society (in particular, health care organizations) to protect and support these workers by giving them the highest priority for vaccinations, providing personal protection equipment, and making disability insurance and death benefits available to workers and their families.[36] What is critical is that pandemic preparedness plans provide clear guidance for health care workers on such issues as their rights and responsibilities in the event of a pandemic influenza. The first scenario addresses this issue of health care professionals' duty to care.

Scenario 1: Duty to Care

Media outlets are reporting that the World Health Organization has officially determined that a pandemic influenza is now under way. The Centers for Disease Control and Prevention has confirmed person-to-person spread in several US cities. Local media are reporting increased demand for emergency room and family physician office visits. Some deaths have been reported, but no one is really certain how serious the problem may be. Little is known about the actual virus at this point.

Maria is a thirty-five-year-old family physician and the mother of three children ages four to eight. She is one of twelve doctors practicing in a primary care clinic in El Paso, Texas. Her husband works in an accounting firm. When her husband hears the media reports, he becomes concerned that Maria may become ill or bring illness home to her family because of her increased exposure at work. He encourages her not to go to work. Maria is concerned about how to care for her children, who attend a local day care center. She is also worried about abandoning her patients and increasing the workload of her colleagues, many of whom, like her, have young families.

Scenario 1: First Set of Questions
1. What are your initial thoughts and feelings about this scenario?
2. What do you think are the most important considerations for Maria in making her decision?
3. Would your opinion change if the day care center was closed? Why?

Maria decides she will go to work, though she is concerned that her clinic lacks the appropriate amount of protective equipment. The clinical group meets and decides that they are committed to providing care to people with influenza, but will only do so if appropriate protective equipment is provided by the clinic or the state department of health. One of Maria's colleagues is close to retirement and also has diabetes and heart disease. He tells the clinic that he will not come to work, as he feels the risk to his own health is too great.

Within two weeks, the influenza pandemic is well advanced, and many people are sick, including a large number of health care workers. Many health care providers in hospitals and clinics are refusing to show up for work because they fear infection.

Scenario 1: Second Set of Questions

1. What do you think of the clinical group's decision?
2. Do you think society has an obligation to health care workers in the event of a pandemic outbreak?
3. In your view, is the health status of a health care worker an acceptable reason for that individual to not respond to a pandemic virus?
4. Should health care providers face consequences for refusing to show up for work?
5. If no, why? If yes, what sorts of penalties do you think would be fair?

If a flu pandemic is as severe as some fear it could be, an extraordinarily high number of sick people around the world will require care, all at the same time and on top of the "normal" demands for health care that often strain medical systems at the best of times. During a pandemic, the human and material resources of health care will be rapidly overwhelmed. There will be scarcities of medicines, equipment, and health care workers in all countries, and less-developed nations will face some of the greatest scarcities. Many of the sick are likely to recover with minimal assistance, but others will be seriously ill and unable to survive without prolonged hospitalization, diagnostic facilities, multiple drugs, access to scarce resources such as mechanical ventilators, and well-trained staff.[37]

During a severe influenza pandemic, there will be a critical shortage of mechanical ventilators, or breathing machines. The US National Vaccine Program Office stated that in a future severe pandemic, "intensive care units at local hospitals will become overwhelmed, and soon there will be widespread shortages of mechanical ventilators for treatment of patients with pneumonia."[38] According to one estimate, a pandemic will require 198 percent of the current supply of ventilators.[39] If this happens, many people in respiratory failure due to influenza or other injury or illness who need mechanical ventilation in order to survive will not receive it. This grave shortage of ventilators will raise unprecedented allocation dilemmas for health care professionals and have a significant impact on individuals and families.

As such, once the federal government declares a public health emergency, the individual disease management decisions of physicians and patients would be subordinated to the larger public health goals of reducing infection, illnesses, and deaths. Decision-makers will need to consider the well-being of the community as a whole while balancing obligations to individuals and individual needs. They will need to decide who will receive vaccines, antiviral drugs, ventilators, and other forms of care, and who will not. It is expected that decision-makers will use priority-setting processes, also known as rationing or resource allocation, with guidance from federal, state, or local pandemic planning documents and guidelines.[40] Consequently, current societal expectations about access to health care will have to change in light of a public health crisis of such major proportions.

Already there are signs of a public debate over choices. For example, when there are shortages of equipment like ventilators and beds in intensive care units, health providers typically ration on a first-come, first-served basis; however, during a pandemic such rationing will likely be done on a different basis—that of saving the greatest number of lives.[41] In most emergency rooms, medical need—those patients who are the worst off and in greatest need—determines which patients are treated first. During a pandemic, saving the greatest number of lives may take priority over patient autonomy. The goal of helping those most in need will clash with the goal of minimizing deaths. Patients with respiratory and multi-organ failure and those whose condition deteriorates over the first few days of treatment have a poor prognosis, so they are most in need.[42] But treating these patients will increase the total number of deaths because their use of a ventilator for many days will preclude the treatment of other patients who need a ventilator for a few days and have a greater chance of survival.

Although such choices are justifiable, it would help to build public support by discussing these issues in an open and transparent manner before a pandemic occurs. The second scenario highlights some of the ethical challenges in the allocation of scarce resources during a pandemic.

Scenario 2: Priority-Setting in an Intensive Care Unit

The Regional Hospital is a major trauma center with a large emergency department and intensive care unit (ICU). During a pandemic influenza crisis, Regional's ICU is filled to capacity with patients suffering from life-threatening medical conditions, including complications from influenza-like bacterial pneumonia. The emergency department calls the ICU seeking to admit Mr. Smith, who has been brought to the emergency room with a severe but potentially reversible brain injury after an automobile accident. One alternative is to move one of the current ICU patients to a medical unit in order to make room for Mr. Smith. However, the ICU staff report that all of their patients need ventilator support, and there are no other ventilated beds available in the hospital. Another alternative is to send Mr. Smith to another unit in the hospital. However, given Mr. Smith's injuries, it is clear that this would overtax the clinical capabilities of the hospital staff who are not trained in critical care and most of whom are already struggling to care for other patients. The final alternative is to transfer Mr. Smith to another health care facility. However, the influenza pandemic has overwhelmed all hospitals in the region, and no ICU beds are available anywhere else.

Scenario 2: First Set of Questions

1. What are your initial responses to this situation? What is your gut reaction?
2. What are the most important considerations in this scenario?
3. What are the features of this case that you find the most compelling?

An ICU patient passes away. A bed is now available in the ICU for Mr. Smith. Just as his transfer is about to be made, an ICU nurse named Ms. Brown is admitted with severe difficulty breathing. It is determined that she has been infected with the influenza virus, which she may have contracted while caring for patients in the hospital's ICU. She needs immediate ventilation support, which is only available in the ICU bed designated for, but not yet occupied by, Mr. Smith. It comes to light that Mr. Smith has aging parents at home who rely on him for help with activities of daily living. Though not a long-standing employee of the hospital, Ms. Brown is well respected by her coworkers.

Scenario 2: Second Set of Questions
1. Have your initial responses to the situation changed in light of this added information?
2. Are there any considerations that you find significant in this additional information?
3. Is there anything compelling about this development?
4. Do these personal details about the two patients' lives affect your perspective?

Until a new flu vaccine is developed or other medications are found that can abate the severity and spread of pandemic flu, restrictive measures may be one of the important public health tools to reduce the spread of this communicable disease. Governments may need to limit three basic personal freedoms that we take for granted: (1) mobility, (2) freedom of assembly, and (3) privacy. For example, public health officials may close schools, cancel public gatherings and sporting events, and impose quarantine, isolation, and even detention where needed in order to manage the spread of the disease.[43] A major flu pandemic could result in very large numbers of people being subjected to such measures, which would impose a heavy burden on those most directly affected. People might be cut off from family, friends, work, shopping, entertainment, travel, and most other activities, including some forms of medical care. People might feel stigmatized if they are put into quarantine or identified as being affected by pandemic flu.[44]

Research conducted in the aftermath of the 2002–2003 SARS epidemic showed that people understood and accepted the need for restrictive measures to control the spread of a communicable disease. However, the research also indicated that if decision-makers expect full compliance with restrictive measures, they need to make their decisions in a fair manner, and those affected by such measures need to support the decisions and conditions.[45] Reciprocity requires that society ensure that those affected receive adequate care and do not suffer unfair economic penalties.

The University of Toronto Joint Centre for Bioethics provides the following recommendations to decision-makers:

> If leaders expect people exposed to or suffering from communicable diseases to act in a manner that does not put others at risk, it is important that they create a social environment that does not leave people without supports. For example, if quarantine is implemented, governments should ensure that people have adequate food supplies and are able to carry out essential functions. Their jobs should be protected, and they should not suffer an undue financial burden.[46]

In the event of a severe pandemic influenza, people in the United States can expect quarantines, but they may also face the possibility of other measures to contain the disease, including mandatory vaccination, surveillance cameras, monitoring devices, and even imprisonment for people who fail to comply with quarantine orders.[47]

Scenario 3 discusses the ethical dilemmas that arise when a quarantine is imposed.

Scenario 3: Measures That Restrict Liberty and Freedom

With the WHO's official determination that an influenza pandemic is under way, the Department of Health and Human Services reports that influenza is confirmed to be spreading in the United States and that several deaths have occurred; further, with large-scale public vaccination programs remaining weeks away, public health officials are strongly recommending the immediate implementation of some restrictive measures to help slow the spread of the infection. Soon many localities have closed community centers and schools and canceled all large public gatherings and events.

One family does not receive this information, which is released just when their daughter, sixteen-year-old Maria, has been killed in a car accident. Information about the closings is disseminated in the English media, and this family does not ordinarily watch TV or listen to the radio in English. Sponsored by her twenty-four-year-old sister Diana to come to the United States, Maria, her brothers Raul and Marcos, and her parents arrived from Colombia less than a year ago, and they all speak little English. The family holds a large memorial service for family and friends the following day. Few people fail to show up because most of them, although they have heard the order by authorities, think that the cancellation of large public gatherings applies to social events, not to a funeral, which is a sacred rite to honor the passing of a loved one. Moreover, the tragedy of this untimely loss over-shadows everyone's concern about a disease outbreak whose seriousness remains unknown. There have been no reported deaths from influenza in their immediate community. Over two hundred people attend the funeral for the young woman.

Scenario 3: First Set of Questions
1. What are your initial thoughts and feelings about this situation?
2. What do you think were the most important considerations for the family in making their decision?
3. What features of this case do you find most compelling?

Immediately following the funeral, state public health authorities issue an order requiring everyone who attended the funeral to stay home for a period of seven days, even though there is still little information about the virus or the extent of the outbreak. Diana wonders whether this is feasible, as her family depends on her income as a sales associate at a local box retailer. Diana started this position as a part-time job and was promoted in the last month to a full-time position, which has enabled her to start receiving health care benefits. Thus, she has no sick leave accrued and cannot take time off from work without losing income. She decides to go to work, where she will be checking out customers, in spite of the order, while the rest of her family stays home.

Scenario 3: Second Set of Questions
1. What do you think of Diana's decision?
2. Do you think people should face consequences if they don't follow an order of quarantine? If yes, what sort of penalties do you think would be fair?

3. Is there anything compelling about this development?

The US government has now declared a state of emergency. Three people who attended the funeral are showing symptoms of influenza, and one person has died from it. Although Diana is aware that the outbreak has now hit close to home, she can't see how it would be possible for her not to go to work. After she continues to ignore the order, public health officials detain Diana. Her family is left with no income and stranded at home with little food.

Scenario 3: Third Set of Questions

1. Have your responses to the situation changed in light of this new information?
2. What do you think of the public health authority's decision to detain Diana?
3. Do you think society has obligations to those ordered into quarantine?
4. Is there anything compelling about this development?

Conclusion

During a major influenza pandemic, it is unlikely that there would be sufficient time to discuss the ethical trade-offs inherent in critical decisions. Personal ethics, like personal fitness, need to be established before one needs them to govern one's behavior. Likewise, it is impossible to anticipate all of the possible key decisions that will need to be made during an emergency. Therefore, it is important to establish a social contract that outlines the ethical principles that society has determined should be considered when deliberating on key decisions. Developing an ethical blueprint in advance of a pandemic, seeking public input into the principles, and then applying these ethical guidelines to the decisions with which decision-makers will be faced will help assure the public that decision-makers are making reasoned responses to the crisis (see Table 5.1.1). The public's acceptance of those responses will increase the likelihood that society will maintain order during the emergency and that people will trust that fair and just decisions are being made to promote the public health and welfare.

TABLE 5.1.1: Ethical Principles to Guide Societal Decision-Making During an Influenza Pandemic

Ethical Principles	Description
Individual liberty	Individual liberty includes some of the basic rights that we value in our society, such as freedom of movement. In an influenza pandemic, restrictions on individual liberty, such as isolation or quarantine, may be necessary to protect the public from serious harm. In addition, some taking of private property may be necessary. Restrictions and takings should: • Be necessary given the nature of the influenza pandemic; • Employ the least restrictive means needed to protect the public; and • Be applied equitably to similarly situated individuals irrespective of race, color, religion, nationality, ethnicity, gender, age, disability, sexual orientation, geography, economic status, or insurance status, unless there are specific clinical reasons why different groups should be treated differently.
Protection of the public from harm	Protecting the public is a fundamental social value. To protect the public from harm and to protect public health, governmental authorities may be required to take actions that impinge on individual liberty, such as quarantine or isolation. In making these determinations, decision-makers should: • Balance the harm to the public that could arise if no action is taken with the harm to the individual(s) that could result if action is taken; • Provide reasons and/or incentives to encourage voluntary compliance; • Employ the least intrusive means needed to protect the public and ensure that the basic necessities of the people subject to quarantine or isolation are being met; • Discontinue protections as soon as circumstances permit; • Specify penalties that will be used to address noncompliance (e.g., jail or fines); and • Establish mechanisms to address actual or perceived inequitable impositions of penalties.
Proportionality	Restrictions to individual liberty, or other measures taken to protect the public from harm, should not exceed what is necessary to address the actual level of risk to or critical needs of the community.
Duty to provide: health care workers	Inherent to all codes of ethics for health care professionals is the duty to provide care and to respond to suffering. Health care professionals, because of their training, knowledge, and commitment to care for the sick and injured, have a heightened obligation to provide health care during an influenza pandemic. Licensed health care professionals have a heightened responsibility to care for the ill because of the special privileges and monopoly conferred on licensed health care professionals. This obligation exists even in the face of increased risk to the health care professional's health or safety. However, health care professionals need to balance their ability to meet the health care needs of individual patients during an influenza pandemic with their ability to care for patients in the future. Health care organizations, and society at large, owe support (reciprocity) to health care workers who may be putting themselves or their families at increased risk during an influenza pandemic.

Ethical Principles	Description
Reciprocity	Certain individuals will be called upon to bear a disproportionate risk to their health or life in the response to an influenza pandemic, including health care professionals and other health care workers, emergency management workers and other first responders, and workers in other critical industries or key professions. Reciprocity requires that society support those who face a disproportionate burden in protecting the public and take steps to minimize this burden as much as possible. In some instances, reciprocity may require additional compensation, services, care, or special considerations for disproportionately burdened individuals.
Equity	Values of distributive justice and equity state that all people have equal moral worth. However, during an influenza pandemic, it may be the case that not all individuals are able to receive all of the health care services they need. Difficult decisions will have to be made about whom to treat and about which health care services to provide and which to defer. Depending on the severity of the health crisis, some individuals may not be able to receive all the health care services needed to treat the flu (such as ventilators). Others may not be able to receive elective surgeries, emergency care, or other necessary services. Decisions about whom to treat and access to needed health care services during an influenza pandemic should not be based on an individual's race, color, religion, nationality, ethnicity, gender, age, disability, sexual orientation, geography, economic status, or insurance status, unless there are specific clinical reasons why different groups should be treated differently. Furthermore, equity concerns may arise in decisions other than treatment. For example, equity issues may arise if certain health care workers are not required to work during a pandemic (e.g., pregnant women or single parents) or if certain workers are required to work longer hours or remain at the worksite.
Trust	Trust is an essential component of the relationships between clinicians and patients, staff and their organizations, and the public and governmental organizations. Decision-makers will be confronted with the challenge of maintaining the public's trust while simultaneously implementing various control measures during an evolving health crisis. Trust is indispensable for expectations of compliance. Trust is enhanced by transparency in decision-making, equity in the application of restrictions and/or allocation of limited resources, and reciprocity toward those with an increased burden.
Collaboration	Response to an influenza pandemic requires collaboration and cooperation within and between governmental officials and organizations, government, public and private health care institutions, health care professionals, other public and private organizations, and individuals. It calls for approaches that set aside narrow self-interest or territoriality.

Source: North Carolina Institute of Medicine, *Stockpiling Solutions: North Carolina's Ethical Guidelines for an Influenza Pandemic*, April 2007, http://epi.publichealth.nc.gov/cd/flu/plan/AppendixO1_2008.

DISCUSSION QUESTIONS

1. What are the ethical problems for health professionals, public administrators, and community members presented in each of the three cases?
2. What were the competing or conflicting ethical principles or values in each case?
3. What are the possible negative or positive consequences of the actions taken by those involved in each case?
4. Review the ethical guidelines in Table 5.1.1. Which of these do you think are most important? Explain.

NOTES

1. Mary Ann Roser, "Health Authorities Troubled by Number of Healthy People Dying from H1N1 Virus," *American-Statesman*, October 20, 2009.

2. Rob Stein, "Swine Flu Deaths Among Youths Rise as Epidemic Spreads," *Washington Post*, October 10, 2009.

3. Marc Lacey and Donald McNeil, "Fighting Deadly Flu, Mexico Shuts Schools," *New York Times*, April 21, 2009.

4. Centers for Disease Control and Prevention, "Updated CDC Estimates of 2009 H1N1 Influenza Cases, Hospitalizations, and Deaths in the United States, April 2009–April 10, 2010," http://www.cdc.gov/h1n1flu/estimates_2009_h1n1.htm/#The%20Numbers (accessed June 30, 2012).

5. Michael Osterholm, "Preparing for the Next Pandemic," *Foreign Affairs* 84 (July–August 2005): 24, cited in US Department of Health and Human Services, HHS Pandemic Influenza Plan, November 2005, http://www.flu.gov/planning-preparedness/federal/hhspandemicinfluenzaplan.pdf.

6. Sarah Lister, "Congressional Research Service Report for Congress: Pandemic Influenza: Domestic Preparedness Effort," updated February, 20, 2007, 11 http://www.fas.org/sgp/crs/misc/RL33145.pdf (accessed June 15, 2012).

7. Christopher McDougall, "Ethical Questions During a Pandemic: Case Studies," National Collaborating Centre for Healthy Public Policy, March 2010, www.ncchpp.ca/docs/Ethics_CaseStudies_EN.pdf (accessed June 1, 2012).

8. Li Chen, "The Writing Committee of the World Health Organization (WHO) Consultation on Human Influenza A/H5: Avian Influenza A (H5N1) Infection in Humans," *New England Journal of Medicine* 353, no. 13 (2005): 1375.

9. US Department of Health and Human Services, Centers for Disease Control and Prevention, "Key Facts About Avian Influenza and Avian Influenza A (H5N1) Virus," June 30, 2006, http://www.cdc.gov/flu/avian/gen-info/facts.htm (accessed September 15, 2011).

10. Ibid., 2.

11. The SARS epidemic in 2002–2003 started in a similar way. See David Heymann, "Past as Prologue?" in *Ethical and Legal Considerations in Mitigating Pandemic Disease: Workshop Summary* (Washington, DC: National Academies Press, 2007), 39.

12. Seasonal influenza has an incubation period of one to four days; see Centers for Disease Control and Prevention, "Seasonal Influenza: Questions and Answers," http://www.cdc.gov/flu/about/qa/disease.htm (accessed October 10, 2011).

13. "Tamiflu Works Against Avian Flu H5N1 Strain," Medical News Today, November 1, 2004, http://www.medicalnewstoday.com/articles/15740.php (accessed October 8, 2011).

14. National Institute of Allergy and Infectious Diseases (NIAID), "Questions and Answers: Avian Influenza Trials," February 2007, http://www.niaid.nih.gov/news/qa/pages/h5n1qanda.aspx (accessed October 8, 2010).

15. US Department of Health and Human Services, "Review of 1918 Pandemic Flu Studies Offers More Questions Than Answers," February 28, 2007, http://www.nih.gov/news/pr/feb2007/niaid-28.htm (accessed October 9, 2010).

16. Osterholm, "Preparing for the Next Pandemic," 24.

17. HHS, "Review of 1918 Pandemic Flu Studies Offers More Questions Than Answers."

18. Ibid., 1.

19. The Congressional Budget Office has developed two pandemic scenarios. In its view, a severe pandemic scenario—one similar to the 1918–1919 influenza episode—could infect 90 million people in the United States and cause the deaths of more than 2 million; and secondly, a milder pandemic resembling the 1957 and 1968 influenza outbreaks might be expected to infect 75 million people and cause roughly 100,000 deaths in the United States. See Congressional Budget Office, "A Potential Influenza Pandemic: Possible Macroeconomic Effects and Policy Issues" (Washington, DC: CBO, July 7, 2006), http://www.cbo.gov/ftpdocs/69xx/doc6946/12–08-BirdFlu.pdf (accessed October 9, 2010).

20. Ibid., 35.

21. US Department of Homeland Security, National Infrastructure Simulation and Analysis Center, *National Population, Economic, and Infrastructure Impacts of Pandemic Influenza with Strategic Recommendations* (Washington, DC: DHS, October 2007), 4, http://www.sandia.gov/nisac/analyses/national-population-economic-and-infrastructure-impacts-of-pandemic-influenza-with-strategic-recommendations/.

22. CBO, "A Potential Influenza Pandemic," 36.

23. Michael Osterholm, "Preparing for the Next Pandemic," *New England Journal of Medicine* 352 (May 2005): 1839.

24. DHS, *National Population, Economic, and Infrastructure Impacts of Pandemic Influenza with Strategic Recommendations.*

25. CBO, "A Potential Influenza Pandemic," 14.

26. Ibid., 16–18.

27. Cited in HHS, *HHS Pandemic Influenza Plan*, appendix D, D-12.

28. CBO, "A Potential Influenza Pandemic," 35. This figure is based on the 2004 labor force total of 147 million people.

29. These estimates are based on the planning assumptions in HHS, *HHS Pandemic Influenza Plan*, 2.

30. According to Roche, the maker of Tamiflu (also known as oseltamivir), production of that drug takes six to eight months and requires scarce ingredients and specialized facilities. See Andrew Pollack, "Is Bird Flu Drug Really So Vexing? Debating the Difficulty of Tamiflu," *New York Times*, November 5, 2005.

31. HHS, *HHS Pandemic Influenza Plan*, 5.

32. A number of planning documents are available, including HHS, *HHS Pandemic Influenza Plan*; North Carolina Institute of Medicine, *Stockpiling Solutions: North Carolina's Ethical Guidelines for an Influenza Pandemic*, April 2007, http://epi.publichealth.nc.gov/cd/flu/plan/AppendixO1_2008.pdf; and Dorothy E. Vawter et al., *For the Good of Us All: Ethically Rationing Health Resources in Minnesota in a Severe Influenza Pandemic*, Minnesota Center for Health Care Ethics, January 30, 2009, www.health.state.mn.us/divs/idepc/ethics/ethics.pdf.

33. National Academy of Sciences, *Ethical and Legal Considerations in Mitigating Pandemic Disease: Workshop Summary* (Washington, DC: National Academies Press, 2007), 154–192.

34. Ibid.

35. Ibid., 171–172.

36. University of Toronto Joint Centre for Bioethics, Pandemic Influenza Working Group, "Stand on Guard for Thee: Ethical Considerations in Preparedness Planning for Pandemic Influenza," 2005, 10, http://www.jointcentreforbioethics.ca/people/documents/upshur_stand_guard.pdf (accessed December 1, 2011).

37. Jaro Kotalik, "Preparing for an Influenza Pandemic: Ethical Issues," *Bioethics* 19, no. 4 (2005): 424.

38. US Department of Health and Human Services, "US National Vaccine Program Office," http://hhs.gov/nvpo/pandemicplan/index.html (accessed December 1, 2011).

39. John Bartlett, "Planning for Avian Influenza," *Annals of Internal Medicine* 145, no. 2 (2006): 141–144.

40. University of Toronto Joint Centre for Bioethics, "Stand on Guard for Thee," 15–17.

41. National Academy of Sciences, *Ethical and Legal Considerations in Mitigating Pandemic Disease*, 193.

42. Ibid., 194.

43. University of Toronto Joint Centre for Bioethics, "Stand on Guard for Thee," 12–14.

44. Ibid.

45. HHS, *HHS Pandemic Influenza Plan*, supplement 8, "Community Disease Control and Prevention."

46. University of Toronto Joint Centre for Bioethics, "Stand on Guard for Thee," 13.

47. HHS, *HHS Pandemic Influenza Plan*, supplement 8, "Community Disease Control and Prevention."

The Impact of Cyber-Security on Critical Infrastructure Protection

The Advanced Persistent Threat

GARY C. KESSLER

Introduction

The advanced persistent threat (APT) is a new type of cyber-threat—a sustained attack on a specific target that employs many types of tools from the hacker's tool kit and adapts to the defenses put up to thwart it. APTs require organization and funding, patience, and a goal—and they appear to be sponsored by nation-states. As such, APTs represent the next escalation in cyber-warfare and present a clear threat to US infrastructures—both physical infrastructures that support the provision of power, water, and food, and systems infrastructures that support health care, manufacturing, banking, and the like. This case will describe the actions of an APT and the evolution of cyber-security threats. The role of nation-states in cyber-security and the impact of APTs on US critical infrastructures will also be explored.

Operation Aurora: The Attack on Google et al.

In January 2010, Google announced on its corporate blog that it had been the target of a cyber-attack. Detected in mid-December 2009, the attack was highly sophisticated, Google reported, and directed at Google's corporate network infrastructure. The attacks, originating from addresses in China, were specifically trying to acquire Google's intellectual property.[1] As Google analyzed the attack, "it soon became clear that what at first appeared to be solely a security incident—albeit a significant one—was something quite different."[2]

According to Google, three factors made this incident different from previous incidents:

1. The attacks targeted specific victims, and Google was not alone. As Google investigated the incident in depth, it discovered at least twenty other corporate victims, including Adobe Systems, Dow Chemical, Juniper Networks, McAfee Labs, Northrop Grumman, Morgan Stanley, and Yahoo.
2. One primary goal of the attack on Google was to access the Gmail accounts of two Chinese human rights activists. The intruders appeared to limit their activity to accessing general account information and message headers (such as date of transmission, recipients, and subject) rather than message content.
3. Investigators discovered that dozens of Chinese, European, and US Gmail accounts belonging to individuals who were advocates of human rights in China had been accessed by one or more unknown third parties. This access, which had been ongoing for an unknown amount of time, appeared to be the result of "phishing"—malware (malicious software) installed on users' computers and other social engineering techniques.[3]

But there were even more differences than these compared to prior incidents. The attackers used a vulnerability in Microsoft's Internet Explorer (IE) browser software to install malware on the victims' computers. McAfee dubbed this attack "Operation Aurora" because the word "aurora" appeared in the file pathname of the malware on the attacker's computer, according to its analysis. Although Microsoft released a patch to fix the IE vulnerability within days of Google's announcement, it was later learned that Microsoft had known about the vulnerability since September 2009.[4] This malware allowed the attackers to gain control of victims' computers and move around the victims' corporate network.

Coincidentally, there was political wrangling between Google and the Chinese government as well, somewhat exacerbating the latter's willingness to use cyber-attacks to access the intellectual property of others and to punish dissidents. Google had initiated a corporate presence in China in 2005 and quickly rose to become the second-largest search engine in that country. In 2006 the Google China search engine (google.cn) was returning results subject to government censorship; the censorship expanded when access to YouTube—which was acquired by Google in late 2006—was blocked. After the attacks on Google were made public in January 2010, Google announced that it was shutting down its China search engine and redirecting all queries from China to its Hong Kong search engine in order to avoid censorship and redirected searches by the Chinese government. It is worth noting that the Operation Aurora attacks did *not* target any Google assets in China but rather Google servers at corporate headquarters in California—because that was where the desired intellectual property resided.

And thus the term "advanced persistent threat" entered the cyber-security vernacular. "Advanced" refers to the fact that these attacks are the result of significant research and intelligence-gathering by the perpetrator. While the actual attack methods employed might not be particularly novel or sophisticated, the combination of methodologies might be very complex and specifically aimed at a given victim. The perpetrators generally have a wide range of intelligence-gathering capabilities, pointing to a highly organized and well-funded group or, more commonly, a national capability. Nothing, however, in the definition of APT limits these attacks to nation-states; they have also been perpetrated by organized, well-funded terrorist and criminal groups. "Persistent" refers to the nature of the event. APTs are not random events that just happen to turn up a potential target that is then, in turn, attacked. Quite the contrary—the attacker chooses the target in order to obtain specific goals and relentlessly pursues that victim using a broad range of tools and a variety of adaptable, mutable attack vectors that respond to the target's defenses and countermoves.[5] APTs are generally "low-and-slow" attacks, meaning that the perpetrator gains access to the victim's cyber-infrastructure and gains control that can be exploited at the attacker's convenience. "Threat" refers to both the capability and intent of the action. APTs are not automated attacks that operate at random; they are specific, intentional, targeted attacks operated by skilled, motivated people who are on a mission and who generally are well funded and well organized. Theoretically, APTs can be carried out by an intelligence or military agency, a terrorist organization, a criminal entity, or any other well-organized, well-funded group with a mission.

APT-class intrusions are the latest evolution of attacks on network-based systems that have been occurring for the last several decades, and they are on the rise since they were first described in 2010.[6] While the exact method of the different attacks varies, they all have several factors in common: they are carried out by professionals; they have a very high success rate; and they leave a way for the attacker to come back later. And because almost all of these attacks appear to have state sponsorship, APTs may very well become a tool in a very real cyber-war, with attacks on national infrastructures and civilian populations.[7]

The Changing Face of Information and Cyber-Warfare

To put the APT into context, it is necessary to step back in time. For many, the terms "information warfare" and "cyber-war" conjure up images of an Internet Armageddon, of Bad Guys—however that is defined—bringing down the Internet. In fact, the notion of an individual or a group crashing the Internet is not—and probably never was—the intent of so-called cyber-war. It is not that disabling the Internet is impossible; it most certainly is possible, and many attacks have shown some of the Internet's critical points of failure (most notably the domain name system[8] and the backbone routers[9]). Bringing down the Internet, however, probably would not serve the purpose of any group that has the capability to do so. The Internet—and its underlying packet-switching technology—is incredibly distributed, resilient, and robust and has no single point of failure. Any adversary that can crash the Internet clearly has to use the Internet and needs the network for its own purposes as well.[10] The analogy in the physical world would be one nation attacking another by destroying all of its roads; once successful, how would the attacker move its own troops around? The importance of the Internet to everyday life around the world has prompted several pleas for the Internet to be a war-free zone.[11]

All this being said, temporarily disrupting the Internet or causing an outage in select portions of it very likely could benefit specific groups— or nation-states—at the expense of others. If some actor can cause a targeted outage at a time of its choosing, it has an enormous advantage over an adversary because of the disruption to the victim's communications, supply chains, and information-gathering capabilities. This is one aspect of the new face of cyber-war.[12]

Cyber-war differs from "traditional" armed conflict, of course, but it also shares many of the kinetic principles of war on land or sea or in the air, including:

1. *Objective:* All military actions (presumably) have a clearly defined and attainable goal. This is clearly also true of cyber-war.

2. *Economy of force:* The ideal circumstance allows a military to place as many of its resources as possible toward obtaining the primary goal and to minimize the resources necessary to effect secondary tasks. Cyber-war is a perfect example of economy of force through asymmetrical warfare.

3. *Maneuver:* Military actions are designed to put an adversary in a position of disadvantage by quickly adapting to the adversary's actions and reactions. This clearly happens in cyber-war, and the movement is generally far more rapid in cyber-space than in "real space" (the physical world).

4. *Unity of command:* Militaries are organized so that command and control comes from the top down. While generally true in some cyber-war operations, some groups perpetrating cyber-war activities (for example, Anonymous) are closer to disorganized militias than to a disciplined army.

5. *Security:* It is important for a military group to not allow its adversary to obtain an unexpected advantage. This is also true in a cyber-war scenario, although there is a greater risk of failure, detection, and having the weapon turned against the original user in cyber-space than in real space.

6. *Surprise:* The element of surprise is essential for quick victory in warfare in both real space and cyber-space; surprise is what allows an attacker to start an incident at the time and place of its choosing. Surprise can be even more of an advantage in cyber-space, where an attack can be launched on a moment's notice and spread extraordinarily quickly.[13]

7. *Simplicity:* A concise, simple plan is easy to execute and understand and less likely to go awry as the situation changes—which it always

does during warfare. This is true in cyber-war as well: simple solutions are the best solutions, and events move rapidly in cyber-space.[14]

Information warfare can be thought of slightly differently than cyber-war. Information warfare is the use of *information*—not necessarily computer data networks—to engage in hostilities with an enemy. Information warfare can include propaganda, misinformation, disinformation, and other forms of communication that can distract or confuse an adversary. Information warfare can also include the theft of another entity's intellectual property for one's own gain, or the destruction or disruption of another entity's information or information systems.

This section confines the discussion to attacks on the Internet as a communications infrastructure. The first such "attack" was the Internet worm. Launched in 1988 while the Internet was still available only to the National Science Foundation and related research sites, the worm nevertheless brought the Internet to its knees in a matter of hours. The perpetrator of the worm was, in fact, a member of the Internet community who was trying to make a point about security vulnerabilities in the communications protocols and whose error in his program caused the worm to infect the Internet at an alarming rate. A result of this event was the formation of the Computer Emergency Response Team/Coordination Center (CERT/CC)[15] to enhance security-related communication; other features were also added to Internet protocols and services that made the network more resilient.[16]

The Internet did not acquire its current commercial, open nature until 1991, and truly widespread use followed after the development of (free) Web server and browser software in 1993. From that point forward, people and groups poked and probed and prodded just about every aspect of Internet sites that they could. In many cases, vulnerabilities were found that were reported to vendors, who, in turn, fixed them. In many other cases, the vulnerabilities were exploited by the people who found them. Over the years, the Internet "backbone" added new protocols and methodologies to make the network more resistant to attack and more robust in its ability to recover and respond to attacks.

For any number of reasons, the Internet makes a great deal of information available that can be used by an attacker because this same information has to be available for basic Internet operations. Take, for example, the ability to learn a server's Internet protocol (IP) address. Without this information, an attacker cannot attack a Web server, but without this information, legitimate users cannot access the server either.

During the first fifteen years or so of the commercial Internet (1991–2006), attacks on the Internet were serious but typically opportunistic. The normal mode of an attack was for a user, for example, to port scan a region of a large network. In the transmission control protocol/Internet protocol (TCP/IP) architecture, an IP address identifies a computer while a "port" identifies an application or process running on the computer. "Port scanning," then, is a means to search a block of IP addresses and identify all running processes at all accessible computers. A person or group could, for example, scan the IP address block that corresponds to the Comcast cable network in Vermont. Upon discovering the IP address and open ports of all hosts, other steps could be taken to identify the actual software being used on the computers. The next step is to search vulnerable databases to find known flaws in the versions of the software running on those systems. Any software that appears vulnerable might then be exploited in order to access information or deface a website. An analogy in the physical world would be to walk through a neighborhood and try jiggling the front door of every house and, on finding an unlocked door, entering the house; once inside, one might just harmlessly look around, steal items, or spray-paint the walls. In any case, intrusion by an uninvited guest is unauthorized and unwanted.

One early, well-publicized defacement in the mid-1990s was of the US Air Force's website. A group changed the color of the site to black, posted a message to some hacker friends, and uploaded a short pornographic video. An example of the escalation and changing motives of these attacks was exemplified in 2009 when the Royal Australian Air Force's website was defaced and the following message was posted:

THIS SITE HACKED BY ATUL DWIVEDI LONG LIVE INDIA THIS IS A WARNING MESSAGE TO AUSTRALIAN GOVT. IMMEDIATELY TAKE ALL MEASURES TO STOP RACIST ATTACKS AGAINST INDIAN STUDENTS IN AUSTRALIA ELSE I WILL PAWN ALL YOUR CYBER PROPERTIES LIKE THIS ONE. JAI HIND[17]

This was an early defacement categorized as "hacktivism," a targeted defacement of a site with the intention of sending a message. Most of the attacks during the early era were sophomoric but effective—they got people's attention. At the time, server system administrators concentrated their defenses on hardware (such as routers, servers, and firewalls) and software (applications and operating systems). Then, over time, the attacks grew more meaningful and more serious.

Characteristics of an Advanced Persistent Threat

The advanced persistent threat is a new form of cyber-attack that is changing the way defenders look at their computers, networks, and data. As the name implies, an APT is targeted at a particular victim, is persistent, and adapts to defenses rather than retreats from them. The defender then might be able to deflect the attack for a while, but the attacker does not go away. Indicative of a very organized type of attack, a cyber-attack is not the work of a pedestrian hacker who is looking for just any site to break into, but of a sponsored organization with plenty of talent that wants to gain access to a particular site.[18]

APTs generally use a variety of attack tools and methodologies such as port-scanning, social engineering,[19] phishing,[20] spear phishing, vishing,[21] smishing,[22] vulnerability exploitation,[23] and other resources in a hacker's tool kit.[24] Target sites often inadvertently help the attacker by providing a large amount of useful inside information on the organization's website. For example, how hard would it be for a user to learn the names of faculty, staff, and students at many, if not most, colleges and universities? Armed with that information, an attacker has an email and telephone number list with which to blast a phishing or vishing attack. Indeed, that information can also aid in social engineering and spear-phishing attacks by providing likely individuals to target.

APTs are currently being carried out by groups in one of three main categories (although the lines between these categories are frequently blurred):

1. Cyber-criminals motivated by monetary gain
2. Nation-states motivated by the political, economic, military, or other strategic advantage gained through espionage and intelligence-gathering
3. Hacktivists or terrorists motivated by politics or ideology

Another important feature of the APT is that it is about so much more than merely defacing websites: it is about gathering information and/or control of the target's servers for the optimal benefit of the attacker. No longer do attackers break in and immediately wreak havoc because they need to prove that they exploited a vulnerability; APT attackers gain entry and wait until the moment is right for them.

Nothing here is meant to suggest that a site cannot defend itself against an APT. It is important for an organization to understand what makes it an attractive target and to identify its potential adversaries. As a pertinent example, InfraGard is an FBI-sponsored public/private-sector information-sharing organization dedicated to protection of the nation's critical infrastructures, with more than fifty thousand members in eighty-six chapters across the United States.[25] In late 2011 and early 2012, many chapters' websites were attacked or defaced, and chapter data leaked to the attackers. In the aftermath of understanding the targeted attacks, several asked why sensitive data were on the InfraGard chapter sites to begin with. Indeed, part of the task of defending data is making judicious choices about how and where it is stored and about the access controls put in place.

Knowing one's adversary might give an organization important insight into the adversary's motivation, intent, available resources, and the lengths to which it might go to launch an attack. That said, if the basic information security processes are not handled well, the motivation does not matter, as the game will be lost anyway: all APT attacks are exploiting real vulnerabilities that need to be identified and mitigated. It is generally accepted in the information security field that 100 percent security in systems is impossible to achieve—and with the rate at which software and operating systems change (think "Patch Tuesday"[26]), new vulnerabilities in individual applications or in the interactions between applications are constantly emerging.

Baseball Hall of Famer Willie Mays once said: "Sandy [Koufax] would strike me out two or three times a game. And I knew every pitch he was going to throw—fastball, breaking ball or whatever. Actually, he would let you look at it. And you still couldn't hit it."[27] The point here is that successfully defending against an APT does not necessarily depend on knowing the enemy or even knowing the attack vector. It is all about user education, proper planning, good policies, and vigilance.

The Exploitation Life Cycle of an APT

An APT has a life cycle, like any good project that has a target and a goal. APTs also employ a series of steps that have much in common with a military, terrorist, or guerrilla action. The typical exploitation cycle of an APT has the following stages:

1. *Reconnaissance:* Prior to launching any sort of attack, attackers learn about their target. The target's website generally contains a wealth of information about the organization, including potential individuals of interest (ranging from the chief financial officer and director of research to the human resources manager and administrative assistant), geographic locations, and partner organizations. Simple hacker tools and public websites can be used to scan the organization's network to learn the IP addresses of servers, information about the domain name and management, locations where servers are hosted, servers' operating system and application platforms, and much more. This research allows the attackers to select a series of attack vectors and methods with which to achieve their goals. Attackers can also obfuscate and add to the fog of war by using so many methods that it is hard to tell which vectors are real and which are red herrings.

2. *Initial intrusion:* The first intrusion is when the attacker actually gains some entry into the target network. One way might be to exploit a flaw in the server software found to be used by the target; for example, if the server scan indicates that the target is using an outdated or unpatched version of an application, the attacker might be able to gain access through the vulnerable software. Another common approach is to use any number of social engineering attacks, such as "spear phishing." Like phishing, spear phishing employs emails that contain malware or bogus website addresses; while phishing is an email blast to a huge number of people, however, spear phishing is targeted, and its falseness is less obvious to the recipient because the email is plausible and not as widespread within the organization (and therefore appears less like spam). As an example, suppose that a group within the target organization recently attended a training session. The APT attackers could spoof an email purportedly coming from one of the trainers and send it just to the group that attended the training session. This spoofed email could have an attachment that contains some form of malware or that sends the reader to a website that contains legitimate

information, along with malware that targets the victim's browser or operating system. Users are more likely to respond to an email coming from a "known" sender, who automatically appears to be trustworthy.

3. *Establishing a backdoor:* Once in, the attacker knows that the intrusion pathway might be discovered and closed. Thus, one of the first actions is to try to create a "backdoor" that will allow the attacker to get back into the network anytime. The most common approach is to gain administrative (or root) privilege on the compromised server and/or network domain, perhaps creating a new user account for use at a later time and even removing traces of the break-in from the system log files. Attackers will attempt to create backdoors on as many systems as possible. They may also employ "stealth malware," which can both avoid detection by host- and network-based scanners and gain system-level access, through a variety of methods. Intruders can keep stealth malware hidden by using a combination of obfuscation methods, such as cryptography, steganography,[28] and going into local system utilities and libraries in order to reduce the size of the executable file.

4. *Obtain user credentials:* After gaining access to a system, an APT intruder generally ensures continued access by using valid credentials in the names of others. Once on a server, the intruder will attempt to copy username databases and break passwords, using an offline attack; the likelihood of finding the passwords for at least a few users with a high level of privilege and/or access rights is pretty high. Once in possession of a set of bona-fide user credentials, the intruder can start to move throughout the network.

5. *Install tools:* Once settled in the network, the intruder can now use some basic hacker tools to continue to learn more about the network—from the inside rather than the outside. The attacker can learn about the operating systems and applications being run on internal systems, servers, and controllers; rootkits[29] can be installed; password databases and email messages can be copied; and data files can be copied, modified, or deleted. Without a doubt, the intruder now owns these systems.

6. *Escalate privilege, move laterally, and exfiltrate data:* At this point, the APT intruder is firmly entrenched in the target network and

can move from system to system in an effort to find a system that will allow an escalation of privilege, which will permit, in turn, additional lateral movement to more systems, more escalation of privilege, and continuance of the cycle. During this process, the intruder can examine data on these systems and remove whatever might be of interest. The exfiltration activity uses the APT client and server software for communication rather than the underlying network infrastructure and generally compresses and encrypts the information. The process may include intermediate servers, and the APT malware generally erases all traces of the activity. The intruder can also modify or delete data after copying.[30]

7. *Maintain persistence:* APT attackers are nothing if not adaptable. The intruder will maintain a presence in the network, dodging and circumventing the owner's mitigation and eradication efforts, and continue to gain access to additional systems, until the attack objectives have been met.[31]

An APT must be detected and stopped at the early phases of this cycle if it is to be stopped at all. In that light, the importance of social engineering to a successful APT cannot be overstated. As an example, consider the intrusion at RSA Corporation in 2011. This intrusion started with a spear-phishing attack directed to low-level employees via a spoofed email purporting to come from an employment recruitment firm. The email contained a spreadsheet attachment; when a recipient opened the spreadsheet, a Flash program was executed that exploited a flaw in Excel that allowed a backdoor program to be installed on the recipient's computer. The backdoor program—called Poison Ivy—then communicated back to the attacker's servers, providing a direct communications path into the network.[32] The attacker then used those few pathways to gain entry to corporate systems, escalate privileges, move laterally, and continue the cycle.

An APT requires a complex combination of tools and human skills, although the majority of the basic tools used by intruders are publicly available. The intrusions are rarely discovered by internal means; in fact, the overwhelming majority of attacks are reported by an external source. Table 5.2.1 shows a breakdown of the industry sectors most targeted by APTs; note that all represent critical infrastructure.

TABLE 5.2.1: Industry Sectors Targeted by APT Attacks, 2012

Sector	Percentage of All APT Attacks
Telecommunications	2
Finance	11
Aerospace and defense	31
Computer hardware and software	3
Legal and consulting	2
Media and entertainment	4
Energy/oil and gas	17
Pharmaceuticals	15
Other	13

Source: Mandiant, "2013 Threat Report," www.mandiant.com/library/M-Trends _2013.pdf (accessed July 20, 2012).

The Role of the State Actor

The initial APT reported by Google was almost certainly launched by a group from China. Many of the APTs targeting other victims, primarily in the United States, have also been thought to originate from China. After the attack on Google, analysts from Northrop Grumman—another target of the initial APT—wrote an in-depth description of the cyber-warfare capabilities and intentions of the People's Republic of China (PRC).[33]

The specific role of the PRC is beyond the scope of this case, but it is important to recognize that many APT attacks are beyond the reach of groups that do not have significant financial support. APTs are widely viewed as a harbinger of a real cyber-war, which would be not just wrongheaded but unethical and perhaps illegal, in the view of most analysts; international treaties specifically outlaw targeting noncombatants during wartime, and a true cyber-war most certainly would be sufficiently indiscriminate as to not be limited to legitimate military targets.[34]

A Chinese group is also thought to be behind an attack dubbed "Operation Shady Rat" by McAfee. First reported in late 2011, Shady Rat was a sustained, five-year operation ostensibly sponsored by the Chinese government and targeting more than seventy organizations in fourteen countries, including the United Nations, the International Olympic Committee, defense contractors, and large businesses. Shady Rat also used steganography, hiding some of the malicious code inside of image files.[35] Interestingly, some in the industry accused McAfee of being alarmist, because the Shady Rat methods were neither new nor particularly sophisticated; in many ways, however, the critics missed the point: the attacks were quite effective and clearly met the criteria of an APT.

Other countries are thought—or known—to be behind APT-type attacks, including Iran, North and South Korea, the Russian Federation, and Turkey.[36] Yet two of the best-known recent APTs are largely thought to be the work of Israel and the United States.

The first attack was called Stuxnet. Discovered in June 2010, Stuxnet was a computer worm that exploited a flaw in the Windows operating system but actually targeted Siemens supervisory control and data acquisition (SCADA) systems. The worm was a programmable logic controller (PLC)[37] rootkit, with the primary target being specific centrifuge models known to be employed at Iranian nuclear research facilities. Specifically designed to damage the centrifuges, Stuxnet was one of the first cyber-attacks intended to cause physical damage. Systems that did not meet specific configuration parameters were unaffected.[38]

Although Iran was ostensibly the primary target of Stuxnet, only 59 percent of the victims were in that country; 18 percent were in Indonesia and 8 percent in India, with other targets being affected in Azerbaijan, Pakistan, and the United States. Analysts quickly realized that Stuxnet was a highly specific attack and probably state-sponsored. When Stuxnet first became known, suspicion fell on Israel and/or the United States as the source, although it was not until June 2012 that news reports "confirmed" that the worm was part of a concerted US and Israeli effort that targeted Iran and was dubbed "Operation Olympic Games."[39] The first variant of Stuxnet was released in June 2009 and the second in early 2010. It is widely believed that the discovery of Stuxnet was inadvertent and due to an error in the program; indeed, like any APT-class threat, Stuxnet was supposed to remain covert until needed.[40]

The second attack was called Flame. Although first detected in May 2012, it is believed by industry analysts to have been active since August 2010, just months after news of Stuxnet was announced. Flame, also thought to have been written in Israel but unrelated to Stuxnet, is a very complex piece of malware. It spreads across a local network or via universal serial bus (USB) devices, after appearing to be a regular Windows update. Flame then uses bogus encryption certificates to authenticate the source code of the malware employed to sniff network traffic, log user keystrokes, capture screenshots, and record audio of conversations. Flame also uses at least five different encryption algorithms in order to evade detection.[41] Although Israel and the United States are again accused of launching this malware in order to negatively affect Iranian nuclear activities, as of this writing this has not yet been confirmed. More than five hundred sites were affected in Egypt, Iran, Israel/Palestine Territory, Lebanon, Saudi Arabia, Sudan, and Syria.[42]

Cyber-war, like war in the physical world (aka real space), involves allies and enemies. There is an appearance that Israel and the United States are starting a cyber-war against Iran's nuclear capability.[43] There are reports that Iran is getting aid from Russian cyber-security experts to build defenses. The United States is the target of cyber-attacks from China, as is Russia—which makes the US-Russian relationship rather complicated. The potential escalation of these activities, as well as the complex and fragile relationships between countries, makes this activity very fraught with danger.

Guns, bombs, and other ordnance are the tools of war in real space and can be employed by armies, criminals, and terrorists alike. Similarly, the tools described here, the tools of cyber-war, have different impacts in the hands of different groups.

Conclusions

There is a close relationship between cyber-security and infrastructure protection. While the information technology and telecommunications sectors are specifically identified as critical infrastructures, every other critical infrastructure sector—such as food, water, financial, transportation, government, and energy—is so dependent on communications and information that any attack on the cyber infrastructure could be made into an attack on any sector.

Consider the attacks on the financial sector in September 2012. In response to a short Internet movie offensive to Muslims, an Islamist cyber-terrorist group called Izz ad-Din al-Qassam Cyber Fighters (a wing of Hamas) launched serious denial-of-service attacks against several US banks, including Bank of America, JPMorgan Chase, PNC Bank, US Bank, and Wells Fargo. Dubbed "Operation Ababil," the attacks were clearly planned, organized, and well executed.[44]

The importance of the APT concept described here goes beyond just protecting the nation's critical infrastructures, because the targets may be outside of what the Department of Homeland Security defines as a critical infrastructure. As we have seen, however, an APT can be launched that goes right to the heart of infrastructure management, operations, and communications facilities, and so we might view the APT as an early version of cyber-warfare.

The attacks on the physical infrastructure are particularly worrisome, and not just for the obvious reasons. Attacks on SCADA devices—which are used to control the electrical grid, oil and gas distribution systems, nuclear power plants, communications networks (including civil defense warning systems), dams, water treatment plants, transportation facilities, food and agriculture, and so many other industrial processes—have been known and documented since the early 1990s.[45] However, the common wisdom has been that if SCADA systems are not connected to the Internet, then the facilities that they control and manage are immune from Internet-based attacks. What APTs such as Stuxnet and Flame have shown is that a sophisticated, multi-tool attack can infect Internet-connected computers that also share a network with SCADA controllers and compromise those very systems. APTs demonstrate a new kind of attack and a new attack vector.

The utility industry in the United States has been neither immune to APTs nor unaware of them. Spear-phishing attacks have been detected against the financial, oil and gas, water, and energy sectors since at least 2009. In February 2011, McAfee released a report about "Night Dragon," a state-sponsored attack utilizing spear phishing, social engineering, and exploitation of Windows systems in order to obtain proprietary information from energy and petrochemical companies.[46]

It is important to remember, however, that not all of the nation's critical infrastructures are physical. Consider the obvious threat of APT-class attacks on infrastructure in commercial facilities, the defense industrial base, emergency services, information technology, banking and finance, and the health care sector if an invader can occupy the network and manipulate the data and the operation at will.

Cyber-war shares many of the same characteristics as war in real space: a specific objective, a strategy, tactics, and command and control. These are the characteristics of the APT events that have occurred since 2010. It does not take too much of a leap of imagination to observe that APTs clearly fall under the characteristics of cyber-war. Couple this with the state sponsorship of many of the attacks and the case becomes even stronger.

Cyber-war has homeland security ramifications that are larger than critical infrastructure protection alone, although these activities clearly put all infrastructures at risk.[47] Cyber-defense and mitigation is beyond the scope of this case, but the essential message for efforts to defend against cyber-war—and APTs—is the same: the definitive way to protect data is at the data itself, through encryption, access control, and other well-known methods. Protection also requires user training and education. Layers of defense are required. And it remains a fact that the best way to keep outsiders away from protected data is to keep those users outside of your network to begin with. An open, "guest" wireless network, for example, may seem like a nice thing to do, but it lets unauthorized users closer to your network than you may want them.

The bottom line to infrastructure protection from attacks in cyber-space is to focus protections on data and workflow, not merely on computers.

DISCUSSION QUESTIONS

1. This case states that "bringing down the Internet" is not the intent of cyber-attacks because then the Internet is lost as a communications channel for the attacker. Consider some arguments to support or refute this assertion.

2. The case suggests that a regional Internet outage could be a goal of attackers. How realistic is this scenario, and how might it be accomplished?

3. The case introduces the APT by describing attacks on major corporations. How do such attacks relate to attacks on the critical infrastructure?

4. Why can attacks such as Stuxnet and Flame be classified as APTs? Why would they not be classified as APTs? Stuxnet and Flame seem to provide a mechanism whereby targeted attacks could be launched on infrastructure to cause regional outages, but is this a realistic scenario? If so, how might such attacks be mitigated?

5. Anonymous is a distributed group of hackers—without clear leadership or organizers—who seem to be able to attack sites pretty much at will. Having been around for ten years, Anonymous is sometimes referred to as an "Internet meme." APTs are generally thought of as being launched by an organized team, usually state-sponsored.

What are some of the factors in defending oneself against a disorganized group that is "everywhere" versus an identifiable group?

6. From the perspective of cyber-security, and APTs in particular, what is the difference between "homeland security" and "national security"?

NOTES

1. David Drummond, "A New Approach to China," Google Official Blog, January 12, 2010, http://googleblog.blogspot.com/2010/01/new-approach-to-china.html; CNBC, "Cyberespionage: The Chinese Threat," CNBC Investigations, Inc., posted on YouTube, July 10, 2012, http://www.youtube.com/watch?v=Js52FjOsgPA (accessed July 22, 2012).

2. Drummond, "A New Approach to China."

3. George Kurtz, "Operation 'Aurora' Hit Google, Others," McAfee Blog Central, January 14, 2010, https://community.mcafee.com/thread/20925.

4. Ibid.

5. "Attack vector" is a term used to denote the pathway or method of a cyber-attack. An attack vector might be a type of hacker tool, a method of gaining information used in an attack, or an exploitation of a vulnerable piece of application software.

6. Mandiant, "M-Trends: The Advanced Persistent Threat," 2010, http://www.princeton.edu/~yctwo/files/readings/M-Trends.pdf (accessed July 20, 2012); Mandiant, "M-Trends: An Evolving Threat," 2012, http://www.greycastlesecurity.com/resources/documents/2012_M_Trends.pdf (accessed July 20, 2012).

7. Mandiant, "M-Trends: The Advanced Persistent Threat."

8. The domain name system (DNS) is the distributed, global database that provides the translation between host names (for example, www.garykessler.net) and Internet protocol (IP) addresses (for example, 207.204.17.246). One of the most effective attacks ever against the Internet occurred in 2002 when most of the DNS root servers were made inaccessible, slowing users' access to the network. It was the equivalent of attacking the freeway system by blocking all of the on-ramps.

9. The Internet is made up of telecommunications facilities that are interconnected by "routers," the traffic cops of Internet data. A data packet from Host A to Host B will be switched through some number of routers—generally no more than twenty—as it traverses the Internet. If the routers fail, data does not get through.

10. Martin C. Libicki, *Conquest in Cyberspace: National Security and Information Warfare* (New York: Cambridge University Press, 2007).

11. Hamadoun I. Touré, *The Quest for Cyber Peace.* International Telecommunication Union and World Federation of Scientists, January 2011, http://www.itu.int/dms_pub/itu-s/opb/gen/S-GEN-WFS.01-1-2011-PDF-E.pdf.

12. Raymond C. Parks and David P. Duggan, "Principles of Cyberwarfare," *IEEE Security and Privacy* 9, no. 5 (September–October 2011): 30–35.

13. The SQL Slammer worm (January 2003), for example, spread worldwide, affecting tens of thousands of systems, within ten minutes.

14. Parks and Duggan, "Principles of Cyberwarfare."

15. When the Internet worm first struck, sites that had not yet been infected removed their systems from the network, and nobody knew who was doing what in order to restore the network to a safe state. In the aftermath, the CERT/CC was formed at Carnegie-Mellon University as a clearinghouse for Internet attack information.

16. Joyce Reynolds, "The Helminthiasis of the Internet," Request for Comments (RFC) 1135, Internet Engineering Task Force, December 1989, http://www.ietf.org/rfc/rfc1135.txt; Eugene H. Spafford, "The Internet Worm: Crisis and Aftermath," *Communications of the ACM* 32, no. 6 (June 1989): 678–687.

17. Chris Duckett, "Hacker Defaces RAAF Site," ZDNet, July 16, 2009, http://www.zdnet.com/hacker-defaces-raaf-site-1339297434/.

18. The term "hacker" is used in this chapter as a synonym for a Black Hat, or criminal hacker, also sometimes called a "cracker."

19. "Social engineering" refers to the technique of manipulating people in order to have them perform some act or provide information. It is a form of tricking a well-meaning person, generally in violation of policy or against their better judgment, into doing something they would not ordinarily do.

20. "Phishing" is the act of setting up a fake website that looks like a real website—such as Amazon.com—for the purpose of acquiring user information, such as username, password, date of birth, credit card number, or social security number. People are generally directed to these fake websites by a number of means, but spam email messages are the primary method.

21. "Vishing" is a form of phishing perpetrated via telephone and voice mail, primarily via voice over Internet protocol (VoIP) systems.

22. "Smishing" is a form of phishing that employs short message service (SMS), or text, messages on mobile phones.

23. Attacks on applications are performed by exploiting vulnerabilities in the programming of the software. A doctrine of computer science is that a program cannot be proven to be correct—that is, it cannot be proven that software will operate correctly 100 percent of the time. The inference from this is that all software might have a flaw, or a vulnerability. Most vulnerabilities are undiscovered, and many merely result in the program stopping. Other vulnerabilities, if discovered, might be exploited to allow an attacker access to application data, to the computer's hard drive, or to the network.

24. The term "hacker's tool kit" refers to the set of software applications and methods that an attacker—aka, a Black Hat hacker—might employ in order to gain unauthorized access to a computer or network.

25. See the InfraGard website at http://www.infragard.net/.

26. Microsoft releases patches on Tuesdays; major patch releases are generally released on the second Tuesday of the month. IT departments schedule their workloads around Patch Tuesdays.

27. Larry Schwartz, "Koufax's Dominance Was Short but Sweet," ESPNClassic, http://espn.go.com/classic/biography/s/koufax_sandy.html (accessed July 20, 2012).

28. "Cryptography" is the science of secret writing, and "steganography" is the science of hidden writing and covert communication.

29. A "rootkit" is malware that operates at the root, or administrator, level and can perform a number of (usually nefarious) tasks. Rootkits are generally stealth malware.

30. Modifying data is generally considered to be worse than deleting data, from the data owner's perspective. Deletions of data are usually detected quickly, and data can be retrieved by recovering from the latest backup. Modifications of data, however, may not be detected for quite some time; recovery is difficult because the owner does not know what backup to use and might overwrite new, legitimate changes to a database that occurred after the intruder's modifications.

31. Mandiant, "M-Trends: The Advanced Persistent Threat."

32. Bruce Schneier, "Details of the RSA Hack," Schneier on Security, August 30, 2011, http://www.schneier.com/blog/archives/2011/08/details_of_the.html; CNBC, "Cyberespionage: The Chinese Threat."

33. Bryan Krekel, "Capability of the People's Republic of China to Conduct Cyber Warfare and Computer Network Exploitation," Northrop Grumman Corporation, October 9, 2009, http://www2.gwu.edu/~nsarchiv/NSAEBB/NSAEBB424/docs/Cyber-030.pdf; Frankie Li, "A Detailed Analysis of an Advanced Persistent Threat Malware," SANS Institute InfoSec Reading Room, October 13, 2011, http://www.sans.org/reading_room/whitepapers/malicious/detailed-analysis-advanced-persistent-threat-malware_33814.

34. Scott D. Applegate, "Cybermilitias and Political Hackers: Use of Irregular Forces in Cyberwarfare," *IEEE Security and Privacy* 9, no. 5 (September–October 2011): 16–22; Parks and Duggan, "Principles of Cyberwarfare."

35. Dmitri Alperovitch, "Revealed: Operation Shady RAT," McAfee, Inc., 2011, http://www.mcafee.com/us/resources/white-papers/wp-operation-shady-rat.pdf (accessed July 20, 2012).

36. Applegate, "Cybermilitias and Political Hackers."

37. A "programmable logic controller" is a special-purpose computer designed to control mechanical devices such as factory-floor machinery, laboratory equipment, and energy systems.

38. Aleksandr Matrosov, Eugene Rodionov, David Harley, and Juraj Malcho, "Stuxnet Under the Microscope: Revision 1.31," Eset, 2011, http://www.eset.com/us/resources /white-papers/Stuxnet_Under_the_Microscope.pdf (accessed July 20, 2012).

39. Kim Zetter, "Report: Obama Ordered Stuxnet to Continue After Bug Caused It to Spread Wildly," Wired, June 1, 2012, http://www.wired.com/threatlevel/2012/06 /obama-ordered-stuxnet-continued/all/.

40. Matrosov et al., "Stuxnet Under the Microscope."

41. sKyWIper Analysis Team, "sKyWIper (a.k.a. Flame a.k.a. Flamer): A Complex Malware for Targeted Attacks," v1.05, Budapest University of Technology and Economics, Laboratory of Cryptography and System Security, May 31, 2012, http://www.crysys .hu/skywiper/skywiper.pdf.

42. Ellen Nakashima, Greg Miller, and Julie Tate, "US, Israel Developed Flame Computer Virus to Slow Iranian Nuclear Efforts, Officials Say," *Washington Post*, June 19, 2012.

43. Agence France-Presse, "US Cyber War on Iran Has Only Just Begun," NDTV Gadgets, July 13, 2012, http://gadgets.ndtv.com/internet/news/us-cyber-war-on-iran-has -only-just-begun-243069.

44. Paul Rothman, "Cyber Terror Rages in the Banking Sector," Security InfoWatch, September 28, 2012, http://www.securityinfowatch.com/blog/10796084/cyber-terror-rages-in -the-banking-sector.

45. Robert Graham and David Maynor, "SCADA Security and Terrorism: We're Not Crying Wolf," Internet Security Systems, http://www.blackhat.com/presentations /bh-federal-06/BH-Fed-06-Maynor-Graham-up.pdf (accessed July 20, 2012).

46. Jim Brenton, "Advanced Persistent Threats to the Electricity Sector," presented at the Grid Security Conference, New Orleans, October 19, 2011, http://www .nerc.com/files/7_Brenton_APT_NERC_GridSecCon_2011-10-19_DRAFT_1.pdf; McAfee Foundstone Professional Services and McAfee Labs, "Global Energy Cyberattacks: 'Night Dragon,'" version 1.4, February 11, 2011, http://www.mcafee.com/ca/resources /white-papers/wp-global-energy-cyberattacks-night-dragon.pdf.

47. Richard A. Clarke and Robert K. Knake, *Cyberwar: The Next Threat to National Security and What to Do About It* (New York: ecco/HarperCollins, 2010).

CHAPTER 6

Transportation Security

T he nation's transportation network is an expansive, open, and accessible set of interconnected systems of roads, tracks, airways, terminals, and conveyances that provide services essential to our way of life. The sector includes several interconnected often independent modes of transportation, each with unique maintenance, operating, and security concerns. Commonly thought of modes of transportation include the following: aviation, freight, rail, highway, maritime, mass transit and passenger rail, cable transport, space transport, and pipeline transport. "In fact, on any given day, transportation assets in the US are used to move approximately eight million truckloads of freight across four million miles of highway; 1.5 million railcars traverse over 170,000 miles of track; 2,400 flights pass through about 400 airports; and roughly 325 seaports transfer more than 25,000 containers."[1] The sheer size and capacity of the sector, which moves, distributes, and delivers billions of passengers and millions of tons of goods each year, makes it a highly attractive target for terrorists, as well as vulnerable to all types of man-made and natural disasters.

The case studies in this chapter not only highlight the vulnerabilities in US transportation systems but also demonstrate how critical these systems are in disaster response and recovery efforts. In the first case, "The Howard Street Tunnel Fire," a train derailment in Baltimore's Howard Street Tunnel, coupled with a fire caused by hazardous materials, led to the loss of access on the nation's main East Coast rail artery. This five-day incident had a significant impact on local businesses and commuters as well as on the movement of freight along the eastern corridor with delays of up to thirty-six hours. In addition, this case raises questions about the transportation of hazardous materials, especially toxic inhalation hazards, through high-threat urban areas (HTUAs) where the release of toxic materials could harm tens of thousands of people. Finally, this case demonstrates the importance of emergency planning for all types of possible disasters at the local level and of cooperation between local, state, and federal agencies in providing mutual aid and outside assistance.

The second case, "The Impact of the 9/11 World Trade Center Attack on Transportation," provides firsthand accounts by Office of Emergency Management (OEM) and New York City Transit (NYCT) personnel on September 11, 2001, and their role in response and recovery efforts. The terrorist attacks on 9/11 clearly showed the vulnerabilities in our nation's air transportation system, but this case also highlights the impact of the attack and the subsequent collapse of the buildings in the World Trade Center (WTC) complex on mass transit in the region. Although the transportation system was a victim of this attack, transportation personnel were key responders who saved lives. When the towers collapsed, the PATH station and the subway lines under it were destroyed, yet no one was killed because of the quick reaction of PATH employees who activated emergency plans and redirected trains around the WTC site and helped evacuate passengers from the area. (PATH is the Port Authority for New York and New Jersey, and they build, operate, and maintain transportation infrastructure for those states.) In addition, New York City Transit personnel played a critical role in search-and-rescue operations, removing debris, shoring up transit tunnel, and making repairs of this critical infrastructure. The role of transportation as a weapon on 9/11 is well known. Less well known is transportation's role as a victim and a responder at the World Trade Center.

NOTES

1. Luke Ritter, Michael Barrett, and Rosalyn Wilson, *Securing Global Transportation Networks* (New York: McGraw-Hill, 2007), xxi.

The Howard Street Tunnel Fire (Baltimore)

FRANCES L. EDWARDS

B altimore's St. Patrick's Day marathon and parade command the city's Inner Harbor waterfront for hours, forcing traffic into the center of town along Howard Street. In 2011, as traffic crawled along Howard Street, a cab driver remarked to his passenger, "That is the manhole they used to get to that big tunnel fire we had. It was ten years ago already, but I can still see that black smoke and all those people running from Camden Yards. Some things just never leave you."[1] The cascading event—a train derailment, hazardous materials on fire, loss of access on the nation's main East Coast rail artery—is a reminder that however thorough emergency planning may be, there is always the event that represents a true "failure of imagination."[2] Most worrisome, this technological accident could be a blueprint for a future intentional act of sabotage or terrorism.[3]

The Unexpected

On July 18, 2001, a northbound freight train running through Baltimore's Howard Street Tunnel had had an uneventful trip from West Baltimore on its way to Philadelphia. The track, owned by CSX, is part of the East Coast's busy north-south corridor, the only freight route connecting New England directly with Washington, DC, and the South. The track passed through the heart of the City of Baltimore, using the Howard Street Tunnel under the business district. The sixty-car train included thirty-one loaded cars, of which eight were hazardous materials tankers regulated by the US Department of Transportation (DOT).[4]

At 3:04 PM, the CSX freight train entered the Howard Street Tunnel, the twelfth train to use the tunnel that day.[5] The brick-faced structure is over one hundred years old and eliminates the need for dangerous grade crossings in the densely populated city. The train consist[6] was three diesel engines pulling the thirty-one loaded cars of mixed freight plus twenty-nine empty cars. Three minutes later, the train crew recalled hearing a grinding noise, the brake pressure dropped, and the train, which had been traveling at twenty-three miles per hour, lurched to a stop.[7] Later reconstruction by the NTSB suggests that the forty-seventh car in the consist derailed, the brake line then broke about three hundred feet later, and the train stopped about five hundred feet after the derailment (see Photo 6.1.1).[8]

PHOTO 6.1.1: Smoke from the south portal of the Howard Street Tunnel.
Source: US Department of Transportation, "Effects of Catastrophic Events on Transportation Management and Operations," January 2003, http://ntl.bts.gov/lib/jpodocs/repts_te/13780.html.

Because the train was in the tunnel's dead zone, the CSX dispatch radio did not work, so a crew member used a cell phone to notify the train master that the train had stopped in the tunnel. The diesel engines were creating considerable exhaust buildup, so the crew uncoupled the engines and pulled them out of the north portal of the tunnel, expecting that this would clear the air and allow for an inspection of the cars in the tunnel. At 3:27 PM, they were able to use the CSX radio to make the official notification to the dispatcher in Jacksonville, Florida, that the train was stuck in the tunnel, blocking the main north-south line. Because the smoke had only steadily worsened after the removal of the engines, the engineers checked the bill of lading and saw that the consist included cars carrying hazardous materials. They immediately called CSX dispatch back and asked that it notify the Baltimore Fire Department that the train apparently had derailed and was on fire, perhaps including the hazardous materials.[9]

By the time the fire department arrived at the scene, thick black smoke was billowing from the south portal of the tunnel, near Camden Yards, where the Baltimore Orioles were playing a doubleheader ball game. The only access to the tunnel was through the ends and through a manhole in the middle of Howard Street downtown that came out at a gallery. The tunnel, built in 1896, is three feet below ground level at Camden Yards and forty-six feet below Martin Luther King Boulevard downtown.

The derailment caused the train's air brakes to lock as the line was severed, and the braking system linkage punctured the tank car full of tripropylene, causing it to ignite. The Department of Transportation's *Emergency Response Guidebook* defines tripropylene as a highly flammable liquid that poses an inhalation hazard for humans and is an environmental pollutant if released. The guidebook further notes that containers may explode when heated.[10] The fire spread to the adjacent cars of paper and wood products, which fueled the fire and caused the thick black smoke.[11] Four of the tankers ignited. At least 2,500 gallons of hydrochloric acid were released.[12]

Transportation Assets

The City of Baltimore is a complex hub of transportation services. The north-south freight rail line runs through the center of the city using the Howard Street Tunnel, the "longest underground conduit of freight on the Atlantic seaboard."[13] CSX Railroad owns the Howard Street Tunnel, which carries about thirty freight trains per day. Norfolk Southern Railroad also serves the city and the port, using the same track. The number of freight trains in the CSX tunnel has been increasing as CSX and the railroad managing system Conrail have tried to move freight off of the Amtrak Northeast Corridor rail line.[14]

The Port of Baltimore is one of the largest cargo ports on the East Coast, with both container ships and roll-on/roll-off general cargo ships. The multimodal transfers include CSX and Norfolk Southern Railroads and the shortline Camden Railroad for local delivery. The port also generates 80,000 truck trips annually.[15]

The interstate highway system also has important nodes in Baltimore, including the direct north-south I-95 corridor and its subsidiary I-695 ring, which serves the Outer Harbor to the east, the Baltimore-Washington International Airport to the south, and the western suburbs, where it intersects with I-70 going west and I-795 going north. I-97 and I-195 serve the southern end of the ring and the airport. I-83 connects downtown to I-695's northern portion and north to Pennsylvania. Coming from the north, US 1 and US 40 parallel I-95. I-83, US 1, and US 40 all converge in the downtown Baltimore core at Howard Street. I-895 serves the Port of Baltimore's Inner Harbor area and its intermodal shipping elements. Maryland 295 connects Baltimore and Washington, DC.

Baltimore also has a robust passenger rail system. The Amtrak Northeast Corridor runs through Baltimore, and that track also hosts one of the local commuter rail service lines to Washington, the Penn Line, while the other, the Camden Line, operates on the CSX track. The Camden Line, which ends near Camden Yards, carries 3,500 passengers per day and was directly impacted by the Howard Street Tunnel fire. The Camden Line serves the baseball stadium.

The Maryland Transit Authority (MTA) offers another layer of commuter services. The light rail lines carry 30,000 passengers per day, the subway line carries 45,000 passengers per day, and the bus system carries 250,000 passengers per day. The Central Light Rail Lines run directly above the Howard Street Tunnel, while city buses run down Howard Street, and other city bus lines cross Howard Street.[16] The subway line goes under the Howard Street Tunnel.

CSX's Howard Street Tunnel runs under the main intersection of Baltimore's business district. The south end of Howard Street is near Camden Yards, the baseball stadium, and the Inner Harbor tourist attractions, such as the aquarium. The north end is near the state government center, the Lyric Opera House, and the Baltimore Symphony Orchestra's Joseph Meyerhoff

Symphony Hall. Hospitals, universities, and the business district are located within two thousand feet of the tunnel. I-395 ends at Howard Street, Maryland 295 has entrances from Howard Street, and US 40 crosses Howard Street. All of Baltimore's major east-west streets cross Howard Street, and it is the spine of the central business district.[17]

Freight Train Management

Freight trains do not begin at one point and travel to another intact. They drop off and pick up cars at sidings and rail yards throughout a trip, often in remote and unguarded areas. The cars are then taken to the customer by short line railroads, or they continue on to their destination by another train going in a different direction. Each time the train stops to drop off or pick up cars it takes time and uses personnel, both of which have financial implications. The movement of cars at each exchange point requires fifteen to twenty minutes and involves both the train crew and the yard or siding crew.[18] Thus, train consists are created for ease and speed of movement during these changes. Each group of cars to be dropped at a location is called a "station block," and the train consist is created with the first station block to be dropped off at the front behind the engine, with each additional station block added behind it in turn.[19]

The makeup of train consists has other limitations. One is the placement of empty and full cars in the consist: the preference is to put empty cars at the rear of the train to avoid derailments.[20] Another important limitation is the placement of hazardous materials tankers, which are mixed among the empty and full cars to ensure that the distance between incompatible chemicals is maintained according to the requirements of the code of regulations, which mandates such placements and distances in a train consist.[21] As a result, empty cars may be placed in the center of the train consist. As mentioned earlier, the train involved in the Howard Street Tunnel derailment and fire included thirty-one loaded and twenty-nine empty cars. The loaded cars included hazardous materials and paper and wood pulp.

First Response

The security director of a hotel above the tunnel called 9-1-1 to report a disturbance to his building that he thought was related to the tunnel. The

CSX dispatcher also called 9-1-1 to request fire department assistance with the fire in the tunnel. Another call to 9-1-1 reported smoke coming from a sewer at Howard and Lombard, which the fire department traced to the portal near Camden Yards. Another fire engine went to the Mt. Royal end of the tunnel, where the train crew and engines had stopped, and got a copy of the consist, which confirmed the presence of hazardous materials and provided emergency response information for them.[22] Hazardous materials technicians determined that the materials were not explosive and that dangerous vapor would not be released, so the incident commander (IC) ordered a "shelter in place" strategy for buildings above the tunnel's path through the city, because of the presence of thick black smoke leaching from the tunnel through faults in the brickwork and street paving. This order included turning off the air conditioning on a hot summer afternoon.

The public alert siren system, which was originally used as a civil defense attack warning device, had been repurposed as a community "alerting" device: the purpose was to motivate members of the community to turn on the radio or television to obtain detailed information on a community disaster.[23] The IC ordered the sirens activated, and radio and television stations broadcast the "shelter in place" information. Camden Yards was evacuated in the middle of a baseball doubleheader game.[24] Joe Foss, an officer with the Baltimore Orioles baseball organization, estimated that 2,500 to 5,000 fans and 2,000 employees present during the game had to be evacuated.[25]

Unfortunately, many residents, having no idea how to respond to the sirens, called 9-1-1 to report a broken siren or ask for information, tying up a vital incident coordination resource. Downtown office workers trying to go home found streets blocked, mass transit dysfunctional, and limited information available on alternate routes or means to get home.[26]

The first forty-five cars of the train that had not derailed had been pulled along by the engines beyond the derailment. Eleven cars were derailed, while the last four cars remained attached to the derailed cars but on the tracks.[27]

The Pipe Break

About 6:15 PM, the city's water system operators noted anomalies suggesting a pipe break somewhere in the downtown section. A security camera showed water breaking through the street at Howard and Lombard, flooding the intersection and flowing down Howard Street and into the tunnel. The city water crew determined that a forty-inch cast-iron water main had broken directly above the tunnel. It took almost six hours for the leaking portion of the system to be isolated and shut off, after a flow of about 14 million gallons of water, much of which went into the tunnel.[28]

The water main break was immediately above the hottest part of the tunnel fire. The National Transportation Safety Board's post-event analysis demonstrated that the fire in the tunnel caused the tunnel, the cast-iron water pipe, and the light rail foundations to all expand, stressing the water main until it broke.[29]

A manhole fifty feet from the water main break had an unexpected connection to an alcove in the tunnel. The fire department was able to use that access to send a fire hose into the tunnel to help fight the fire. Later that access allowed the fire department to introduce pressurized air into one derailed tanker car and pump the hydrochloric acid out of it, lessening the danger to the community and speeding the end of the incident.[30]

Continuing Response

The environmental effects of the smoky fire and polluted runoff were also a concern, owing to the large concentration of population in the area of the fire and its proximity to the Inner Harbor. Specialists from the Maryland Department of the Environment (MDE) Emergency Response Division (ERD) collaborated with South Baltimore Industrial Mutual Aid Plan (SBIMAP) members to determine potential environmental impacts. SBIMAP, founded in 1982 and made up of state and local government agencies and local businesses, plans for responses to hazardous materials accidents in the city. Two chemists from member businesses confirmed that an evacuation was not necessary, but ERD personnel nevertheless established air and water quality monitoring.[31]

The fire reached 1,500 degrees, making it impossible for firefighters to approach the blaze.[32] The 14 million gallons of water from the broken pipeline did mitigate the fire by wetting down potential fuel sources, but it could not adequately cool down the chemical-fueled fire, which had to burn itself out.[33] Five days after the derailment, the fire was declared under control. Heavy equipment was used to remove the last four cars that were still on the tracks—and then the smoldering derailed cars—from the tunnel. This removal effectively destroyed any evidence of why the derailment occurred.[34]

The Incident Command System (ICS) and Interagency Coordination

In the incident command system (ICS) put in place, the Baltimore city fire chief was the incident commander for the tunnel fire. The incident command structure included the Baltimore Police Department, the Baltimore Public Works Department, and the Mayor's Office of Emergency Management (MOEM); the Maryland Emergency Management Administration (MEMA), the Maryland Department of Transportation, and the Maryland Department of the Environment (MDE); and the US Environmental Protection Agency (EPA) and the Coast Guard.[35] City personnel focused first on immediate response actions, including public notification and press coordination.

Initially there were three competing priorities: (1) extinguish the fire, (2) maintain the city's and region's transportation systems, and (3) protect the population and environment from hazardous materials leaks, vapors, and potential explosions. The fire department's desire to enter the tunnel to evaluate the fire was interdicted by the state environmental staff, whose concern was the hazardous materials implications: sending personnel into a relatively enclosed environment where air monitoring was inadequate and explosive limits had been detected. The longer the fire burned and generated smoke the greater the effect on the transportation system. CSX's immediately available paperwork aided the Maryland Department of the Environment's quick evaluation of the hazardous materials safety concerns, which allowed the IC to determine that a large-scale evacuation was not needed because the hazardous materials posed a minimal threat to firefighters and the surrounding area. Thus, the priority became fire suppression and traffic control.

The Maryland Department of Transportation had a variety of divisions actively involved in the remediation and recovery efforts. The headquarters staff focused on coordinating with city public works personnel to develop a plan for highway repairs. This included site survey, the procurement process for hiring a contractor for immediate repair work, and a traffic management plan for the construction. The Maryland State Highway Administration used its fixed and mobile signs to notify interstate drivers of the status of roadway access. It also activated the highway advisory radio system to provide motorists with routing information around the closed roadways. The Mass Transit Administration managed the bus system routing and light rail operations in the city during the fire, including the development of bus bridges around the closures. It also managed the MARC commuter rail system and the Metro subway operation, both of which were impacted by the fire and route changes. The Maryland Transportation Authority (MTA) managed the closure of I-395 during the initial fire response as well as the I-95 traffic.

Two other state agencies provided support to the ICS structure. The Maryland Department of the Environment coordinated with SBIMAP to obtain professional advice on management of the hazardous materials impacts of the derailment and fire. The MDE monitored air and water quality and watched for leaks or discharge from the fire into the Inner Harbor, ultimately setting up absorbent booms to protect the harbor from leaking material related to the fire. When the fire was out, the MDE monitored the railcars removed from the tunnel and oversaw disposal of the hazardous materials from the train. The Maryland Emergency Management Administration coordinated state assistance to the city and also assisted with media relations and rumor control.

In addition to the local response organizations, two federal agencies were part of the ICS structure. The US Environmental Protection Agency supported the evaluation of the hazardous materials impacts, including monitoring air and water quality. The Coast Guard, at that time part of the US Department of Transportation, closed the Inner Harbor and focused on marine environmental impacts.

The Immediate Impact on Transportation

Within the first hour after the fire began, the transportation system had begun to feel the impact. "MARC commuter rail, MTA's Central Light Rail Line, and rail freight movement [were] disrupted by the tunnel street fire. MTA initiated a bus bridge to bring MARC passengers from Dorsey Station south of Baltimore to the City."[36] The fire chief had also ordered all major routes into the city closed, including I-395, I-83, and US 40.

Within the second hour, the police department and public works personnel had rerouted all downtown traffic, closing Howard Street and all streets that crossed over the tunnel. The Coast Guard had closed the Inner Harbor to boat traffic. By the third hour, smoke entering the subway tunnel from the fire had caused the closure of the Metro State Center station. Within five hours, the interstates had been reopened, although the Howard Street area closures remained in place (see Map 6.1.1).

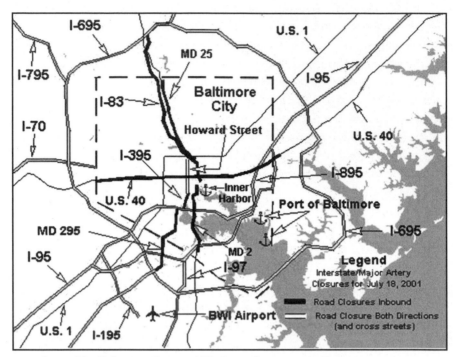

MAP 6.1.1: The Baltimore Regional Highway System with Closures
Source: US Department of Transportation, "Effects of Catastrophic Events on Transportation Management and Operations," January 2003, http://ntl.bts.gov/lib/jpodocs/repts_te/13780.html.

Initially drivers found themselves trapped, as no traffic could cross Howard Street and freeway access was blocked. Commuters went to bus stops, but the buses had been rerouted. City police and public works personnel worked to get signs in place, and the MTA used supervisors to go to bus stops to advise passengers of new pickup locations. The Metro State Center station remained closed, owing to the heavy smoke, but the rest of the system continued to operate normally. Even though the tunnel fire developed and worsened throughout the rush hour, the transportation organizations were able to clear the downtown traffic by 8:00 PM, only two hours later than normal. Streets remained congested and bus routes disrupted until July 24, when all but the area immediately adjacent to the pipe break was reopened.

Light rail disruption lasted longer because the water main break broke the street surface and damaged the light rail foundation. The MTA established a bus bridge to carry riders around the disrupted section of light rail. This service continued until the pipe and street repairs were complete. The bus bridge carried about 15,000 riders per day.

While disruption to city and regional transportation was managed by city and state agencies, the loss of the Howard Street Tunnel had wider implications for freight service. There are only two direct north-south freight routes along the eastern corridor. One is owned by CSX and uses the Howard Street Tunnel. The other, the Norfolk Southern Railroad line, runs through Maryland and Harrisburg and Reading, Pennsylvania, and is less direct and already at capacity. After the fire, freight coming from Chicago had to go through Selkirk, New York, and New Jersey, a delay of eighteen to twenty-four hours. Freight going to southern states experienced twenty-four- to thirty-six-hour delays on the alternate route. Only six trains each day could be added to the Norfolk Southern line, including the Florida "juice train" carrying time-critical loads of fresh orange juice. Freight going north of Philadelphia was diverted through Ohio.

The tunnel was closed for five days as the fire burned itself out, the debris was removed, and the track was repaired. Freight trains for local short hauls were allowed in the tunnel on July 23, and regional freight service was restored July 24. For the next three weeks, the tunnel was closed periodically for additional restoration, slowing the freight schedule, but this was less disruptive than the long detours.

Long-Term Transportation Disruption

Although the rail line in the tunnel was restored in a matter of days, repair of the water main required twelve days, and the surface street damage took fifty-three days to repair. The Central Light Rail Line was the transportation mode most affected by the Baltimore tunnel fire. The light rail line ran above the tunnel, and when the water main broke, the water washed away the fill under the concrete slab that holds the light rail track. Repairs to the water main required destruction of other portions of the light rail's foundation. Ground-penetrating radar was used to determine if the ground underneath the foundation where the water poured in was adequate to support the repaired structure. Ultimately a new foundation with embedded light rail track was constructed. The concrete had to cure before service could be restored. The slab was monitored for several years for possible changes in the underlying disturbed soil.

The closure of the line allowed MTA engineers to investigate a vibration problem that had been noted for several years; that the vibration was loosening the fasteners that connected the track to the slab. During the closure for the pipe-break-related repair, the engineers designed and installed rubber insulation that resolved the vibration problem.

The water main break cut the light rail line into two segments. Equipment that was on the southern segment at the time of the break could not reach the normal maintenance facility. The MTA was forced to excavate a pit below a storage rail and create a temporary service facility. This allowed the MTA to keep all light rail equipment in service during the disruption to the line.

The MTA bus system was used to create a bridge between the two light rail segments. This forced the MTA to use 100 percent of its equipment to ensure that mandated service occurred, and scheduling challenges arose. Driver schedules also had to be carefully monitored to ensure that "drivers maintained compliance with hours of service regulations," as mandated by the US Department of Transportation.[37] During the bus bridge phase, light rail ridership dropped to about half of its 15,000-per-day average, but was restored within two months of line restoration.

Wider Community Disruption

Rail line rights of way have long been used by communications systems. Initially telegraph wires paralleled the tracks, then telephone lines, and now Internet connections follow the rails. The Howard Street Tunnel carried an "Internet pipe" that served the seven largest Internet service providers (ISPs) in the country. The fire caused disruptions in service that were first thought to be a virus but were eventually tracked to the tunnel, where the fire had burned through the pipe and "severed fiber optic cable used for voice and data transmission."[38] The damage affected service along the East Coast, including the loss of email and Web pages for the Hearst Corporation, and areas as far away as Africa, where the US embassy in Lusaka, Zambia, had email disruptions. Service was restored within thirty-six hours, with 24,000 feet of new cable required for the repair.

Downtown businesses were impacted in various ways. Some businesses were flooded, and the flooding disrupted phone service to downtown buildings. Businesses along Howard Street lost 80 percent of their revenue during the five days when the street was closed. The Baltimore Orioles baseball team had to cancel three games, with a direct revenue loss of $1.5 million to $2 million. In addition, local businesses lost the income from restaurant sales, parking lots, and stores around the stadium, and the state lost the related sales tax.

Legal Actions

For four and a half years, while the NTSB conducted its detailed investigation, the city and the railroad blamed each other for the accident in the tunnel. The city blamed the railroad for maintenance and inspection failures, while CSX claimed that the water main break caused the derailment. Ultimately, the time-stamped security camera photos of water rising from the street and the NTSB's evaluation demonstrated that the fire led to the pipe rupture.[39]

CSX paid $2 million for Baltimore's emergency response costs after a four-year legal battle. The railroad also paid $300,000 for city worker overtime,[40] and it previously had paid merchants for their losses.[41] Perhaps a more important consequence of the fire is that the Baltimore Police Department and the CSX police will now share a communications frequency, and the city will get access to a camera feed from inside the tunnel. The railroad has also agreed to share information with the city on the chemicals that have passed through the tunnel within the previous year.

No one died in this disaster, there were only five minor injuries during the emergency response, and the ultimate cost of the event was estimated at $12 million by the NTSB. But other costs—loss of revenue for merchants and businesses, mass transit fare losses, tax losses, and freight disruption—greatly exceed this number.

Transporting Hazardous Materials Through Urban Areas

The Baltimore tunnel fire demonstrates why some security and terrorism experts oppose the transportation of hazardous materials, especially toxic inhalation hazards (TIHs), through high-threat urban areas (HTUA). In 2001 over eighty-three tons of hazardous materials were shipped by rail, much of it through cities.[42] Hazardous materials accidents demonstrate how a terrorist organization might engineer an accident that could release toxic materials in a crowded area. Little information about the movement of hazardous materials is released to the public for security reasons. The placards on the outside of the railcars indicate the class of materials as a warning to first responders that they need to get the details from the train consist package before beginning an emergency response.[43] It does not generally specify the exact items being transported.[44]

In 2007 there was another CSX train derailment in Baltimore, near the M&T Bank stadium, in which twelve cars left the tracks. Three cars were carrying hazardous materials, but this time there were no leaks. The mayor's reaction was to ask CSX to "limit rail traffic during events at M&T stadium and Camden Yards."[45] In 2001 a city council member introduced legislation "to restrict shipments of some hazardous chemicals through the downtown tunnel. The legislation never made it out of committee," noted *Baltimore Sun* reporter Madison Park. "He called Saturday's incident 'deja vu all over again.'"[46]

In 2008 the US Department of Transportation required rail carriers to analyze routes for hazardous cargoes through urban areas, but did not mandate rerouting because of the economic implications of longer train routings and the potential for additional removal and adding of station blocks to avoid urban routes.[47]

The Transportation Security Administration (TSA) began to evaluate the dangers of hazardous materials in urban areas in 2006. Several bulletins and supplements urged rail carriers to work with the Department of Homeland Security (DHS), the DOT, and the TSA to evaluate urban routes, especially for the proximity of sensitive receptors to siding and rail yards where hazardous materials might be staged and left unguarded. "The security plans for railroads operating in HTUAs had to be updated to include additional provisions for the secure storage of TIH cars in HTUAs, and the minimization of the time that full TIH cars remain unattended in HTUAs."[48]

Although in-transit hazardous materials might be rerouted, terrorism expert Stephen Flynn has noted that many of the TIHs are headed for HTUAs for public and private uses, such as processing drinking water and refining petroleum products.[49] Frances Edwards and Daniel Goodrich have noted that "cities could use bleach instead of chlorine for water processing, and refineries could use sulfuric acid in place of hydrofluoric acid for petroleum refining."[50] Furthermore, the American Association of Railroads notes that changing the routes just changes the communities that are exposed to the hazards and that the new routes would extend the time of transit and therefore exposure, since the current routes are the most efficient.[51] Sending the hazardous materials on rural routes might actually make matters worse, as rural areas seldom have the sophisticated training and equipment necessary for the successful management of a hazardous materials accident.[52]

In the post-9/11 world, the specter of terrorist activity hangs over emergency management preparations in all major American cities. Having now seen the unimaginable act of commercial airliners being used as missiles, city emergency managers are dedicated to not failing to imagine the worst again. However, how realistic is it to postulate hazardous materials railcars as terrorist weapons? In the Howard Street Tunnel fire, the tripropylene tanker was punctured by part of the train's own braking mechanism and then set on fire by an unknown action, possibly sparks from the derailment. This suggests that a dedicated engineer could take the NTSB report on the Baltimore tunnel fire and design an intentional event with the same results, but using a tanker filled with a more toxic substance.

However, unlike planes controlled by the Federal Aviation Administration (FAA), trains run on approximate schedules that are coordinated in segments. Track use is managed by signals and sidings. The length of the rail system and the remoteness of much of its infrastructure, even in urban areas, serve as a kind of security. Derailing a train is actually very difficult, as demonstrated by the Office of Strategic Services (OSS), precursor to the Central Intelligence Agency (CIA), and the American military in a World War II training film.[53] Although the NTSB report details several potential causes of train derailment, it notes that none of them caused the CSX derailment in Baltimore. Derailments can be caused by sand on the tracks, defective track, or foreign objects on the track, but there was no evidence of any of these conditions, and eleven other trains had passed through the tunnel safely that day.[54] Thus, this accident could be seen as a demonstration of the serendipitous nature of train derailments and their unpredictability as a weapon.

CSX was faulted for poor record-keeping related to its tunnel inspections. There were no records of the repairs and modifications to the tunnel over the years.[55] In addition, the heat of the fire and the quantity of water that poured into the tunnel obliterated evidence. "The National Transportation Safety Board, after an exhaustive investigative effort, could not identify convincing evidence to explain the derailment of CSX freight train L-412-16 in the Baltimore, Maryland, Howard Street Tunnel on July 18, 2001," the report concluded.[56]

Lessons Learned

Baltimore was well prepared for a disaster. It had local plans in place using the incident command system and involving the whole community through SBIMAP. It was well connected to state and federal agencies that could provide mutual aid and outside assistance. The challenge was that the training and exercise scenarios had not postulated an event with both a fire and a hazardous materials event. Unfortunately, the city had not coordinated with the railroad and had not planned for an event inside the tunnel.[57]

Although state and local agencies do not often work together, they supported each other effectively in the disaster. The Maryland Department of Transportation and city public works personnel coordinated the infrastructure repair plan and collaborated effectively on traffic management between the interstate system and the city streets. The MTA provided the fire department with the equipment to remove the train cars from the tunnel.[58]

Initially, the various agencies had problems with communications. Agency-to-agency notification procedures also needed to be improved. The MTA provided a mobile command post that provided communications capabilities to support all the participating agencies. While cell-phone coverage on the day of the event was poor owing to high call volumes, Nextel equipment provided to agencies in advance performed well.[59]

Public information about the availability of the various transit systems was very effective. The use of professional public information officers and the provision of regular updates to the media kept the community informed about the progress of the tunnel fire. Road closures, alternate routes, and information about operating mass transit assisted the public in avoiding the closure areas.

Public notification was effective, but a lack of comprehensive pre-event public education on the sirens made the use of radio and television announcements less effective. The sirens generating 9-1-1 calls from the public created a loss of efficiency for dispatchers during the response.

Technology made a positive contribution to the management of the situation. Fixed and portable electronic signboards on the highways guided motorists. The highway advisory radio system provided additional information on highway detours and closures. Maryland's CHART (Coordinated Highways Action Response Team) website, which provided ongoing information about the event and its impact on transportation systems, had over 35,000 hits on the day after the fire.[60]

The fire demonstrated that the Nuclear Regulatory Commission (NRC) design specifications for nuclear waste casks may be inadequate. The current requirement is for the cask to withstand a fire of 1,475 degrees for eight hours; the Baltimore tunnel fire reached higher sustained temperatures. The National Institute of Standards and Technology (NIST) estimated that the tunnel fire burned at 1,800 degrees for the first three hours and that the walls of the tunnel reached 1,500 degrees.[61] The local newspaper reported that the fire burned out of control for over twenty-four hours, which exceeds the NRC standards.[62]

The 2007 CSX derailment near the stadium demonstrated that many of the lessons of the 2001 derailment had been learned and were being applied. Agencies reported more rapid notifications. They shared a command post to facilitate rapid decision-making. Communication between CSX and government agencies had also improved by 2007.[63]

Perhaps the most important lesson learned was the need for redundancy in all critical infrastructure. The Baltimore tunnel fire demonstrated that America's freight rail system is close to capacity. After the fire, the Federal Railroad Administration (FRA) undertook a study of the use of the Howard Street Tunnel for hazardous materials transport along the Eastern Seaboard. The FRA recognized that new modern tunnels would be a better option, but the cost ranged from $1 billion to $3 billion in 2004, with no funding source.[64] Until a truly redundant system is created, the FRA recommends "identifying chokepoints and redundant systems (to the extent feasible) that can be used to compensate for a major transportation system disruption."[65] The loss of Internet capability through burned fiber-optic cable in the tunnel also demonstrates the need for redundancy in communications systems.

Conclusions

The response to the 2001 CSX derailment in Baltimore demonstrates the value of planning, training, and exercising, but it also shows that even a well-developed plan may not consider all possible disasters. Communication among potential responding agencies and good advance public education on disaster response are important factors in the success of any disaster response, but especially one that is unexpected.

Hazardous materials are critical to public health, fuel, and other economically important activities. Finding a balance between efficiency and safety is the challenge for transporters, manufacturers, and consumers.

DISCUSSION QUESTIONS

1. What are the pros and cons of shipping hazardous materials through high-threat urban areas? What are the economic aspects of changing the current system?
2. What lessons about managing hazardous materials in transit can be learned from the Baltimore tunnel fire?
3. What "best practices" can you identify that assisted in managing the event and minimizing losses?

NOTES

1. Thomas Wynn, cab driver, interview with the author, Baltimore, March 13, 2011.

2. National Commission on Terrorist Attacks Upon the United States, *The 9/11 Commission Report: Final Report of the National Commission on Terrorist Attacks upon the United States* (2004). "A Failure of Imagination" was the subtitle of the congressional 9/11 report.

3. Mark R. Carter, Mark P. Howard, Nicholas Owens, David Register, Jason Kennedy, Kelley Pecheux, and Aaron Newton, "Effects of Catastrophic Events on Transportation System Management and Operations: Howard Street Tunnel Fire, Baltimore City, Maryland—July 18, 2001," US Department of Transportation, ITS (Intelligent Transportation Systems) Office, July 2002.

4. National Transportation Safety Board (NTSB), *Railroad Accident Brief: Accident Number DCA-01-MR-004, Baltimore, Maryland* (Washington, DC: NTSB, April 2008).

5. Ibid.

6. A train "consist" refers to the cars that make up the train and the order in which they are placed.

7. Carter et al., "Effects of Catastrophic Events on Transportation System Management and Operations."

8. NTSB, *Railroad Accident Brief.*

9. Carter et al., "Effects of Catastrophic Events on Transportation System Management and Operations."

10. US Department of Transportation, Hazardous Materials Safety Administration, *2012 Emergency Response Guidebook: A Guidebook for First Responders During the Initial Phase of*

a Dangerous Goods/Hazardous Materials Transportation Incident, Guide 128: Tripropylene, http://phmsa.dot.gov/staticfiles/PHMSA/DownloadableFiles/Files/Hazmat/ERG2012.pdf.

11. NTSB, *Railroad Accident Brief.*

12. Hilary C. Styron, "CSX Tunnel Fire Baltimore, Maryland," US Fire Administration (USFA) Technical Report Series USFA-TR-140, US Department of Homeland Security /USFA/National Fire Data Center, July 2001, http://www.usfa.fema.gov/downloads/pdf /publications/tr-140.pdf (accessed March 12, 2012).

13. Carter et al., "Effects of Catastrophic Events on Transportation System Management and Operations," 6.

14. Ibid.

15. Ibid.

16. Ibid.

17. Ibid.

18. R. E. Thompson, E. R. Zamejc, and D. R. Ahlbeck, *Hazardous Materials Placement in a Train Consist,* vol. 1, *Review and Analysis* (Washington, DC: US DOT, Federal Railroad Administration, Office of Research and Development, 1992).

19. Frances Edwards and Daniel Goodrich, *Introduction to Transportation Security* (Boca Raton, FL: CRC Press, 2012).

20. Thompson et al., *Hazardous Materials Placement in a Train Consist.*

21. See 49 CFR Part 174 Subpart D; see also Thompson et al., *Hazardous Materials Placement in a Train Consist.*

22. NTSB, *Railroad Accident Brief.*

23. Carter et al., "Effects of Catastrophic Events on Transportation System Management and Operations."

24. NTSB, *Railroad Accident Brief.*

25. Carter et al., "Effects of Catastrophic Events on Transportation System Management and Operations."

26. Ibid.

27. NTSB, *Railroad Accident Brief.*

28. Ibid.

29. Ibid.

30. Carter et al., "Effects of Catastrophic Events on Transportation System Management and Operations."

31. Ibid.

32. NTSB, *Railroad Accident Brief.*

33. Carter et al., "Effects of Catastrophic Events on Transportation System Management and Operations."

34. NTSB, *Railroad Accident Brief.*

35. Discussion in the next three sections is based in large part on Carter et al., "Effects of Catastrophic Events on Transportation System Management and Operations."

36. Ibid., 11.

37. Ibid., 19.

38. Ibid., 20.

39. NTSB, *Railroad Accident Brief.*

40. Michel Dresser, "CSX to Pay $2 million to Baltimore; Settlement Assigns No Fault for 2001 Railroad Tunnel Fire," *Baltimore Sun,* February 14, 2006.

41. Carter et al., "Effects of Catastrophic Events on Transportation System Management and Operations."

42. Peter F. Guerrero and Norman J. Rabkin, "Rail Security: Some Actions Taken to Enhance Passenger and Freight Rail Security, but Significant Challenges Remain," report to the Senate Committee on Commerce, Science, and Transportation, GAO 04–598T, March 23, 2004.

43. Edwards and Goodrich, *Introduction to Transportation Security.*

44. Carter et al., "Effects of Catastrophic Events on Transportation System Management and Operations."

45. Madison Park, "Stadium Safety at Issue in Rail Crash; Mayor Urges CSX to Cut Traffic During Events," *Baltimore Sun*, November 26, 2007.

46. Ibid.

47. Ibid.

48. Edwards and Goodrich, *Introduction to Transportation Security,* 235.

49. Flynn quoted in Eben Kaplan, "Rail Security and the Terrorist Threat," Council on Foreign Relations, March 12, 2007, http://www.cfr.org/united-states/rail-security -terrorist-threat/p12800.

50. Edwards and Goodrich, *Introduction to Transportation Security,* 236.

51. American Association of Railroads, "Security Plan," 2011, http://www.aar.org /Safety/Rail-Security.aspx (accessed July 23, 2011).

52. Carter et al., "Effects of Catastrophic Events on Transportation System Management and Operations."

53. Office of Strategic Services, Field Photographic Branch, "Derailment: An Experiment Performed by the National Defense Research Committee on the Claiborne-Polk Military Railroad, March 8–10, 1944" (film), http://www.youtube.com/watch?v=D-8g V4DJZUw (accessed on YouTube, July 23, 2011).

54. NTSB, *Railroad Accident Brief.*

55. Ibid.

56. Ibid., 18.

57. Carter et al., "Effects of Catastrophic Events on Transportation System Management and Operations."

58. Ibid.

59. Ibid.

60. Ibid.

61. Marvin Resnikoff, "Baltimore Tunnel Fire," presentation to the National Academy of Sciences, Committee on Transportation of Radioactive Waste, July 25, 2003.

62. Carter et al., "Effects of Catastrophic Events on Transportation System Management and Operations."

63. Park, "Stadium Safety at Issue in Rail Crash."

64. NTSB, *Railroad Accident Brief.*

65. Carter et al., "Effects of Catastrophic Events on Transportation System Management and Operations," 25.

The Impact of the 9/11 World Trade Center Attack on Transportation

FRANCES L. EDWARDS

A s neighbors watched the dismantling of the skeleton of the Deutsche Bank Building at 130 Liberty Street in January 2011, they commented that it was the end of an era with "a lot of sad history."[1] As the last of the buildings damaged in the attacks of September 11, 2001, on New York's World Trade Center, the Deutsche Bank Building had been the last physical reminder of a day that British prime minister Tony Blair called "attacks on the basic democratic values in which we all believe so passionately and on the civilised world."[2]

The Unexpected

September 11, 2001, was a beautiful day in New York City, with the kind of clarity to the air that only comes in the fall. Sixty thousand people worked in New York's World Trade Center (WTC), and that day those on the higher floors had a panoramic view of the metropolitan area. Ninety thousand people might have visited the Twin Towers on a given day to do business with the buildings' tenant companies, to buy half-priced theater tickets, to stand on the observation platform atop World Trade Center 2 (WTC 2, Tower 2, or the South Tower), or eat in the famous Windows on the World Restaurant under the television antenna of World Trade Center 1 (WTC 1, Tower 1, or the North Tower).[3]

At 8:46 AM, when the first plane hit WTC 1, people were starting to arrive at their offices. Although the bond firms' employees and international bankers came in early to get a jump on the market, most businesses located at the WTC opened at 9:00 AM. At 8:46 AM, people were stopping to buy a paper, a cup of coffee, or a snack to take to work. Some people were delayed and had not yet arrived in their Twin Towers offices because they voted in New York City's primary election before going to work. Because of this accident of timing, thousands of lives were doubtless saved. According to Sergeant Rick Bylicki of the New York Police Department (NYPD), 99 percent of the people on the floors below the point of aircraft impact survived the damage to the towers. No one on the floors above the crash-related fires survived.[4]

The plane that crashed into Tower 1 was an American Airlines flight from Boston to Los Angeles carrying ninety-two people. It was assumed by many to be an accident. However, when a second plane crashed into Tower 2 at 9:03 AM, it became apparent that this was a coordinated attack.[5] The second plane, a United Airlines flight also from Boston headed for Los Angeles, had sixty-four people on board.[6] At 10:00 AM, Tower 2 collapsed as television viewers watched a cloud of debris engulf lower Manhattan. Just as the dust began to settle, Tower 1 collapsed at 10:28 AM, killing the command staff of the Fire Department of New York (FDNY), who were operating the incident command post in the lobby by the fire annunciator board.[7] At 5:20 PM, World Trade Center 7 (WTC 7) collapsed as a result of the infrastructure damage caused by the collapses of the two skyscrapers.[8]

The World Trade Center Complex

The World Trade Center, built by the Port Authority of New York and New Jersey, opened on April 4, 1973. Excavation of the site required the removal of 1.2 million cubic yards of dirt. The excavated dirt was placed as fill on the margins of Manhattan Island, into the Hudson River, creating Battery Park Center, a new area for housing and commercial buildings just west of the WTC and the World Financial Center. The lower portions of Manhattan south of Canal Street are below the water line in many areas and have to be protected from water incursion.[9] A trench seventy feet deep and three feet wide was created around the sixteen-acre site and filled with slurry to support the movement of the WTC buildings while keeping out water.[10]

The Twin Towers were the centerpieces of the seven-building complex, with 40,000 square feet per floor, for a total of 12 million square feet. Each tower was 110 stories tall, with an observation deck on the top of Tower 2 and a television antenna serving the metropolitan area on Tower 1.[11] The Port Authority had its dispatch center and corporate offices in the towers.[12]

In addition to the two iconic towers, the WTC complex had five other major buildings. WTC 3 was the twenty-one-story Marriott Hotel, and WTC 4, 5, and 6 were smaller buildings that housed various financial entities and public organizations. All shared the raised plaza with the Twin Towers. WTC 7 was across Vesey Street and housed many government agencies, including New York City's Emergency Operations Center.

Beneath the plaza on which the Twin Towers sat was a multi-story substructure built in a sixteen-acre, seventy-foot-deep hole. Its seven layers included a two-level shopping mall; a station for several New York City Transit (NYCT) subway lines, the 1&9 and the N&R; three levels of parking; and at the very bottom, a station for the Port Authority Trans-Hudson (PATH) commuter rail from New Jersey. The N&R line stations were adjacent to the WTC complex. The 1&9 line ran down Greenwich Street, under WTC 7 and beneath the plaza between Tower 1 and Tower 2.[13] The hole was below the waterline, and its waterproof "bathtub"—seventy feet deep by three feet wide all around the plaza perimeter—had been subjected to the pressure of the collapsing buildings above.[14]

To the west of the WTC complex was the World Financial Center, home to more banking and financial institutions, such as American Express and Merrill Lynch. To the east of WTC 7 was the Federal Building and to the west was the Verizon Building, nerve center for all telecommunications in the New York metropolitan area.[15] To the south of the plaza was 130 Liberty Street, the Deutsche Bank Building that would stand for ten years draped in black netting, filled with dust and human remains from the collapse of the Twin Towers.[16] Next to it was the FDNY station for Engine 10/Ladder 10, whose members were the first into the damaged buildings on 9/11 and who perished while evacuating victims.[17]

The Immediate Impacts on Transportation

Commuter traffic was a problem for people on the morning of September 11, 2001. The tunnels into the city seemed slower than usual, and one banker stuck in the Holland Tunnel despaired of getting to her desk before the New York Stock Exchange opened at 9:00 AM. As it turned out, the snarled traffic saved more lives by slowing the arrival of the commuters, who heard that their workplace had been attacked with jet planes while they sat in gridlock in their cars. The banker entered the Holland Tunnel and lost radio contact while passing under the river. When she emerged from the tunnel, the radio reception had improved, but the announcer's voice was now strained as he described the plane crash into WTC 1, reflecting the confusion of his listeners.[18]

Sergeant Bylicki of the NYPD was in his Office of Emergency Management (OEM) office on the twenty-third floor of WTC 7 on the morning of 9/11. OEM staff members had arrived at work early to prepare for "Operation Tripod," the exercise that would test the plan to mass-medicate the entire city population during a bioterror attack. The exercise was planned for September 12, the next day, using police and fire cadets as the simulated population. Pier 92 was set up as a model distribution station where mock victims of a bioterrorist event who needed to receive antibiotics would be treated.

Afterward, OEM staff reported hearing a plane flying over their building, an unusual sound for that location, and then heard a popping sound. The Kevlar-lined walls of the Emergency Operations Center (EOC, also located at WTC 7) deadened the sound of the plane crashing into WTC 1, the 110-story North Tower directly across from their location in WTC 7. When the building shook at 8:46 AM, NYPD inspector John Odermatt, OEM's commissioner, thought the event was a freak accident with a ground-to-air missile. The OEM staff members present began to open the command center on the twenty-third floor. Shortly thereafter, OEM received a message that in fact a plane had hit the North Tower. From their window, OEM staff could see the fireball and people running from the building as paper floated through the air.[19]

First Response

WTC 7 housed not only New York's OEM and EOC but other government agencies as well. The Central Intelligence Agency (CIA), the Drug Enforcement

Administration (DEA), the Federal Bureau of Investigation (FBI), and the Bureau of Alcohol, Tobacco, and Firearms (ATF) were among the tenants. The building had its own power supply and private building security, and it had been built to be flood- and storm-resistant. Hours later, when WTC 1 collapsed, federal staff members were laboring to remove boxes of contraband and evidence from WTC 7 to safeguard it.[20]

OEM had its own dispatch center overlooking the emergency operations center, which monitored all the other New York City agency frequencies. It was used as a phone bank and to do personnel callback for its assigned staff of 104 people. Because OEM did not have its own budget, its staff was provided by various city agencies, but principally by the NYPD, its original home department. As OEM staff began calling in from all over the city, dispatch center staff heard the second plane hit WTC 2, the South Tower, at 9:03 AM, over their radio. This attack caused the internal alarms in WTC 7 to activate, warning of no water pressure and activating the generator. OEM staff shared a sudden realization that this was not an accident!

OEM staff immediately called for air support for air security over New York City. Sergeant Bylicki called the Federal Aviation Administration (FAA) and was directed to use NYPD and Port Authority Police Department air assets to clear the airspace around the World Trade Center.[21] OEM staff were assured that federal support was on its way. They were also warned that the tower at John F. Kennedy International Airport was tracking an unaccounted-for plane heading for New York. This was the plane that ultimately crashed in Pennsylvania.

Inspector Odermatt ordered staff to evacuate WTC 7 immediately as a precaution. This was before the plane being tracked at JFK Airport crashed in Pennsylvania, so the staff had no sense of urgency, still assuming that the plane crashing into Tower 1 had been an accident. As people collected personal belongings and began removing OEM records, Deputy Director Richie Rotans, who was also an FDNY captain, urged people to abandon the search for their belongings and leave the building quickly. This call for immediate evacuation saved the lives of the OEM staff.

OEM staff members began responding to the field. Sergeant Bylicki, who had been assigned to OEM by the NYPD, was sent to the FDNY command post in the South Tower along with Rotans. As they made their way across the plaza they observed people jumping from above the fire, their blood splattering the tower's intact floor-to-ceiling windows as they landed. Rotans and Bylicki entered the lobby of WTC 2 just before 10:00 AM in search of Fire

Chief Peter J. Gianci Jr. and the fire command post to establish coordination. There were already many dead in the area.

Collapse

Once inside the South Tower, Rotans and Bylicki felt the floor vibrate like a small earthquake. Instinctively, each sought shelter behind one of the massive pillars in the lobby as everything went black. The vibration lasted for about thirty seconds. The doors they had entered were knocked out, and they watched a huge ball of flame and sparks created by the diesel fuel from the building's own rooftop generator's supply roll from the elevator shaft and out the doors of WTC 2, consuming everything in its path.

When the movement stopped, Bylicki found Rotans, who had a concussion but no other physical injuries. Realizing that the doorway was still clear, they called about forty people together and urged them out the door toward the Marriott Hotel at WTC 3. As Bylicki and Rotans were assisting a Port Authority police officer who had been injured in the collapse from the building, the officer said his partner had been killed right next to him. As the three walked to the ambulance at street level, they met the team of personnel carrying out the body of Father Mychal Judge, the fire department's chaplain who had been killed in the collapse.

After delivering the injured officer to the ambulance, Bylicki and Rotans headed back toward WTC 2, but an NYPD officer told them that they could not return to the building because it had collapsed. This was the first they knew that the building had fallen down around them. They thought the FAA's missing third plane had arrived. Bylicki had his OEM radio, the only thing he had grabbed as he left WTC 7. The radio was broadcasting an all call for OEM personnel to gather to reestablish government.

Although the rapid evacuation of WTC 7 saved the OEM staff, they were deployed to a variety of response points that continued to keep them in harm's way. Odermatt was trapped in the fire station across from the South Tower—Engine 10/Ladder 10, now the site of a shrine to the firefighters lost that day. Calvin Drayton, the operation director for OEM, was trapped near the command post area. Rotans, though he had suffered a concussion in the collapse of Tower 2, returned to WTC 7 to ensure that the OEM staff had all evacuated, but the collapse of the North Tower had set the face of WTC 7 on fire. Early in the response, the lobby of WTC 7 became a triage station for those injured in the collapses of WTC 1 and WTC 2. Dave Longshore, an OEM staff member and emergency preparedness specialist, was working in the triage center alongside colleagues when the urge for a cigarette overcame him. He stepped outside for one cigarette, and WTC 7 came down.[22]

WTC 7 was across from WTC 1, with only narrow Vesey Street between. It sat next to the Federal Office Building with the area's main post office. As a result of the damage to the area and the collapse of WTC 7, the mail from that post office was tied up for two weeks. In this one event, the city of New York lost office space equivalent to the entire office square footage in the city of Atlanta.[23] Managing the rescue, emergency response, and recovery operation would be a months-long task.[24]

Alternate Emergency Operations Centers

Staff members had already requested the OEM command bus, with its radios, computers, and weather station, for use as a mobile EOC, or on-scene command post. Because the WTC 7 EOC had been built with redundant systems and independent power supplies, emergency planners relied on internal redundancy to store emergency plans and vital records, but those records and plans were inaccessible. OEM staff members were able to implement their emergency action plans from memory and combined knowledge while copies of the city's emergency operations plans were retrieved from other agencies and personal storage. OEM's well-equipped communications center bus was brought to Warren Street, within six blocks of the World Trade Center, and became OEM's immediate command center.

Bylicki headed to the OEM bus. He was one block away when the North Tower collapsed at 10:28 AM. He was pulled into a building by a colleague as the dust enveloped the street. When all OEM staff had assembled, the bus was dispatched to Sixth Avenue and Thirty-Sixth Street, which became the new OEM location near the corner fire station, with Mayor Rudy Giuliani, OEM Commissioner Odermatt, and surviving FDNY and NYPD leadership present.

Unsettling events continued in the midst of the unfolding World Trade Center tragedy. A panel truck with a painting of a plane flying into the World Trade Center was stopped near the temporary command post and immediately assumed to be a truck bomb. It proved to be rented to a group of ethnic Middle Eastern people who did not speak English. Odermatt and Bylicki took charge of the truck. The police department evacuated a block, called out the bomb squad, and detained the occupants until a thorough search was made. It turned out to be a delivery truck, but its appearance and timing caused great concern.

Next the OEM function was moved to an alternate EOC at the Police Academy on East Twentieth Street. This space was quickly outgrown. Because Pier 92 was already set up for the planned pill distribution exercise, OEM staff members were able to convert that space into a large EOC adequate to support the complex task of managing the nation's largest catastrophic building collapse. In thirty-one hours, the OEM staff had a functional facility with air conditioning, heat, carpet, and furnishings. They also established a help center at the Jacob K. Javits Convention Center nearby at West Thirty-Ninth Street. There were 175 agencies represented at Pier 92. Each agency had its own emergency response plan, but not all the plans were integrated. There was a Federal Emergency Management Agency (FEMA) representative at Pier 92, but FEMA took over Pier 90 for its own EOC. Pier 94 became the family assistance unit, including the American Red Cross.

Pier 92 was both a work site and a rest area, with fifty beds for staff members who could not get home, and it served over one thousand meals each day. Water-side access to the pier was protected by a Coast Guard patrol, and cement barges were positioned to protect the working areas of the pier. The Javits Center was headquarters for the urban search-and-rescue teams from across the United States, deployed by FEMA as part of the federal response plan to support the New York City emergency responders.

The Impact on the Transit System

Every day thousands of commuters passed through the transit points at the World Trade Center on their way to work. On September 11, the woman in charge of PATH operations was concerned for the safety of the PATH equipment once the first tower had been hit. She ordered all PATH trains to proceed to the end of the line and stay there, and she stopped additional trains from leaving their New Jersey stations. The PATH trains came in directly under the WTC concourse between Tower 1 and Tower 2. The track for PATH was still visible in the cleared area at the WTC site months later (see Photo 6.2.1). The PATH escalators and underpass were built below the 1&9 line tracks, and the 1&9 tunnel was built over the original PATH tubes to the old Hudson and Manhattan station at Church Street

PHOTO 6.2.1: The PATH train entrance at the World Trade Center.
Source: Photo by Frances Edwards.

(see Photo 6.2.2). Built in 1918, the tunnel had less than ten feet of dirt above it, with the base of the rail approximately ten feet below groundwater. The bathtub wall built prior to the construction of the World Trade Center prevented settlement of the subway during WTC construction.[25]

Upon hearing of the plane crashes, New York City Transit dispatchers activated their emergency plans. One train was approaching Cortlandt Street when the driver received word of the crash from the operations center. He moved rapidly through the station and pulled the train and its passengers to safety. All NYCT buses and subways went to the end of the line, bypassing the World Trade Center stations, according to plan. According to Inspector Francis O'Hare of the NYPD (retired), "Rapid evacuation was the key factor in NYCT sustaining no employee or customer fatalities."[26]

In the crucial first moments after the plane crash, NYCT subway trains were ordered to bypass all World Trade Center locations, pending police investigation of the apparent accident. Line superintendents were dispatched to the WTC stations, while the police closed the Cortlandt Street station as a precaution, owing to its proximity to the accident scene. NYCT personnel

PHOTO 6.2.2: The box tunnel for lines the 1&9 line at the World Trade Center. *Source:* Photo by Frances Edwards.

walked the tracks and tunnels in the areas near the World Trade Center to ensure complete evacuation of all stations and tunnels.

As a result, not one commuter's life was lost in the transit levels of the WTC as the towers fell, even as the stations were damaged and the 1&9 line was ruined.[27]

NYCT had a long-standing plan for emergencies. All trains were to go to the closest station and evacuate passengers and crew pending fire department response and NYCT evaluation. Since the New York subway system has surface ventilation, the plan was to use the stations as safe zones. During the Fourteenth Street subway accident some years before, NYCT discovered that the temperature rose to over 120 degrees even in the ventilated areas, owing to the operation of the generators. At that time fans were added to increase the movement of air from the outside, and workers were given headlights to enable them to use their hands for response work. These infrastructure improvements made the subway search faster and safer.[28]

During the construction of the World Trade Center, a curtain wall had been created around the excavation to protect the city from the encroachment of water. When the towers fell, some of this protective infrastructure was lost. As a result, the tracks and tunnels of the 1&9 line were flooded in places, and NYCT was forced to stop service in lower Manhattan and determine the damage.[29]

NYCT's offices are located at 2 South Broadway, just east of the damaged area. The collapse of the WTC towers felt like an earthquake to the staff of NYCT. The building was covered with dust and debris from the collapse, causing the headquarters facility to be closed for one week. There was neither electricity nor phone service in the area, and the dust compromised the building's ventilation system. Bowling Green Park and Battery Park nearby were "like military zones," filled with first responders.[30]

The Brooklyn center ordered all the subway trains to the yard pending evaluation of the system. Because of physical damage from the collapse and vibrations and flooding of some track, the N&R trains and the IRT's 1&9 were out of service. The rest of the service was restarted later that day, with partial closings on the Lexington Avenue line, as many companies let people go home early.[31] Frightened, fleeing victims walked across bridges or took ferries to anywhere just to get out of the devastated city. Fiberglass in the air from the collapse dust was causing most people respiratory distress.[32]

According to Bill Ciaccio, a senior director with NYCT, "the whole area was one thick black cloud." Ciaccio was off-site for training in midtown Manhattan when the attack occurred. He went to his lower Manhattan home with some colleagues from work, and from his home he had a view over the impacted area. There were crowds of people everywhere. He went to Cabrini Hospital to give blood and heard of people getting on ferries to anywhere just to escape from the dust and horror of the attack scene.[33]

Transit response was key to the city's economic and social recovery. Mass transit across the city, represented at the EOC at Pier 92 by the Metropolitan Transit Authority (MTA), included buses, subways, and rail connections. OEM had developed good relations with the transit system through collaboration to shut down subway lines when older buildings had collapsed. With New York's old infrastructure and building stock, an average of two hundred structures per year are lost to decay and dry rot. Building collapse is so common in New York that a special fire unit was established to respond specifically to these emergencies.[34]

OEM had worked with the transit agencies to support emergency evacuations and to provide temporary shelters using mass transit buses. Just before the 9/11 terrorist attack, OEM and the transit agencies had jointly developed an emergency response plan for using mass transit buses for hurricane evacuations. They were still in discussions to resolve the issues of driver risk and safety. The mass transit bus plans would end up supporting the urgent response to the WTC building collapses.[35]

New York City's emergency plan had taken into account a variety of potential disasters that could disrupt the city's transportation network. The city is in the path of hurricanes, and there is an earthquake fault at 125th Street in Manhattan. In the summer of 2000, New York City had conducted a tabletop exercise for top city officials using a scenario of a biological warfare agent released at a sporting event. The police commissioner's response at the tabletop exercise was to "shut down" Manhattan, forbidding traffic movement into or out of the borough. A method for limiting traffic movement was discussed, and that led to an informal understanding among first responders of how best to handle the need to stop traffic through the tunnels and on the bridges. The plan, which was used on 9/11, was that initially all traffic would be one way out of the city, and then the routes would be closed.[36]

On September 11, the traffic management plan that grew out of the tabletop exercise was implemented, along with restrictions on transit. Surface transportation was sealed off below Houston Street until January 2002, with access only for residents and emergency vehicles. Although necessary for security reasons, this limitation made it difficult for businesses to restart, since employees had limited means of getting to work. Furthermore, many small businesses that depended on foot traffic and tourists did not reopen. Chinatown merchants and small businesses that served the Financial District were especially hard hit.[37]

Emergency Response Actions by Mass Transit

Immediately upon learning of the attack, NYCT activated its departmental EOC. The first task was to begin assembling equipment and workers to assist in the rescue operations. Once subway service was suspended, buses were activated to remove people from the WTC site. Within two hours of the attack, a two-mile-long convoy of NYCT equipment and 3,500 transit personnel were en route to what had become known as "Ground Zero."[38]

All electric power to the attack area was lost. The NYCT has a cache of generators to use in its construction projects, and these were delivered to support power to traffic signals, illuminate stations for damage assessment, and illuminate the attack area for the fire department's rescue efforts. Other generators were lent to Verizon to assist it in maintaining telephone networks and keeping fiber-optics node sites in operation.[39]

The NYCT ironworkers were sent to Ground Zero to assist the fire department in search-and-rescue attempts by cutting steel and removing debris. Workers from every NYCT division, readily recognized by their orange vests, staffed bucket brigades to remove debris from the search-and-rescue areas. There were more transportation employees at the site than from any other department or profession as everyone, including construction and maintenance workers, assisted with excavating the burning pile of debris.[40]

With a strong suspicion of terrorism as the cause of these horrific incidents, security around the NYCT facilities was immediately intensified. Barriers and bollards were installed at key points, and other enhancements to access controls were added. Perimeter security was enhanced, including extra patrol officers.[41]

NYCT's first priority was to preserve the undamaged portions of the system and protect the rest from flooding. NYCT officials were also concerned about the load of rubble and heavy equipment now working above transit tunnels. They engineered shoring operations in the transit tunnels, with the dual goals of preserving the NYCT structures and keeping the rescuers working above them safe. Service restoration was also a goal.[42]

NYCT workers laid discharge lines from flooded tunnels to working sewers. The normal outlets for tunnel runoff went to crushed sewers that just recirculated the water back to the flooded area. They pumped 4,000 gallons per minute from the flooded tunnel for three days before the New York City Department of Engineering and Planning was able to shut off the water. To contain the flooding, two concrete bulkheads were constructed at Park Place to the north and Cedar Street to the south, within the 1&9 subway tunnel. The Port Authority implemented dewatering along West Street and Liberty Street to reduce the lateral load on the slurry wall. The Port Authority also issued an emergency contract to create a bulkhead against a large water inflow that might occur with a failure of the WTC site's retaining wall, which could have flooded NYCT facilities with several feet of water. Steel dowels were used to secure the plug.[43]

The tunnel under the World Trade Center plaza was bearing extra weight from the cranes and other equipment used in the rescue effort. The heavy crane used by the New York City Department of Design and Construction to clear and remove debris was located directly over the 1&9 subway roof at the PATH escalators. The tunnel was shored up with posting and bracing to prevent a collapse as removals and demolition continued above. Instrumentation that measured spatial orientation and vibrations was added to monitor the effects of the removals and demolitions on the NYCT property. The levels and inclinometers showed changes in the NYCT subway structures, and the vibration measurements estimated the effect that the NYCT operations might have on nearby structures.[44]

Subway service repairs were focused on the areas of track needed for system service restoration. The N&R train facilities were intact except for the Cortlandt Street station exits and some facilities rooms. The E exit in the World Trade Center was ruined, and the 1&9 line required lengthy engineering studies to determine how it could best be repaired after the loss of 1,400 linear feet of tunnel and two fan plants. The tunnel was also flooded between Vesey and Barclay Streets from a broken water main in the area. NYCT engineers' quick fixes to essential track areas led to the reopening of the N&R line without the Cortlandt Street station on October 21, 2001. However, the 1&9 line could not pass through the World Trade Center site, so stations at Cortlandt, Rector, and South Ferry remained closed.[45]

Transit Loss and Medical Issues

Dr. Dario Gonzales was the full-time medical director for OEM, so he was attuned to the human and health consequences of disasters. He had coordinated with transit agencies and members of the medical community on disaster response and mitigation. He noted that some self-dispatched patients, the "walking wounded," showed up at the hospitals nearest to the World Trade Center, but others went to New Jersey on the ferry, following the instinct to flee the damaged area before seeking medical attention. Patients who sustained injuries at the WTC and self-transported on public transit were reported as far away as Long Island, Connecticut, and upstate New York.[46]

Dr. Lorraine Giordano of the New York City Health Department had a challenge in moving and allocating patients to medical care immediately after the attack on the WTC. Historically, NYCT has cooperated with the health department in providing buses to move patients, taking the moderately injured, sometimes called "greens" for the color of their triage tags, or "walking wounded," to medical facilities farther from the event site to conserve nearby resources for the seriously injured. The health department uses its own incident management system, a variation on the incident command system, to coordinate its responses.[47]

The New York City emergency medical system manages approximately one thousand multiple-casualty-incident responses (multiple patients generated at one event) annually, such as bus accidents. These events provide opportunities for repeated training, and as Dr. Giordano said, "Good training is the key." The Port Authority was developing its own Office of Emergency Management and doing incident command training at its airports. The Port Authority found that meeting ahead of time with its partners—both medical and otherwise—led to success in actual responses. Dr. Giordano noted that "you cannot plan too much, but you have to remain flexible."[48]

Even with all this experience, the decision to seal off a portion of lower Manhattan had unexpected and severe medical consequences for homebound elderly patients. The area had lost power and telephone service from the multiple system damage, and radio and television reception had disappeared with the collapse of the North Tower, with its major antenna for the metropolitan area. Many isolated elderly residents were left unaware of the disaster.[49]

The New York City Health Department had to create teams to visit the homebound elderly in the closed-off areas of lower Manhattan to check on their medical status.[50] Loss of power is often a problem for homebound, medically dependent people, especially those using ventilators or oxygen generators. Ordinarily, medical equipment rental companies would provide backup power for short outages, but battery backup was inadequate for this prolonged event.[51] Many of the low-income elderly had relied on the mass transit routes that were closed by the disaster. The teams facilitated their receipt of continuing medical care for chronic conditions, including delivery of prescription refills.[52]

Recovery

During the first few months after September 11, there were periodic bomb scares in the subways, and anthrax threats closed subway lines and stations a few times. The smoke lasted for months. According to Bill Ciaccio, "The area looked like Pompeii with ash in the street." Finally, the area opened in stages. First, city building officials confirmed the structural soundness of buildings to be reoccupied. Then owners had to contract with private firms to remove all the dust and ash from their building facades. Many buildings had severe window damage: as many as 75 percent of the panes facing the collapse of the towers had to be replaced.[53] Some buildings, including the graduate school dormitories of New York University, had to be secured for weeks as part of the crime scene, while debris and body parts were carefully removed. Only when the investigative work was completed could the cleanup and repair begin.[54]

The area east of Broadway was reopened first, with street cleaning followed by building cleaning. Dust removal and disposal was a problem for building owners as well as business and residential tenants. Because there were toxic substances like asbestos and fiberglass in the dust, a thorough professional cleanup was required. Eventually the area of exclusion was moved south from Houston Street to Canal Street, followed by Canal east of Broadway, and finally Chambers Street was reopened.[55]

NYCT studied alternatives to rebuilding the 1&9 line exactly as it had been. They recognized a need for compliance with the Americans with Disabilities Act (ADA) and a desire to create new connections among transit assets in lower Manhattan. The existing capital program remained the priority, and by carefully selecting repair and restoration strategies, NYCT was able to keep its capital program on time. New capital projects were added in lower Manhattan, and security projects were added.[56]

New York City is densely populated and economically dependent on mass transit. There is little available parking, and what is available is expensive. Transit service not damaged by the WTC collapse was restarted quickly to maintain service to parts of the city outside of the exclusion areas, thus mitigating the economic damage. The MTA agencies followed their own emergency plans. The damaged stations were refurbished rapidly, enabling the N&R trains to function before the end of 2001.[57]

Recognizing the importance of these transit links to New York's economy, the governor issued an order to resume 1&9 line service to the South Ferry Terminal station by November 2002. One mile of the 1&9 line was rebuilt in a box tunnel across the WTC property; it was opened in October 2002. The project included demolishing the tunnel between Barclay and Liberty Streets, including the Cortlandt Street station on the 1&9 line.[58] System elements that were restored or repaired included the signal system, DC power, communications, tracks, lighting for stations and tunnels, and pumps and ventilation equipment. The track replacement runs from South Ferry station to Chambers Street station.[59]

As part of the overall project, additional improvements were undertaken, including two new fan plants to improve fire protection and ventilation. A connection between the 1&9 and N&R Rector Street stations was constructed, providing ADA access for both stations. A new head house was constructed at street level. The project was completed by December 2005.[60]

Lessons Learned by Mass Transit Systems

OEM staff members developed stronger bonds with transit agencies as a result of the World Trade Center disaster. There are now plans in place to add cars to trains or alter bus service to respond to disaster needs. OEM has stronger linkages to all transit agencies, including rail. MTA has now designated two of its employees as liaison officers to help make and confirm transit/OEM coordination of emergency plans. In future events, these staff members would be the lead staff to coordinate the emergency response between OEM and MTA, representing the transit community. One of the original staff members, Gary Hearn, was a retired New York Police Department member who worked in transit during his career and knew the transit system infrastructure, especially Penn Station, very well. He helped to write the disaster plan for Penn Station.[61]

The other original OEM member from MTA was Detective Charles Wendel. Before the 9/11 attacks, each MTA agency had its own evacuation plan in place, but not all were coordinated with each other or with OEM. Detective Wendel, as liaison to OEM for MTA, and also as an OEM responder to the scene of emergencies and disasters, was able to provide coordination across agencies on-scene. Before 9/11, the NYPD did not use the standard incident command system espoused by FEMA, but by 2002 it had developed better on-scene, cross-agency communication. Port Authority Police officers are certified as both law enforcement officers and firefighters, so they are familiar with ICS.[62]

OEM has an all-hazards emergency response plan that anticipated the use of MTA assets in disasters. MTA has always had a seat in the resources section of the New York City EOC. Emergency plans include strategies for specific disaster events, such as hurricanes. Buses have been used for evacuation of threatened areas, movement of victims, transport of first responders and emergency equipment to a disaster scene, and temporary shelters for victims. Commuter trains, buses, subways, PATH, and the Long Island Rail Road (LIRR) provide a rich mixture of resources for disaster response.[63] Some emergency response capabilities were created in response to the pressing needs of the 9/11 event without preplanning, such as the use of ferries to move people stranded by the loss of other mass transit assets. Placement of MTA representation within the day-to-day planning structure of OEM should help to institutionalize the best of those improvised plans.[64]

MTA now has unannounced drills more frequently. NYCT has improved security in its facilities, using emergency plans and emergency response guidance from British Transit. Plans include increased police presence and closer surveillance of key infrastructure. Staff members are studying the threats to the transit system and the best ways to handle them.[65]

Another concern for NYCT is the maintenance of a centralized and consistent field emergency response plan. Because NYCT shares some stations with PATH, the railroads, and other transit providers, the problem of multiple jurisdictions within the stations arises. The solution to this problem would seem to be more tactical planning and a greater emphasis on interagency cooperation.[66]

NYCT has a large infrastructure footprint, including old tunnels and abandoned underground work areas. Workers must ensure that all tunnel facilities and rooms are locked when not in use. More than four thousand locations have been identified, and sensitive locations have been prioritized. Underwater tunnels, selected towers, and other sensitive locations receive special security oversight.[67]

Conclusions

The role of transportation as a weapon on 9/11 is well known. Less well known is transportation's role as a victim and responder at the site of the World Trade Center collapse. Damage to critical transportation infrastructure was managed by the rapid response of thousands of transportation personnel who stopped the flooding, shored up the plaza, and assisted with debris removal and search operation in the critical first hours of 9/11.

DISCUSSION QUESTIONS

1. Was it reasonable for Inspector Odermatt and Sergeant Bylicki to assume that a panel truck with a painting of a plane flying into the World Trade Center and found near a command post might contain a bomb? What events preceding the 9/11 attacks used truck bombs to attack an American building?

2. What lessons about developing security for mass transit can be learned from the response to the WTC attack? What "best practices" can you identify that assisted in saving lives after the attack?

3. What role did NYCT personnel play in the response and recovery efforts?

NOTES

1. Karen Matthews, "Deutsche Bank Building Finally Coming Down," *Huffington Post*, January 9, 2011, http://www.huffingtonpost.com/2011/01/09/deutsche-bank-building -fi_n_806553.html (accessed April 12, 2012).

2. Prime Minister Tony Blair, speech to the House of Commons, September 14, 2001, http://www.patriotresource.com/wtc/intl/0914/uk.html (accessed April 15, 2012).

3. Brian M. Jenkins and Frances Edwards-Winslow, *Saving City Lifelines: Lessons Learned in the 9-11 Terrorist Attacks* (San Jose, CA: Mineta Transportation Institute, September 2003). Excerpts from the author's work in this publication have been used in this case by permission of the publisher.

4. Sgt. Rick Bylicki, Planning and Research, City of New York Office of Emergency Management, interview with the author, Brooklyn, NY, July 24, 2002.

5. Ibid.

6. Joseph N. Siano, PE, "Restoration of Passenger Transportation to Lower Manhattan," presentation to American Society of Civil Engineers, North Jersey Branch, The Newark Club, February 21, 2002.

7. Bylicki, interview with the author, July 24, 2002.

8. Joseph F. Trainor, PE, Program Manager, Station Complexes, Elevators, and Escalators, New York City Transit (NYCT), "Rebuilding the NYC Transit System Post 9/11" (NYCT, May 2002).

9. Ashok Patel, PE, Lead Construction Manager, Line Equipment, Shops, Yards, and Facilities Program, Capital Program Management, NYCT, interview with the author, NYCT/MTA headquarters, New York, July 25, 2002.

10. Siano, "Restoration of Passenger Transportation to Lower Manhattan."

11. Ibid.

12. Bylicki, interview with the author, July 24, 2002.

13. William Ciaccio, Senior Director, Line Equipment, Shops, and Yards, Capital Program Management, New York City Transit Authority, interview with the author, NYCT/MTA headquarters, New York, July 16 and 25, 2002.

14. Dennis Overbye, "Engineers Tackle Havoc Beneath Trade Center," *New York Times*, September 18, 2001, A6.

15. Francis M. O'Hare, Inspector, Operations Commander, Transit Bureau, NYPD (retired), interview with the author, Crown Plaza Hotel, San Jose, CA, August 13, 2002.

16. Matthews, "Deutsche Bank Building Finally Coming Down."

17. Bylicki, interview with the author, July 24, 2002.

18. Joanne Matchett, bank vice president, New Jersey, telephone interview with the author, September 12, 2001.

19. Bylicki, interview with the author, July 24, 2002.

20. The following three sections are based in large part on the account of Sgt. Bylicki, interview with the author, July 24, 2002.

21. Both the New York Police Department and the Port Authority of New York and New Jersey own helicopters and fixed-wing aircraft, and they were immediately deployed to the area around the WTC to deny access to the area to media and sightseeing aircraft until the FAA could activate formal restricted airspace.

22. Dave Longshore, Emergency Preparedness Specialist, New York City Office of Emergency Management, interview with the author, Office of Emergency Management, Brooklyn, NY, July 24, 2002.

23. Siano, "Restoration of Passenger Transportation to Lower Manhattan."

24. O'Hare, interview with the author, August 13, 2002.

25. Ciaccio, interview with the author, July 16 and 25, 2002.

26. O'Hare, interview with the author, August 13, 2002.

27. Ciaccio, interview with the author, July 16 and 25, 2002.

28. Ibid.

29. Patel, interview with the author, July 25, 2002.

30. Ciaccio, interview with the author, July 16 and 25, 2002.

31. Ibid.

32. Dario Gonzales, MD, Medical Director, City of New York Office of Emergency Management, interview with the author, Office of Emergency Management, Brooklyn, NY, July 24, 2002.

33. Ciaccio, interview with the author, July 16 and 25, 2002.

34. Bylicki, interview with the author, July 24, 2002.

35. Sid Dinsay, Public Information Officer, City of New York Office of Emergency Management, interview with the author, Office of Emergency Management, Brooklyn, NY, July 16, 2002.

36. Ibid.

37. Ibid.

38. Ciaccio, interview with the author, July 16 and 25, 2002.

39. Patel, interview with the author, July 25, 2002.

40. Ciaccio, interview with the author, July 16 and 25, 2002.

41. O'Hare, interview with the author, August 13, 2002.

42. Patel, interview with the author, July 25, 2002.

43. Ciaccio, interview with the author, July 16 and 25, 2002.

44. Patel, interview with the author, July 25, 2002.

45. Ciaccio, interview with the author, July 16 and 25, 2002.

46. Gonzales, interview with the author, July 24, 2002.

47. Lorraine Giordano, MD, Director of Medical Compliance, New York City Health Department, interview with the author, New York City Health Department, New York, July 25, 2002.

48. Ibid.

49. Gonzales, interview with the author, July 24, 2002.

50. Giordano, interview with the author, July 25, 2002.

51. Gonzales, interview with the author, July 24, 2002.

52. Giordano, interview with the author, July 25, 2002.

53. Ciaccio, interview with the author, July 16 and 25, 2002.

54. O'Hare, interview with the author, August 13, 2002.

55. Ciaccio, interview with the author, July 16 and 25, 2002.

56. Siano, "Restoration of Passenger Transportation to Lower Manhattan."

57. Ciaccio, interview with the author, July 16 and 25, 2002.

58. Siano, "Restoration of Passenger Transportation to Lower Manhattan."

59. Ciaccio, interview with the author, July 16 and 25, 2002.

60. Cosema Crawford, PE, Vice President and Chief Engineer, Capital Programs Management, New York City Transit Authority, "Rebuilding After 9-11," PowerPoint presentation (undated).

61. Charles W. Wendel, Detective, Office of Technology, System Development, and Communications, Metropolitan Transportation Authority Police Department, interview with the author, Office of Emergency Management, Brooklyn, NY, July 16, 2002.

62. Ibid.

63. Kevin Clark, City of New York Office of Emergency Management, interview with the author, Office of Emergency Management, Brooklyn, NY, July 16, 2002.

64. O'Hare, interview with the author, August 13, 2002.

65. Ciaccio, interview with the author, July 16 and 25, 2002.

66. Ibid.

67. O'Hare, interview with the author, August 13, 2002.

CHAPTER 7

Emergency Management

A fter the events of September 11, 2001, there was a widespread sense in the United States and in many other parts of the world that humanity was entering a new and more dangerous era. Subsequent events, such as the Japanese 8.9 magnitude earthquake and tsunami of 2011, the Haiti earthquake in 2010, the Gulf Coast hurricanes of Katrina and Rita in 2005, and subsequent terrorist attacks by Al-Qaeda and its affiliates in Madrid (2004), in London (2005), and against the US consulate in Benghazi, Libya (2012) have, if anything, strengthened that feeling.[1] The sheer complexity and interdependencies of modern society clearly make us enormously vulnerable, whether it is to natural or man-made disasters or to terrorist attacks. In this new world, it is essential that we anticipate such events and their potential impacts. It is impossible to know exactly what form they will take, how severe they will be, or where and when they will occur, but the value of planning for both natural and man-made disasters has been amply demonstrated. Our ability to plan, respond to, and recover from a broad range of disasters in the future will be determined in large part by the quality of our local, state, and national emergency management systems as well as our homeland security policies and programs.

The two cases in this chapter highlight the importance of emergency management in our homeland security efforts. Emergency management has been defined as "the governmental function that coordinates and integrates all activities to build, sustain, and improve the capability to prepare for, protect against, respond to, recover from, or mitigate against threatened or actual natural disasters, acts of terrorism or man-made disasters."[2] While it is inevitable that costly natural and man-made disasters will continue to affect communities and nations around the world, as highlighted with the Haiti earthquake in 2010 and the San Bruno gas pipeline explosion in 2010, it is critical that we try to mitigate or reduce these risks to people and property and improve the management of disaster response and recovery operations.

The first case, "The San Bruno Gas Pipeline Explosion," discusses the natural gas pipeline explosion and fire on September 9, 2010, in San Bruno, California, and the response and recovery operations that followed from the perspective of first responders and local government officials. For this case, data were collected from personal interviews with key leaders involved in the response, including leaders in the local American Red Cross chapter, the City of San Bruno, and the San Bruno police and fire departments. This case highlights the shortcomings and successes associated with mitigation response and recovery and identifies important lessons learned by those responsible for emergency planning and community preparedness.

People of all nations face risks associated with natural and man-made disasters, and almost all nations eventually become victim to disaster, as we see in the second case, "Lessons Learned from the 2010 Haiti Earthquake." The capacity for a nation or region to respond and recover can be linked to several factors, including: level of risk for specific disasters; local, regional, and national economic resources; availability of technological, logistical, and human resources; extent of various mitigation efforts; and level of preparedness. The 2010 earthquake devastated the already impoverished Haiti, caused a flood of aid from around the globe to converge on the tiny island nation, and simultaneously crippled the infrastructure and the capacity of the Haitian government to mount effective operations. In the wake of large-scale disasters, many developing nations, like Haiti, simply do not have the resources or capacity to adequately respond and recover and must call for outside assistance from other nations, international organizations, and nongovernmental organizations (NGOs). Although this case is critical of the lack of mitigation and preparedness efforts undertaken in Haiti at the time, it is important to understand that countries ranking lower on development indices have placed disaster management very low in budgetary priority.[3] "These nations' resources tend to be focused on more socially demanded interests such as education and base infrastructure, or on their military, instead of on projects that serve a preparatory or mitigative need, such as retrofitting structures with hazard-resistant construction."[4] Future large-scale disasters in the developing nations should be of concern because these events will not only challenge the capabilities and organizational capacities of international disaster management agencies but may also undermine the development of these nations and contribute to regional instability.

NOTES

1. Stephen Lee Myers, "Clinton Suggests Link to Al-Qaeda Offshoot in Deadly Libya Attack," *New York Times*, September 26, 2012.

2. See Post Katrina Emergency Management Reform Act of 2006, Title 6, 40; PL 109-295 (120 Stat. 1394).

3. George Haddow and Jane Bullock, *Introduction to Emergency Management* (New York: Butterworth-Heinemann, 2003), 165.

4. Ibid., 166.

The San Bruno
Gas Pipeline Explosion

DAVID A. McENTIRE

Introduction

On September 9, 2010, a natural gas pipeline located in a residential neighborhood exploded in the city of San Bruno, California. The pipeline failure and subsequent fire had significant consequences. Eight people were killed in the inferno, and nearly sixty individuals were injured. Thirty-eight homes were destroyed, and over seventy other homes were damaged, resulting in a total estimated cost of $1.6 billion.[1] Although the incident is undoubtedly small in comparison to events like 9/11 or Hurricane Katrina, it is still highly relevant to those involved in emergency management and homeland security.

With this in mind, the following case study provides the context of the incident and explains the methodology used for the research. Details pertaining to the case are discussed, as well as the shortcomings and successes of mitigation, response, and recovery efforts. The case study concludes with valuable lessons for the myriad of individuals and organizations responsible for emergency planning and community preparedness.

The Context

San Bruno is a small, suburban city located in Northern California twelve miles south of San Francisco. The jurisdiction is adjacent to San Francisco International Airport and has a total land area of 6.4 miles. According to the US Census Bureau, San Bruno has an estimated population of about 40,000 people.[2] The populace is relatively young (median age is 38.2 years), and it includes a diverse ethnic profile comprising Caucasians, Asians, and Hispanics. Those living in San Bruno are relatively wealthy (with a median household income of $74,375), and a majority of residents live in single-unit homes.

At 6:11 PM on September 9, 2010, the Crestmore neighborhood was jolted by an explosion that occurred near the intersection of Glenwood Drive and Earl Avenue. Line 132, a thirty-inch steel natural gas pipeline owned by Pacific Gas and Electric (PG&E), erupted in a ball of fire. The blast produced a crater seventy-two feet long and twenty-six feet wide, and it hurled a twenty-eight-foot-long segment of the pipe one hundred feet south of the point of origin.[3] PG&E estimates that 47.6 million standard cubic feet of natural gas were released in the fire. The blaze reached from one hundred to one thousand feet high, and the radiant heat combined with moderate to high northeasterly winds to cause the fire to encroach upon nearby homes and vegetation.[4]

The pipeline explosion resulted in significant response and recovery operations, which included fire suppression, evacuation and sheltering, damage assessment, public information, disaster assistance, and infrastructure and home repairs (see Photo 7.1.1). Subsequent investigations also revealed several shortcomings that had increased the risk of such an incident occurring in the first place.

Methodology

In order to gather data for this study, the author (and colleagues from the University of North Texas and the University of Delaware) used qualitative methods involving traditional quick-response disaster research. Quick-response research is data collection (mainly through interviews) immediately after an event to collect perishable data. In this case, the researchers traveled to San Bruno from January 11 to January 14, 2011. A number of key leaders

PHOTO 7.1.1: Aerial view of the pipeline fire.
Source: National Transportation Safety Board, "Pacific Gas and Electric Company Natural Gas Transmission Pipeline Rupture and Fire, San Bruno, CA, September 9, 2010," Accident Report NTSB/PAR 11/01, www.ntsb.gov/doclib/reports/2011/PAR1101.pdf.

intimately involved in the response to this incident were interviewed as part of the study. These individuals represented local public and private organizations such as the American Red Cross Bay Area Chapter, the City of San Bruno, Millbrae Fire Department, the San Bruno police and fire departments, California Recycle (CalRecycle), and the San Mateo County Environmental Health Services Department. Each interview lasted approximately one hour and was based on semistructured questions such as:

- What was the cause of the explosion?
- What was/were the major problem(s) you faced when it occurred?
- What did you do to respond to the incident?
- How did recovery operations proceed after the fire?
- What lessons did you learn from your experience?
- What could be done in the future to avert this type of event or to be better prepared to respond to it?

After these interviews were completed, the recorded interviews were transcribed throughout the summer and fall of 2011. In order to bolster our findings we obtained additional information from sources on the Internet or from National Transportation Safety Board (NTSB) reports regarding the incident. Thus, the data for this study included qualitative interviews and a survey of news and official government documents.

Unanticipated Risk

A lengthy investigation by the National Transportation Safety Board uncovered several mistakes relating to mitigation in the San Bruno gas pipeline explosion. It appears that insufficient efforts were undertaken before the incident to reduce the risk of such an incident, minimize the probability of its occurrence, and decrease its impact. First, and most importantly, the NTSB discovered that the creation and installation of the pipeline where the explosion occurred was faulty. The NTSB determined that one of the seams connecting pipe sections along line 132 was only partially welded. It is believed that the fabrication of the sections "in 1956 would not have met generally accepted industry quality control and welding standards then in effect, indicating that those standards were either overlooked or ignored."[5] This partial weld was the point of origin of the gas leak and the primary cause of the pipeline explosion.

Second, development decisions, based on incomplete understanding of the risks associated with this pipeline, were also to blame. Line 132—a high-pressure distribution system—was established in 1956, before the peak of urban expansion in this part of Northern California. While some of the homes in the Crestmore neighborhood were built during the same period when the transmission line was laid, the majority were constructed between 1970 and 1994. Therefore, residential development was allowed to occur directly over line 132. This urban sprawl near a major gas pipeline obviously put more people and property at risk. Making matters worse, government officials admitted that they were not fully cognizant of the location of the pipeline before or when the incident occurred. Had there been more awareness about the pipeline grid, decisions pertaining to residential development could have been made that would have decreased vulnerability and enhanced preparedness.

Third, evidence suggests that the maintenance program for the aging pipeline was inadequate. According to the independent review panel of the

California Public Utilities Commission, "The capital investment by PG&E in the gas transmission pipeline system has been minimal. There was no plan to modernize the system and seek opportunities to improve the risk [profile] associated with operating the system."[6] Safety regulators believe that proper and regular testing of the highly pressurized system could have detected and resolved the gas leak before the explosion occurred.

A final problem related to PG&E's ability to control the flow of gas in its distribution systems. "Contributing to the severity of the accident were the lack of either automatic shutoff valves or remote control valves on the line and PG&E's flawed emergency response procedures and delay in isolating the rupture to stop the flow of gas."[7] In other words, there were not enough valves (whether automatic or manual) to stop the flow of gas in the pipeline. In addition, PG&E employees could not shut down the line for approximately ninety minutes. The complexity of the pipeline system and the lack of planning, training, and execution resulted in more homes being destroyed after the explosion occurred.

A Successful Response

While mitigation activities reveal several shortcomings, the response to the San Bruno gas pipeline explosion was generally successful. Post-disaster activities got off to a fortuitous start in spite of major challenges and obstacles encountered by first responders and other disaster-related organizations. The immediate response included fire suppression, sheltering, damage assessment, and public information activities.

Fire Suppression
Because the pipeline ruptured only two blocks away from Fire Station 52, the response to the incident was almost instantaneous. Firefighters heard the blast and immediately exited the building, thinking that the shaking was the result of an earthquake or plane crash. When they peered outside the station, they noticed a huge fireball in the sky. They called 9-1-1 to report the fire and self-dispatched to the scene.

After repositioning the first engine to arrive on the scene (the extensive radiant heat of the fire had made the initial approach down Earl Avenue problematic), firefighters helped evacuate residents and began fire suppression activities. They went door to door to warn residents and told them to leave the area right away because the fire was spreading rapidly. Even though eight people could not be saved, the human toll would have undoubtedly been higher if this decisive action had not been taken as the event unfolded. Firefighters also laid down hoses and started to connect them to hydrants, only to find that the blast had taken out the water main in the immediate vicinity. This required some exploration away from the scene to find the nearest working hydrants. Once they were discovered, extra hoses were connected and the fire was attacked at the source and as it spread elsewhere. Meanwhile, police officers had arrived to block off traffic where hoses were crossing roads; these "water tenders" ensured that the flow of water was not interrupted.

Because the gas line was emitting so much fuel, the battalion chief issued further alarms. Additional fire departments (both in and outside of the city) arrived to battle the growing blaze and shuffle water tenders to the neediest areas (since there was still a lack of water at the scene). The assistance of CalFire was also requested to help control and push back the flames that were now encroaching upon the trees and vegetation in Crestmore Canyon. Involving CalFire in a residential area was a somewhat unique decision for an urban conflagration, and this measure required coordination with fire units to keep firefighters safe on the ground during aerial drops. This action slowed the progression of the blaze, and fire units began to gain control of the fire, particularly after PG&E was able to shut off the gas line ninety minutes into the incident. Nevertheless, a prolonged response would be needed to fully extinguish the fire, and various mutual aid partners were called in to assist with fire operations. A total of forty-two fire agencies responded with over five hundred personnel and ninety pieces of apparatus. The fire was not officially pronounced controlled until 8:00 PM on Saturday.

Sheltering

When firefighting operations began, there was serious concern that the blaze would continue to spread to other parts of the neighborhood (see Photo 7.1.2). As noted earlier, several homes were completely destroyed, and scores of others caught on fire. A decision was therefore made to evacuate the entire neighborhood (which comprised about three hundred homes). Because people were forced to leave their homes for an unknown period of time, the American Red Cross and city leaders started to focus on the sheltering function.

Two approaches were utilized to provide mass care services. First, an evacuation center was established at the Bayhill Shopping Center. This was a location where evacuees could obtain information about the unfolding situation

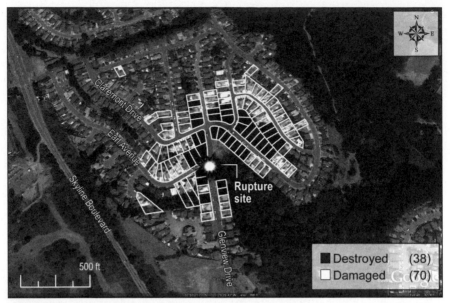

PHOTO 7.1.2: Area of damage from blast and fire.

Source: National Transportation Safety Board, "Pacific Gas and Electric Company Natural Gas Transmission Pipeline Rupture and Fire, San Bruno, CA, September 9, 2010," Accident Report NTSB/PAR 11/01, www.ntsb.gov/doclib/reports/2011/PAR1101.pdf.

while shelter operators could learn about individual and family needs. After coming to this "waypoint" or "pit stop" evacuation center, evacuees were directed to one of two Red Cross shelters. One was located at the Veterans Memorial Recreation Center and the other at the San Bruno Senior Center. Only about forty people used the shelters that first evening, and no one remained in a shelter after that. It is believed that many evacuees stayed with family and friends or received lodging vouchers from PG&E.

Following a recommendation by the California Emergency Management Agency (CalEMA), the Veterans Memorial Recreation Center was converted into a local assistance center (LAC). This was a location where residents impacted by the fire could go to access a variety of emergency resources provided by the City of San Bruno, PG&E, the San Mateo Red Cross, the Salvation Army, and a number of other community groups and faith-based organizations.

Damage Assessment

Shortly after the pipeline explosion on September 9, a small group of building inspectors assembled at city hall to assess the damages. Because fire suppression operations were still in the active phase, the building officials used the downtime to gather supplies (pens, forms, clipboards, tape, staple guns, and so on) and coordinate how they would complete the damage assessment the following day.

On September 10, the building inspectors arrived at the scene early in the morning, as determined from their meeting the night before, and set up their field headquarters in the bay of Fire Station 52. Using a laptop computer opened to an Excel spreadsheet, they divided up the neighborhood and gave each of the five assessment teams a geographic assignment. Inspectors then walked the neighborhood to collect information. Within forty-five minutes, everyone, including the damage assessment teams, was asked to leave the area. It is believed that the police wanted to gain more control over who was in the most dangerous parts of the neighborhood. There was also concern about privacy issues regarding the retrieval of the remains of those who had perished in the fire. This led to some disagreements between the building department and the police department about the decision and the importance of their respective roles. The police department was justified in its concern over access, but the building officials needed to complete the damage assessment as soon as possible.

After three or four hours, the building inspectors were allowed to resume their evaluation of the damages. All homes in the neighborhood were tagged with red, yellow, or green tags according to guidelines in the *ATC-20-1 Field Manual* (a document developed in California to guide procedures for the safe evaluation of buildings after earthquakes).[8] Homes that sustained total or major damage were regarded as unsafe and condemned and were given red tags. Yellow-tagged homes were those that sustained moderate damage and were thought to be potentially unsafe. Green tags were placed on homes that were considered habitable, with full utility services. This information was used by the city to determine who could return to the area and how recovery activities would proceed (see Photo 7.1.3).

Public Information

From the very beginning of the incident, the mayor and the city manager recognized the importance of public information. Extra city personnel were therefore brought in the very night of the explosion to answer calls from concerned citizens. In addition, the city held a number of press briefings in a parking lot where the Red Cross had staged some of its mobile communications vehicles. This required the delivery of a microphone, a podium, and speakers. The timing of these

PHOTO 7.1.3: A burned car in front of destroyed homes.

Source: National Transportation Safety Board, "Pacific Gas and Electric Company Natural Gas Transmission Pipeline Rupture and Fire, San Bruno, CA, September 9, 2010," Accident Report NTSB/PAR 11/01, www.ntsb.gov/doclib/reports/2011/PAR1101.pdf.

briefings had to be coordinated with various department spokespersons and the media. Major media outlets on the East Coast also requested information on one occasion, and this required a very early start to the day for city officials (owing to the difference in time zones). City hall continued to bring in extra staff and hold press briefings over the next several days.

On September 11, the city also held a town hall meeting at St. Robert's Church. Over 650 local citizens, including disaster victims, attended the afternoon meeting. City staff and representatives from PG&E, CalEMA, and the police, fire, building, planning, and public works departments attended to discuss what they were doing to help the community. Congresswoman Jackie Speier also showed up to advocate for the needs of the victims and the affected community. The press was there to ask questions and keep readers and audiences informed about the response to the incident. During the town hall meeting, PG&E representatives gave out pamphlets that listed where victims could get assistance. Later on, the Red Cross used social media outlets (Twitter and Facebook) to share up-to-date information about mass care services.

Short- and Long-Term Recovery Activities

The reaction to the San Bruno gas pipeline explosion did not end with the immediate response operations. A variety of recovery activities, including evacuee reentry, debris removal and environmental restoration, disaster assistance, and infrastructure and housing repairs, were also required. Long-term recovery continues to this day.

Evacuee Reentry

Because the neighborhood was contaminated from the fire and many homes were unsafe to enter, the city and county issued various emergency laws on September 9, on September 11, and again on September 14. These ordinances placed restrictions on public access in the most affected areas and were enforced with additional police presence and the help of physical barriers brought in by National Rent-A-Fence. The emergency ordinances also allowed government workers to enter private properties to collect hazardous waste (for example, paints, propane, and pesticides). However, public officials wanted to get people back into their homes as soon as possible, so they devised a plan to make this happen. Reentry procedures were prepared in the city's emergency operations center on September 10 and 11.

On Sunday, September 12, the reentry process began in a highly coordinated fashion. Victims and evacuees met at Skyline College, where they were required to prove ownership or occupancy in the affected neighborhood with a driver's license. At this point, the evacuees were given tags to determine the order of reentry (based on the severity of the damages). All of the individuals and families with green-tagged homes were allowed to return that day, and it took about six hours to accomplish this task. The owners or occupants of homes with yellow or red tags were not allowed to return to their properties until Tuesday, September 14. These individuals were required to attend a briefing session about potential safety concerns and put on personal protective equipment (for example, Tyvek suits, hard hats, gloves, and dust masks). They were then accompanied by firefighters and building officials for up to a two-hour period each day over the following week. This allowed survivors to sort through the remains of their homes and gather information to share with insurance companies.

Debris Removal and Environmental Remediation

As mentioned earlier, the incident scene was replete with numerous hazards, ranging from spoiled food to broken glass, sharp nails, and twisted metal. On Saturday, county personnel and residents gathered enough hazardous materials to fill ten 55-gallon drums. However, there was also a lot of other debris in the affected area, including damaged concrete foundations, partially collapsed chimneys, charred wood, and even cars gutted by fire. A right-of-entry permit was drafted by government lawyers and distributed to property owners. This was important, since city and county personnel needed legal justification to work on private property and remove debris that was considered a public health hazard. On September 17, the city met with residents to allow CalRecycle (a waste management agency) and Pacific States Environmental to remove this debris. Although some owners were initially reluctant to transfer responsibility for debris removal to the government and its contractors, all of the owners of red-tagged homes eventually consented.

Heavy equipment arrived in the area on September 20, and a complicated debris removal process was under way a few days later. This included the segregation of different types of debris (wood, concrete, metals) so that the materials could be recycled or go to the proper landfills. An impressive 58 to 65 percent of debris was recycled to prevent excessive environmental impact. All of the ash and contaminated soil was also removed and hauled to a class II or III waste management facility. By October 17, the debris removal process was virtually complete. Fortunately, PG&E paid for debris removal, which is estimated to have cost $1.8 million.

As debris removal operations took place, the environment was monitored continuously. Air and soil samples were frequently taken by the county public health department, and the streets were cleaned regularly to keep dust levels down. In addition, the denuded hillside in Crestmore Canyon was stabilized with silt fences, straw wattles, and hydra-seed to prevent erosion into the San Francisco Bay water supply.

Disaster Assistance

The San Bruno pipeline explosion resulted in a noteworthy outpouring of disaster assistance. Donations came in from local and external sources and included both in-kind and monetary gifts. For instance, citizens dropped off clothing, furniture, and miscellaneous goods for disaster victims. Gift cards from local businesses were also given to the Red Cross to distribute to those in need. Unfortunately, the need to sort, store, and distribute the unsolicited donations created additional work for voluntary agencies. Also, some gift cards did not prove useful, such as ones to be used in stores that carried products unlikely to be needed by disaster victims (for example, scented candles).

Corporations and concerned individuals also opened up their wallets to those in need. PG&E, feeling responsible for the pipeline explosion, distributed $15,000, $25,000, or $50,000 to individuals and families based on the level of impact to their property. About $400,000 was also collected by the city for the Glenview Fire Relief Fund. Although the distribution of these funds was the source of some debate, a decision about how to disperse the relief was finally made several months later. Thirty-eight individuals/families whose homes were destroyed received $6,000 each, and sixteen owners of the moderately damaged properties were given $4,000 each. Other occupants of the remaining properties collected $1,000 each. Moreover, another $49,000 was reserved to address the long-term needs of the fire victims. The San Bruno Resource and Recovery Center was established on September 15 to help with mental health support, housing services, and other needs.

Infrastructure Repair and Housing Construction

Over the next several months, utilities were restored and housing recovery was initiated. Water and sewer lines damaged in the explosion were repaired, but since line 132 brought up painful memories of the conflagration, citizens and city leaders demanded that the natural gas distribution pipe be deactivated. The flow of gas was diverted to other parts of the distribution system. The crater created in the rupture will remain open for quite some time to permit a full investigation by the NTSB.

The city also established policies and procedures to help victims rebuild their damaged and destroyed homes. The permitting process was expedited for fire victims, and all fees pertaining to planning and rebuilding were waived as well. Information meetings were held to educate victims about the rebuilding process and resolve concerns along the way. As of May 2012, three homes had been rebuilt and fourteen properties had been issued a permit. The remaining homes were in the planning review stages.

Overall Lessons

This examination of the San Bruno gas pipeline explosion provides countless important lessons for those individuals and agencies involved directly or indirectly in emergency management. Five are particularly noteworthy:

1. It is imperative that jurisdictions consider pipeline explosions as part of their threat and hazard identification and risk assessments (THIRAs). The seriousness of these technological hazards tends to be overlooked by emergency managers, and awareness of location, probable occurrence, and potential impacts remains low among both public administrators and the general populace. The potential for sabotage or terrorist attacks combined with the potential perils of our aging and crumbling infrastructure suggests that more effort should be given to protecting pipelines and mitigating ruptures and explosions, whether they are caused by pipeline failure, earthquakes, or other hazards.

2. The San Bruno pipeline explosion severely stretched all types of first response and emergency management capabilities. Although this was a relatively small event, government officials admitted that they were lucky to be able to rely on personnel and equipment from neighboring jurisdictions. Had this been a regionwide earthquake instead of a localized pipeline explosion, mutual aid partners would have been significantly less available. The central implication of this finding is that emergency planners should give more thought to worst-case scenarios and to building independent capacity.

3. Individuals and agencies involved in emergency planning must also consider and incorporate a wide variety of participants and functions in order to be effective. Emergency management is not solely related to first responders and emergency managers, but includes a plethora of activities ranging from fire suppression and damage assessment to public information and rebuilding. Partners at all levels of government in addition to the public and nonprofit sectors must therefore be integrated into the system if overall preparedness levels are to be increased. Coordination during an incident will certainly suffer if such proactive steps are not taken in advance of an emergency or disaster.

4. Those reacting to emergencies should allow for flexibility and improvisation during response operations. In several instances in the response to the San Bruno explosion, first responders and other emergency management personnel had to depart from standard operating procedures or even "make up" the response as the situation unfolded. For instance, the fire department issued multiple alarms at one time in order to quickly acquire resources to fight the growing blaze. It also exhibited creativity in obtaining water and utilizing air support in a residential neighborhood. Moreover, city and county leaders had to spontaneously plan how to conduct reentry and debris removal operations. They recognized that planning-on-the-fly was necessary for successful post-disaster operations.

5. It is necessary to remember that an incident is not over when immediate needs have been met. Because of the variety of the victims' medical, emotional, and other needs, disaster assistance activities can last for months, if not longer. Infrastructure repairs and the reconstruction of housing can take years. In addition, pipeline explosions like the one in San Bruno will often result in lengthy investigations as well as drawn-out litigation.

Conclusions

The San Bruno gas pipeline explosion is an important case for those involved in emergency management and homeland security. It reveals a number of shortcomings pertaining to the mitigation of this type of hazard associated with critical infrastructure. The incident also provides some positive examples of response operations and demonstrates the breadth of the other activities that must begin immediately after an emergency occurs. The lessons of this incident should be considered by practitioners involved with infrastructure protection and emergency planning. Learning from prior emergencies and disasters is imperative if emergency management and homeland security are to be improved.

DISCUSSION QUESTIONS

1. What were the causes of the San Bruno gas pipeline explosion, and how could the explosion have been prevented?

2. How did city and county emergency management personnel respond to the incident?

3. In what ways did decision-makers and emergency personnel impro-
    vise their responses?
4. Why is planning for recovery imperative?

NOTES

1. National Transportation Safety Board (NTSB), "Pacific Gas and Electric Company Natural Gas Transmission Pipeline Rupture and Fire, San Bruno, CA, September 9, 2010," Pipeline Accident Report 11/01 (Washington, DC: NTSB, August 30, 2011), http://www.ntsb.gov/news/events/2011/san_bruno_ca/index.html, hereafter "NTSB Pipeline Report." The full report is available at: http://www.ntsb.gov/doclib/reports/2011/PAR1101.pdf.

2. US Census Bureau, "2005–2009 American Community Survey Five-Year Esti-mates," June 20, 2011, http://quickfacts.census.gov/qfd/states/06/0665028lk.html.

3. NTSB, "Operations Group Chairman Factual Report," docket no. SA-534, exhibit no. 2-A (Washington, DC: NTSB).

4. NTSB, "Fire Scene Factual Report," docket no. SA-534, exhibit no. 5-A (Wash-ington, DC: NTSB).

5. NTSB Pipeline Report.

6. Independent Review Panel, "Report of the Independent Review Panel: San Bruno Explosion," prepared for the California Public Utilities Commission, June 24, 2011, http://www.cpuc.ca.gov/NR/rdonlyres/85E17CDA-7CE2-4D2D-93BA-B95D25CF98B2/0/cpucfinalreportrevised62411.pdf.

7. NTSB Pipeline Report.

8. Applied Technology Council (ATC), *ATC-20-1 Field Manual: Postearthquake Safety Evaluation of Buildings*, 2nd ed. (Redwood City, CA: ATC, 2005).

Lessons Learned from the 2010 Haiti Earthquake

JOSHUA KELLY AND DAVID A. McENTIRE

Introduction

On January 12, 2010, the Republic of Haiti was struck by a 7.0 magnitude earthquake that killed between 210,000 and 300,000 people, displaced 1.3 million individuals, and forced approximately 26,671 others to evacuate the country (mainly to Florida and New York).[1] The earthquake devastated the already impoverished Haiti, caused a flood of aid from around the globe to converge on the tiny island nation, and simultaneously crippled the infrastructure and Haitian government's capacity to mount effective operations.

The 2010 Haiti earthquake (alternately referred to as the 2010 Port-au-Prince earthquake) is an important case for the study of international disasters and catastrophes because of the magnitude of the event, the extreme poverty in the country, and a number of other extenuating factors. Since the initial attention and outpouring of support have faded, Haiti has continued to struggle in its attempt to recover. This case study explores the lessons learned from the 2010 Haiti earthquake, discusses some of the complex issues associated with catastrophes and international responses, and educates students on what did and did not work in order to improve future response efforts.

Background

To gain a better understanding of the challenges facing Haiti in this disaster, this section provides information on the demographics of Haiti, a geographic profile to illustrate the logistics of relief efforts, a review of Haiti's emergency management culture prior to the event, and a snapshot of the traditional hazards that Haiti has faced over the course of its existence.

The Republic of Haiti was founded in 1804 when it gained independence from France after a prolonged and bloody civil war. Haiti has a population of approximately 10 million, with 900,000 residing in the capital city of Port-au-Prince.[2] Haiti is an impoverished nation: 70 percent of the population lives on less than US$2.00 a day,[3] and Haiti receives roughly 30 percent of its annual GDP from the international diaspora community.[4] Reflecting the history of the country, the official languages of Haiti are French and Creole. In addition, Haiti is a developing nation with a small manufacturing base, and 38 percent of its population work in farming-related professions.[5]

MAP 7.2.1: The Earthquake Impact Area in Haiti

Source: Hearts and Hands website, http://heartsandhandsforhaiti .org/media/Haiti_Quake_Map_viawikinews.png.

Geographically speaking, Haiti is a tropical nation located on the western half of the Hispaniola island (the other half being the Dominican Republic) (see Map 7.2.1). Haiti is a comparatively small nation, with a landmass slightly smaller than the US state of Maryland. Haiti's terrain is divided between mountainous and coastal regions, with 1,771 kilometers of coastline being its dominant feature.

Haiti's disaster response capabilities are managed by the Directorate for Civil Protection (DPC)—the Haitian equivalent to the Federal Emergency Management Agency (FEMA) in the United States. Unlike FEMA, however, the DPC has historically been criticized for its lack of resources and political support. The emergency management system is also supported by a patchwork of local civic groups as well as domestic and international non-governmental organizations (NGOs). Beyond Haiti's own disaster response capability, the country is heavily supported by the Caribbean Disaster Emergency Management Agency (CDEMA), a mutual aid coalition of eighteen regional disaster response organizations—such as the Jamaican Defense Force and the Bahamas National Emergency Management Agency—that pool resources in times of disasters.

Haiti is a nation prone to a variety of hazards and accustomed to disaster events (see Table 7.2.1). Since 1751, Haiti has been struck by ten major disasters, suffered approximately 327,000 disaster-related deaths, and lost US$12.7 billion in monetary resources.[6] The primary hazards that frequently affect Haiti are hurricanes, earthquakes, and flooding. The frequency of these natural disasters is due to several factors. First, Haiti lies within the hurricane-prone Caribbean. Second, Haiti has an undeveloped emergency management structure.[7] Finally, Haiti's tropical climate makes the country susceptible to drought and erosion conditions, exacerbating the population's vulnerability.

With this contextual information in mind, this case study of the 2010 Port-au-Prince earthquake will illustrate that, beyond a heightened vulnerability due to its location in the disaster-prone Caribbean, Haiti suffers disproportionately from a corrupt and ineffective government, poorly enforced zoning regulations, subpar building practices and materials, and a lack of resources geared toward disaster and emergency management priorities.[8]

The case study is divided into four sections, based on the phases of the disaster management cycle: mitigation, preparedness, response, and recovery. This case study uses Damon Coppola's definitions of the four emergency

TABLE 7.2.1: Disasters in Haiti

Hazard	Date	Impact
7.4–7.5 magnitude earthquake	1751	Roughly 75 percent of Port-au-Prince's masonry homes were destroyed
7.5 magnitude earthquake	1770	250 killed
8.1 magnitude earthquake	1842	10,000 killed
Hurricane Flora	1963	Killed roughly 8,000 in Haiti, the Dominican Republic, and Cuba and resulted in $150 million in damage to Haiti
Hurricane Cleo	1964	Killed 192 and caused $17 million in damages to Haiti
Hurricane Gordon	1994	Killed over 1,000
Tropical Storm Jeanne/mudslide	2004	Killed over 2,500 and left 200,000 homeless
Hurricanes Fay, Gustav, Hanna, and Ike	2008	Killed over 800, caused $1 billion in damages, and destroyed roughly 60 percent of Haiti's harvest
7.0 magnitude earthquake	2010	Killed over 300,000, injured over 300,000, displaced 1.3 million, and left damages estimated at $11.5 billion
Severe cholera outbreak	2010	Killed 4,500 and affected roughly 300,000

Source: PreventionWeb, "Haiti: Disaster Statistics," http://www.preventionweb.net /english/countries/statistics/?cid=74 (accessed September 5, 2012).

management phases.[9] The mitigation section discusses how pre-event miti-gation procedures, or the lack thereof, contributed to and affected the extent of the disaster when the earthquake struck Haiti on January 12, 2010. The preparedness section reviews planning efforts that helped shape the event. The response section details the earthquake, the immediate response efforts, and the successes and failures that were evident in the response. The recovery section analyzes the current state of Haiti two and a half years later. The case study concludes by presenting some lessons learned and the relevance of the 2010 Haiti earthquake and its place in disaster history.

Mitigation

The benefits of mitigation are increasingly accepted around the world. For instance, in the United States it has been reported that efforts to reduce risk may result in a four-to-one savings of dollars spent to dollars saved after a disaster event.[10] In spite of this widespread recognition of the benefits of mitigation, the practice has been largely ignored in Haiti. That country's failure to successfully operationalize accepted mitigation practices, owing to lax building codes and limited professional engineering standards, was one of many factors that exacerbated the loss of life during the earthquake.

Historically, Port-au-Prince has been constructed in a sort of patchwork system: residents tend to build homes on available land, with little oversight or interference from public officials. Building codes either do not exist or they are not properly enforced. In addition, there historically has been little standardization and proper certification of engineers that has further hampered professional building standards.[11] Thus, there is a clear shortage of professional engineers to properly oversee construction of buildings and perform building inspections.

The lack of codes, enforcement, and engineering licensures has left Haitians with little if any knowledge of mitigation principles and practices when they construct their own homes. Haitians often build their own residences based on their own limited resources. By using materials such as thin, hollow bricks, held together by improperly mixed cement and unreinforced masonry (that is, insufficient rebar), Haitians constructed many buildings in Port-au-Prince that were unable to cope with the 7.0 magnitude earthquake on January 12.

The failure of buildings during the earthquake for these reasons is illustrated by the fact that even some of the highest-profile buildings in Port-au-Prince, such as the prime minister's residence, collapsed during the earthquake. Weak materials, insufficient standards, lack of enforcement, and a dearth of engineers are the most important reasons why so many people perished in Haiti on January 12, 2010.

Preparedness

In Haiti, pre-event preparedness measures, which play a large role in disasters, can be categorized into two realms: (1) domestic emergency management organizations and (2) international and nonprofit humanitarian organizations.

Haiti's domestic emergency management efforts are coordinated by the Directorate for Civil Protection under the general secretariat, with the participation of various other departments and local community groups. Prior to the 2010 earthquake, disaster preparedness efforts in Haiti were minimal and received little support, owing to a shortage of resources and a lack of political will.[12] The only exception to this general rule was the establishment of permanent disaster response committees, which are small teams of approximately six individuals (similar to the SWAT team model in the United States) who are ready to deploy when disasters occur. While the permanent disaster response committees are a positive step toward preparedness, they have been criticized for operating only in small-scale, high-frequency events and not in large catastrophes like the 2010 Port-au-Prince earthquake.

Additionally, the response committees lacked resources in 2010 and were criticized for not having enough members to deal with the scope of the earthquake.[13] Contributing to Haiti's lack of domestic preparedness is the fact that firefighters and emergency response personnel receive low pay and status, they are granted limited resources, and the jobs attract a limited number of quality recruits.[14] Ultimately, this lack of resource commitment combined with the lack of societal buy-in to emergency response personnel to handicap those responders already on the ground. There is simply not enough planning, training, practice, and community education to adequately prepare Haitians for impending disasters.

Regionally, preparedness efforts fall to the Caribbean Disaster Emergency Management Agency. CDEMA consists of twenty-one member nations, various nonprofit organizations, and private-sector entities such as the Caribbean Association of Industry and Commerce.[15] One of the successful preparedness takeaways prior to the 2010 Haiti earthquake was the foresight of regional governments in establishing CDEMA in the area and ensuring that it developed operational capability and maintained a high degree of regional legitimacy.

Response

The response phase of a disaster is the most publicly visible and criticized aspect of the emergency management cycle. In the immediate aftermath of the

2010 Port-au-Prince earthquake, the response had to deal with the massive loss of housing, the decimation of government and United Nations facilities and the deaths of personnel, insufficient medical care for the injured, and the difficult task of dealing with thousands of fatalities.[16]

When the earthquake struck, 300,000 thousand homes were damaged or destroyed. This resulted in homelessness for over 1.5 million people.[17] Even if their homes remained intact, residents often immediately decided to leave them and stay outside. They feared aftershocks and did not want to be trapped in buildings, as happened to so many victims on that fateful day.

Although people were fearful of building collapses, many citizens attempted to retrieve those who were trapped in the rubble. Unfortunately, they did not have equipment and training to do this safely and effectively. Making matters worse, the local government was a victim of the catastrophe as well: government buildings collapsed, and many government departments lost personnel in the disaster. The DPC itself was therefore ill equipped for such a major disaster and lacked heavy machinery to help with search-and-rescue operations.[18] The United Nations also suffered extensive losses in the disaster. On January 12, the UN reported that a number of its personnel were unaccounted for on the ground in Port-au-Prince. MINUSTAH, the UN stabilization mission in Haiti, later confirmed that 102 UN personnel were killed as a direct result of the 2010 Port-au-Prince earthquake. This was the largest loss of UN personnel in a single event in UN history.[19]

For these reasons, there was a serious dearth of medical personnel and supplies to care for the wounded. Doctors, nurses, blood, medicines, bandages, and other medical necessities were woefully inadequate for the number of casualties. Even days and weeks after the event the medical capabilities of the country and outside organizations were insufficient for those who needed care, surgery, and follow-up.

Not all of the initial response personnel, however, were hampered. Following the 2010 Port-au-Prince earthquake, the regional response was quickly deployed. Within twenty-four hours, the CDEMA was on the ground performing damage assessment and providing medical personnel.[20] Among CDEMA's primary preparedness activities were coordinating the UN teams, pre-identifying vital resource needs, and deploying emergency response personnel.[21] Overall, eleven countries contributed to the CDEMA response effort (see Photo 7.2.1).[22]

PHOTO 7.2.1: The US Army supporting the CDEMA response effort.
Source: US Army, http://upload.wikimedia.org/wikipedia/commons/1/16/2010_Haiti_earthquake
_relief_efforts_by_the_US_Army.jpg.

Not only did emergency management personnel have to coordinate large-scale search-and-rescue operations and ongoing medical care to victims, but they also had to deal with the massive number of fatalities. The difficulty of locating, identifying, processing, and managing fatalities after the earthquake may be regarded as a secondary disaster in itself. From an emergency management perspective, this situation was categorized as a mass fatality management (MFM) incident. David McEntire defines mass fatality management as a "situation where there are more bodies than can be handled using existing local resources."[23] In Haiti's case, this secondary blow was devastating.

Citizens piled bodies on the street or took them to hospitals and morgues (where capacity was quickly overwhelmed). Because no one was able to deal with over 200,000 bodies, they quickly started to decompose and putrefy. Annoyed with the pungent smell, some citizens doused bodies with gasoline and lit them on fire. Eventually, the government developed a plan to collect bodies with heavy equipment and dump them into mass graves in Titanyen. In his study of the MFM incident during the aftermath of the 2010 Haiti earthquake, McEntire noted that "the Haiti earthquake was a worst-case scenario for the Haiti government and the international community. . . . [The earthquake] created an insurmountable challenge for those in charge of body handling; so much so that the Haiti government had to issue directives for mass burials."[24]

Recovery

Recovery is perhaps the least understood phase of the four phases of emergency management. Combined with continuing shelter and housing challenges, the effects of the cholera outbreak, and ongoing debris management operations, this is just one of the reasons why recovery will be a very long process for Haiti.

One of the stories coming out of Haiti immediately after the earthquake was that 1.5 million people had been displaced from their homes and forced to find alternative shelters such as ad-hoc displacement camps.[25] The challenge of transitioning these displaced individuals from temporary to permanent housing has been a major impediment to Haiti's recovery process.

In conjunction with the massive shelter operation under way after the earthquake, authorities began to be concerned when the Haiti National Public Health Laboratory began to report cases of cholera in October 2010. Cholera, in the most basic terms, is an infectious bacterial disease that is caused by the ingestion of contaminated water and results in severe dehydration, diarrhea, and in some cases death. After an intensive investigation, the outbreak was determined to be the result of United Nations relief personnel failing to properly dispose of waste at a campsite north of Port-au-Prince. The cholera outbreak ended up killing an additional 4,500 individuals, affected roughly 300,000, and hampered repatriation efforts of evacuees.[26]

Another hindrance to the recovery process was the slow pace of debris removal operations. Six months after the January 2010 earthquake, 98 percent of the original debris had not been cleared. A shortage of heavy machinery, a lack of accurate mapping information about damages, and strict tariffs on incoming relief supplies all contributed to the slow debris removal process.[27] It is likely that debris removal will take years or even decades. This, along with limited resources, will continue to limit the extent to which Haitians will be able to return to permanent housing.

As can be seen, Haiti has faced many roadblocks to recovery. If recovery is to be successful, a large commitment of further resources will be needed. In addition, patience and flexibility will be required. It will be interesting to see how Haiti recovers as the international community forgets about the earthquake and other nations turn inward to resolve their own important domestic economic problems.

Lessons Learned

The consequences of the 2010 Haiti earthquake seen in its aftermath were a result of a combination of many factors and agents. The lack of pre-event mitigation, insufficient preparedness, inadequate response, and the ongoing challenges facing recovery have made this a monumental disaster. In this final section, we discuss additional takeaway lessons learned during and after the Port-au-Prince earthquake, including the importance of pre-event relationships for development organizations, the emergence of text-to-donate (TTD) campaigns as a disaster recovery tool, disaster aid transparency issues, the value of mitigation as a practice, and the need for careful planning when deploying active response personnel.

Because Haiti hosts over eight thousand international nonprofit organizations (the highest nonprofit density of any country in the world), it has been referred to as "the Republic of NGOs."[28] In the aftermath of the Haiti earthquake, responses by nonprofits were often hampered by their poor communication with one another and by their failure to pool resources effectively. For these reasons, establishing pre-event relationships and clearing communication issues in advance of a disaster would not only help minimize duplication of services but also help maximize the efficiency of the resources already on the ground.

The 2010 Haiti earthquake also showed for the first time the viability of the "text-to-donate" (TTD) philanthropic method as a fund-raising tool. Nonprofit organizations, such as the International Red Cross, allowed individuals to donate $5 or $10 to the Haiti earthquake response and recovery effort by texting "donate" to a predetermined number. This simple method of streamlining donations raised over $8 million for the Red Cross alone and should be used as a template for future disaster response and recovery events.[29]

Another issue that received widespread attention following the 2010 Haiti earthquake was that of aid transparency. The American Red Cross and other aid agencies received criticism about their spending habits and for the lack of public access to their fund distribution methods.[30] In order to maintain public support and donor trust, organizations that are soliciting donations following a disaster event need to be transparent about their response capabilities and revenue expenditures. Failing to do so is likely to result in lower donations after major disasters.

Another major lesson learned from the January 12, 2010, Haiti earthquake is the value of mitigation as a disaster management tool. Haiti had few, if any, codes for buildings and few adequately trained personnel to enforce standards. This resulted in major damages and loss of life, especially when we compare the impact of the Haiti earthquake to the effects of Chile's 8.8 magnitude earthquake the next month, on February 27.[31] While obvious differences exist between the two nations, Haiti should try to emulate its neighbor to the south by pushing for proper, affordable, and sustainable building practices in the rebuilding and simultaneous redevelopment of Port-au-Prince. Failure to do so will only increase Haiti's vulnerability to the next earthquake.

Finally, it should be recognized that the October 2010 cholera outbreak was a preventable and deadly reminder of the impact of poor planning by relief organizations. In order to avoid secondary public health emergencies, relief personnel need to be acutely aware of local geography, infrastructural limitations, and cultural practices—such as the Haitian practice of bathing and drawing drinking water from the Artibonite River, which, according to an independent UN investigatory panel, was one of the main contributing factors to the spread of the 2010 cholera outbreak.[32]

Conclusions

As this case study has illustrated, the 2010 Port-au-Prince earthquake reshaped the physical and social landscape of the Republic of Haiti. In this sense, it is similar to other large events, such as the Great Chicago Fire of 1871 and the 1906 San Francisco earthquake. These disasters can serve as catalysts for development and renewal, although there are no guarantees for Haiti. Haiti cannot secure a stable future without a sustained focus on rebuilding Port-au-Prince in such a way as to reduce vulnerability. It will also be important to improve NGO coordination, renew funding for the regional disaster response organizations, and build emergency management capabilities in Haiti.

DISCUSSION QUESTIONS

1. What mitigation measures were not implemented prior to the 2010 Port-au-Prince earthquake that exacerbated the negative consequences of the earthquake?
2. What were the failures of preparedness that ultimately led to the struggles during the response?
3. What are the key issues surrounding disaster response efforts that presented major challenges to national and international aid organizations in the aftermath of the 2010 Haiti earthquake?
4. What are the roadblocks to recovery in Haiti that have hampered and slowed efforts to rehabilitate the country?

NOTES

1. Rhoda Margesson and Maureen Taft-Morales, "Haiti Earthquake: Crisis and Response," Congressional Research Service Report for Congress, February 19, 2010, http://fpc.state.gov/documents/organization/139280.pdf (accessed July 25, 2012).

2. Central Intelligence Agency (CIA), "The World Factbook: Central America and Caribbean: Haiti," https://www.cia.gov/library/publications/the-world-factbook/geos/ha.html (accessed February 12, 2012).

3. François Grünewald and Andrea Binder, with Yvio Georges, "Inter-Agency Real-Time Evaluation in Haiti: Three Months After the Earthquake," Global Public Policy Institute, August 30, 2010, http://www.unicef.org/evaluation/files/Haiti_IA_RTE_final_Eng.pdf (accessed July 12, 2012).

4. Christian D. Klose and Christian Webersik, "Long-Term Impacts of Tropical Storms and Earthquakes on Human Population Growth in Haiti and Dominican Republic," NaturePrecedings, August 4, 2010, http://dx.doi.org/10.1038/npre.2010.4737.1 (accessed July 12, 2012).

5. CIA, "The World Factbook: Central America and Caribbean: Haiti."

6. PreventionWeb, "Haiti: Disaster Statistics," http://www.preventionweb.net/english/countries/statistics/?cid=74 (accessed September 5, 2012); see also Erin Fordyce, Abdul-Akeem Sadiq, and Grace Chikoto, "Haiti's Emergency Management: A Case of Regional Support, Challenges, Opportunities, and Recommendations for the Future," in *Comparative Emergency Management: Understanding Disaster Policies, Organizations, and Initiatives Around the World*, ed. David A. McEntire (Washington, DC: Federal Emergency Management Agency Higher Education and the US Department of Homeland Security).

7. Ibid.

8. Ibid.

9. Damon P. Coppola, *Introduction to International Disaster Management*, 2nd ed. (Burlington, MA: Elsevier, 2011), 209, 251, 305, and 377.

10. Adam Rose et al., "Benefit-Cost Analysis of FEMA Hazard Mitigation Grants," *Natural Hazards Review* (November 2007): 1.

11. Build Change, "2010 Annual Report," http://www.buildchange.org/pdfs /ANNUAL%20REPORT%202010_Build%20Change.pdf (accessed September 7, 2012).

12. Fordyce et al., "Haiti's Emergency Management."

13. PreventionWeb, "CDEMA: Regional Progress Report on the Implementation of the Hyogo Framework for Action (2009–2011)," 2011, http://www.preventionweb.net /english/hyogo/progress/reports/v.php?id=17512&pid:183.

14. ICMA, "Building Firefighting Capacity in Haiti," July 11, 2012, http://icma.org/en /icma/newsroom/highlights/Article/102298/Building_Firefighting_Capacity_in_Haiti.

15. PreventionWeb, "CDEMA: Regional Progress Report," 5.

16. Edith M. Lederer and John Heilprin, "Haiti Earthquake: UN Peacekeeping Headquarters Collapses," Huffington Post, January 13, 2010, http://www.huffingtonpost .com/2010/01/13/haiti-earthquake-un-peace_n_421336.html.

17. United Nations Development Programme, "Rebuilding Haiti," http://www.undp .org/content/undp/en/home/ourwork/crisispreventionandrecovery/projects_initiatives /crisis_in_haiti/.

18. Fordyce et al., "Haiti's Emergency Management."

19. MINUSTAH UN Stabilization Mission in Haiti, "Haiti Earthquake—One Year Anniversary," January 12, 2011, http://www.un.org/en/peacekeeping/missions/minustah /rememberance.shtml.

20. Fordyce et al., "Haiti's Emergency Management."

21. Pan American Health Organization (PAHO), "The Interview [with CDEMA executive director Jeremy Collymore]," *Disasters: Preparedness and Mitigation in the Americas* 114 (October 2010): 1–3.

22. Ibid.

23. David McEntire, *Disaster Response and Recovery: Strategies and Tactics for Resilience* (Hoboken, NJ: John Wiley and Sons), 159.

24. David McEntire, Abdul-Akeem Sadiq, and Kailash Gupta, "Unidentified Bodies and Mass-Fatality Management in Haiti: A Case Study of the January 2010 Earthquake with a Cross-Cultural Comparison," *International Journal of Mass Emergencies and Disasters* (November 2012): 35.

25. United Nations Development Programme, "Rebuilding Haiti."

26. Dr. Alejandro Cravioto et al., "Final Report of the Independent Panel of Experts on the Cholera Outbreak in Haiti," 3, http://www.un.org/News/dh/infocus/haiti/UN-cholera-report-final.pdf.

27. Margesson and Taft-Morales, "Haiti Earthquake: Crisis and Response."

28. Steven Lawry, "Building Back Better: Revisiting the Roles of Government, Donors, and INGOs in Haiti's Reconstruction," Harvard University, Hauser Center for Nonprofit Organizations, January 31, 2010; see also Margesson and Taft-Morales, "Haiti Earthquake: Crisis and Response."

29. "Haiti Text Donations to Red Cross Exceed $8 Million," Fox News, January 15, 2010, http://www.foxnews.com/story/0,2933,583082,00.html.

30. Disaster Accountability Project, "One Year Report on Transparency of Relief Groups Responding to 2010 Haiti Earthquake," January 5, 2011, http://www.disasteraccountability.org/blog2/2011/01/one-year-report-on-transparency-of-relief-groups-responding-to-2010-haiti-earthquake/.

31. "Magnitude 8.8—Offshore Bio-Bio, Chile," US Geological Survey, February 27, 2010, http://earthquake.usgs.gov/earthquakes/recenteqsww/Quakes/us2010tfan.php#details (accessed October 7, 2012).

32. Cravioto et al., "Final Report of the Independent Panel of Experts on the Cholera Outbreak in Haiti," 3.

Conclusion

LINDA KILTZ AND JAMES RAMSAY

As we were completing the manuscript for this book, we wondered what the next set of case studies might be. Examining current events and the larger social issues at the time, we noticed two major incidents dominating the press: the Sandy Hook Elementary School shooting and Hurricane Sandy.

The shooting took place on December 14, 2012, at the Sandy Hook Elementary School in the village of Sandy Hook in the town of New-town, Connecticut. The incident left twenty grade-school children and seven adults dead, including the shooter's mother, and as such, it was the second-deadliest school shooting.[1] The lone gunman, Adam Lanza, forced his way into the school after killing his mother in his home, and he began shooting children in one of the kindergarten classes with a .223 caliber Bushmaster rifle. Teachers who attempted to shield the children from harm were also shot and killed. In the aftermath of this tragedy, the nation not only tried to identify the reasons for these horrific acts but also began analyzing possible causes, such as the lack of gun control policies and an inadequate mental health care system.

As with previous active shooter events, the nation will mourn the dead and then cry out for legislative action of some kind to prevent such an act from occurring in the future. The school shooting in Newtown was the seventh mass killing event in 2012, which made it a record year in the number of casualties, with 138 people injured or killed.[2] Research published in *USA Today*, stemming from FBI data, found that four or more people died in a mass killing about every two weeks in the United States.[3] These attacks ranged from robberies to public shooting sprees like the massacre in Newtown. From 2006 to 2012, there were 156 incidents of mass killings that resulted in 774 deaths, including at least 161 children.[4] Given the number of casualties and the resources involved in planning for and responding to such domestic violence events, the security question is this: Do these sorts of issues fall within the domain of homeland security? And if so, how?

Severe weather, which causes more destruction, more death, and more economic chaos than any other type of incident, poses quite a different sort of challenge to the nation from the Sandy Hook incident. But are natural disasters per se homeland security issues? A number of scholars have argued there is no clear consensus on how homeland security is defined or characterized.[5] We know that homeland security is often described as an interdisciplinary enterprise that involves a vast array of academic disciplines and fields of practice.[6] The dynamic nature of this enterprise is evident looking at its ten-year history. For instance, following the attacks on September 11, 2001, homeland security efforts primarily focused on preventing and responding to acts of terrorism. However, the impact of Hurricane Katrina in 2005 revealed the weaknesses of our homeland security efforts up to that time, particularly in the areas of emergency preparedness and response, critical infrastructure protection, and resilience integration. Consequently, the homeland security enterprise has begun to shift its focus to an all-hazards approach that recognizes that natural and man-made disasters, as well as terrorism, pose significant, albeit different, threats to the homeland.[7]

This text is unique in being one of the first to include environmental security as an academic area of homeland security. While most texts in homeland security discuss terrorism, intelligence, emergency management, and so on, this text has presented two case studies on environmental security: one on the security implications of the thawing Arctic region, and the other on the security implications of Hurricane Katrina. Such diverse cases demonstrate the importance of building resilience and environmental security concepts into homeland security strategy.

The emergent security challenges posed by climate-related hazards and by extreme weather events were clearly highlighted in 2012. From unprecedented drought to killer cold, 2012 was a year of weather extremes. The United States suffered eleven weather-related events that cost $1 billion apiece, according to an estimate prepared by the National Oceanic and Atmospheric Administration (NOAA).[8] Economic losses from Hurricane Sandy and the yearlong drought are estimated to be about $50 billion each.[9] Sandy, which was a post-tropical cyclone when it made landfall on October 30, will go down in the record books as the second-costliest storm in US history. Its tremendous storm surge, coupled with a high tide, wreaked havoc along the New Jersey and New York coastlines. Sandy left 132 people dead, about 380,000 homes and buildings damaged or destroyed, and over 8 million people without power across 17 states.[10] Mayor Michael Bloomberg of New York City publicly stated that he believed climate change had contributed to the devastation caused by Sandy. According to climatologists, future storms are likely to hit even harder as the effects of climate change increase.[11] Such increases can be seen with rising sea levels (three inches in the past century) and with the rise in the global average temperature by up to 2.0 degrees Celsius by 2052.[12] The negative impacts are already being felt with more droughts, floods, and extreme weather events.

Further, 2012 was the hottest year on record in the United States. Daily temperature records melted across the country as heat waves and drought gripped the nation. In June alone, 164 all-time-high temperature records were tied or broken, according to government records.[13] With extreme heat comes drought, and in July just under *56 percent of the country was experiencing drought conditions,* a record.[14] As ongoing drought combined with a crippling heat wave throughout the summer of 2012, the effects on people, animals, and crops were lethal. With 56 percent of the continental United States in the grip of a drought, agriculture, particularly corn production, was threatened, prompting the US Department of Agriculture (USDA) to declare a disaster in more than one thousand counties in twenty-six states—the largest disaster in USDA history.[15] The USDA further announced that the drought would push retail food prices up by 3 to 4 percent in 2013, which is higher than average annual increases.[16]

The year 2012 also earned notice as one of the worst years for wildfires. Wildfires raged through Colorado and throughout the Southwest in early summer before shifting west and north to hit Washington, Montana, and Idaho. The 2012 wildfire season had 55,050 fires that burned 9.15 million acres, setting a record for the most acres burned per fire.[17]

Given the links between climate change, natural hazards, and economics, future curricula in emergency management and homeland security should include topics related to the adverse physical, social, health, and security impacts of climate change on the United States. Although some uncertainties remain regarding the extent and speed of climate change, the overwhelming global scientific consensus is that the Earth's atmosphere is warming rapidly, perhaps at an unprecedented rate, and that much of this warming is due to human activity. Climate change is expected to have a number of adverse socioeconomic impacts within the global environment, including: (1) shortfalls in water for drinking and irrigation, with concomitant risks of thirst and famine; (2) changes and possible declines in agricultural productivity stemming from altered temperature, rainfall, or pest patterns; (3) spikes in the rates and extended geographic scope of malaria and other diseases; (4) associated shifts in economic output and trade patterns; (5) changes and possibly large shifts in human migration patterns; and (6) larger economic and human losses attributable to extreme weather events such as hurricanes.[18]

The United Nations Intergovernmental Panel on Climate Change (IPCC) warns that coastal populations in North America will be increasingly vulnerable to climate change—and nearly 50 percent of Americans live within fifty miles of the coast.[19] Other predicted impacts of climate change increasing hazards in the United States include an increased likelihood of flooding throughout the nation, more intense hurricanes in the Gulf of Mexico, an increase in the number and duration of urban wildfires, and more severe and longer heat waves.[20] Climate change is likely to impact the location, frequency, and occurrence of a variety of natural hazards, from cyclones and floods to wildfires and winter storms. Thus, the historical data that are typically the basis of hazard identification and risk assessment may not accurately forecast future events. Consequently, future emergency managers and homeland security professionals will need to evaluate and better understand how climate change could affect the identification and selection of disaster mitigation strategies, the types of preparedness activities that jurisdictions should undertake, the execution of response operations, and the implementation of long-term recovery strategies.

Although the case studies in this textbook highlight the interdisciplinary nature and all-hazards approach to homeland security, they also represent only a small sample of the possible topics in this field. Given that natural disasters are likely to increase in number and severity with global climate change, perhaps even more of our focus in homeland security should be placed on planning for and mitigating the new environmental hazards we are surely going to face in the years ahead. Hence, our goal in the next textbook of case studies will be to include more topics such as narco-terrorism, risk management and decision-making, food and water security, port and maritime security, disaster preparedness, response and recovery from an international perspective, business continuity planning, science and technology, and the impact of global climate change on homeland security and emergency management.

NOTES

1. James Barron, "Nation Reels After Gunman Massacres 20 Children at School in Connecticut," *New York Times,* December 15, 2012.

2. Mark Follman, Gavin Aronsen, and Deanna Pan, "A Guide to Mass Shootings in America," *Mother Jones,* December 15, 2012.

3. Meghan Hoyer and Brad Heath, "Mass Killings Occur in USA Once Every 2 Weeks," *USA Today,* December 19, 2012.

4. Ibid.

5. Linda Kiltz and James D. Ramsay, "Perceptual Framing of Homeland Security," *Homeland Security Affairs* 8, no. 16 (August 2012), http://www.hsaj.org/?article=8.1.16; see also Christopher Bellavita, "Changing Homeland Security: What Is Homeland Security?" *Homeland Security Affairs* 4, no. 2 (June 2008), http://www.hsaj.org/?article=4.2.1.

6. James D. Ramsay, Daniel Cutrer, and Robert Raffel, "Development of an Outcomes-Based Undergraduate Curriculum in Homeland Security," *Homeland Security Affairs* 6, no. 2 (May 2010), http://www.hsaj.org/?article=6.2.4.

7. This shift was nicely described by former DHS secretary Michael Chertoff in a series of meta-lectures presented through the Brookings Institution. See, for example, "The Future of Homeland Security," September 5, 2008, http://www.brookings.edu/~/medi a/events/2008/9/02%20chertoff/20080902_chertoff (accessed January 2, 2013).

8. "Countdown: 2012's Wildest Weather," *Our Amazing Planet,* December 21, 2012, http://www.ouramazingplanet.com/3914-wild-weather-countdown-2012.html.

9. Ibid.

10. Andrew Newman, "Hurricane Sandy vs. Hurricane Katrina," *New York Times,* November 27, 2012.

11. Jorgan Randers, *2052: Global Forecast for the Next Forty Years* (White River Junction, VT: Chelsea Green, 2012), 241.

12. Ibid.

13. "Countdown: 2012's Wildest Weather."

14. Ibid.

15. Wynne Parry, "How Bad Is the US Drought?" *Live Science,* July 18, 2012, http://www.livescience.com/21681-drought-us-disaster.html.

16. "The Cost and Consequences of the US Drought," *Time,* October 26, 2012.

17. Bill Gabbert, "2012: Third Highest Number of Wildfire Acres Burned," *Wildfire Today,* November 23, 2012, http://wildfiretoday.com/2012/11/23/2012-third-highest-number-of-wildfire-acres-burned/.

18. Intergovernmental Panel on Climate Change (IPCC), *Climate Change 2007: Synthesis Report,* 2007, http://www.ipcc.ch/publications_and_data/publications_ipcc_fourth_assessment_report_synthesis_report.htm.

19. Ibid.

20. Thomas Karl, Jerry Melillo, and Thomas Peterson, *Global Climate Change Impacts in the United States* (New York: Cambridge University Press, 2009).

Further Resources

1. LAW AND POLICY

Alexander, Yonah. *Evolution of US Counterterrorism Policy*, vol. 1. New York: Praeger, 2008.

Carafano, James Jay. "Homeland Security in the Next Administration," Lecture 1085. Washington, DC: Heritage Foundation, May 16, 2008, http://www.heritage.org /Research/Lecture/Homeland-Security-in-the-Next-Administration.

Cato Institute. "Domestic Security." In *Cato Handbook for Policymakers,* 7th ed. Washington, DC: Cato Institute, 2008.

Cohen, Dara Kay, Mariano-Florentino Cuellar, and Barry R. Weingast. "Crisis Bureaucracy: Homeland Security and the Political Design of Legal Mandates." *Stanford Law Review* 59, no. 3 (December 2006): 673–759.

Cusic, Jerry R. "The Confusion of Homeland Security with Homeland Defense." Strategy Research Project. Carlisle Barracks, PA: US Army War College, March 24, 2009, http://handle.dtic.mil/100.2/ADA500868.

Faddis, Charles S. *Willful Neglect: The Dangerous Illusion of Homeland Security.* Guilford, CT: Lyons Press, 2010.

Flynn, Stephen E., and Daniel B. Prieto. *Neglected Defense: Mobilizing the Private Sector to Support Homeland Security.* New York: Council on Foreign Relations, March 2006, http://www.cfr.org/content/publications/attachments/NeglectedDefenseCSR.pdf.

Forest, James J. F. *Homeland Security: Protecting America's Targets.* Westport, CT: Praeger, 2006.

Kamien, David, ed. *The McGraw-Hill Homeland Security Handbook.* New York: McGraw-Hill, 2012.

Kettl, Donald F. *System Under Stress: Homeland Security and American Politics,* 2nd ed. Washington, DC: Congressional Quarterly Press, 2007.

Monahan, Torin. *Surveillance in the Time of Insecurity.* New Brunswick, NJ: Rutgers University Press, 2010.

Posner, Richard A. *Not a Suicide Pact: The Constitution in a Time of National Emergency.* New York: Oxford University Press, 2006.

Raskin, Marcus G., and Robert Spero. *The Four Freedoms Under Siege: The Clear and Present Danger from Our National Security State.* Westport, CT: Praeger, 2007.

Sauter, Mark, and James Jay Carafano. *Homeland Security: A Complete Guide to Understanding, Preventing, and Surviving Terrorism.* New York: McGraw-Hill, 2005.

US Department of Homeland Security. *Quadrennial Homeland Security Review Report: A Strategic Framework for a Secure Homeland.* Washington, DC: US Department of Homeland Security, February 2010, http://www.dhs.gov/xlibrary/assets/qhsr_report .pdf.

US Executive Office of the President. *National Security Strategy.* Washington, DC: The White House, May 2010, http://www.whitehouse.gov/sites/default/files/rss_viewer /national_security_strategy.pdf.

US Executive Office of the President. Homeland Security Council. *National Strategy for Homeland Security.* Washington, DC: US Executive Office of the President, Homeland Security Council, October 2007, http://handle.dtic.mil/100.2/ADA472950.

US Naval Postgraduate School. Center for Homeland Defense and Security. Homeland Security Digital Library, https://www.hsdl.org/.

2. TERRORISM

Chenoweth, Erica, and Susan E. Clarke. "All Terrorism Is Local: Resources, Nested Institutions, and Governance for Urban Homeland Security in the American Federal System." *Political Research Quarterly* 63, no. 3 (September 2010): 495–507.

Danzig, Richard J. *Preparing for Catastrophic Bioterrorism: Toward a Long-Term Strategy for Limiting Risk.* Washington, DC: US National Defense University, Center for Technology and National Security Policy, May 2008.

Danzig, Richard J., Rachel Kleinfeld, and Philipp C. Bleek. *After an Attack: Preparing Citizens for Bioterrorism.* Washington, DC: Center for a New American Security, June 2007, http://www.cnas.org/files/documents/publications/DanzigBleekKleinfeld _Bioterror_June07pdf.

Davis, Lois M., et al. *Long-Term Effects of Law Enforcement's Post-9/11 Focus on Counterterrorism and Homeland Security.* Santa Monica, CA: RAND, 2010, http://www.rand .org/pubs/monographs/2010/RAND_MG1031.pdf.

May, Peter J., Joshua Sapotichne, and Samuel Workman. "Widespread Policy Disruption: Terrorism, Public Risks, and Homeland Security." *Policy Studies Journal* 37, no. 2 (May 2009): 171–194.

3. ENVIRONMENTAL SECURITY

Ackerman, John T. "Climate Change, National Security, and the Quadrennial Defense Review: Avoiding the Perfect Storm." *Strategic Studies Quarterly* 2, no. 1 (Spring 2008): 56–96, http://www.au.af.mil/au/ssq/2008/Spring/ackerman.pdf.

Brigham, Lawson. "New US Arctic Policy." *Proceedings: US Naval Institute* 135, no. 5 (May 2009): 46–47.

Busby, Joshua W. "Who Cares About the Weather? Climate Change and National Security." *Security Studies* 17, no. 3 (July–September 2008): 468–504.

Eggers, Jeffrey W. "The Oil Gauge of National Security." *Proceedings: US Naval Institute* 134, no. 6 (June 2008): 10.

Goodman, Sherri, William Kratz, and Terry A. Yonkers. "Climate Change and National Security." *Military Engineer* 101, no. 657 (January–February 2009): 41–42, http://themilitaryengineer.com/tme_past_issues/2009-01-JanFebTME-SM.pdf.

4. INTELLIGENCE

Clark, J. Ransom. *Intelligence and National Security: A Reference Handbook.* Westport, CT: Praeger, 2007.

George, Roger Z. *Analyzing Intelligence: Origins, Obstacles, and Innovations.* Washington, DC: Georgetown University Press, 2008.

Hayden, Michael Vincent. "Protecting America and Winning the Intelligence War." *Heritage Lectures* 1167 (September 27, 2010), http://thf_media.s3.amazonaws.com/2010/pdf/hl_1167.pdf.

Logan, Keith Gregory. *Homeland Security and Intelligence.* Westport, CT: Praeger, 2010.

Lowenthal, Mark M. *Intelligence: From Secrets to Policy,* 4th ed. Washington, DC: Congressional Quarterly Press, 2009.

US Central Intelligence Agency (CIA). Home page, https://www.cia.gov.

US Defense Intelligence Agency (DIA). Home page, http://www.dia.mil.

US Director of National Intelligence. Intelligence.gov. http://www.intelligence.gov.

———. *The National Counterintelligence Strategy of the United States of America.* Washington, DC: US Director of National Intelligence, 2008, http://www.ncix.gov/publications/strategy/docs/2008_Strategy.pdf.

———. *The National Intelligence Strategy.* Washington, DC: US Director of National Intelligence, August 2009, https://www.fas.org/irp/offdocs/nis2009.pdf.

5. CRITICAL INFRASTRUCTURE PROTECTION

Bucci, Steven P. "A Most Dangerous Link: The Most Likely Major Cyber Threat to the United States Is a Homeland Security Problem." *Proceedings: US Naval Institute* 135, no. 10 (October 2009): 38–42.

Collins, Pamela Ann. *Homeland Security and Critical Infrastructure Protection*. Westport, CT: Praeger, 2009.

Donahue, William. "Fearless About Cyberspace." *C4ISR* 9, no. 1 (January–February 2010): 36–37, http://www.c4isrjournal.com/story.php?F=4372254.

Grosskruger, Paul L. "Analysis of US Water Infrastructure from a Security Perspective." Strategy Research Project. Carlisle Barracks, PA: US Army War College, March 15, 2006, http://handle.dtic.mil/100.2/ADA449651.

Kramer, Franklin D., Stuart H. Starr, and Larry K. Wentz, eds. *Cyberpower and National Security*. Washington, DC: National Defense University Press/Potomac Books, 2009.

Libicki, Martin C. *Cyberdeterrence and Cyberwar*. Santa Monica, CA: RAND, 2009, http://www.rand.org/pubs/monographs/2009/RAND_MG877.pdf.

Moteff, John D. *Critical Infrastructures: Background, Policy, and Implementation*. Washington, DC: Library of Congress, Congressional Research Service, July 11, 2010, http://www.fas.org/sgp/crs/homesec/RL30153.pdf.

US Department of Homeland Security. *National Infrastructure Protection Plan: Partnering to Enhance Protection and Resiliency*. Washington, DC: US Department of Homeland Security, 2009, http://www.dhs.gov/xlibrary/assets/NIPP_Plan.pdf.

6. TRANSPORTATION SECURITY

Anthony, Hodges. "America's International Ports and Intermodal Transportation System: Ill-Prepared for Biological Weapons of Mass Destruction." Strategy Research Project. Carlisle Barracks, PA: US Army War College, March 8, 2006, http://handle.dtic.mil/100.2/ADA449367.

Edwards, Frances, and Goodrich, Daniel C. *Introduction to Transportation Security*. New York: CRC Press, 2012.

The White House. *Surface Transportation Security Priority Assessment*. Washington, DC: The White House, March 2010, http://www.whitehouse.gov/sites/default/files/rss_viewer/STSA.pdf.

7. EMERGENCY MANAGEMENT

Birkland, Thomas A. "Disasters, Catastrophes, and Policy Failure in the Homeland Security Era." *Review of Policy Research* 26, no. 4 (July 2009): 423–438.

Gecowets, Gregory A. S., and Jefferson P. Marquis. "Applying Lessons of Hurricane Katrina." *Joint Force Quarterly* 48 (First Quarter 2008): 70–76.

Getha-Taylor, Heather. "Preparing Leaders for High-Stakes Collaborative Action: Darrell Darnell and the Department of Homeland Security." *Public Administration Review* 66, no. 6 (December 2006): 159–160.

Herrick, Charles. "Homeland Security and Citizen Response to Emergency Situations: A Perspective on the Need for a Policy Approach to Information Access." *Policy Sciences* 42, no. 3 (August 2009): 195–210.

Kiefer, John J., and Robert S. Montjoy. "Incrementalism Before the Storm: Network Performance for the Evacuation of New Orleans." *Public Administration Review* 66, no. 6 (December 2006): 122–130.

Miskel, James F. *Disaster Response and Homeland Security: What Works, What Doesn't.* Stanford, CA: Stanford Security Studies, 2008.

Schrader, Dennis R. "Unfinished Business at FEMA: A National Preparedness Perspective." Heritage Lectures 1125 (June 26, 2009), http://www.heritage.org/Research/Lecture/Unfinished-Business-at-FEMA-A-National-Preparedness-Perspective.

US Centers for Disease Control and Prevention (CDC). Emergency Preparedness and Response. Washington, DC: CDC, http://www.bt.cdc.gov.

US Department of Health and Human Services (HHS). Assistant Secretary for Preparedness and Response. Public Health Emergency. Washington, DC: HHS, http://www.phe.gov/preparedness/pages/default.aspx.

US Department of Homeland Security (DHS). *National Incident Management System.* Washington, DC: DHS, December 2008, http://www.fema.gov/pdf/emergency/nims/NIMS_core.pdf.

———. *National Response Framework* [replaces National Response Plan]. Washington, DC: DHS, January 2008, http://www.fema.gov/pdf/emergency/nrf/nrf-core.pdf.

US Federal Emergency Management Agency (FEMA). Home page, http://www.fema.gov.

Wise, Charles R. "Organizing for Homeland Security After Katrina: Is Adaptive Management What's Missing?" *Public Administration Review* 66, no. 3 (May–June 2006): 302–318.

Acknowledgments

We would like to thank our families, especially our spouses, for their support and understanding while we worked on the writing and editing of this book. A special thank-you to all of the authors who contributed the cases featured in this book. We appreciate their time, effort, and professionalism as they worked to complete compelling and scholarly case studies. Finally, we have appreciated the support and encouragement we have received from scholars in the fields of homeland security and emergency management in writing this textbook, and in particular we would like to thank the following reviewers for their thoughtful feedback: Jeff Bumgarner (University of Minnesota), Pamela Everett (Wayne State College), Bruce Liebe (MacMurray College), and Phillip Schertzing (Michigan State University).

About the Editors
and Authors

EDITORS

James D. Ramsay (PhD, MA, CSP) has almost twenty years of experience in public health education, emergency management and occupational safety, and environmental health. Dr. Ramsay is currently a certified safety professional, professor of homeland security, and chair of the Department of Security Studies and International Affairs at Embry-Riddle Aeronautical University. Dr. Ramsay also began the homeland security program in 2006. Dr. Ramsay teaches environmental security, emergency management, exercise design and evaluation, strategic planning and decision-making, and terrorism origins and ideologics, and he directs the internship program and the senior capstone consulting project. Dr. Ramsay was recently appointed by the US Secretary of Health and Human Services to serve on the Board of Scientific Counselors to the Director of the National Institute of Occupational Safety and Health in the CDC. Dr. Ramsay also serves on the board of directors for ABET, Inc. In addition, Dr. Ramsay serves on the education standards committees for both the International Association for Intelligence Education (IAFIE) and the American Society of Safety Engineers (ASSE), where he also chairs the committee. Dr. Ramsay has also been a frequent scientific reviewer for the National Occupational Research Agenda and currently serves on the editorial review board for *Homeland Security Affairs Journal,* the *Journal of Homeland Security and Emergency Management,* and the *Journal of Homeland Security Education.* Dr. Ramsay has served as a subject matter expert and consulted on a wide range of emergency management planning and evaluation issues as well as occupational safety and health challenges for many organizations. Dr. Ramsay will complete his third book, *Fundamentals of Environmental Security,* by fall/winter 2014.

Linda Kiltz, PhD, has over fifteen years of experience in leadership and management positions in government and nonprofit organizations. Dr. Kiltz is the Program Director for the Master of Public Administration, Master of Public Policy, and Master of Science in Nonprofit Management and Leadership Programs at Walden University. Dr. Kiltz was an Assistant Professor of Public Administration in the Master of Public Administration Program and Program Director for the Graduate Certificate in Homeland Security at Texas A&M University–Corpus Christi from 2008 to 2012. Dr. Kiltz's research interests include measuring and evaluating community resilience, developing a theory of homeland security, and analyzing how climate change will impact homeland security and emergency management policies, practices, and operations. Dr. Kiltz is the author of a number of articles that have been published in the *Journal of Homeland Security and Emergency Management, Homeland Security Affairs Journal,* and *Journal of Homeland Security Education.* Dr. Kiltz received her PhD in public administration and policy from Portland State University in 2008. Her area of expertise is in public administration and management as well as in homeland security policy, emergency management, and terrorism. Dr. Kiltz has extensive public service experience, including service as an air defense artillery officer for six years in the US Army, specializing in security, counterterrorism, training, and human resource management. In addition, Dr. Kiltz has over eight years of experience in law enforcement as a police officer, reserve sheriff's deputy, crime prevention specialist, police trainer, and training manager in Montana and Oregon. Dr. Kiltz has served as a community educator and victim's advocate for nonprofit organizations dedicated to preventing family violence, has extensive training and experience in emergency management, community preparedness, and emergency response coordination, and has served as a FEMA educator.

AUTHORS

Frances L. Edwards, MUP, PhD, CEM, is Deputy Director of the National Transportation Security Center at Mineta Transportation Institute (MTI) and Professor of Political Science and Director of the MPA program at San Jose State University. Her most recent book is *Introduction to Transportation Security,* written with Dan Goodrich, and she has recently published "Effective Disaster Response in Cross-Border Events" in the *Journal of Contingency and Crisis Management.* She is co-author of two books in the NATO Science Series and co-author of nine monographs for MTI. Dr. Edwards's research in climate change adaptation, cultural competency, emergency management, and homeland security has led to chapters in professional books and over thirty articles. She has consulted with NATO, the European Union, and government agencies in Japan and Turkey and has over twenty years of experience as a director of emergency services in California, including a term on the California Seismic Safety Commission. She is a certified emergency manager and a professional continuity practitioner.

Tobias T. Gibson earned his PhD in political science from Washington University in St. Louis. His dissertation is a look at the role of the Office of Legal Counsel in advising the president about issuing executive orders. He is currently an Associate Professor of Political Science and the Chair of the Security Studies Program at Westminster College, in Fulton, Missouri. He is the author of several articles and book chapters related to the president and the legal bureaucracy in the executive branch.

Joshua Kelly received his master's in public administration, with a concentration in emergency management, from the University of North Texas in the spring of 2012. He holds a bachelor's degree from the University of Delaware, from which he graduated with dual degrees in sociology and criminal justice in 2010. In the past, Joshua has worked in local emergency management and since 2009 has worked as an undergraduate/graduate research assistant at the University of Delaware's Disaster Research Center and at the University of North Texas. His research interests include multi-organizational coordination issues, organizational resilience, and improvisation. He has worked as a research assistant on multiple projects, some funded either partially or fully by the National Science Foundation—including a study of the improvised waterborne evacuation of Manhattan following 9/11, a study determining the resilience of the I-95 corridor to a winter hazard event, a quick-response funded study looking at the reception of evacuees following the 2010 Haiti earthquake, and most recently a quick-response study that looked at spontaneous planning during the 2010 San Bruno gas pipeline explosion.

Gary C. Kessler, PhD, CCE, CISSP, is an Associate Professor of Homeland Security at Embry-Riddle Aeronautical University, specializing in cyber-security. Dr. Kessler is also a member of the North Florida Internet Crimes Against Children (ICAC) Task Force and an adjunct Associate Professor at Edith Cowan University (Perth, Western Australia). He is a certified information systems security professional, a certified computer examiner, and on the board of directors of the Consortium of Digital Forensic Specialists (CDFS). Dr. Kessler is the co-author of two professional texts and over sixty articles and papers, a frequent speaker at industry events, and Editor in Chief of the *Journal of Digital Forensics, Security, and Law.* He is also a member of the Professional Association of Dive Instructors (PADI), a PADI Divemaster and Master SCUBA Diver Trainer, and a US Coast Guard–licensed captain. More information about Dr. Kessler can be found at his website, http://www.garykessler.net.

John Lanicci is a Professor of Applied Meteorology and the Coordinator for the Master in Aeronautics Program at Embry-Riddle Aeronautical University. He joined the Embry-Riddle faculty in 2006 after completing a twenty-seven-year career in the US Air Force. His assignments included two staff tours at the Pentagon; tours as a weather forecaster and as Chief of Model Development at AF Global Weather Central (now the AF Weather Agency), Offutt AFB, Nebraska; an assignment as a research scientist and project manager at the AF Research Laboratory at Hanscom AFB, Massachusetts; and three command assignments, the last of which was as Commander of the Air Force Weather Agency. Dr. Lanicci received a BS degree (summa cum laude) in physics from Manhattan College, Bronx, New York, in 1979; a BS degree (with highest distinction) in meteorology from The Pennsylvania State University in 1980; and MS and PhD degrees in meteorology from Penn State in 1984 and 1991 through Air Force Institute of Technology sponsorship. He served for three years on the faculty at Air War College, Maxwell AFB, Alabama, where he was also Chief Information Officer for the college, and two years as an Adjunct Assistant Professor with Embry-Riddle's Worldwide Campus Program. Dr. Lanicci has taught undergraduate and graduate courses in synoptic and mesoscale meteorology, weather analysis and forecasting, aviation meteorology, and environmental security. His research interests include the effects of climate change on national and international security, the integration of weather information into aviation decision-making, and central Florida severe-storms. Dr. Lanicci is Chair of the American Meteorological Society's Committee on Environmental Security, which is part of the AMS Commission on the Weather and Climate Enterprise. He also is a member of the AMS Board on Higher Education, which is part of the AMS Commission on Education and Human Resources. Since 2008, he has been the national co-chair of the annual AMS Student Conference.

David A. McEntire is a Professor in the Emergency Administration and Planning Program in the Department of Public Administration at the University of North Texas. Dr. McEntire's research interests include emergency management theory, vulnerability reduction, community preparedness, response coordination, international disasters, and terrorism. Dr. McEntire is the author of several books, including *Disaster Response and Recovery, Introduction to Homeland Security,* and *Disciplines, Di-*

sasters, and Emergency Management. He has published articles in many academic and professional journals and received awards for his work in the *International Journal of Disaster Resilience in the Built Environment* and in *Disaster Prevention and Management.* Dr. McEntire is the recipient of the Dr. B. Wayne Blanchard Award for Academic Excellence in Emergency Management Higher Education.

Richard T. Sylves has been a Professor and Senior Research Scientist at The George Washington University's Institute for Crisis, Disaster, and Risk Management since 2009. He is also an Emeritus Professor of Political Science and International Relations at the University of Delaware (UD), as well as a former Senior Policy Fellow at the UD Center for Energy and Environmental Policy, and on the affiliated faculty of the UD Disaster Research Center. Dr. Sylves authored *The Nuclear Oracles* (1986) as well as *Disaster Policy and Politics* (2008) and co-edited two books with William Waugh, *Cities and Disaster* and *Disaster Management in the US and Canada.* He has taught courses on emergency management and disaster policy since 1988 and is an expert on presidential declarations of major disaster and emergency. Dr. Sylves is an Advisor to the Emergency Management Accreditation Program, served on the National Academy of Sciences (NAS) panel "Estimating the Costs of Natural Disasters" in 2000, was a member of the NAS Disasters Roundtable from 2002 to 2005, and created grant-supported courseware for the FEMA Higher Education Program on "The Politics and Policy of Emergency Management."

Steve Young, PhD, began teaching at Sam Houston State University in the fall of 2005, following his retirement from eighteen years as an Operations Officer with the CIA's Clandestine Service, in which role his primary area of expertise was counterterrorism. His postings included Europe, the Middle East, and South Asia, as well as temporary duty assignments in Iraq and Afghanistan. From 2001 to 2005, he worked with Houston FBI's Joint Terrorism Task Force (JTTF). At Sam Houston State University, Dr. Young is the Coordinator for the Master of Science in Security Studies within the College of Criminal Justice. He also teaches primarily graduate courses in homeland security, global terrorism, and national security intelligence. Dr. Young is a contributor to *Counterterrorism* magazine and the *Journal of Strategic Security.*

Index